S. T. Coleridge

S. T. Coleridge

Interviews and Recollections

Edited by

Seamus Perry
Lecturer in English Literature
University of Glasgow

First published 2000 by
PALGRAVE
Houndmills, Basingstoke, Hampshire RG21 6XS and
175 Fifth Avenue, New York, N. Y. 10010
Companies and representatives throughout the world

PALGRAVE is the new global academic imprint of
St. Martin's Press LLC Scholarly and Reference Division and
Palgrave Publishers Ltd (formerly Macmillan Press Ltd).

ISBN 0–333–68159–2

This book is printed on paper suitable for recycling and
made from fully managed and sustained forest sources.

A catalogue record for this book is available
from the British Library.

Library of Congress Cataloging-in-Publication Data
S.T. Coleridge : interviews and recollections / edited by Seamus Perry.
     p. cm.
   Includes bibliographical references and index.
   ISBN 0–333–68159–2
    1. Coleridge, Samuel Taylor, 1772–1834. 2. Coleridge, Samuel Taylor,
1772–1834—Friends and associates. 3. Poets, English—19th century–
–Biography. I. Perry, Seamus.
   PR4483 .S15 2000
   821'.7—dc21
   [B]
                                                        00–055684

10   9   8   7   6   5   4   3   2   1
09   08   07   06   05   04   03   02   01   00

Printed and bound in Great Britain by
Antony Rowe Ltd, Chippenham, Wiltshire

For my parents

Contents

Acknowledgements

I gratefully acknowledge, for permission to reprint material: Oxford University Press, for a passage from Nicholas Roe, *Wordsworth and Coleridge. The Radical Years* (1988), and for a passage from *The Letters of Samuel Taylor Coleridge*, ed. Earl Leslie Griggs (1956-71); The English Association, for the sonnet quoted from Edmund Blunden, 'Elia and Christ's Hospital', *Essays and Studies* XXII (1936); and the Hampshire Record Office, for the letter from Sir George Beaumont (reference no. 38M49/C6/25/2), as printed by Tom Mayberry in *The Coleridge Bulletin* (NS 1 (Winter 1992-3), 5-7). I gratefully acknowledge the help of several publishers and editors in the search for permissions, particularly the editor of the Huntington Library Quarterly, who kindly answered my enquiries about the memoir by Samuel Teulon Porter, as printed by Griggs (*HLQ* XVII (1953-4), 365-78). Every attempt has been made to locate copyright-holders, but if any have been inadvertently overlooked I shall be very pleased to learn about them and make good my oversight.

Anyone working on Coleridge has the immense good fortune of using the excellent bibliography of Coleridge and Coleridgean scholarship prepared by Richard Haven, and Walter and Ann Crawford, and I am much indebted to their scholarship. I have also leant heavily upon the achievements of the Bollingen *Collected Works of S.T. Coleridge* (London and Princeton, NJ; general editor, Kathleen Coburn): especially R.A. Foakes's edition of *Lectures 1808-1819 on Literature* (1987) and Carl Woodring's edition of *Table Talk* (1990). I referred repeatedly, especially in the early stages, to the anthology *Coleridge the Talker*, edited by Richard W. Armour and Raymond F. Howes (Ithaca, NY, 1940); Ralph Pite's *Coleridge*, in the *Lives of the Great Romantics* series (1997), was also very useful. Besides the normal reference works (especially the *DNB*), I have relied upon Earl Leslie Griggs's edition of Coleridge's letters (6 vols.; Oxford, 1956-71), and P.P. Howe's of Hazlitt's works (21 vols.; 1930-4); Claude A. Prance's *Companion to Charles Lamb. A Guide to People and Places 1760-1847* (1983); Valerie Purton's *A Coleridge Chronology* (Basingstoke, 1993); and Mark L. Reed's *Wordsworth. The Chronology of the Early Years 1770-1799* and

Wordsworth. The Chronology of the Middle Years 1880-1815 (Cambridge, Mass., 1967; 1975).

During the preparation of this book, I have been fortunate enough to read in the following libraries: The Bodleian Library, Oxford; The British Library, Bloomsbury, and now St. Pancras; The English Faculty Library, Oxford; The London Library, St. James's Square; The National Library of Scotland, Edinburgh; the University Library, Glasgow; and the Library of the Wordsworth Trust, Dove Cottage, Grasmere. I am most grateful to the staff of all these institutions. I am indebted to many colleagues at Glasgow for assistance with various tangles, especially to Robert Cummings for his help in identifying several tags and allusions; and I am grateful too to Matthew Scott and Kazuyoshi Oishi, who took time away from their own work to check some of my transcriptions. Nicholas Roe kindly sent me material. At my publishers, Charmian Hearne and, latterly, Eleanor Birne, have been exemplarily supportive, patient far beyond duty with an editor of near-Coleridgean procrastination and deferred promises. I am hugely indebted to Nicola Trott for suggestions, help in the checking, and much else besides. The book is dedicated to my parents, whose support has always been unwavering and invaluable.

S.P.
Glasgow, February 2000.

Editorial Note

This is a deliberately eclectic gathering of texts, ranging from private journal and chatty letter, to reverential biography and formal obituary; and it is obviously not sensible to annotate them all equally thickly. In the notes I have restricted myself to identifying those people who importantly crop up—both those who cross Coleridge's path, and those about whom he talks—and to naming a source for tags and what seemed the more important allusions. I have also pointed out some of the parallels between the opinions attributed to Coleridge in these memoirs and views expressed in his works. Many snippets, too scrappy to be included in the main body of the work, are to be found in the notes, as well as bibliographical references and cross-references for those who are interested. I have, where possible, chosen texts from early editions, and usually the first; but an absolute policy of textual purism is hardly appropriate to a collection like this, and I have not hesitated in a few cases to use later versions, where they are very much easier to locate. Full details of publications are given on initial appearance, and subsequently only when the first citation is inconveniently distant or buried in notage; place of publication, unless otherwise noted, is London. Variants on words with several reasonable spellings (including 'Shakespeare'), have been left without the notice of a '[sic]', which I have used sparingly in other cases. I have silently brought 'Mr', 'Dr', and so on into stopped conformity ('Mr.', 'Dr.'), except where this threatened to over-tidy an informal piece of private writing. The ordering of single and double inverted commas has been regularised; and I have occasionally added some punctuation or the odd letter in square brackets, where I thought it might help. Otherwise orthography has been left as it stands, variously, in the originals: I have been especially keen not to tidy the vividly non-standard practice of some letter-writers and journal-keepers. My own elisions are marked '[…]': where they occur immediately before a paragraph break, the reader is to understand that the next paragraph comes from a new page of the original (as specified in the headnote); but where they occur within a paragraph, they replace a relatively small amount of text omitted from within a single page of the original text. Footnotes appearing in the original texts have (where it seemed worthwhile) been printed at the end of the excerpt; my own notes are grouped at the end of each section.

Shakespeare is cited from *The Riverside Shakespeare*, ed. G. Blakemore Evans *et al.* (Boston, 1974); classical texts from the Loeb editions; and Biblical texts from the King James version.

The following abbreviations have been used throughout:

AR   Samuel Taylor Coleridge, *Aids to Reflection*, ed. John Beer (London and Princeton, 1993).

BL   Samuel Taylor Coleridge, *Biographia Literaria, or Biographical Sketches of My Literary Life and Opinions*, ed. James Engell and W. Jackson Bate (2 vols.; London and Princeton, 1983).

CL   *The Collected Letters of Samuel Taylor Coleridge*, ed. Earl Leslie Griggs (6 vols.; Oxford, 1956-71).

CM   Samuel Taylor Coleridge, *Marginalia*, ed. H.J. Jackson and George Whalley (4 vols. to date; London and Princeton, 1980-).

CN   *The Notebooks of Samuel Taylor Coleridge*, ed. Kathleen Coburn and (vol. IV) Merton Christensen (4 double vols. to date; London and Princeton, 1957-).

CPW   *The Complete Poetical Works of Samuel Taylor Coleridge [...]*, ed. E.H. Coleridge (2 vols.; Oxford, 1912).

CT   Richard W. Armour and Raymond F. Howes (eds.), *Coleridge the Talker. A Series of Contemporary Descriptions and Comments* (Ithaca, NY, 1940).

DWJ   *Journals of Dorothy Wordsworth*, ed. E. de Selincourt (2 vols.; 1941).

EOT   Samuel Taylor Coleridge, *Essays on his Times*, ed. David V. Erdman (3 vols.; London and Princeton, 1978).

F   Samuel Taylor Coleridge, *The Friend*, ed. Barbara E. Rooke (2 vols.; London and Princeton, 1969).

H&C   *Samuel Taylor Coleridge. An Annotated Bibliography of Criticism and Scholarship*, ed. Richard Haven and Josephine Haven, and Walter B. Crawford with Ann M. Crawford (3 vols.; NY, 1976-96).

L1795 Samuel Taylor Coleridge, *Lectures 1795 On Politics and Religion*, ed. Lewis Patton and Peter Mann (London and Princeton, 1971).

LL   Samuel Taylor Coleridge, *Lectures 1808-1819 On Literature*, ed. R.A. Foakes (2 vols.; London and Princeton, 1987).

LS   Samuel Taylor Coleridge, *Lay Sermons*, ed. R. J. White
        (London and Princeton, 1972).

OED   *Oxford English Dictionary.*

MY   *The Letters of William and Dorothy Wordsworth. The Middle
        Years*, ed. Ernest de Selincourt, rev. Mary Moorman and
        Alan G. Hill (2 vols.; Oxford, 1969-70).

SWF   Samuel Taylor Coleridge, *Shorter Works and Fragments*, ed.
        H. J. Jackson and J.R. de J. Jackson (2 vols.; London and
        Princeton, 1995).

TT   Samuel Taylor Coleridge, *Table Talk Recorded by Henry
        Nelson Coleridge (and John Taylor Coleridge)*, ed. Carl Wood-
        ring (2 vols.; London and Princeton, 1990).

Introduction

This book aims to present the most important reminiscences of Coleridge written by his contemporaries—which are not always the reminiscences written by his most important contemporaries—arranged (as well as may be deduced) in chronological order of the episodes and incidents which they report. Around them, I have provided a commentary sketching in the more important events of Coleridge's life: so the book amounts, in a way, to a composite biography; and I hope it will prove informative to the non-specialist, as well as useful to the card-carrying Coleridgean.

Meeting Coleridge, and—what usually amounted to the same thing—hearing him *talk*, was one of the great experiences of the romantic age. In what Hazlitt identified, in *The Spirit of the Age*, as 'an age of talkers', Coleridge was surely pre-eminent, his only serious rival as a conversationalist the now obscure figure of Sir James Mackintosh (of whom Coleridge took a very low view—perhaps partly because of the challenge to his celebrity). His habits as a talker leant him readily to satire: 'He is very great in monologue, but he has no idea of dialogue', as Mme. de Staël famously said, and there is evidence enough here that others felt the same. 'Coleridge has been talking for two whole days', Lady Lansdowne is reported as saying, after enduring an exhausting house-visit. On the other hand, response could be rapturous: 'He talked on for ever,' Hazlitt generously recalled, years after his disillusionment with Coleridge seemed complete, 'and you wished him to talk on for ever'. Others, again, found a more responsive conversationalist: William Rowan Hamilton remembered that 'he took very graciously, and in good part, any few words I ventured to throw in; and allowed them to influence, and in some degree to guide his own great, and sweet, and wondrous stream of speech'.

What may we learn from the accounts collected here (some for the first time since their original appearance)? Firstly, of course, they have the importance of any biographical document: it is interesting to learn (and it may prove useful to know) that Coleridge was reading Berkeley in early 1798, as he prepared for the Unitarian ministry; or that, on the evening of 29 January 1829, he found himself seized with a fit of—unfashionable—enthusiasm for Donne's poetry. His life-long fascination with the Gospel of

John is amply testfied. But more than that, the reports of his conversation in these documents, however imperfect their record may be, represent small but significant additions to the body of Coleridge's works. There are some little bits of impromptu verse, mostly frivolous or witty, that will, I suppose, belong in a comprehensive *Collected Poems* ('We went, the younger Parry bore our goods / O'er d— bad roads through d— delightful woods'); scattered images and metaphors that deserve saving from the library stacks ('That wave (said he) seems to me *like a world's embrace*'); and even, as reported by his nephew, a spooky short story, 'The Phantom Portrait'. Besides those real but doubtless minor additions to the canon, the immense number of recorded opinions and remarks also deserve their place alongside the great *Collected Coleridge*. This is not special pleading: many of the works for which Coleridge is best known, like *Biographia* and *The Friend*, were first composed by dictation, and the *Literary Lectures* survive, in large part, by second-hand report; so the attempts, collected here, to transcribe his talk, difficult though it inevitably proved, form a natural continuation of the idiosyncratic gathering of works (including notebooks and marginalia) that has come down to us as the Coleridgean *oeuvre*.

There are many fine things here, typically capturing with a winning colloquial ease thoughts that emerge more knottily in the formal prose. Of Wordsworth, who inspired many of Coleridge's best thoughts: 'He strides on so far before you, that he dwindles in the distance!'; yet also of Wordsworth (anticipating the mixed feelings of *Biographia*), 'that there was a something corporeal, a *matter-of-fact-ness*, a clinging to the palpable, or often to the petty, in his poetry'; or, as he says later, 'With "malice prepense" he fixes on objects of reflection, which do not naturally excite it'. Of other poets: 'Gray's personifications [...] were mere printer's devils' personifications'; Erasmus Darwin 'was like a pigeon picking up peas, and afterwards voiding them with excrementitious additions'; 'Byron's perpetual quarrel with the world was as absurd as if the spoke of a wheel should quarrel with the movement of which it must of necessity partake'. On Shakespeare's characters: 'Shakespeare, while his eye rested upon an individual character, always embraced a wide circumference of others, without diminishing the separate interest he intended to attach to the being he pourtrayed'. On poetry in general: 'He is the truest poet who can apply to a new purpose the oldest occurrences, and most usual appearances'; 'the ears of these couplet-writers might be charged with having short memories, that could not retain the harmony of whole passages'; and on art: 'A Gothic cathedral [...] is like a petrified religion', 'Grecian architecture is a thing, but the Gothic is an idea', or, again, 'I can make a Grecian temple of two brick-bats and a cocked hat'. And on the abiding topic of his life: 'All Theology [...] depends on mastering the term, Nature', or 'Nature is the Opposite to God [...] God can not be seen *in* Nature'. This last, of course, was a striking reversal of the youthful beliefs with which he remained associated in the popular mind, and reminders of his earlier views could provoke outbursts: '*I* think God and Nature the same!' he protested to an unwise Professor, 'I think Nature is the devil in a strait-waistcoat'.

Secondly, and more generally, we can glimpse in these pages a much more various Coleridge than the poet or thinker we usually read and study now: a more human presence than the visionary poet of 'Kubla Khan', or the Sage of Kantianised Christianity. Several critics in recent years have sought to challenge 'romantic' notions of the solitary genius; and here we have an STC thoroughly socialised: here, we find Coleridge the diner, the lion of literary London, the punster, the anecdotalist, the drinker, the political commentator, the charmer. His kindness is often remarked; and his encouragement of the young. A sense of high spirits recurs, even when excess and disease had ruined him: his last recorded words are 'I could even be witty'. Leigh Hunt was exasperated by what he saw as canting theology; but Lamb continued to enjoy Coleridge's 'g—g—reat deal of fun'—a light but profound remark, with, as John Beer has suggested, pregnant implications for our full sense of Coleridge.

And thirdly, on a rather different tack. Although the records gathered here come out of real-life encounters, they are themselves, in variously ambitious ways, works of imagining, or re-imagining. Some are by the most distinguished writers of the period: any collection of the best romantic prose will contain portraits of Coleridge by Lamb, De Quincey, and Hazlitt; Coleridge inspired some of Wordsworth's greatest lines, an inimitable poetry of mingled intimacy, anxiety and awe. Those are the highlights. Considering the body of memoir as a whole, I think we can make out an interesting development—beginning with the visionary of Wordsworth's verse, and extending down, through Gillman's loyal *Life*, to Carlyle's satire, and beyond: the establishment of a distinctive (and tenacious) portrait of Genius. The language used by the memoirists to describe his speech is very often drawn from the same imaginative repertoire as Coleridge's (and Wordsworth's) own: rivers, streams and torrents gush and flash through the pages ahead, favourite romantic figures for the never-ending fluency and fluidity of human consciousness. Accurate reporting was clearly hopeless in such a case, and Coleridge himself lamented that he had no Boswell; at other times, though, the impossibility was a point of pride: Johnson's capacity to talk in pointed, atomistic, transcribable epigrams was precisely what implied the limits of his imagination. By contrast, the on-flowing stream of Coleridge's all-encompassing and holistic mind—no slave to those false powers Wordsworth deplored in *The Prelude*, which divide the world up into discriminative categories and separable concepts—gloriously resisted transcription. Many writers of the accounts collected here profess their sad incompetence, lamenting the inadequacy of their language—so Coleridge's garrulous consciousness becomes, in itself, the new object of a kind of wonder, encountered in the domestic comfort of Mrs. Gillman's Highgate garden, but quite as beyond normal articulation or rational containment as more traditional sources of sublimity. At the same time, this new digressive sublime has its dark aspect: there is a sense in many of these accounts that such power has been purchased at a terrible cost, and that Coleridge is as much its victim as its beneficiary. And here again, the memoirists are picking up on a Coleridgean idiom, though of a more troubling kind: the compelling grey eye of the inspired Genius (the detail of Coleridge's face repeatedly singled out) is often likened to the fixing, tormented eye of the Ancient Mariner. Charismatic, distracted, unworldly, self-involuted, suffering, this figure of Genius is really a *myth* of Coleridge—quite at odds (we should remember) with the jokey or gamesome, socialised or wittily adept man who appears elsewhere. But, deplored or venerated, this mythical type is itself a remarkable element of the immense, disorganised Coleridgean legacy which we are still experiencing; and it is in these recorded interviews and recollections that we can watch it taking its impressive shape.

In the evening at Charles Lamb's. He was serious,
and therefore very interesting. I accidentally made use of the
expression 'poor Coleridge!' Lamb corrected me, not angrily,
but as if really pained. 'He is,' he said, 'a fine fellow,
in spite of all his faults and weaknesses. Call him Coleridge;
I hate *poor*, as applied to such a man. I can't bear
to hear such a man pitied.'

Henry Crabb Robinson's Diary, 3 August 1811

One
Childhood, School, Cambridge 1772-94

Boy

(i) JOSEPH COTTLE

From Joseph Cottle, Early Recollections; *chiefly relating to the late Samuel Taylor Coleridge, during his long residence in Bristol (2 vols.; 1837), I, 241. Joseph Cottle (1770-1835), himself a minor poet, was publisher of Coleridge and Wordsworth (among others). He presumably heard this story from Coleridge's own lips — making it evidence at one remove of Coleridge's powers as a raconteur.*

Little Sammy Coleridge had heard of fishing, and thought he could catch fish as well as his elders. With this impression strong on his mind he went to his sister Ann, (older than himself)[1] and asked for a hook and line, when she crooked a pin, and tying it to a piece of thread, told him to go and bring home all the fish he could catch in the gutter flowing through the street. Little Sammy thought he should never be able to catch any thing better than eels, in that ignoble current, and having an ambition to catch a whale, he hurried off toward the River Otter. The evening was coming on, and not finding a whale, in one part of the river, he posted off further down; and proceeding still in his lofty pursuit, he wandered to a great distance; till, overcome with weariness, he lay down on the bank of the river, and there fell fast asleep.

(ii) WILLIAM JERDAN

From 'Men I Have Known: Samuel Taylor Coleridge', Leisure Hour *XI (1862) 679-80, 680. Jerdan (1782-1869) was a man of letters and editor of the* London Literary Gazette *— where a version of this anecdote first appeared ('Coleridge's Table Talk',* London Literary Gazette *957 (23 May 1835) 340-2, 342). Another version crops up in his* Autobiography *(4 vols.; 1852-3), III, 313.*

I have not yet noticed a vein of sportive humour which he occasionally displayed, and which was exceedingly amusing when it accompanied the relation of any whimsical anecdote. The lustre of his large eye, the gravity of his look, the silvery tone of his voice, and a slightly drawling manner in the delivery of his narrative, gave a peculiar significance to these little stories, of which no idea can be formed from the matter, divorced from the accessories of person, emphasis, and a playful action. I remember one case in point. He described his school-days, and, I think, when a junior pupil in a boarding-school kept by his father.[2] It was speech and breaking-up day, and the parents were gratified with the exhibition of a drama enacted by their sons. Among the rest, Coleridge had to say something, attended by a laugh, which he unhappily uttered without an attempt at cachinnation, 'Ha! ha! ha!' The father, who had bestowed great pains on the passage, and was dreadfully provoked, as one of the *irritabile genus vatum*[3] ought to be, by its being 'come tardy off,'[4] leapt upon the platform, and, seizing the delinquent by the ears, vociferated a *laugh* by way of example, though hardly more genial than the first offence. At any rate, it was out of time and place; and the more he shook him, shouting 'Ha, ha, haw!' the more the culprit failed in his imitation, till at last his doleful 'ha!' was emitted with a blubber and a howl, which set the whole audience in a roar.

NOTES

[1] Anne ('Nancy') (1767-1791) was to die of tuberculosis. STC was called 'Sam' or 'Sammy' by his family, names he detested (see *CL*, II, 1126).
[2] John Coleridge was Vicar of Ottery St Mary's, and headmaster of the Grammar School, from 1760. STC joined the school in 1778.
[3] 'Irritable race of poets': Horace, *Epistles*, II.ii, l.102.
[4] *Hamlet*, III.ii, l.25. Part of Hamlet's advice to the players.

The Inspired Charity-Boy

(i) 'ELIA' (CHARLES LAMB)

From 'Christ's Hospital Five and Thirty Years Ago', collected in Elia. Essays *which have Appeared under that Signature in the London Magazine (1823), 47-48. Lamb (1775-1834), essayist, poet, and officer of India House, was one of Coleridge's most devoted and amused friends.*

Come back into memory, like as thou wert in the day-spring of thy fancies, with hope like a fiery column before thee—the dark pillar not yet turned[1]—Samuel Taylor Coleridge—Logician, Metaphysician, Bard!—How have I seen the casual passer through the Cloisters stand still, intranced with admiration (while he weighed the disproportion between the *speech* and the *garb* of the young Mi-randula),[2] to hear thee unfold, in thy deep and sweet intonations, the mysteries of Jamblichus, or Plotinus[3] (for even in those years thou waxedst not pale at such philosophic draughts), or reciting Homer in his Greek, or Pindar—while the walls of the old Grey Friars[4] re-echoed to the accents of the *inspired charity-boy!*—Many were the "wit-combats," (to dally awhile with the words of old Fuller,)[5] between him and C.V. Le G——[6], "which two I behold like a Spanish great gallion, and an English man of war; Master Coleridge, like the former, was built far higher in learning, solid, but slow in his performances. C.V.L., with the English man of war, lesser in bulk, but lighter in sailing, could turn with all tides, tack about, and take advantage of all winds, by the quickness of his wit and invention."

(ii) JAMES GILLMAN

From James Gillman, The Life of Samuel Taylor Coleridge *(1838), 17-20. Gillman (1792-1839) was Coleridge's physician-cum-disciple for almost his last twenty years, and his biographer. Only one volume of the* Life *appeared. It is one of our best sources for the early years, though we should remember that much of it is oblique autobiography. 'I had often pressed him to write some account of his early life, and of the various circumstances connected with it', Gillman says, 'But the aversion he had to read or write anything about himself was so great, that I never succeeded, except in obtaining a few notes, rather than a detailed account' (*Life*, 9). Early episodes, like the following, were based upon these notes.*

Never was a friend or schoolfellow more fondly attached to another than Lamb to Coleridge. The latter from his own account, as well as from Lamb and others who knew him when at school, must have been a delicate and suffering boy. His principal ailments he owed much to the state of his stomach, which was at that time so delicate, that when compelled to go to a large closet (shoe-bin, its school name,) containing shoes, to pick out a pair easy to his feet, which were always tender, and he required shoes so large that he could walk in them, rather than with them, and the smell, from the number in this place, used to make him so sick, that I have often seen him shudder, even in late life, when he gave an account of it. In this note, continuing an account of himself at school, he says, 'From eight to fourteen I was a playless day-dreamer, a *helluo librorum*,[7] my appetite for which was indulged by a singular incident: a stranger, who was struck by my conversation, made me free of a circulating library in King Street, Cheapside.' The incident, indeed, was singular: going down the Strand, in one of his day-dreams, fancying himself swimming across the Hellespont, thrusting his hands before him as in the act of swimming, his hand came in contact with a gentleman's pocket; the gentleman seized his hand, turning round and looking at him with some anger, 'What! so young, and so wicked?' at the same time accused him of an attempt to pick his pocket; the frightened boy sobbed out his denial of the intention, and explained to him how he thought himself Leander, swimming across the Hellespont. The gentleman was so struck and delighted with the novelty of the thing, and with the simplicity and intelligence of the boy, that he subscribed, as before stated, to the library, in consequence of which Coleridge was further enabled to indulge his love of reading. In his bathing excursions he had greatly injured his health, and reduced his strength; in one of these bathing exploits he swam across the New River[8] in his clothes, and dried them in the fields on his back: from these excursions commenced those bodily sufferings which embittered the rest of his life, and rendered it truly one of sickness and suffering. When a boy he had a remarkably delicate, white skin, which was once the cause of great punishment to him. His dame had undertaken to cure him of the itch, with which the boys of his ward had suffered much; but Coleridge was doomed to suffer more than his comrades, from the use of sulphur ointment, through the great sagacity of his dame, who with her extraordinary eyes, aided by the power of glasses, could see the malady in the skin deep and out of common vision; and consequently, as often as she employed this miraculous sight, she found or thought she found fresh reasons for continuing the friction, to the prolonged suffering and mortification of her patient. This occurred when he was about eight years of age, and gave rise to his first attempt at making a verse, as follows:

> 'O Lord, have mercy on me!
> For I am very sad!
> For why, good Lord? I've got the itch,
> And eke I've got the *tad*,'

the school name for ringworm. He was to be found during play-hours often with the knees of his breeches unbuttoned, and his shoes down at the heel, walking to and fro, or sitting on a step, or in a corner, deeply engaged in some book. This had attracted the notice of Middleton,[9] at that time a deputy grecian, and going up to him one day, asked what he was reading; the answer was

'Virgil.' 'Are you then,' said M. 'studying your lesson?' 'No,' said C., 'I am reading it for pleasure;' for he had not yet arrived at Virgil in his class studies. This struck Middleton as something so peculiar, that he mentioned it to the head master, as Coleridge was then in the grammar school (which is the lower part of the classical school), and doing the work of the lower boys. The Rev. James Bowyer, who was at that time head master, a quick discerning man, but hasty and severe, sent for the master of the grammar school, and inquired about Coleridge;[10] from him he learnt that he was a dull and inapt scholar, and that he could not be made to repeat a single rule of syntax, although he would give a rule in his own way. This brought Coleridge before Bowyer, and to this circumstance may be attributed the notice which he afterwards took of him: the school and his scholars were every thing to him, and Coleridge's neglect and carelessness never went unpunished. I have often heard him say, he was so ordinary a looking boy, with his black head, that Bowyer generally gave him at the end of a flogging an extra cut; 'for,' said he, 'you are such an ugly fellow!'

(iii) CHARLES VALENTINE LE GRICE

'Sonnet in Remembrance of the Poet Coleridge'; quoted in Edmund Blunden, 'Elia and Christ's Hospital', Essays and Studies XXII (1936) 37-60, 57. Le Grice (1773-1858) was another 'Grecian': one of the handful of boys prepared by Headmaster Bowyer for University. (Lamb was a Deputy Grecian.) Le Grice went up to Trinity, and remained part of Coleridge's circle. Later, ordained and settled in Cornwall, he became an indefatigable man of letters. (The poem is dated 16 June 1852.)

Coleridge, of Boyhood in the early dawn
Oppress'd I felt not, nor of hope forlorn,
Grasping your hand. You spake, as though our School
Were of a sep'rate world the vestibule;
And we it's inhabitants. — In cloister'd walk
While such of opening scenes your cherish'd talk,
I listen'd breathless; — and I saw you prove
Your boded triumphs in the College grove.
Thence, by a sudden plunge, amid their strife,
You sprang into the waves of this world's life;
Nor paused. — Far, far away 'twas mine to hear
Fame of your struggles, and th'applauding cheer. —
At last of wond'rous Boy, of Bard, of Sage
Sank beneath Friendship's roof the shelter'd Age.

(iv) THOMAS HARTWELL HORNE

From Thomas Hartwell Horne, Reminiscences Personal and Bibliographical *(1862), 4-5; 5-6. Horne (1780-1862), also at Christ's Hospital, was later Prebend in St. Paul's Cathedral, and a librarian at the British Museum. He casts a side-light on school life, and on Coleridge's pre-eminence within it.*

'My next remove was into the Royal and Ancient Foundation of Christ's Hospital, on the presentation of Mr. Graham's intimate friend, the celebrated barrister and dramatic author, Arthur Murphy, Esq..[11] Here I received the rudiments of a classical education between the years 1789 and 1795. During two years I was contemporary with the subsequently eminent poet, Samuel Taylor Coleridge, at that time head-Grecian or senior scholar; who evinced his gratitude for my father's hospitalities to him by giving me private instruction in the summer school vacation of 1790.

This enabled me to attain such proficiency, that I was removed many months earlier than I otherwise could have been, from the under grammar school into the upper school, which was then under the able superintendence of the devoted head-master, the Rev. James Boyer, M.A., of whose scholastic discipline and peculiarities Mr. Coleridge has given a graphic delineation in the first volume of his "Biographia Literaria."'[12] [...]

It was not unusual for the Grecians to give private lessons to younger boys, whose friends showed them kindness in return;[13] and, as Coleridge was himself an orphan with scarcely any connections in London, my grandfather's invitations could not have been unacceptable.[14] The late matron of Christ's Hospital, Mrs. Green, who resided more than fifty years within its walls, recollected frequently giving 'Little Horne' a ticket of leave to accompany Coleridge to my grandfather's house on holidays. Among other things, Coleridge taught my father the Greek alphabet. At that early period the future poet evinced his prevailing taste by declaiming verses as he went about the school-grounds.

(v) REV. CHARLES LEAPIDGE SMITH

From 'Reminiscences of an Octogenarian', Leisure Hour *IX (1860) 633-35, 633-34. Smith confirms Coleridge's fascination with the 'Arabian Nights'.*

As you wish for something relative to my old satrap, S.T. Coleridge, permit me to inform you that in my early days I performed the onerous duty, among others, of cleaning his shoes; and well do I remember that they were too often for my comfort very dirty, for he was not very nice in his person or in his dress. He seldom had two garters at one time, in consequence of which his stockings used to drop into a series of not very elegant folds. I have a pleasing remembrance of even Coleridge's old shoes; for, as he was not very particular *how* they were cleaned, and I was not very particular how I cleaned them, the Grecian and myself agreed pretty well on that matter; but woe to my head if he caught me taking the liberty to read in his study. There was not much there to tempt me, however, for my taste was then quite in another direction. Instead of Homer and Virgil, I much preferred 'The Seven Champions,' or even 'Jack the Giant-killer.' Unluckily, as it happened, he had an odd volume of the 'Arabian Nights' Entertainments,' in the vulgar tongue, and one day he caught me very cozily reading this work; on which discovery he most unceremoniously, or perhaps I should say very ceremoniously, kicked me out, prefacing the act with an animated speech. Yes, I well remember his wrath at my impudence, as he angrily called it. What may have increased his indignation on the occasion was, that he found me in the act of eating a remnant of mince-pie, which, in my juvenile innocence, I fancied to be my perquisite as his study boy. Well do I remember the furious look he assumed as he put back his long black curls from his face, and the wrathful curl of his lip in the disappointment of his lost mince-pie, when he hurled the empty plate after me as I quickly retreated from his presence.

I remember his entering his study one afternoon in a state of great irritation against Dr. Bowyer, the head master, who had deeply offended his majesty by sneering at his definition of some Greek word, which I have forgotten, and then sending me for a rush candle (the night light of those times). After lighting it, he desired me to go to the doctor's house, immediately opposite, and present it to him with Coleridge's duty, particularly informing the doctor that Coleridge had lighted it. I did not much relish the task, but on presenting myself to the doctor and delivering my message (lighted rush in hand), he laughed most heartily, and replied, 'Tell Colly (he always called him so when pleased) that he is a good fellow.' As, from my ignorance of Greek, I never could comprehend this, I must leave the solution thereof to those learned Thebans who may be competent to unriddle the enigma.[15]

Although Coleridge was somewhat of a hard task-master, yet I parted from him, on his leaving for the university, with as deep a regret as a boy could feel for one so superior to himself. In person he was a tall, dark, handsome young man, with long black flowing hair; eyes, not merely dark, but black and keenly penetrating; a fine forehead, a deep-toned harmonious voice; a manner never to be forgotten, full of life, vivacity, and kindness; dignified in his person, and, added to all these, exhibiting the elements of his future greatness. Yet there was something awful about him, for all his equals in age and rank quailed before him. No wonder, therefore, if I did, who was selected to be his 'boy' or attendant; he was to me the very impersonation of majesty, and stern indeed he could be when offended.

NOTES

[1] Exodus 13.21-22, 14.19.

[2] Giovanni Pico della Mirandola (1463-94), polymathic philosopher and poet.

[3] Neoplatonists Iamblichus (c.245-c.325), and Plotinus (205-169/70). STC describes his early study of Platonists in BL (I, 144), so Lamb's account may not be as hyperbolic as it first appears.

[4] Christ's Hospital was founded by Edward VI in 1552, on the site of a Franciscan monastery, as a free school for the children of poor gentry.

[5] Lamb here adopts Thomas Fuller's description of 'wit-combats' between Jonson and Shakespeare in his History of Worthies of England (1662).

[6] Charles Valentine Le Grice: for whom, see headnote above.

[7] i.e. 'glutton for books'.

[8] An artificial waterway between Hertfordshire and London.

[9] Thomas Middleton; for whom, see headnote below.

[10] James Boyer or Bowyer (1736-1814), Upper Master during STC's time, and a severe disciplinarian. He once flogged STC for atheism (TT, I, 143-4).

[11] Arthur Murphy (1727-1805), farceur. Boys were presented to enter Christ's Hospital; STC was presented in April 1782 by Judge Buller, a former student of his father (CL, I, 388). John Coleridge had died suddenly on 4 October 1781.

[12] BL, I, 8-11.

[13] The Reminiscences are edited with commentary by Horne's daughter, Sarah Anne Cheyne, who here takes over the account from her father.

[14] STC described himself as an orphan-schoolboy (BL, I, 16), but he was not without family. His maternal uncle, a tobacconist and clerk called Bowden, put the boy up for ten weeks on his arrival in London. STC later recalled being displayed by him as a 'prodigy' in taverns and coffee-houses (CL, I, 388).

[15] The best suggestions are offered by John Beer, 'Coleridge at School', N&Q 203 (1958) 114-116, 115-16. The point may be the way that some verbs can mean both 'to do something' and 'to make to do something': thus, 'to light' can mean 'to kindle' and 'to illuminate'.

A Cambridge Figure

Coleridge went up to Jesus College, Cambridge in October 1791. In his first year, already awarded an Exhibition and a Scholarship, he won the Sir William Brown Gold Medal for a Greek Ode (on the slave trade); and in January 1793, he was one of the four finalists for the University's Craven Scholarship. In the event, that went to Samuel Butler, later Headmaster of Shrewsbury;[1] but Jesus awarded him £33 a year for 'the Librarian and Clerk Chapel's Place' (*CL*, I, 45; 46). The next year, he was *proxime accessit* in the Brown prize to John Keate, later Headmaster of Eton. (The poem is lost, but we have Southey's translation). In May 1793, the Frend trial blew up, and Coleridge's life took a radically different turn.

(i) THOMAS MIDDLETON

From The Country Spectator *XVI (22 January 1793), 128; 129. The 'truly learned, and every way excellent' Thomas Fanshaw Middleton (1769-1822), first Protestant Bishop of Calcutta, was at school with Coleridge, and, three years older, his 'patron and protector' (BL, I, 13). He overlapped with Coleridge at Cambridge for a year, going down in 1792 – removing a crucial stabilising influence on the younger man (CL, III, 69). Middleton produced* The Country Spectator *(1792-3) from Gainsborough (where he was curate). This passage comes from a letter, supposedly by a disappointed graduate, whose thoughts dwell sadly on Cambridge days, and especially on a thinly disguised Coleridge.*

I look back to the hours, which I spent at College, with pleasing fond regret, and in vain sigh for their return. My feelings at this moment are admirably expressed in some charming lines of *Cowley's Dedicatory Elegy;*[2] and as they happily have not been 'blown upon' (to use the phrase of *Addison*)[3] by the swarm of learned flies, who do little else than quote, I will subjoin the whole passage, together with a *Sonnet* written in imitation of it.

> *O mihi jucundum Grantæ super omnia nomen!* [...]

> CAMBRIDGE! dear name, at whose transporting sound
> A pang of fond remembrance thrills my breast,
> O could those hours return, which Friendship blest,
> Which Letter'd Ease, the Muse, and C******** crown'd.
> How calm my soul, when oft at parting day
> CAM saw me musing by his willowy side,
> The while I would recite some raptur'd lay,
> Whose lingering murmurs floated down the tide.
> Yet ah! too short is Youth's fantastic dream,
> Ere manhood wakes th'unweeting heart to woe!
> Silent and smooth CAM's loitering waters flow;

So glided Life, a smooth and silent stream:
Sad change! for now by choking cares withstood
It scarcely bursts its way, a troubled boisterous flood.

(ii) GEORGE DYER

From The Monthly Magazine; or, British Register *XVII (1804), 125. Dyer (1755-1841), Grecian and Cantab., was a prolific author and journalist. This piece appears in 'Cantabrigiana', a regular gathering of university stories which Dyer contributed to the* Monthly. *The anecdote earned a rebuff from Coleridge (CL, II, 1091), denying that he was 'of the genus irritabile; and must resign all claim to the poetic inspiration, if irritability be an essential character of it' (which anticipates BL, I, 30-47). Feelings weren't hurt: the letter ends with three epigrams which Dyer published in the next column (CL, II, 1092n.2).*

The poetical abilities of Mr. Coleridge, formerly of Jesus College, are well known. He obtained one of the prizes at Cambridge, and but one, for a Greek ode. Being once in company with a person who had gained two prizes, the latter carried himself with an air of superiority and triumph, and seemed to estimate his own abilities above Coleridge's, in the ratio of at least two to one. A person in company growing, at length, indignant at the vaunting airs of the conceited young fellow, exclaimed, 'Why zounds, Sir, a man's leg may as easily be too big for the boot, as your's just fitted it.'[4]

(iii) CHARLES VALENTINE LE GRICE

From 'Cergiel', 'College Reminiscences of Mr. Coleridge', Gentleman's Magazine NS II (1834) 605-7, 606. This memoir appeared shortly after Coleridge's death, and disputes an obituarist's statement that Coleridge 'did not obtain, and indeed did not aim to obtain, the honours of the University'. Le Grice cites Coleridge's Browne medal, and his near-success in the scholarship competition; and goes on to discuss the effect which that last failure had upon him.

Unfortunately, at that period there was no classical Tripos; so that, if a person did not obtain the classical medal, he was thrown back among the totally undistinguished; and it was not allowable to become a candidate for the classical medal, unless you had taken a respectable degree in mathematics. Coleridge had not the least taste for these, and here his case was hopeless; so that he despaired of a Fellowship, and gave up what in his heart he coveted, college honours, and a college life. He had seen Middleton (late Bishop of Calcutta) quit Pembroke under similar circumstances. Not *quite* similar, because Middleton studied mathematics so as to take a respectable degree, and to enable him to try for the medal: but he failed, and therefore all hopes failed of a Fellowship—most fortu-

nately, as it proved in after-life for Middleton, though he mourned
at the time most deeply, and exclaimed, 'I am Middleton, which is
another name for Misfortune !' [...] – But to return to Coleridge.
When he quitted college, which he did before he had taken a degree, in a moment of mad-cap caprice – it was indeed an inauspicious hour! – 'In an inauspicious hour I left the friendly cloisters
and the happy grove of quiet, ever-honoured Jesus College, Cambridge.'[5] Short but deep and heartfelt reminiscence! In a literary
Life of himself, this short memorial is all that Coleridge gives of his
happy days at college. Say not that he did not obtain, and did not
wish to obtain classical honours! He did obtain them, and was eagerly ambitious of them; but he did not bend to that discipline
which was to qualify him for the whole course. He was very studi-
ous, but his reading was desultory and capricious. He took little
exercise merely for the sake of exercise; but he was ready at any
time to unbend his mind in conversation, and for the sake of this,
his room (the ground-floor room on the right hand of the staircase
facing the great gate) was a constant rendezvous of conversation-
loving friends, – I will not call them loungers, for they did not call
to kill time, but to enjoy it. What evenings have I spent in those
rooms! What little suppers, or *sizings*, as they were called, have I
enjoyed; when Æschylus, and Plato, and Thucydides were pushed
aside, with a pile of lexicons, &c. to discuss the pamplets of the
day. Ever and anon, a pamphlet issued from the pen of Burke.
There was no need of having the book before us. Coleridge had
read it in the morning, and in the evening he would repeat whole
pages verbatim. Frend's trial was then in progress. Pamphlets
swarmed from the press. Coleridge had read them all; and in the
evening, with our negus, we had them *viva voce* gloriously. O
Coleridge! it was indeed an inauspicious hour, when you quitted
the friendly cloisters of Jesus.

(iv) HENRY GUNNING

From Henry Gunning, Reminiscences of the University, Town and County
of Cambridge *(2 vols.; 1854), I, 299-301. William Frend (1757-1841), was a
fellow of Jesus. By the time Coleridge arrived in Cambridge, he had already lost
his college tutorship for urging abolition of the Religious Tests then required for
fellowships. He had welcomed the Revolution in France, and wrote in favour of
radical reform – including Church reform – in* Peace *and* Union *(1793), which
he was called upon to defend before both University and College. Throughout May
1793, the Vice-Chancellor's court met in the Senate House. Finally, faced with the*

charge that the pamphlet was seditious, Frend refused to retract. The trial was a
sensation, and undergraduates attended in large numbers, supporting Frend
noisily, Coleridge among them. Gunning (1768-1854), a student in the 1780s,
became esquire bedell in 1789, and later senior esquire bedell.

The Undergraduates were unanimous in favour of Mr. Frend, and
every satirical remark reflecting upon the conduct and motives of
his prosecutors was vociferously applauded. At length the Court
desired the Proctors to interfere. Mr. Farish, the Senior Proctor,
having marked one man who had particularly distinguished
himself by applauding, and noted his position in the gallery,
selected him as a fit subject for punishment. He went into the
gallery, and having previously ascertained the exact situation of
the culprit, he touched a person, whom he supposed to be the
same, on the shoulder, and asked him his name and college. The
person thus addressed assured him that he had been perfectly
quiet. Farish replied, 'I have been watching you for a long time,
and have seen you repeatedly clapping your hands.' 'I wish this
was possible,' said the man, and turning round, exhibited an arm
so deformed that his hands could not by any possibility be brought
together: this exculpation was received with repeated rounds of
applause, which continued for some minutes. The name of the
young man was Charnock, and his college Clare Hall; the real
culprit was S.T. Coleridge, of Jesus College, who having observed
that the Proctor had noticed him, and was coming into the gallery,
turned round to the person who was standing behind him, and
made an offer of changing places, which was gladly accepted by
the unsuspecting man. Coleridge immediately retreated, and
mixing with the crowd, entirely escaped suspicion. This conduct on
the part of Coleridge, was severely censured by the
Undergraduates, as it was quite clear that, to escape punishment
himself, he would have subjected an innocent man to rustication or
expulsion.[6]

Coleridge was an excellent classical scholar; he affected a peculiar style in conversation, and his language was very poetical. An
instance has at this moment occurred to me. Speaking of the dinners in Hall, he described the veal which was served up to them
(and which was large and coarse) in the following words, — 'We
have veal, Sir, tottering on the verge of beef!'[7] The topic upon
which Coleridge much delighted to converse, was the establishment of a society consisting of twelve members, each of whom,

after having learned some handicraft (I think he was learning to be a carpenter), should select a highly accomplished woman, who should accompany them to some remote and uninhabited country, where they should form a colony of themselves.[8] He and Southey married two sisters, whom they first saw in Bristol.[9] The projected colonization never took place, but a button-manufacturer at Birmingham (who was to have been one of the party)[10] defrayed all the expenses that had been incurred to carry out this wild scheme.

(v) WILLIAM ROUGH

From Edith J. Morley, 'Some Contemporary Allusions to Coleridge's Death'; in Coleridge. Studies by Several Hands on the Hundredth Anniversary of his Death, *ed. Edmund Blunden and Earl Leslie Griggs (1934) 89-95, 92-3. Rough, later Lord Chief Justice of Ceylon, was an intimate of Crabb Robinson (see chapter 4), to whom, in 1835, upon Coleridge's death, he wrote the letter from which this passage comes. It nicely sketches the radical excitement of Coleridge's Cambridge.*

The first Individual of those with whom I early associated at Cambridge, was Satterthwaite:[11] (a Man of no mean natural powers). He was the first cut off from us—a Memento not lost upon me. Poor Coleridge has since followed! I recall a juvenile Scene to my mind, in which both of these were with myself engaged—I think, in my first or second Term at Trinity. Frend, the Algebraist, had published a pamphlet named Peace & Union, and was called upon to answer for the Opinions expressed in it before the Vice Chancellor's Court, in the Senate House. He appeared to Us an oppressed Man and a party was suddenly made up to chalk his Name in triumph upon the University Walls. Copley, although of a higher Year, joined Us, and also so did the late Legh Richmond,[12] who afterwards adopted opinions like those of Cargill & Mason. Richmond had a stump leg, but was very active—the Pavement rang with his Steps and drew after Us the Proctor and his Beadles—it became necessary for Richmond to screen himself under a Post. The work however was prosecuted and hardly was a Wall of a College left unmarked by 'Frend for Ever.' We were at it three or four Hours.

(vi) ROBERT OWEN

From The Life of Robert Owen. *Written by Himself (2 vols.; 1857-8), I, 35-6.*
Owen (1771-1858), industrialist and reformer, and author of A New View of
Society or Essays on the Principle of the Formation of the Human
Character *(1813-17). His autobiography is distinguished by neither accuracy*
nor modesty, and Owen's account of effortless triumph here looks unlikely; but it
is interesting to learn that Coleridge visited the Manchester Academy (in late
1793),[13] implying the depth of his involvement in non-conformist circles.

At this period John Dalton, the Quaker, afterwards the celebrated
Dr. Dalton the philosopher, and a Mr. Winstanley, both intimate
friends of mine, were assistants in this college under Dr. Baines;[14]
and in their room we often met in the evenings, and had much [*sic*]
and frequent interesting discussions upon religion, morals, and
other similar subjects, as well as upon the late discoveries in
chemistry and other sciences, — and here Dalton first broached his
then undefined atomic theory. We began to think ourselves philosophers. Occasionally we admitted a friend or two to join our
circle, but this was considered a favour. At this period Coleridge
was studying at one of the universities, and was then considered a
genius and eloquent. He solicited permission to join our party, that
he might meet me in discussion, as I was the one who opposed the
religious prejudices of all sects, though always in a friendly and
kind manner, having now imbibed the spirit of charity and kindness for my opponents, which was forced upon me by my knowledge of the true formation of character by nature and society. Mr.
Coleridge had a great fluency of words, and he could well put
them together in high-sounding sentences; but my words, directly
to the point, generally told well; and although the eloquence and
learning were with him, the strength of the argument was generally admitted to be on my side. Many years afterwards, when he
was better known and more celebrated, I presented him with a
copy of my 'Essays on the Formation of Character,' and the next time I
met him after he had read them, he said — "Mr. Owen, I am really
ashamed of myself. I have been making use of many words in
writing and speaking what is called eloquence, while I find you
have said much more to the purpose in plain simple language,
easily to be understood, and in a short compass. I will endeavour
to profit by it."

(vii) CHRISTOPHER WORDSWORTH

From Christopher Wordsworth, Social Life at the English Universities in the Eighteenth Century *(Cambridge, 1874), 589-90. Christopher Wordsworth (1774-1846), the poet's brother, was at Trinity (and would later become Master). His diary for November 1793 contains several glimpses of Coleridge.*

Tuesday, Nov. 5 Roused about nine o'clock by Bilsborrow and Le Grice with a proposal to become member of a literary society: the members they mentioned as having already come into the plan, Coleridge, *Jes[us].*, Satterthwaite, Rough, and themselves, *Trin[ity] C[ollege]*, and Franklin, *Pembroke.* Heard Allen's dissertation on K. William; was to have gone to Coleridge's to wine, to consult on the plan, had I not been engaged at home with the Howeses and Strickland. Went with them to the coffee-house. On my going out met Bilsborrow: returned back with him. Soon after came in Le Grice, Coleridge, and Rough. Got all into a box and (having met with the Monthly Review of my Brother's Poems),[15] entered into a good deal of literary and critical conversation on Dr. Darwin, Miss Seward, Mrs. Smith, Bowles,[16] and my Brother. Coleridge spoke of the esteem in which my Brother was holden by a society at Exeter,[17] of which Downman and Hole were members, as did Bilsborrow (which he had before told me) of his repute with Dr. Darwin, Miss Seward, &c., &c., at Derby. Coleridge talked Greek, Max. Tyrius he told us,[18] and spouted out of Bowles. At nine o'clock called on Satterthwaite, and sat awhile with him.

Thursday, 7. Rose at half-past eight. Lectures began, went to them at nine. Breakfasted with Rough. Met with Vaughan. Coleridge called on Rough: we sat in criticism on some of his poems. In one of them he wished he were a Woodbine bower, a Myrtle, the Zephyr to fan the folds of her garment, neck, hair, &c.; a Dream; and finally he wished

> to be the Heaven that he aloft 'might rise
> And gaze upon her with unnumber'd eyes,'[19]

which, by the bye, is borrowed from an epigram of Plato. Vid. Brunck.[20]

There was one idea, however, in its application to me new, which may compensate for the above. Somehow thus:

> The waving poplar 'sleeps upon the stream'[21]
> ('How sweet the moonlight *sleeps* upon this bank, &c.'). —
> *Merch. Ven.*[22] [...]

Friday, 8. Chapel. Lectures. Considered of a subject for my essay on Wednesday se'nnight. Drank Wine with Coleridge. Present, *the Society.* Chapel. Read *Morning Chronicle.* Found in it an ode to Fortune, by Coleridge, which I had seen at Rough's yesterday.[23] [...] *Wednesday, 13.* Satterthwaite and Malcolm, Trin., drunk Wine with me. The Society, this evening, met at my rooms for the first time. Time before supper was spent in hearing Coleridge repeat some original poetry (he having neglected to write his essay, which therefore is to be produced next week), and other men each his voluntary contribution. After supper, in debating and adjusting the Rules of the Society.

NOTES

1 In 1834, Butler wrote to the *Analyst* disputing its obituary of STC, which had described his negligence of academic honours. Butler cites the prize Ode and near-success in the Scholarships: 'I believe no other opportunity occurred for his exertions during his stay at College, he may, therefore, be fairly said to have distinguished himself on every occasion of competition for first-rate honours while at the University' (*Analyst,* I (1834), 227). A respectful letter from STC to Butler survives (*CL,* I, 82).

2 'Elegia Dedicatoria, ad Illustrissimam Academiam Cantabrigiensem', l.33ff.

3 *The Spectator,* no. 464 (22 August 1712).

4 Cf. the Cambridge anecdote recalled in the *Notebook* in November 1803: Frere assumes that STC is bound to win a university prize; STC reassures him that, on the contrary, he or some other King's man will win it. '"But why?" — Why, Sir! the Boot fits you, Sir! I cannot get my leg in.' (*CN,* I, 1656)

5 Cf. *BL,* I, 179.

6 The reviewer in *The Athenæum* (cited in the second edition of *Reminiscences* (2 vols.; 1855), I, 275n.) quotes Gunning's account of Frend's trial, and corrects it:

> Party feeling ran very high at the moment, and Charnock was one of those who, like Coleridge, felt strongly in favour of the accused: it had been previously agreed that Coleridge should be most violent in opposition to the Vice-Chancellor, and that if his conduct in hissing one side and applauding the other by clapping his hands, excited angry observation, that when the Proctor was sent up he should slip away, and leave Charnock to take his place, and bear the brunt of the affray. This arrangement was probably not known to many at the time, and hence the censure which Mr. Gunning tells us was bestowed upon Coleridge. In after-life the poet not unfrequently alluded to the transaction, and always maintained that the suggestion proceeded from Charnock himself, upon whom, of course, no punishment could be inflicted, and who sent the zealous Proctor away deceived and disconcerted. (*The Athenæum* 1400 (26 August 1854) 1038-1040, 1038-9).

7 STC's student fame as a conversationalist lingered for years. Touring the colleges in February 1866 in the company of William Whewell (1794-1866),

polymathic former Master of Trinity, the young Elizabeth Wordsworth was told: '"This was Coleridge's College. A man here used to tell stories of his keeping his fellow-collegians half an hour after Hall, with his interesting talk"' (Elizabeth Wordsworth, *Glimpses of the Past* (1912), 66).

[8] Pantisocracy was devised during the summer of 1794, a year after Frend's trial: Gunning may be recalling stories of STC's conversations during the autumn of 1794, when he was sometimes in Cambridge. There *was* talk of a plan to 'learn the theory and practice of agriculture and carpentry' (*CL*, I, 97).

[9] STC married Sara Fricker on 4 October, and Southey, Edith on 14 November.

[10] Gunning conflates Joseph Priestley (who lived in Birmingham and emigrated to America in 1794), the banker Lloyd (of Birmingham, whose son Charles lived with the Coleridges in 1796-7 as pupil and lodger), and the Wedgwoods, who offered STC money in 1797 and granted him an annuity in 1798. There was some suggestion that Priestley might join the Pantisocrats (*CL*, I, 98).

[11] James Satterthwaite (1772-1827), a Cockermouth man, was chaplain to George III before returning to the Lakes as Rector of several churches (*Alumni Cantabrigienses*, ed. J.A. Venn (10 vols.; Cambridge, 1953), Pt. II, vol.V, 423).

[12] John Singleton Copley, Baron Lyndhurst (1772-1863), later Lord Chancellor; Legh Richmond (1772-1827), later a celebrated evangelical preacher.

[13] The date argued for by John Unsworth, 'Coleridge and the Manchester Academy', *Charles Lamb Bulletin* NS XXXII (October 1980), 149-58.

[14] The 'college' is the Manchester Academy, with which Owen was associated. John Dalton (1766-1844) was the first to describe colour-blindness, and formulated the atomic theory. Winstanley was in fact a student, and 'Baines' is really Thomas Barnes, the Principal (Unsworth, 153; 151). The Academy led a peripatetic life, before finally settling in Oxford as Manchester College.

[15] Wordsworth's *An Evening Walk* and *Descriptive Sketches* were published in January 1793. Holcroft's review appeared in the *Monthly Review* for October.

[16] Erasmus Darwin, (1731-1802), physician, naturalist, and poet, author of *The Botanic Garden* (1789-92); Anna Seward (1747-1809), 'The Swan of Lichfield', poet, author of *Louisa* (1784); Charlotte Smith (1749-1806), novelist and poet, author of *Emmeline; or, The Orphan of the Castle* (1788) and *Ethelinde; or, the Recluse of the Lake* (1789). For Bowles, see headnote below.

[17] STC had heard 'An Evening Walk' recited at a literary society in Exeter during the previous summer vacation.

[18] Maximus of Tyre (2nd. C.), whose *Dialexeis* are full of Homer and Platonism.

[19] 'Lines on an Autumnal Evening', ll.69-70, *var.* (*CPW*, I, 53).

[20] Richard Francois Philippe Brunck (1729-1803); his edition of Greek epigrams appeared in 1773. In *Poems* (1796), STC apologises for the lack of originality in ll.57-70: 'every thought is to be found in the Greek Epigrams' (*CPW*, I, 52n.).

[21] Misremembering STC's 'Songs of the Pixies', ll.71-2 (*CPW*, I, 43).

[22] *Merchant of Venice*, V.i, l.54.

[23] 'To Fortune...', *The Morning Chronicle*, 7 November 1793 (*CPW*, I, 54-55).

Silas Tomkyn Comberbache

By November 1793, Coleridge was badly in debt. He bought a forlorn ticket in the Irish lottery, sending to the *Morning Chronicle* the poem which Christopher Wordsworth had seen, on fortune: his first published poem. Fleeing to London (according to Gillman)[1] he saw an advertisement for the Dragoons, and enlisted in the 15th or King's Light Dragoons on 2 December 1793, as Silas Tomkyn Comberbache. Before joining, he told some of 'the young men at Christ's Hospital' (*CL*, I, 62), and news reached his elder brother George; by April 1794, he had been bought out, discharged insane. Back at Jesus, he was gated; but by the year's end his university career was over anyway: he had met Southey and become a Pantisocrat.

(i) JAMES GILLMAN
From Gillman, Life, 59–62; 60n..

The same amiable and benevolent conduct which was so inter-woven in his nature, soon made him friends, and his new com-rades vied with each other in their endeavours to be useful to him; and being, as before described, rather helpless, he required the as-sistance of his fellow-soldiers. They cleaned his horse, attended particularly to its heels, and to the accoutrements. At this time he frequently complained of a pain at the pit of his stomach, accom-panied with sickness, which totally prevented his stooping, and in consequence he could never arrive at the power of bending his body to rub the heels of his horse, which alone was sufficient to make him dependent on his comrades; but it should be observed that he on his part was ever willing to assist them by being their amanuensis when one was required, and wrote all their letters to their sweethearts and wives. It appears that he never advanced beyond the awkward squad, and that the drill-sergeant had little hope of his progress from the necessary warnings he gave to the rest of the troop, even to this same squad to which he belonged; and, though his awkward manœuvres were well understood, the sergeant would vociferously exclaim, 'Take care of that Comber-bach, take care of him, for he will ride over you,' and other such complimentary warnings. From the notice that one of his officers took of him, he excited, for a short time, the jealousy of some of his companions. When in the street, he walked behind this officer as an orderly, but when out of town they walked abreast, and his comrades not understanding how a soldier in the awkward squad merited this distinction, thought it a neglect of themselves, which, for the time, produced some additional discomfort to Coleridge. I believe this officer to have been Capt. Ogle, who I think visited him in after life at Highgate. It seems that his attention had been drawn to Coleridge in consequence of discovering the following sentence in the stables, written in pencil, 'Eheu! quam infortunii miserrimum est fuisse felicem!' [2] but his more immediate discovery arose from a young man who had left Cambridge for the army, and in his road through Reading to join his regiment, met Coleridge in the street in his Dragoon's dress, who was about to pass him, but, said he, 'No, Coleridge, this will not do, we have been seeking you these six months; I must and will converse with you, and have no hesitation in declaring that I shall immediately inform your friends that I have found you.' This led to Coleridge's return to Cambridge [...] He returned to Cambridge, but did not long remain there; and quitted it without taking a degree. [...]

There is another incident which I shall here relate that raised him in the esteem of his comrades. One of them was seized with confluent small-pox, and his life was considered in great danger. The fear of the spread of this had produced such alarm in his quarters, that the sufferer was nearly deserted. Here Coleridge's reading served him; and, having a small quantity of medical knowledge in addition to a large share of kindness, he volunteered his services, and nursed the sick man night and day for six weeks. His patient recovered, to the joy of Coleridge and of his comrades. The man was taken ill during a march, and in consequence of the fears of the persons of the place, he and Coleridge (who had volunteered to remain with him) were put into an out-building, and no communication held with them. — Coleridge remaining the whole time in the same room with the man (who, during part of his illness, was violently delirious) nursing and reading to him, &c.[.]

(ii) JOSEPH COTTLE

From Cottle, Early Recollections, *II, 56-7; 58-60; 64-5. Cottle casts his account of Coleridge in the dragoons as a comic interlude, one 'chiefly collected from Mr. C.'s own mouth, but not inconsiderably, from the information of other of his more intimate friends', particularly Robert Lovell, fellow Pantisocrat (II, 53; 51).*[3]

Mr. Coleridge, in the midst of all his deficiencies, it appeared, was liked by the men, although he was the butt of the whole company; being esteemed by them as next kin to a natural, though of a peculiar kind—a talking natural. This fancy of theirs was stoutly resisted by the love-sick swain, but the regimental logic prevailed; for, whatever they could do, with masterly dexterity, he could not do at all, ergo, must he not be a natural? There was no man in the regiment who met with so many falls from his horse, as Silas Tomken Cumberbatch [sic]! He often calculated with so little precision his due equilibrium, that, in mounting on one side, (perhaps the wrong stirrup) the probability was, especially, if his horse moved a little, that he lost his balance, and, if he did not roll back on this side, came down ponderously on the other! when the laugh spread amongst the men, 'Silas is off again!' Mr. C. had often heard of campaigns, but he never before had so correct an idea of hard service. [...]

[The officers] kindly took pity on the 'poor scholar,' and had Mr. C. removed to the medical department, where he was appointed 'assistant' in the regimental hospital. This change was a vast improvement in Mr. C.'s condition; and happy was the day, also, on which it took place, for the sake of the sick patients; for, Silas Tomken Cumberbatch's amusing stories, they said, did them more good than all the 'doctor's physic!' Many ludicrous dialogues sometimes occurred between Mr. C. and his new disciples; particularly with the 'geographer.' The following are some of these dialogues.

If he began talking to one or two of his comrades, (for they were all on a perfect equality, except, that those who went through their exercise the best, stretched their necks a little above the 'awkward squad;' in which ignoble class Mr. C. was placed, as the preeminent member, almost by acclamation.) If he began to speak, notwithstanding, to one or two, others drew near, increasing momently, till by and by the sick beds were deserted, and Mr. C. formed the centre of a large circle.

On one occasion, he told them of the Peloponnesian war, which lasted twenty-seven years, 'There must have been famous promotion there,' said one poor fellow, haggard as a death's head. Another, tottering with disease, ejaculated, 'can you tell, Silas, how many rose from the ra[n]ks?'

He now still more excited their wonderment, by recapitulating the feats of Archimedes. As the narrative proceeded, one restrained his scepticism, till he was almost ready to burst, and then vociferated, 'Silas, that's a lie!' 'D'ye think so?' said Mr. C. smiling, and went on with his story. The idea, however, got amongst them, that Silas's fancy was on the stretch, when Mr. C. finding that this tact would not do, changed his subject, and told them of a famous general, called Alexander the Great. As by a magic spell, the flagging attention was revived, and several, at the same moment, to testify their eagerness, called out, 'The general! The general!' 'I'll tell you all about him,' said Mr. C. when impatience marked every countenance. He then told them whose son this Alexander the Great was; no less than Philip of Macedon. 'I never heard of him,' said one. 'I think I have,' said another, (ashamed of being thought ignorant) 'Silas, wasn't he a Cornish man? I knew one of the Alexanders at Truro!'[4] [...]

The inspecting officer of his regiment, on one occasion, was examining the guns of the men, and coming to one piece which was rusty, he called out in an authoritative tone, 'Whose rusty gun is this?' when Mr. C. said, 'is it *very* rusty, Sir?' 'Yes Cumberbatch, it *is*,' said the officer, sternly. 'Then, Sir,' replied Mr. C. 'it must be mine!' The oddity of the reply disarmed the officer, and the 'poor scholar' escaped without punishment.

Mr. Coleridge was a remarkably awkward horseman, so much so, as generally to attract notice. Some years after this, he was riding along the turnpike road, in the county of Durham, when a wag, approaching him, noticed his peculiarity, and (quite mistaking his man) thought the rider a fine subject for a little sport; when, as he drew near, he thus accosted Mr. C.[.] 'I say, young man, did you meet a *tailor* on the road?' 'Yes,' replied Mr. C. (who was never at a loss for a rejoinder) 'I did; and he told me, if I went a little further I should meet a *goose!*' The assailant was struck dumb, while the traveller jogged on.[5]

(iii) WILLIAM LISLE BOWLES

From 'Miscellanea: Coleridge a private Soldier', The Athenæum 355 *(16 August 1834), 613-14. Bowles (1762-1850), was a poet and clergyman, over whose sonnets STC had enthused since school (BL, I, 14; 17); later, they became acquainted. After Coleridge's death, Bowles told the story of his military career, prompted by an obituary (*The Athenæum 353 (2 August 1834), 574-5)*. Bowles not only had the story from Coleridge: he was also a friend 'from our school days, and at Oxford, with that very officer [...] who alone procured his discharge.'*

The regiment was the 15th Elliot's Light Dragoons; the officer was Nathaniel Ogle, eldest son of Dr. Newton Ogle, Dean of Winchester, and brother of the late Mrs. Sheridan; he was a scholar, and leaving Merton College, he entered this regiment a cornet. Some years afterwards, I believe he was then Captain of Coleridge's troop, going into the stables, at Reading, he remarked written on the white wall, under one of the saddles, in large pencil characters, the following sentence, in Latin,

'Eheu! quam infortunii miserrimum est fuisse felicem!'

Being struck with the circumstance, and himself a scholar, Captain Ogle inquired of a soldier whether he knew to whom the saddle belonged. 'Please your honour, to Comberback,' answered the dragoon. 'Comberback!' said his captain, 'send him to me.' Comberback presented himself, with the inside of his hand in front of his cap. His officer mildly said, 'Comberback, did you write the Latin sentence which I have just read under your saddle?' 'Please your honour,' answered the soldier, 'I wrote it.' 'Then, my lad, you are not what you appear to be. I shall speak to the commanding officer, and you may depend on my speaking as a friend.' The commanding officer, I think, was General Churchill. Comberback* was examined, and it was found out, that having left Jesus College, Cambridge, and being in London without resources, he had enlisted in this regiment. He was soon discharged, — not from his democratical feelings, for whatever those feelings might be, as a soldier he was remarkably orderly and obedient, though he could not rub down his own horse. He was discharged from respect to his friends and his station. His friends having been informed of his situation, a chaise was soon at the door of the Bear Inn, Reading, and the officers of the 15th cordially shaking his hands, particularly the officer who had been the means of his discharge, he drove off, not without a tear in his eye, whilst his old companions of the tap-room† gave him three hearty cheers as the wheels rapidly rolled away along the Bath road to London and Cambridge.

* When he enlisted he was asked his name. He hesitated, but saw the name Comberback over a shop door near Westminster Bridge, and instantly said his name was 'Comberback.'

† It should be mentioned, that by far the most correct, sublime, chaste, and beautiful of his poems, *meo judicio*, 'Religious Musings,' was written, *non inter sylvas academi*, but in the tap-room at Reading.[6] A fine subject for a painting by Wilkie.[7]

(iv) MARY RUSSELL MITFORD

From Mary Russell Mitford, Recollections of a Literary Life; or, Books, Places, and People *(3 vols.; 1852), III, 14-16. Mitford (1787-1855) was a poet and novelist, best known for the hugely popular* Our Village *(1824-32).*

Everybody has heard the often told story of Coleridge's enlisting in a cavalry regiment under a feigned name, and being detected as a Cambridge scholar in consequence of his writing some Greek lines, or rather, I believe, some Greek words, over the bed of a sick comrade, whom, not knowing how else to dispose of him, he had been appointed to nurse. It has not been stated that the arrangement for his discharge took place at my father's house at Reading. Such, however, was the case. The story was this. Dr. Ogle, Dean of Winchester, was related to the Mitfords, as relationships go in Northumberland, and having been an intimate friend of my maternal grandfather, had no small share in bringing about the marriage between his young cousin and the orphan heiress. He continued to take an affectionate interest in the couple he had brought together, and the 15th Light Dragoons, in which his eldest son had a troop, being quartered in Reading, he came to spend some days at their house. Of course Captain Ogle, between whom and my father the closest friendship subsisted, was invited to meet the Dean, and in the course of the dinner told the story of the learned recruit. It was the beginning of the great war with France; men were procured with difficulty, and if one of the servants waiting at table had not been induced to enlist in his place, there might have been some hesitation in procuring a discharge. Mr. Coleridge never forgot my father's zeal in the cause, for kind and clever as he was, Captain Ogle was so indolent a man, that without a flapper, the matter might have slept in his hands till the Greek kalends. Such was Mr. Coleridge's kind recognition of my father's exertions, that he had the infinite goodness and condescension to look over the proof sheets of two girlish efforts, 'Christina' and 'Blanch,'[8] and to encourage the young writer by gentle strictures and stimulating praise.

NOTES

1 According to Gillman's unlikely (but no doubt Coleridgean) story, he enlisted to cure himself of his 'violent antipathy to soldiers and horses' (*Life*, 57).

2 Cf. Boethius, *De Consolatione*, II.iv: 'Nam in omni adversitate fortunae infelicissimum est genus infortunii fuisse felicem' ('In all fortune's adversities, the most unhappy is to have known happiness').

3 Cottle says that his account of STC's military career is confirmed by Josiah Wade (II, 63n.), a friend of STC's from Bristol days. Wade is reported by Cottle telling a less frivolous anecdote of STC's time in the hospital: 'One of the men in Mr. C.'s company, had, it appeared, a bad case of the small pox, when Mr. C. was appointed to be his nurse, night and day. The fatigue, and anxiety, and various inconveniences, involved in the superintendence on this his sorely diseased comrade, almost sickened him of hospital service' (II, 63-4n.).

4 Other stories circulated of STC's impromptu army lectures:

> a gentleman gave a lecture on some subject intimately connected with literature; Coleridge was present, and after the lecture, differed with many in opinion as to its merits, and undertook to deliver a better one the following evening on the same subject, which he actually did to the admiration of a numerous audience, who came prejudiced against the presumption of this oratorical son of Mars. ('Portraitures of Modern Poets. No XII. S.T. Coleridge, Esq.', *The Ladies' Monthly Museum* 17 (1823) 203-7 and 256-9, 259)

5 Stories of STC's horsemanship form a minor genre of nineteenth-century humour. Publishing a comic poem, 'Contemplations of Coleridge in a Cavalry Regiment' ('which stamped the Private as a poet of the *no-mistake* order in the estimation of his regi-mental, though not mental superiors': p. 423), Maginn (for whom, see below) offered another example (no doubt from the horse's mouth):

> On one occasion, when, according to his duty, the poet was singeing his horse's beard, the animal looked at him with a peculiar twinkle of the eye, nearly approaching to a wink. Coleridge checked his hand, and became absorbed in thought as to what could be the meaning of this singular intimation on the part of his horse. In deep abstraction he revolved all that had ever passed, not only between him and that particular horse, but between him and any other horse whatever. With nothing, however, could he reproach himself. He then tortured his speculative spirit on the subject of the transmigration of souls, in vain. A long self-examination left him just as wise as before. In the mean time, by some slip or other, the horse had got loose, and, scenting a truss of hay behind him, had disrespectfully turned his tail where his head should be; namely, under the poet's nose. Still ruminating, Coleridge almost mechanically resumed his singeing, much to the astonishment of the steed; who, as Smollett says, was surprised at being taken in tail, and resented the indignity by kicking out most lustily. We are happy, however, to add, that, following a sort of poetic intuition, Coleridge slipped between the two out-kicking legs, and then dexterously saving his own person, resumed his operations at the other extremity of his steed; and, considering the circumstances, dressed his

beard after a very regimental fashion. ('The Book of the Season', *Fraser's* XI (1835) 414-27, 422)

(The Smollett joke appears in the first chapter of *Sir Launcelot Greaves*.) And cf.:

Coleridge was acknowledged to be a bad rider. One day, riding through a street, he was accosted by a would-be wit: 'I say, do you know what happened to Balaam?' Came the answer sharp and quick: 'The same as happened to me. An ass spoke to him!' (*Harper's New Monthly Magazine* XXXII (1865-6), 544)

6 The poem's subtitle claims it was written on Christmas Eve in 1794.

7 Sir David Wilkie (1785-1841), celebrated for his paintings of historical incidents and genre scenes.

8 Mitford's *Christina, the Maid of the South Seas* was published in 1811; *Blanche of Castille* in 1812. Mitford's father sought STC's advice about both poems, which he gave, even supplying some lines of his own to include. (See the headnote, *CL*, III, 301-2.)

Two
Radical, Pantisocrat, Visionary
1794-97

The gating over, Coleridge set off with an acquaintance, Hucks, for a walking tour of Wales. They paused at Oxford to see Allen, an old friend of Coleridge's, who, in turn, took them to see Robert Southey, a student at Balliol. They ended up staying for three weeks, during which time Pantisocracy was born. Finally, on 5 July Coleridge and Hucks set off.

On Tour

JOSEPH HUCKS

From Joseph Hucks, A Pedestrian Tour through North Wales, in a Series of Letters *(1795), 24-6. Hucks (1772-1800), a student at St. Catharine's – 'a Man of cultivated, tho' not vigorous, understanding' (CL, I, 83-4) – wrote up the tour in a book which contrives to omit every episode of Coleridgean interest. This is the nearest we come to an escapade: revolutionary enthusiasm meeting loyalist vehemence at an inn in Bala. The incident is recounted more colourfully in Coleridge's letters: in one version, he gave the toast to Washington himself, in another to Priestley; in both, controversy ends in reconciliation (CL, I, 89; 91).*

We were yesterday much diverted with a curious political conversation carried on at the inn, in the room which we in part occupied, at a table by ourselves; at another were seated the clergyman, the exciseman, the attorney, the apothecary, and I suppose, by his appearance, the barber of the place, &c. these were met upon business over a bowl of punch, which seemed to constitute the chief part of it; whilst in an opposite corner of the room, two more decent looking people were enjoying themselves in a similar manner. The clergyman gave aloud 'Church and King,' as a toast, and soon after one of our neighbours at the other table, proposed 'General Washington' to his friend; this created a great commotion amongst the large party; for the clergyman immediately standing up gave as his second toast 'may all *Demicrats* be *gullotin'd*,' when the other filling *his* glass, added, 'may all fools be gullotin'd, and then I knows who'll be the first'; after this ensued a violent and dreadful battle of tongues, in which these people excel in an extraordinary degree. The clergyman defended his toast, on the grounds that it shewed his zeal in a good cause, forgetting that it was necessary first to prove the merit of the sentiment, as united by him, and after that, to shew that his zeal was best made known as a clergyman, by his benevolent and truly pious wish. But majors and minors were things which this zealous and humane defender of the church and king had little regard for. The clamour at length became so loud, that we soon withdrew ourselves from the scene of contention, and left the combatants to settle the point in the best manner they could[.]

At 'The Salutation and Cat'

CHARLES LAMB

From Thomas Noon Talfourd, Final Memorials of Charles Lamb *(2 vols.; 1848), I, 26-7;* The Letters of Charles Lamb, with a Sketch of his Life *(2 vols.; 1837), I, 41;* Final Memorials, *I, 68 (letters to Coleridge, 8-10 June; 13-16 June; and 2 December 1796). By the middle of December 1794, Coleridge was in London, mostly at the Salutation and Cat, an inn at 17, Newgate Street. (It burnt down in 1884.) A brilliant Cambridge career was over.[1] In London, his friendship with Lamb flourished; Lamb's later letters poignantly sketch their bachelor life.*

You came to town, and I saw you at a time when your heart was yet bleeding with recent wounds. Like yourself, I was sore galled with disappointed hope;[2] you had

> — 'many an holy lay
> That, mourning, soothed the mourner on his way;'[3]

I had ears of sympathy to drink them in, and they yet vibrate pleasant on the sense. When I read in your little volume, your nineteenth effusion, or the twenty-eighth or twenty-ninth, or what you call the 'Sigh,'[4] I think I hear *you* again. I image to myself the little smoky room at the Salutation and Cat, where we have sat together through the winter nights, beguiling the cares of life with Poesy. When you left London, I felt a dismal void in my heart. I found myself cut off, at one and the same time, from two most dear to me. 'How blest with ye the path could I have trod of quiet life!' In your conversation you had blended so many pleasant fancies that they cheated me of my grief. But in your absence, the tide of melancholy rushed in again and did its worst mischief by over-whelming my reason.[5] I have recovered, but feel a stupor that makes me indifferent to the hopes and fears of this life. [...]

I have been drinking egg hot[6] and smoking Oronooko, (associated circumstances, which ever forcibly recall to my mind our evenings and nights at the Salutation,) my eyes and brain are heavy and asleep, but my heart is awake; and if words came as ready as ideas, and ideas as feelings, I could say ten thousand kind things. Coleridge, you know not my supreme happiness at having one on earth (though counties separate us)[7] whom I can call a friend. [...]

That sonnet, Coleridge, brings afresh to my mind the time when you wrote those on Bowles, Priestly [sic], Burke;[8] — 'twas two Christmases ago, and in that nice little smoky room at the Salutation, which is ever now continually presenting itself to my recollection, with all its associate train of pipes, tobacco, egg-hot, welsh-rabbits, metaphysics, and poetry. — Are we *never* to meet again?

NOTES

1 As a sharp review of *Literary Memoirs of Living Authors of Great Britain* noted:

> 'Squire *Coleridge* was educated at Christ's hospital, and sent thence to Jesus college, whence this worthy gentleman and splendid genius ran away, nobody knew why, nor whither he was gone; in consequence of which, the master and fellows had ordered him to be written off the books; and a general court of Christ's hospital, on April 24, 1795, ordered the exhibitions which they allowed him to cease. And the next news heard of him was, that he was become as ex-alted a democrat as Mr. Thelwall or Mr. Horne Tooke. Let the memoir-writer, who mourns over his 'disappointed hope and distressful adversity,' say *who* is the cause of it. (*Gentleman's Magazine* LXVIII (1798) 411-14 and 773-6, 774)

2 Lamb was unhappily in love with Ann Simmons, STC with Mary Evans.

3 Lamb is quoting STC's 'Preface' to his 1796 *Poems* (*CPW*, II, 1136).

4 'On a Discovery Made Too Late', 'The Kiss', 'Imitated from Ossian', and 'The Sigh' (*CPW*, I, 72; 63; 38; 62).

5 Lamb spent six weeks in a madhouse in Hoxton at the end of 1795.

6 A drink made of beer, eggs, sugar, and nutmeg.

7 STC had been ushered back to Bristol by an insistent Southey in January.

8 'Sonnets on Eminent Characters' appeared in the *Morning Post* in December 1794 and January 1795 (*CPW*, I, 79-90).

The Pantisocrat
(i) JOSEPH COTTLE

From Cottle, Early Recollections, I, 2-3; 7; 17; 28-9; 30-2. Coleridge met Cottle in Bristol in August 1794, returning from Wales. In early 1795 he moved to the city, lodging with Southey and George Burnett, preparing for Pantisocracy.[1] Cottle's account is comical, but does give some sense of the group and of Coleridge's dominance within it.

At the close of the year 1794, a clever young quaker, of the name of Robert Lovell, who had married a Miss Fricker,[2] informed me, that a few friends of his from Oxford and Cambridge, with himself, were about to sail to America, and on the banks of the Susquehannah, to form a 'Social Colony;' in which there was to be a community of property, and where all that was selfish was to be proscribed. None, he said, were to be admitted into their number, but tried and incorruptible characters; and he felt quite assured, that he and his friends would be able to realize a state of society, free from the evils and turmoils that then agitated the world, and present an example of the eminence to which men might arrive under the unrestrained influence of sound principles. He now paid me the compliment of saying, they would be happy to include *me* in this select assemblage, who, under a state which he called PANTISOCRACY,[3] were, he hoped, to regenerate the whole complexion of society, and that, not by establishing formal laws, but by excluding all the little deteriorating passions; injustice, 'wrath, anger, clamour, and evil speaking,' and thereby setting an example of 'Human Perfectability.' [...]

After some considerable delay, it was at length announced, that, on the coming morning, Samuel Taylor Coleridge would arrive in Bristol, as the nearest and most convenient port; and where he was to reside but a short time, before the favouring gales were to waft him and his friends, across the Atlantic. Robert Lovell, at length, introduced Mr. C.[.] I instantly descried his intellectual character; exhibiting as he did, an eye, a brow, and a forehead, indicative of commanding genius. Interviews succeeded, and these increased the impression of respect. [...]

Soon after, finding Mr. Coleridge in rather a desponding mood, I urged him to keep up his spirits, and recommended him to publish a volume of his poems. 'Oh,' he replied, 'that is a useless expedient.' He continued: 'I offered a volume of my poems to different booksellers in London, who would not even look at them! The reply being, "Sir, the article will not do." At length, one, more accommodating than the rest, condescended to receive my MS. poems, and, after a deliberate inspection, offered me, for the copy-right, six guineas, which sum, poor as I was, I refused to accept.' 'Well,' said I, 'to encourage you, I will give you twenty guineas.' It was very pleasant to observe the joy that instantly diffused itself over his countenance. 'Nay,' I continued, 'others publish for themselves, I will chiefly remember you. Instead of giving you twenty guineas, I will extend it to thirty, and without waiting for the completion of the work, to make you easy, you may have the money, as your occasions require.' The silence and the grasped hand, showed, that, at that moment, one person was happy. [...]

It may be proper to state, that all three of my young friends, in that day of excitement, felt a detestation of the French war, then raging, and a hearty sympathy with the efforts made in France to obtain political ameliorations. Almost every young and un-prejudiced mind, participated in this feeling; and Muir, and Palmer, and Margarot, were regarded as martyrs in the holy cause of freedom.[4] The successive enormities, however, perpetrated in France and Switzerland, by the French,[5] tended to moderate their enthusiastic politics, and progressively to produce that effect on them which extended also to so many of the soberest friends of rational freedom. Mr. Coleridge's zeal, on these questions, was by far the most conspicuous, as will appear by some of his Sonnets, and, particularly, by his Poem of 'Fire, Famine, and Slaughter;' though written some considerable time after.[6] When he read this Poem to me, it was with so much jocularity, as to convince me, that, without bitterness, it was designed as a mere joke. [...]

Mr. Coleridge, though, at this time, embracing every topic of conversation, testified a partiality for a few, which might be called stock subjects. Without noticing his favorite Pantisocracy, (which was an everlasting theme of the laudatory) he generally contrived, either by direct amalgamation, or digression, to notice, in the warmest encomiastic language, Bishop Berkeley, David Hartley,[7] or Mr. Bowles; whose sonnets he delighted in reciting. He once told me, that he believed, by his constant recommendation, he had sold a whole edition of some works; particularly amongst the fresh-men of Cambridge, to whom, whenever he found access, he urged the purchase of three works, indispensable to all who wished to excel in sound reasoning, or a correct taste; namely; Simpson's Euclid;[8] Hartley on Man; and Bowles's Poems.

In process of time, however, when reflection had rendered his mind more mature, he appeared to renounce the fanciful and brain-bewildering system of Berkeley; whilst he sparingly extolled Hartley; and was almost silent respecting Mr. Bowles. I noticed a marked change in his commendation of Mr. B. from the time he paid that man of genius a visit. [...] Whether their canons of criticism were different, or that the personal enthusiasm was not mutual; or whether there was a diversity in political views; whatever the cause was, an altered feeling toward that gentleman was manifested after his visit, not so much expressed by words, as by his subdued tone of applause.[9]

The reflux of the tide had not yet commenced, and Pantisocracy was still Mr. Coleridge's favourite theme of discourse, and the banks of the Susquehannah the only refuge for permanent repose. His eloquence, those who heard knew to be founded in pure fallacy, but, to himself, all he said was the essence of wisdom. It will excite marvellous surprise in the reader, to understand, that Mr. C.'s cooler friends could not ascertain that he had received any specific information respecting this notable river.[10] 'It was a grand river;' but there were many other grand and noble rivers in America; (the Land of Rivers!) and the preference given to the Susquehannah, seemed almost to arise solely from its imposing name, which, if not classical, was at least, poetical; and it, probably, by mere accident, became the centre of all his pleasurable associations. Had this same river been called the Miramichi, or the Irrawaddy, it would have been despoiled of half its charms, and have sunk down into a vulgar stream; the atmosphere of which might have suited well enough Russian boors, but which would have been pestiferous to men of letters.

(ii) THOMAS POOLE

From Mrs. Henry (i.e. Elizabeth) Sandford, Thomas Poole and his Friends *(2 vols.; 1888), I, 96-9. Poole (1765-1837) was one of Coleridge's greatest admirers, a generous and loyal friend throughout his life: 'the man', said Coleridge, 'in whom first and in whom alone, I had felt an* anchor!' *(CL, I, 491). Poole made a comfortable living as a tanner, a business he took over from his father (also Thomas); he lived, unmarried and with a good library, in Nether Stowey, in North Somerset. Family tradition maintained that Poole met Coleridge in a London inn, where Coleridge, in the guise of a private soldier, startled Poole, in the guise of a workman, by his conversation (I, 83); more likely they met through common associates in West Country radical circles. Poole's first report is in a letter of 22 September 1794, describing a recent meeting. Pantisocracy was discussed.*

I received your obliging letter a day or two ago, and will with pleasure give you all the information I can respecting the emigration to America to which you allude. But first, perhaps, you would like to have some idea of the character of the projectors of the scheme. Out of eight whom they informed me were engaged, I have seen but two, and only spent part of one day with them; their names are Coldridge [*sic*] and Southey.[11]

Coldridge, whom I consider the Principal in the undertaking, and of whom I had heard much before I saw him, is about five and twenty, belongs to the University of Cambridge, possesses splendid abilities—he is, I understand, a shining scholar, gained the prize for Greek verses the first or second year he entered the University, and is now engaged in publishing a selection of the best modern Latin poems with a poetical translation.[12] He speaks with much elegance and energy, and with uncommon felicity, but he, as it generally happens to men of his class, feels the justice of Providence in the want of those inferiour abilities which are necessary to the rational discharge of the common duties of life. His aberrations from prudence, to use his own expression, have been great; but he now promises to be as sober and rational as his most sober friends could wish. In religion he is a Unitarian, if not a Deist; in politicks a Democrat, to the utmost extent of the word.

Southey, who was with him, is of the University of Oxford, a younger man, without the splendid abilities of Coldridge, though possessing much information, particularly metaphysical, and is more violent in his principles than even Coldridge himself. In Religion, shocking to say in a mere Boy as he is, I fear he wavers between Deism and Atheism.

Thus much for the characters of two of the Emigrators. Their plan is as follows: —

Twelve gentlemen of good education and liberal principles are to embark with twelve ladies in April next. Previous to their leaving this country they are to have as much intercourse as possible, in order to ascertain each other's dispositions, and firmly to settle every regulation for the government of their future conduct. Their opinion was that they should fix themselves at—I do not recollect the place, but somewhere in a delightful part of the new back settlements; that each man should labour two or three hours in a day, the produce of which labour would, they imagine, be more than sufficient to support the colony. As Adam Smith observes that there is not above one productive man in twenty, they argue that if each laboured the twentieth part of time, it would produce enough to satisfy their wants.[13] The produce of their industry is to be laid up in common for the use of all; and a good library of books is to be collected, and their leisure hours to be spent in study, liberal discussions, and the education of their children. A system for the education of their children is laid down, for which, if this plan at all suits you, I must refer you to the authors of it.[14] The regulations relating to the females strike them as the most difficult; whether the marriage contract shall be dissolved if agreeable to one or both parties, and many other circumstances, are not yet determined.[15] The employments of the women are to be the care of infant children, and other occupations suited to their strength; at the same time the greatest attention is to be paid to the cultivation of their minds. Every one is to enjoy his own religious and political opinions, provided they do not encroach on the rules previously made, which rules, it is unnecessary to add, must in some measure be regulated by the laws of the state which includes the district in which they settle. They calculate that each gentleman providing £125 will be sufficient to carry the scheme into execution. Finally, every individual is at liberty, whenever he pleases, to withdraw from the society.

These are the outlines of their plan, and such are their ideas. Could they realise them they would, indeed, realise the age of reason; but, however perfectible human nature may be, I fear it is not yet perfect enough to exist long under the regulations of such a system, particularly when the Executors of the plan are taken from a society in a high degree civilised and corrupted. America is certainly a desirable country, so desirable in my eye that, were it not for some insuperable reasons, I would certainly settle there. At some future period I perhaps may. But I think a man would do well first to see the country and his future hopes, before he removes his connections or any large portion of his property there. I could live, I think, in America, much to my satisfaction and credit, without joining in such a scheme as I have been describing, though I should like well to accompany them, and see what progress they make.

NOTES

[1] News of the scheme got around. Dyer mentions it (respectfully) in his account of Southey in *Public Characters of 1799-1800* (1799), 224. (STC complained about the piece (*CL*, I, 549), perhaps because of perceived insinuations about his marriage: 'The three young poetical friends, Lovel, Southey, and Coleridge, married three sisters. Southey is attached to domestic life, and, fortunately, was very happy in his matrimonial connection' (p. 225).)

[2] Lovell (?1770-96) had married Mary Fricker, sister of Sara and Edith.

[3] Originally 'Pantocracy'; STC's term for 'System of no Property' (*CL*, I, 84; 90).

[4] The 'illustrious Triumvirate' (*L1795*, 14), Thomas Muir, Thomas Fysshe Palmer, and Maurice Margarot, found guilty of sedition and transported.

[5] The French invaded Switzerland in January 1798; STC's 'France: An Ode', (published in the *Morning Post* in April) protested against the aggression.

[6] *CPW*, I, 237-40. It is a denunciation of Pitt, although STC later added an 'apologetic preface', claiming that he had always supported Pitt.

[7] George, Bishop Berkeley (1685-1753), author of *Principles of Human Knowledge* (1710) and *Siris* (1744): STC was declaring himself 'a Berkleian' in July 1797 (*CL*, I, 335). David Hartley (1705-57), divine and associationist, whose *Observations on Man* (1749), mediated by Priestley, was a formative influence on STC.

[8] *The Elements of Euclid* [...], ed. Robert Simpson (1756).

[9] Enthusiasm had cooled by 1802 (*CL*, II, 864). He later recalled: 'I injured myself irreparably with him by devoting a fortnight to the correction of his Poem – he took the corrections and never forgave the Corrector' (*CL*, IV, 694).

[10] This was the story STC told Gillman (*Life*, 69); but in fact he found the Susquehannah recommended in Thomas Cooper's *Some Information Respecting America* (1794): see J.R. MacGillivray, 'The Pantisocracy Scheme and its Immediate Background'; in Malcolm W. Wallace (ed.), *Studies in English [...]* (Toronto, 1931) 131-69, 150-2.

[11] Those signed up included STC, Southey, Lovell, Robert Allen (1772-1805), Robert Favell (1775-1812) — both schoolfriends of STC — George Burnett (1776-1811), a Balliol man, the Fricker sisters, their mother, and Southey's mother.

[12] The 'prize' was the Brown Medal. STC's *Imitations of the Modern Latin Poets* was advertised in the *Cambridge Intelligencer* (*CL*, I, 77n.), but didn't appear.

[13] For the preponderance of unproductive labourers, see *Wealth of Nations*, I.iii.

[14] STC wished the children be not taught '*Christianity*, — I mean — that mongrel whelp that goes under it's name'. No prospectus appeared (*CL*, I, 123; 96-7).

[15] Possibly a difference between STC — who told Thelwall that '*Marriage is indissoluble*' (*CL*, I, 213) — and a more Godwinian Southey. William Godwin (1756-1836), later a member of STC's circle (see below), was a leading radical voice in the 1790s, thanks to his *Enquiry concerning Political Justice* (1793). STC remained equivocal (at least) about many of Godwin's positions, especially his atheism, and — to return to the present point — his advocacy of the abolition of marriage, which he saw as but 'a branch of the prevailing system of property' (*Political Justice* (1793), VIII.vi).

'Shamefully hot with Democratic rage'

(i) JOHN POOLE

From Sandford, Thomas Poole, I, 103-4. John was Thomas Poole's cousin; his branch of the family lived at Marshmill in Over Stowey. This comes from his journal for August 1794 (translated from his Latin by Sandford).

Rise about eight. After breakfast go to Mr. Lewis's and get the loan of Boswell's *Life of Johnson* from him. About one o'clock, Thomas Poole and his brother Richard, Henry Poole, and two young men, friends of his, come in. These two strangers, I understand, had left Cambridge, and had walked nearly all through Wales. One is an undergraduate of Oxford, the other of Cambridge. Each of them was shamefully hot with Democratic rage as regards politics, and both Infidel as to religion. I was extremely indignant. At last, however, about two o'clock, they all go away. After dinner I betake myself to the *Life of Johnson*. About seven o'clock Mr. Reekes comes from Stowey; he is very indignant over the odious and detestable ill-feeling of those two young men, whom he had met at my Uncle Thomas's. They seem to have shown their sentiments more plainly there than with us. But enough of such matters.[1]

(ii) THOMAS POOLE

From Sandford, Thomas Poole, I, 125-6. Poole's admiration grew; by February 1796 he was referring to 'my beloved friend Coleridge' (I, 134). Poole recorded the Marshmill visit in verses (with a rather last-minute, footnoted stanza about Sara).

Hail to thee, Coldridge [*sic*], youth of various powers!
    I love to hear thy soul pour forth the line,
To hear it sing of love and liberty
    As if fresh breathing from the hand divine.

As if on earth it never yet had dwelt,
    As if from heaven it now had wing'd its way;
And brought us tidings how, in argent fields,
    In love and liberty blest spirits stray.

I love to mark that soul-pervaded clay,
    To see the passions in thine eyeballs roll —
Their quick succession on thy weighty brow —
    Thy trembling lips express their very soul.

I love to view the abstracted gaze which speaks
    Thy soul to heavenwards towering — then I say,
He's gone — for us to cull celestial sweets
    Amid the flowerets of the milky way.

And now at home, within its mortal cage,
    I see thy spirit pent — ah me! — and mourn
Thy sorrow sad, that weighs it down to earth,
    As if the Cherub Hope would ne'er return.

And then I mark the starting tear that steals
    Adown thy cheek, when of a friend thou speak'st,
Who erst, as thou dost say, was wondrous kind,
    But now, unkind, forgets — I feel and weep.

I hear thee speak indignant of the world,
    Th'unfeeling world crowded with folly's train;
I hear thy fervent eloquence dispel
    The murky mists of error's mazy reign.*

And thou, Religion, white-robed Maid of Peace,
    Who smil'st to hear him raise his voice on high
To fix thy image on the Patriot's breast —
    Remove the bitter tear, the fearful sigh.

September 12, 1795. T.P.

*   Anon thy Sarah's image cheers thy soul,
     When sickening at the world, thy spirits faint;
   Soft balm it brings—thou hail'st the lovely maid,
     Paint'st her dear form as Love alone can paint.

The Lecturer

(i) JOSEPH COTTLE

From Cottle, Early Recollections, *I, 37-40; 41-2. To subsidise their emigration, Coleridge and Southey offered some lectures: Coleridge chose 'Political and Moral subjects' (to espouse his own brand of non-conformist radicalism) and Southey 'History' (I, 19). Cottle here contrasts professional Southey and erratic Coleridge.*

These Lectures of Mr. Southey were numerously attended, and their composition was greatly admired; exhibiting, as they did, a succinct view of the various subjects commented upon, so as to chain the hearers' attention. They, at the same time, evinced great self-possession in the lecturer; a peculiar grace in the delivery; with reasoning so judicious and acute, as to excite astonishment in the auditory, that so young a man should concentrate so rich a fund of valuable matter in lectures, comparatively, so brief, and which clearly authorized the anticipation of his future eminence.

From this statement it will justly be inferred, that no public lecturer could have received stronger proofs of approbation, than Mr. S. from a polite and discriminating audience. Mr. Coleridge now solicited permission of Mr. Southey, to deliver his fourth lecture, 'On the Rise, Progress, and Decline of the Roman Empire,' as a subject 'to which he had devoted much attention'. The request was immediately granted, and, at the end of the third lecture, it was formally announced to the audience, that the next lecture would be delivered by 'Mr. Samuel Taylor Coleridge, of Jesus College, Cambridge.'

At the usual hour the room was thronged. The moment of commencement arrived. No lecturer appeared! Patience was preserved for a quarter, extending to half an hour!—but still no lecturer! At length it was communicated to the impatient assemblage, 'that a circumstance, exceedingly to be regretted! would prevent Mr. Coleridge from giving his lecture, that evening, as intended.' Some few present learned the truth, but the major part of the company retired, not very well pleased, and under the impression that Mr. C. had either broken his leg, or that some severe family affliction had occurred. Mr. C.'s rather habitual absence of mind, with the little importance he generally attached to engagements, renders it likely, that, at this very time he might have been found, at No. 48, College-Street, composedly smoking his pipe, and lost in profound musings on his divine Susquehannah! [...]

Proceeding on my principle of impartial narration, I must here state, that, after dinner, an unpleasant altercation occurred between—no other than the two Pantisocratians! When feelings are accumulated in the heart, the tongue will give them utterance. Mr. Southey, whose regular habits scarcely rendered it a virtue in him, never to fail in an engagement, expressed to Mr. Coleridge, his deep feelings of regret, that his audience should have been disappointed, on the preceding evening; reminding him that unless he had determined punctually to fulfil his voluntary engagement, he ought not to have entered upon it. Mr. C. thought the delay of the lecture of little, or no consequence. This excited a remonstrance, which produced a reply. At first I interfered with a few conciliatory words, which were unavailing; and these two friends, about to exhibit to the world a glorious example of the effects of concord and sound principles, with an exemption from all the selfish and unsocial passions, fell, alas! into the common lot of humanity, and, in so doing, must have demonstrated, even to themselves, the rope of sand, to which they had confided their destinies!

In unspeakable concern and surprise, I retired to a distant part of the room, and heard with dismay, the contention continued, if not extending; for now the two young ladies entered into the dispute, (on adverse sides, as might be supposed) each confirming, or repelling, the arguments of the belligerents. A little cessation in the storm, afforded me the opportunity of stepping forward, and remarking, that, 'however much the disappointment was to be regretted, it was an evil not likely again to occur, (Mr. S. shook his head) and that the wisest way, was, to forget the past, and to remember only the pleasant objects before us.' In this opinion the ladies concurred, when placing a hand of one of the dissentients in that of the other, the hearty salutation went round, and, with our accustomed spirits, we prepared once more for Piercefield and the Abbey.[2]

(ii) 'THE OBSERVER'

From 'THE OBSERVER. PART 1st. BEING A TRANSIENT GLANCE AT ABOUT FORTY YOUTHS of Bristol' (Bristol, 1794); as quoted in a letter of J. Livingston Lowes, 'Coleridge and the "Forty Youths of Bristol"', TLS 1393 (11 October 1928), 736. 'S.T. Coler**ge' appears among thirty-six contemporaries.

THIS Cantab is well versed in Greek and in Latin; indeed he is a superior Scholar to most of his years: that love of his species, that detestation of human butchery and legalized murder called War, are worthy traits in his character. He has delivered many Lectures here, one of which (on the Slave-trade) is a proof of the detestation in which he holds that infamous traffic.[3] As all his lectures are about to be published, it would be useless to treat of them in this place. The Public, I will dare to predict, will be highly gratified in them. He has my hearty tribute of praise for the disseminating that knowledge which so nearly concerns us all, that is, *political*. Undaunted by the storms of popular prejudice, unswayed by magisterial influence, he spoke in public what none had the courage in this City to do before—he told Men that they have Rights.—I must now remark what are the exceptionable features belonging to him; his speech is perfect monotonism; his person is slovenly; a clean appearance is as good a criterion whereby to know a scholar as the person of mean appearance: it is exemplified in the preceding character. Mr. C—— would therefore do well to appear with cleaner stockings in public, and if his hair were combed out every time he appeared in public it would not depreciate him in the esteem of his friends.

NOTES

[1] Charlotte, John's sister, also met Coleridge at Marshmill, and recorded her impression on 19 September 1795: 'Tom Poole has a friend with him of the name of Coldridge [*sic*]: a young man of brilliant understanding, great eloquence, d sperate fortune, democratick principles, and entirely led away by the i... es of th moment' (Sandford, *Thomas Poole*, I, 124). They met again in May 1796: 'w o should arrive but the famous Mr. Coldridge!' —

I cannot form an opinion of him in so short a time, but could have discovered, if I had not before heard it, that he is clever, and a very short acquaintance will unfold that he is extremely vain of it. (I, 146).

2 The tour becomes a series of minor disasters, and ends at Tintern Abbey.
3 STC's lecture on the slave trade was given 16 June 1795.

'Your godlike scheme ...'

CHARLES LLOYD

*From 'To ******, Written in Worcestershire, July 1797'; in* Charles Lloyd and Charles Lamb, *Blank Verse (1798), 9–12; 12–13. Charles Lloyd (1775–1839), son of the Quaker banker and philanthropist, moved in with the Coleridges in September 1796 as a private pupil (CL, I, 235–6). He returned home in November after a series of fits, but rejoined them in February 1797 as a lodger. Coleridge included some of his poems (and Lamb's) in the second edition of his* Poems *(1797).[1] The following year, Lloyd and Lamb published* Blank Verse; *this poem from that volume nostalgically recalls an intoxicating Coleridgean brew of pastoral, politics, and religious intensity.*

> Often in no uninterested mood
> I've told thee that there were of noble souls
> Who deem'd it wise, e'en in the morn of youth,
> To quit this world'! (a scene in my poor thought
> Deliver'd over long by outrag'd Heaven
> To wasting fiends, and unrepenting guilt,)
> They counted still beyond the Atlantic deep
> To find those virtues, of whose sweets bereft
> The unearthly soul calleth its sojourn here
> A most impure enthralment! Oh my best friend,
> That I had liv'd in high-soul'd fellowship
> With such as fancy pictures these might be,
> Tried spirits, and unspotted from the world!
> But I must sicken thy awaken'd soul,
> Storying their blasted hopes! Yet, honour'd few,
> The seeds that ye have sown, the unworldly dreams,
> The lofty thoughts, disinterested loves,
> That ye have nurs'd, silently long shall work
> In beings unknown, regenerating thus
> Full many a guilt-vex'd mind, that, but for you,
> Had sunken in dismay (now animate

With noblest emulation), and to truth
Leavening each baser wish, shall perfect them!
Yes! it shall rise again, your godlike scheme;
And every fleshly lust, and every sin,
Pampering the subtleties of selfish pride,
Shall vanish swiftly, as the morning cloud,
From its most holy influence; and all those,
Who struggled with the spirit of this world,
Shall come forth with unutterable joy,
And (as with recognition of dear friends
Long lost, and sought for) join the elect† of Heaven. [...]
Then let us, * * * * * * *, watch aloof,
Till the long night be past, that, so prepar'd,
We, with the first redeem'd from this bad world,
May hail the promis'd time, when pain and grief
Shall be no more; of love and blessedness
The hallow'd advent; and with unstain'd hands
Circle the grassy altar which shall rise
In every grove and mead, when *equal man*
Shall deem the world his temple, to that God,
Who destin'd all his creatures *to be good*,
And who, with sympathies of holiest love,
Shall teach best fellowship with kindred souls,
Or loftier breathings of devoutest praise.

* This alludes to a plan projected by S.T. Coleridge and Robert Southey, together
with some common friends, of establishing a society in America, in which all
individual property was to be abandoned.

† Wherever the word elect is used in the following pages, the authors by no
means intend the arbitrary dogma of Calvinism. They are both believers in the
doctrine of philosophical necessity, and in the final happiness of all mankind.[2]
They apply the word elect therefore to those persons whom *secondary causes*,
under providence, have fitted for an immediate entrance into the paradisiacal
state.

From Charles Lloyd, Edmund Oliver (2 vols.; Bristol, 1798), I, 14-15; 66-7. In
April 1798, Coleridge was disturbed to discover that Cottle had published a novel
by Lloyd (dedicated to Lamb) which featured a portrait of himself, complete with
'love-fit, debaucheries, leaving college & going into the army' (CL, I, 404).
Despite its satirical edge, Edmund Oliver contains one of the best accounts of
young Coleridge, and it is far from consistently unsympathetic. Some passages
very effectively evoke the conversational energy that had intoxicated Lloyd.[3]

I had received strong and delicate sensibilities from nature: having
in my early life, from the morose and reserved character of my father, who hated the intercourse of his neighbours, been uniformly

confined at home, I had acquired much timidity of temper. My mind was active, but slow to receive impressions from others: it felt its own shapings more interesting than any ideas suggested from foreign sources: it was too full of itself to be passive to the mouldings of authority or experience. From this restlessness of spirit, supported by a warm and impetuous temperament, and connected with solitariness of habits, I soon acquired imagination; or the faculty of ever combining the moral with the physical world; or, on the other hand, of embodying intellectual conceptions in the borrowed shapes of the visible elements. [...]

I passed my infancy and youth in solitude; my feelings were ever more than commensurate with the objects which acted upon them! I combined and recombined. I panted for happiness which I had not heard of! from this circumstance may be traced my dissatisfaction with the state of society in which I was educated; and my subsequent ardour for the introduction of more generous and impartial principles among men.

Even strong physical feelings repelled and thrown back on the mind which associates them with moral shapings, filtrate, and minister to the growth of intellect. Appetites and passions connect us with, and give a character to every surrounding object; teach us to insinuate ourselves into the souls of others, and make us as it were a part of their identity: these, if not gratified, remain as materials for fresh combination, and initiate us into all the motiveless obliquities of human agency. It is to these sources that I trace the formation of my character[.]

From Edmund Oliver, *I, 100-4; 105-7. We cannot come much closer to the young Coleridge than this imagined monologue, which, in its concern with necessity (Oliver advocates 'the sublime system of optimism': I, 72), the self, and the egocentrism of modern life, echoes the preoccupations (and rhetorical forms) of the 1795 lectures. Lloyd appears to catch some genuine Coleridgean habits, like the philosophical appeal to ordinary linguistic use, and the coining of new terms.*

I employed the morning in traversing the streets of this great city. How irksome, how horribly irksome, is this wilderness of men! You meet thousands of fellow beings, and not one that has a sympathy with yourself! In large cities, from each individual, being under the necessity to struggle with a multitude, for his own emolument, every face seems to have acquired an unwholesome calosity, an unnatural acuteness. The very manner in which a London man passes in the street, is that of consequential bustle, and a sticking out of the elbows, accompanied with a look that says, 'Retire you here, and you there, I must mind MY OWN business.'

When my soul is full—when it aches to be understood, and to feel a common existence with another soul, how loathsome is this desert of human kind, this waste, this chaos of existence! The unnatural flocking together of the species hardens and *unsocializes* the heart more perhaps than uniform solitude.

Human intercourse becomes so cheap that it is disregarded. The pains associated with it from its burthensome frequency, and from the aspect of personal interest, which it always wears in towns, overbalance the pleasures;[4] so that in the end a citizen, when he would snatch a brief taste of enjoyment, shuns with a monstrous perversion his fellow beings, and hugs himself in the security of a misanthropic retirement.

In short, I hardly know which is the most unfavourable to the social virtues, an anchoritical seclusion, or a continual jostling with common natures, rendered uncongenial by jarring arms. Cities are the very graves, the cemetries of human virtue! Sincerity, simplicity of heart, genius, and purity of principle, all necessarily die away in them. I never see a concourse of men, but I feel a sad oppression of soul; nor a *city*, but with a prophetic assurance that the guilt of its inhabitants encreases in proportion to its aggregative prosperity.

Oh Charles! will the time ever arrive when men will sink their individual feelings in the general mass of existence? Is human nature capable of divesting itself of that sensation of private emolument which now coalesces with all the active motives of man? We are all unhappy; all complaining; all friendless; all lamenting the want of an object in life! When, if we would but annihilate selfishness;[5] regard the interests of others as our own; narrow our physical sphere, and widen our intellectual one; sink our own wants, and live in the happiness of others: throw aside the panoply of artificial and personal distinction, and feel a common identity with mankind at large, we might be happy at all times, ever feel our souls raised and exalted by the most august of spectacles, a general diffusion to sentient beings of progressive and illimitable felicity! [...]

While the words *mine* and *thine* last, it is impossible that this complete self-abasement should be familiarized to the mind. We cannot see, and come in contact with objects without connecting ideas and sensations with them; and in proportion as the objects are beautiful and desirable, the associated impressions will be vivid and lasting. Now wealth procures to weak man so many sources of delight; it so envelopes him with beauties of his own creation; with forms to which the fascinating sensation of '*mine*' subtly coalesces, that it is impossible a being in this predicament should ever arrive at the state I have been describing: the laws of nature, and mental association forbid it. Now, a complete self-annihilation and abasement, is the doctrine held out by Revelation as the indispensable mean [*sic*] to happiness hereafter.[6] But we have seen that this cannot be obtained by the great and honourable of this world, I therefore believe that 'meek man, and lowliest of the sons of men,' when he says,[7] 'It is *easier* for a camel to go through the eye of a needle, than for a rich man to enter the kingdom of Heaven.'[8]

NOTES

[1] Relations deteriorated after STC published parodic sonnets by 'Nehemiah Higginbottom', offending not only Lloyd and Lamb, but also Southey, all of whom took themselves for the target of satire.

[2] STC told Southey 'I am a compleat Necessitarian' (*CL*, I, 137).

[3] See John Beer, *Coleridge the Visionary* (1959), 54-6.

[4] A Coleridgean rhetoric of rural pleasure and urban pains: e.g. *L1795*, 225-6.

[5] For self-annihilation, cf. 'Religious Musings', ll.154-7 (*CPW*, I, 115).

[6] As a Unitarian, the young STC did not believe that the Revelation of Christ showed him to be divine. Christ was human, but exemplarily perfect; and his perfection lay in his being 'all of Self regardless' ('Religious Musings' (1796), l.21; *CPW*, I, 109n.).

[7] 'Religious Musings' (1796), l.26 (*CPW*, I, 109n.).

[8] Cf. Matthew 19.24; Mark 10.25.

Three
Poet and Traveller
1797-1806

Hopes of Pantisocracy had died by the end of 1795. Coleridge's radicalism wasn't finished: he spent the first months of 1796 launching his journal, *The Watchman*, but closed it after ten issues. Hartley Coleridge was born in September. Coleridge saw Nether Stowey as an ideal place of retirement (*CL*, I, 242), and he brought his wife and child to a small cottage there in December 1796. Their garden met Poole's in a lime-tree bower.

'... a wonderful man ... '

(i) DOROTHY WORDSWORTH

From Christopher Wordsworth, Memoirs of William Wordsworth (2 vols.; 1851), I, 98-99. Dorothy Wordsworth (1771-1855) was a crucial element in the Coleridge-Wordsworth collaboration. The poets had first met in 1795; they admired one another's poetry;[1] but now, in 1797, their friendship suddenly blossomed. The Wordsworths were living at Racedown in Dorset; Coleridge paid them a visit in June, returning a call that Wordsworth had made to Stowey earlier in the Spring. Coleridge was soon declaring his friend 'a great man' (CL, I, 327); and the Wordsworths' response was no less enthusiastic. This comes from a letter to Catherine Clarkson (1772-1856), an old friend of Dorothy's, and the wife of Thomas (1760-1846), the celebrated slave campaigner.

You had a great loss in not seeing Coleridge. He is a wonderful man. His conversation teems with soul, mind, and spirit. Then he is so benevolent, so good-tempered and cheerful, and, like William, interests himself so much about every little trifle. At first I thought him very plain, that is, for about three minutes: he is pale, thin, has a wide mouth, thick lips, and not very good teeth, longish, loose-growing, half-curling, rough, black hair. [...] But, if you hear him speak for five minutes you think no more of them. His eye is large and full, and not very dark, but grey, such an eye as would receive from a heavy soul the dullest expression; but it speaks every emotion of his animated mind: it has more of 'the poet's eye in a fine frenzy rolling'[2] than I ever witnessed. He has fine dark eyebrows, and an overhanging forehead.

The first thing that was read after he came was William's new poem, 'Ruined Cottage,' with which he was much delighted; and after tea he repeated to us two acts and a half of his tragedy, 'Osorio.' The next morning, William read his tragedy, 'The Borderers.'[3]

(ii) WILLIAM WORDSWORTH

From Letters of the Wordsworth Family from 1787 to 1855, *ed. William Knight (3 vols.; 1907), III, 327. In a late letter (7 November 1845) from Mary, his wife, to Sara, Coleridge's daughter, Wordsworth recalled Coleridge's appearance at Racedown almost fifty years before. Wordsworth's own voice takes over half-way.*

With my husband's tender love to you he bids me say, in reply to a question you have put to him through Miss Fenwick, that he has not as distinct a remembrance as he could wish of the time when he first saw your father and your uncle Southey; but the impression upon his mind is that he first saw them both, and your aunt Edith at the same time, in a lodging in Bristol. This must have been about the year 1795. Your father, he says, came afterwards to see us at Racedown, where I was then living with my sister. We have both a distinct remembrance of his arrival. He did not keep to the high road, but leaped over a gate and bounded down a pathless field, by which he cut off an angle. We both retain the liveliest possible image of his appearance at that moment. My poor sister[4] has just been speaking of it to me with much feeling and tenderness.

(iii) JOHN ANSTER

From Alaric Alfred Watts, Alaric Watts. A Narrative of his Life [...] *(2 vols.; 1884), I, 246-7. This story comes from a letter (3 October 1835), from John Anster (1793-1867), translator of* Faust, *to Watts (1797-1864), poet and man of letters. Coleridge's short career as a reviewer for the* Critical Review *took place in the late 1790s, so Anster's mention of the Lake Country is mistaken; otherwise, the anecdote closely resembles a story that Coleridge told elsewhere (CL, VI, 733).*

I will conclude this dull letter by telling you an anecdote of Coleridge. He told me, that when he first thought of literature as a means of support, he formed some connection with one of the Reviews, I think the *Critical:* he was at that time living somewhere in the Lake country, together with Wordsworth. A parcel of books were [*sic*] sent down to be reviewed; among the rest, a volume of poems, he did not tell me the name, and I believe he had forgotten it. He wrote a smart review of the work; every sentence of his article was, he said, an epigram.[5] When he had concluded, he read his review aloud to the ladies of the family. One of them, Wordsworth's sister, burst into tears, and asked how he could write it? 'I was thinking,' said she, 'how I must feel if I were to read such a review of a poem of yours or William's. And has not this poor man some sister or wife to feel for him?' Coleridge described himself as so affected that he never afterwards wrote a review, and he appeared to me to have even a morbid feeling on the subject.

Is not the circumstance a striking and characteristic one?

NOTES

[1] See Robert Woof, 'Wordsworth and Coleridge: Some Early Matters'; in *Bicentenary Wordsworth Studies*, ed. Jonathan Wordsworth (Ithaca, 1970), 76-91.

[2] Cf. *A Midsummer Night's Dream*, V.i, l.12.

[3] A version of 'The Ruined Cottage' was written in Spring 1797. *Osorio* was written for Drury Lane, but turned down; *The Borderers* was meant for Covent Garden, and was also rejected.

[4] Dorothy suffered from a form of dementia from 1829.

[5] A mangled reference to the review of Lewis's *The Monk* (*SWF*, I, 57-65)?

Writing *Lyrical Ballads*

WILLIAM WORDSWORTH

From The Prelude, or Growth of a Poet's Mind; An Autobiographical Poem *(1850), 369-70 (XIV, ll.388-454). Coleridge brought the Wordsworths to Stowey, and they quickly arranged to rent Alfoxden Park, a large house nearby. On 13 July, barely a month after Coleridge's visit to Racedown, they moved in.*

> Whether to me shall be allotted life,
> And, with life, power to accomplish aught of worth,
> That will be deemed no insufficient plea
> For having given the story of myself,
> Is all uncertain: but, beloved Friend!
> When, looking back, thou seest, in clearer view
> Than any liveliest sight of yesterday,
> That summer, under whose indulgent skies,
> Upon smooth Quantock's airy ridge we roved
> Unchecked, or loitered 'mid her sylvan combs,
> Thou in bewitching words, with happy heart,
> Didst chaunt the vision of that Ancient Man,
> The bright-eyed Mariner, and rueful woes
> Didst utter of the Lady Christabel;
> And I, associate with such labour, steeped
> In soft forgetfulness the livelong hours,

Murmuring of him who, joyous hap, was found,
After the perils of his moonlight ride,
Near the loud waterfall; or her who sate
In misery near the miserable Thorn;[1]
When thou dost to that summer turn thy thoughts,
And hast before thee all which then we were,
To thee, in memory of that happiness,
It will be known, by thee at least, my Friend!
Felt, that the history of a Poet's mind
Is labour not unworthy of regard:
To thee the work shall justify itself.

From Prose Works of William Wordsworth, *ed. Alexander B. Grosart (3 vols.; 1876), III, 16-18. In old age, Wordsworth dictated notes for his poems to Isabella Fenwick. Recalling the circumstances of 'We Are Seven', he recollected his role in 'The Ancient Mariner'. It is startling how much was Wordsworth's contribution.*

In reference to this poem, I will here mention one of the most remarkable facts in my own poetic history, and that of Mr. Coleridge. In the spring of the year 1798, he, my sister, and myself, started from Alfoxden pretty late in the afternoon, with a view to visit Linton, and the Valley of Stones near to it; and as our united funds were very small, we agreed to defray the expense of the tour by writing a poem, to be sent to the *New Monthly Magazine*, set up by Phillips, the bookseller, and edited by Dr. Aikin.[2] Accordingly, we set off, and proceeded, along the Quantock Hills, towards Watchet; and in the course of this walk was planned the poem of the 'Ancient Mariner,' founded on a dream, as Mr. Coleridge said, of his friend Mr. Cruikshank. Much the greatest part of the story was Mr. Coleridge's invention; but certain parts I myself suggested; for example, some crime was to be committed which would bring upon the Old Navigator, as Coleridge afterwards delighted to call him, the spectral persecution, as a consequence of that crime and his own wanderings. I had been reading in Shelvocke's *Voyages*,[3] a day or two before, that, while doubling Cape Horn, they frequently saw albatrosses in that latitude, the largest sort of sea-fowl, some extending their wings twelve or thirteen feet. 'Suppose,' said I, 'you represent him as having killed one of these birds on entering the South Sea, and that the tutelary spirits of these regions take upon them to avenge the crime.' The incident was thought fit for the purpose, and adopted accordingly. I also suggested the navigation of the ship by the dead men, but do not recollect that I had anything more to do with the scheme of the poem. The gloss with which it was subsequently accompanied was not thought of by either of us at the time, at least not a hint of it was given to me, and I have no doubt it was a gratuitous after-thought. We began the composition together, on that to me memorable evening: I furnished two or three lines at the beginning of the poem, in particular—

> 'And listen'd like a three years' child;
> The Mariner had his will.'[4]

These trifling considerations, all but one, (which Mr. C. has with unnecessary scrupulosity recorded,)[5] slipt out of his mind, as they well might. As we endeavoured to proceed conjointly (I speak of the same evening), our respective manners proved so widely different, that it would have been quite presumptuous in me to do anything but separate from an undertaking upon which I could only have been a clog.[6] We returned after a few days from a delightful tour, of which I have many pleasant, and some of them droll enough, recollections. We returned by Dulverton to Alfoxden. The 'Ancient Mariner' grew and grew till it became too important for our first object, which was limited to our expectation of five pounds; and we began to talk of a volume which was to consist, as Mr. Coleridge has told the world, of Poems chiefly on natural subjects, taken from common life, but looked at, as much as might be, through an imaginative medium.[7] Accordingly I wrote 'The Idiot Boy,' 'Her Eyes are wild,' &c., and 'We are Seven,' 'The Thorn,' and some others. To return to 'We are Seven,' the piece that called forth this note:—I composed it while walking in the grove of Alfoxden. My friends will not deem it too trifling to relate, that while walking to and fro I composed the last stanza first, having begun with the last line. When it was all but finished, I came in and recited it to Mr. Coleridge and my sister, and said, 'A prefatory stanza must be added, and I should sit down to our little tea-meal with greater pleasure if my task was finished.' I mentioned in substance what I wished to be expressed, and Coleridge immediately threw off the stanza, thus:

> 'A little child, dear brother Jem.'[8]

I objected to the rhyme, 'dear brother Jem,' as being ludicrous; but we all enjoyed the joke of hitching in our friend James Tobin's name, who was familiarly called Jem.[9] He was the brother of the dramatist; and this reminds me of an anecdote which it may be worth while here to notice. The said Jem got a sight of the 'Lyrical Ballads' as it was going through the press at Bristol, during which time I was residing in that city. One evening he came to me with a grave face, and said, 'Wordsworth, I have seen the volume that Coleridge and you are about to publish. There is one poem in it which I earnestly entreat you will cancel, for, if published, it will make you everlastingly ridiculous.' I answered, that I felt much obliged by the interest he took in my good name as a writer, and begged to know what was the unfortunate piece he alluded to. He said, 'It is called "We are Seven."' 'Nay,' said I, 'that shall take its chance, however;' and he left me in despair.

From Edward Whately, 'Personal Recollections of the Lake Poets', Leisure Hour 19 (1870) 651-53, 653.

Coleridge I never saw, nor did I ever hear his son Hartley or Wordsworth say much respecting him. Hartley always spoke of his father with affection, but never, to my knowledge at least, related any anecdotes respecting him. I once heard Wordsworth speak of him, but it was only about his personal appearance. He remarked, that he could not be called a handsome man, and that the great fault in his face was his mouth; the best feature, his eyes. He once gave an interesting account of the origin of 'We Are Seven,' the 'Ancient Mariner,' and some other poems, the names of which I forget. He and Coleridge agreed to take a tour together, I think, into Devonshire; and in order to pay their expenses, resolved to write some poems, which, I think, were composed during the tour, but I am not sure. They gave each other a certain amount of assistance in their respective compositions. In the 'Ancient Mariner' it is remarkable that the idea of the dead men pulling the ropes, which would seem more likely to have emanated from the mind of Coleridge than of Wordsworth, was suggested by the latter. The first verse of the poem 'We are Seven' was written by Coleridge. Wordsworth composed this poem backwards, beginning at the last verse and going upwards. He and Coleridge were staying in a friend's house at the time of its composition. Wordsworth was summoned to tea when he had finished all but the last verse, and Coleridge told him to go into the drawing-room, and he would complete it for him.

NOTES

[1] 'The Ancient Mariner' was written November 1797 – March 1798; 'Christabel, I', 'The Idiot Boy' and 'The Thorn' in the Spring and early Summer of 1798.

[2] Sir Richard Phillips (1767-1840), journalist, editor and bookseller; and publisher of the *Monthly Magazine*, edited by Dr John Aikin (1747-1822).

[3] Shelvocke's *A Voyage Round the World, by Way of the Great South Sea* (1726).

[4] 'The Rime of the Ancient Mariner', ll.15-16 (*CPW*, I, 187).

[5] STC credits Wordsworth with ll.226-7 (*CPW*, I, 196n.1).

[6] Wordsworth told Alexander Dyce: 'I had very little share in the composition of it, for I soon found that the style of Coleridge and myself would not assimilate' (quoted in *The Poems of S.T. Coleridge*, ed. Derwent and Sara Coleridge (1852), 323-4).

[7] *BL*, II, 6 — according to which, this was Wordsworth's half of the *Ballads*; STC was to address 'persons and characters supernatural, or at least romantic'.

[8] Cf. 'We Are Seven', l.1.

[9] James Webbe Tobin (1767-1814), friend of STC and Wordsworth, and brother of John, the dramatist.

The Stowey Circle

(i) JOHN THELWALL

From 'Lines, written at Bridgewater, in Somersetshire, on the 27th of July, 1797; during a long excursion, in quest of a peaceful retreat'; in John Thelwall, Poems Chiefly Written in Retirement *(1801), 129-31. Coleridge wrote to 'Citizen' Thelwall (1764-1834), the prominent radical, in April 1796, enclosing a copy of his poems. In July 1797, Thelwall came to stay at Stowey. He wrote home enthusing about 'the delightful society of Coleridge and of Wordsworth':*

> We have been having a delightful ramble to-day among the plantations, and along a wild, romantic dell in these grounds, through which a foaming, rushing, murmuring torrent of water winds its long artless course. There have we ... a literary and political triumvirate, passed sentence on the productions and characters of the age, burst forth in poetical flights of enthusiasm, and philosophised our minds into a state of tranquillity, which the leaders of nations might envy, and the residents of cities can never know. (*Sandford,* Thomas Poole, *I, 232-3*)

Coleridge later recalled: 'I said to him – "Citizen John! this is a fine place to talk treason in!" "Nay, Citizen Samuel!" replied he, 'it is a fine place to make a man forget that there is any necessity for treason"' (TT, I, 180-1) – an often-told story.[1] Thelwall's poem recalls his visit, casting it as a Utopian vision of permanent settlement, and implies the way that the Pantisocratic vision was being kept alive: a potent mixture of domesticity, sentiment, intermittent farming, puns and metaphysics.

> Ah! let me then, far from the strifeful scenes
> Of public life (where Reason's warning voice
> Is heard no longer, and the trump of Truth
> Who blows but wakes The Ruffian Crew of Power
> To deeds of maddest anarchy and blood)

Ah! let me, far in some sequestr'd dell,
Build my low cot; most happy might it prove,
My Samuel! near to thine, that I might oft
Share thy sweet converse, best-belov'd of friends! —
Long-lov'd ere known: for kindred sympathies
Link'd, tho far distant, our congenial souls.
        Ah! 'twould be sweet, beneath the neighb'ring thatch,
In philosophic amity to dwell,
Inditing moral verse, or tale, or theme,
Gay or instructive; and it would be sweet,
With kindly interchange of mutual aid,
To delve our little garden plots, the while
Sweet converse flow'd, suspending oft the arm
And half-driven spade, while, eager, one propounds,
And listens one, weighing each pregnant word,
And pondering fit reply, that may untwist
The knotty point — perchance, of import high —
Of Moral Truth, of Causes Infinite,
Creating Power! or Uncreated Worlds
Eternal and uncaus'd! or whatsoe'er,
Of Metaphysic, or of Ethic lore,
The mind, with curious subtilty, pursues —
Agreeing, or dissenting — sweet alike,
When wisdom, and not victory, the end.
And 'twould be sweet, my Samuel, ah! most sweet
To see our little infants stretch their limbs
In gambols unrestrain'd, and early learn
Practical love, and, Wisdom's noblest lore,
Fraternal kindliness; while rosiest health,
Bloom'd on their sun-burnt cheeks. And 'twould be sweet,
When what to toil was due, to study what,
And literary effort, had been paid,
Alternate, in each other's bower to sit,
In summer's genial season; or, when, bleak,
The wintry blast had stripp'd the leafy shade,
Around the blazing hearth, social and gay,
To share our frugal viands, and the bowl
Sparkling with home-brew'd beverage: — by our sides
Thy Sara, and my Susan, and, perchance,
Allfoxden's musing tenant, and the maid
Of ardent eye, who, with fraternal love,
Sweetens his solitude. With these should join
Arcadian Pool [sic], swain of a happier age,

When Wisdom and Refinement lov'd to dwell
With Rustic Plainness, and the pastoral vale
Was vocal to the melodies of verse—
Echoing sweet minstrelsey. With such, my friend!—
With such how pleasant to unbend awhile,
Winging the idle hour with song, or tale,
Pun, or quaint joke, or converse, such as fits
Minds gay, but innocent: and we would laugh—
(Unless, perchance, pity's more kindly tear
Check the obstreperous mirth) at such who waste
Life's precious hours in the delusive chace
Of wealth and worldly gewgaws, and contend
For honours emptier than the hollow voice
That rings in Echo's cave; and which, like that,
Exists but in the babbling of a world
Creating its own wonder. Wiselier we,
To intellectual joys will thus devote
Our fleeting years; mingling Arcadian sports
With healthful industry. O, it would be
A Golden Age reviv'd!—

(ii) 'SPY NOZY'

From Nicholas Roe, Wordsworth and Coleridge. The Radical Years *(Oxford, 1988), 260-1. Thelwall was not the only person keen to listen: so was a government agent, James Walsh, who had been trailing Thelwall. When he arrived in Stowey, Thelwall had already left; so he turned his attention to the 'Sett of Violent Democrats' which he found at Alfoxden (see Roe, 257-62). In* Biographia *(BL, I, 194), Coleridge nicknames Walsh 'Spy Nozy': allegedly, the spy mistook the poets' talk of Spinoza for unkind references to his large nose (a likely story). Walsh's report to HQ (16 August 1797) contains this portrait of the 'Sett'.*

The house was taken for a Person of the name of Wordsworth, who came to It from a Village near Honiton in Devonshire, about five Weeks since. The Rent of the House is secured to the Landlord by a Mr. Thomas Poole of this Town. Mr. Poole is a Tanner and a Man of some property. He is a most Violent Member of the Corresponding Society[2] and a strenuous supporter of Its friends, He has with him at this time a Mr Coldridge and his Wife both of whom he has supported since Christmas last. This Coldridge came last from Bristol and is reckoned a Man of superior Ability. He is frequently publishing, and I am told is soon to produce a new work. He has a Press in the House and I am inform'd He prints as well as publishes his own productions.

Mr. Poole with his disposition, is the more dangerous from his having established in this Town, what He Stiles *The Poor Mans Club*,[3] and placing himself at the head of It, By the Title of the *Poor Mans Friend*. I am told that there are 150 poor Men belonging to this Club, and that Mr. Poole has the intire command of every one of them. When Mr. Thelwall was here, he was continually with Mr. Poole.

(iii) CORNELIA A.H. CROSSE

From Cornelia A.H. Crosse, 'Thomas Poole', Temple Bar 87 (1889) 354-70, 364-5. Reviewing Sandford's Thomas Poole, Crosse repeats some stories told by John Kenyon, a friend of Southey's who lived near Nether Stowey.

Another trifling anecdote of the Quantock days occurs to me, but this time Coleridge is the hero. Whenever he could borrow a steed of tolerable meekness, he was fond of making an expedition over the hills to Taunton, where he had, in early days, many friends amongst the Unitarian Community. He preached in their chapel more than once, in his blue coat with brass buttons. On one occasion, when riding over the hills, his horse cast a shoe, and he stopped at a village to have it replaced. He chanced to ask the smith what time it was? 'I'll tell 'ee present, sir,' said the man, lifting a hind foot of the horse, and looking across it attentively, added, 'half-past eleven.' 'How do you know?' asked Coleridge. 'Do 'ee think as I've shoed hosses all my life and don't know by sign what o'clock it is?' Coleridge went away puzzled; and returning the same way in the evening he offered the blacksmith a shilling to show him how he could tell the time by a horse's hoof. 'Just you get off your hoss, sir,' said the smith with a twinkle in his eye. 'Now do 'ee stoop down and look through the hole in yon pollard ash, and you'll see the church clock.'

A very Philistine recollection of Coleridge exists in a letter written by the mother of an old friend of mine. In it she describes having paid a visit in the same house with Coleridge. 'He drank up all the brandy in the house, and used up all the snuff in the village,' she writes, adding:—

'I think him a most absent-minded opiniated [*sic*] man, talking everybody down, and going on about subjects that the rest of the company care nothing for. His conversation is always working, working on, and most fatiguing to listen to.'

Poor lady, it is evident she did not understand what Charles Lamb called 'Coleridge's fun.'

NOTES

[1] Thelwall was evidently surprised by the vehemence of STC's politics: 'Mount him but upon his darling hobby horse "the republic of God's own making", & away he goes like hey go mad, spattering & splashing thro thick & thin & scattering more *levelling* sedition, & constructive treason, than poor *Gilly*, or myself ever dreamt of' (letter of 3 March 1798; quoted in Nicholas Roe, '"Atmospheric Air Itself": Medical Science, Politics and Poetry in Thelwall, Coleridge and Wordsworth'; in Richard Cronin (ed.), *1798: The Year of the Lyrical Ballads* (Basingstoke, 1998) 185-202, 198-9).

[2] The London Corresponding Society, the most famous of the many societies founded to champion democratic reform.

[3] Presumably the 'Benefit Club' that STC mentions in a letter (*CL*, I, 342).

Preacher

(i) WILLIAM HAZLITT

From 'Mr. Coleridge's Lay Sermon. To the Editor of The Examiner' (12 January 1817); collected in Political Essays, with Sketches of Public Characters *(1819) 137-39, 137-8. Hazlitt (1778-1830), critic and essayist, never fully overcame his youthful fascination with Coleridge, although he overcame very successfully his early admiration. This reminiscence comes in a letter, purportedly written in response to Hazlitt's own damning review of Coleridge's* Lay Sermon. *As prospective incumbent, Coleridge needed to deliver a sermon to the Unitarian chapel in Shrewsbury, near Wem, where Hazlitt's father was Unitarian minister.*

It was in January, 1798, just 19 years ago, that I got up one morning before day-light to walk 10 miles in the mud, and went to hear a poet and a philosopher preach. It was the author of the 'Lay-Sermon.' Never, Sir, the longest day I have to live, shall I have such another walk as this cold, raw, comfortless one, in the winter of the year 1798. — Mr. Examiner, *Il y a des impressions que ni le tems ni les circonstances peuvent effacer. Dusse-je vivre des siècles entiers, le doux tems de ma jeunesse ne peut renaitre pour moi, ni s'effacer jamais dans ma mémoire.*[1] When I got there, Sir, the organ was playing the 100th psalm, and when it was done, Mr. C. rose and gave out his text, 'And he went up into the mountain to pray, HIMSELF, ALONE.'[2] As he gave out this text, his voice 'rose like a steam of rich distill'd perfumes,'[3] and when he came to the two last words, which he pronounced loud, deep, and distinct, it seemed to me, Sir, who was then young, as if the sounds had echoed from the bottom of the human heart, and as if that prayer might have floated in solemn silence through the universe. The idea of St. John came into my mind, 'of one crying in the wilderness, who had his loins girt about, and whose food was locusts and wild honey.'[4] The preacher then launched into his subject, like an eagle dallying with the wind. *That* sermon, like *this* Sermon, was upon peace and war; upon church and state—not their alliance, but their separation[5]—on the spirit of the world and the spirit of Christianity, not as the same, but as opposed to one another. He talked of those who had 'inscribed the cross of Christ on banners dripping with human gore.' He made a poetical and pastoral excursion,—and to shew the fatal effects of war, drew a striking contrast between the simple shepherd boy, driving his team afield, or sitting under the hawthorn, piping to his flock, as though he should never be old, and the same poor country-lad, crimped, kidnapped, brought into town, made drunk at an alehouse, turned into a wretched drummer-boy, with his hair sticking on end with powder and pomatum, a long cue at his back, and tricked out in the loathsome finery of the profession of blood.

> 'Such were the notes our once-lov'd poet sung.'[6]

And for myself, Sir, I could not have been more delighted if I had heard the music of the spheres. Poetry and Philosophy had met together, Truth and Genius had embraced, under the eye and with the sanction of Religion. This was even beyond my hopes. I returned home well satisfied. The sun that was still labouring pale and wan through the sky, obscured by thick mists, seemed an emblem of the *good cause:* and the cold dank drops of dew that hung half melted on the beard of the thistle, had something genial and refreshing in them; for there was a spirit of hope and youth in all nature, that turned everything into good.

(ii) 'R.A.'

From 'R.A.', 'Presbyterian Meeting-House, Shrewsbury', Christian Reformer NS 3 (1847) 323-332, 330n..

The late Mr. Joseph Swanwick, of Chester, a gentleman admirably qualified by his talents and education to appreciate any intellectual effort, was accustomed to speak of Mr. Coleridge's pulpit addresses, at this time, with high admiration. On one occasion, when preaching in Mr. Hazlitt's pulpit at Wem, on the being of a God, Mr. Coleridge delighted the few who could follow him, by the closeness of his reasoning, the variety of his illustrations, and the exquisite beauty of his language. So completely was the orator carried away by his own eloquence, that dispensing with the ordinary close of the service, a hymn and prayer, he burst from the sermon, which he abruptly terminated, into a fervent address to the Deity. That prayer impressed all present as the most sublime devotional exercise they had ever heard.

NOTES

[1] A conflation of passages from *La Nouvelle Héloïse* (1761), Part VI, letter 7.
[2] A cross between Matthew 14.23 and John 6.15.
[3] Cf. *Comus*, l.555.
[4] Matthew, 3.3-4.
[5] STC became an eloquent supporter of the established church.
[6] Cf. Pope, 'Epistle to Robert Earl of Oxford, and Earl Mortimer', l.1.

'and you wished him to talk on for ever'
WILLIAM HAZLITT

From William Hazlitt, 'My First Acquaintance with Poets', The Liberal. Verse and Prose from the South II (1823) 23-46, 26-7; 29-36; 38-9; 41-6. After the memorable sermon, Coleridge returned to the Hazlitt household.

On the Tuesday following, the half-inspired speaker came. I was called down into the room where he was, and went half-hoping, half-afraid. He received me very graciously, and I listened for a long time without uttering a word. I did not suffer in his opinion by my silence. 'For those two hours,' he afterwards was pleased to say, 'he was conversing with W.H.'s forehead!' His appearance was different from what I had anticipated from seeing him before. At a distance, and in the dim light of the chapel, there was to me a strange wildness in his aspect, a dusky obscurity, and I thought him pitted with the small-pox. His complexion was at that time clear, and even bright—

'As are the children of yon azure sheen.'[1]

His forehead was broad and high, light as if built of ivory, with large projecting eyebrows, and his eyes rolling beneath them like a sea with darkened lustre. 'A certain tender bloom his face o'erspread,'[2] a purple tinge as we see it in the pale thoughtful complexions of the Spanish portrait-painters, Murillo and Velasquez. His mouth was gross, voluptuous, open, eloquent; his chin good-humoured and round; but his nose, the rudder of the face, the index of the will, was small, feeble, nothing—like what he has done. It might seem that the genius of his face as from a height surveyed and projected him (with sufficient capacity and huge aspiration) into the world unknown of thought and imagination, with nothing to support or guide his veering purpose, as if Columbus had launched his adventurous course for the New World in a scallop, without oars or compass. So at least I comment on it after the event. Coleridge in his person was rather above the common size, inclining to the corpulent, or like Lord Hamlet, 'somewhat fat and pursy.'[3] His hair (now, alas! grey) was then black and glossy as the raven's, and fell in smooth masses over his forehead. This long pendulous hair is peculiar to enthusiasts, to those whose minds tend heavenward; and is traditionally inseparable (though of a different colour) from the pictures of Christ. It ought to belong, as a character, to all who preach *Christ crucified*, and Coleridge was at that time one of those! [...]

No two individuals were ever more unlike than were the host and his guest. A poet was to my father a sort of non-descript: yet whatever added grace to the Unitarian cause was to him welcome. He could hardly have been more surprised or pleased, if our visitor had worn wings. Indeed, his thoughts had wings; and as the silken sounds rustled round out little wainscoted parlour, my father threw back his spectacles over his forehead, his white hairs mixing with its sanguine hew; and a smile of delight beamed across his rugged cordial face, to think that Truth had found a new ally in Fancy! Besides, Coleridge seemed to take considerable notice of me, and that of itself was enough. He talked very familiarly, but agreeably, and glanced over a variety of subjects. At dinnertime he grew more animated, and dilated in a very edifying manner on Mary Wolstonecraft [*sic*] and Mackintosh. [4] The last, he said, he considered (on my father's speaking of his *Vindiciæ Gallicæ*[5] as a capital performance) as a clever scholastic man—a master of the topics,—or as the ready warehouseman of letters, who knew exactly where to lay his hand on what he wanted, though the goods were not his own. He thought him no match for Burke, either in style or matter. Burke was a metaphysician, Mackintosh a mere logician. Burke was an orator (almost a poet) who reasoned in figures, because he had an eye for nature: Mackintosh, on the other hand, was a rhetorician, who had only an eye to common-places.

On this I ventured to say that I had always entertained a great opinion of Burke, and that (as far as I could find) the speaking of him with contempt might be made the test of a vulgar democratical mind. This was the first observation I ever made to Coleridge, and he said it was a very just and striking one. I remember the leg of Welsh mutton and the turnips on the table that day had the finest flavour imaginable. Coleridge added that Mackintosh and Tom. Wedgwood (of whom, however, he spoke highly) had expressed a very indifferent opinion of his friend Mr. Wordsworth, on which he remarked to them—'He strides on so far before you, that he dwindles in the distance!' Godwin had once boasted to him of having carried on an argument with Mackintosh for three hours with dubious success; Coleridge told him—'If there had been a man of genius in the room, he would have settled the question in five minutes.' He asked me if I had ever seen Mary Wolstonecraft, and I said, I had once for a few moments, and that she seemed to me to turn off Godwin's objections to something she advanced with quite a playful, easy air. He replied, that 'this was only one instance of the ascendancy which people of imagination exercised over those of mere intellect.' He did not rate Godwin very high (this was caprice or prejudice, real or affected) but he had a great idea of Mrs. Wolstonecraft's powers of conversation, none at all of her talent for book-making. We talked a little about Holcroft.[6] He had been asked if he was not much struck *with* him, and he said, he thought himself in more danger of being struck *by* him. I complained that he would not let me get on at all, for he required a definition of every the commonest word, exclaiming, 'What do you mean by a *sensation*, Sir? What do you mean by an *idea*?' This, Coleridge said, was barricadoing the road to truth:—it was setting up a turnpike-gate at every step we took. I forget a great number of things, many more than I remember; but the day passed off pleasantly, and the next morning Mr. Coleridge was to return to Shrewsbury. When I came down to breakfast, I found that he had just received a letter from his friend, T. Wedgwood, making him an offer of £150 a-year if he chose to wave his present pursuit, and devote himself entirely to the study of poetry and philosophy.[7] Coleridge seemed to make up his mind to close with this proposal in the act of tying on one of his shoes. It threw an additional damp on his departure. It took the wayward enthusiast quite from us to cast him into Deva's winding vales,[8] or by the shores of old ro-

mance. Instead of living at ten miles distance, of being the pastor of
a Dissenting congregation at Shrewsbury, he was henceforth to
inhabit the Hill of Parnassus, to be a Shepherd on the Delectable
Mountains. Alas! I knew not the way thither, and felt very little
gratitude for Mr. Wedgwood's bounty. I was presently relieved
from this dilemma; for Mr. Coleridge, asking for a pen and ink,
and going to a table to write something on a bit of card, advanced
towards me with undulating step, and giving me the precious
document, said that that was his address, *Mr. Coleridge, Nether-
Stowey, Somersetshire*; and that he should be glad to see me there in
a few weeks' time, and, if I chose, would come half-way to meet
me. I was not less surprised than the shepherd-boy (this simile is to
be found in Cassandra) when he sees a thunder-bolt fall close at his
feet. I stammered out my acknowledgments and acceptance of this
offer (I thought Mr. Wedgwood's annuity a trifle to it) as well as I
could; and this mighty business being settled, the poet-preacher
took leave, and I accompanied him six miles on the road. It was a
fine morning in the middle of winter, and he talked the whole way.
The scholar in Chaucer is described as going

—— 'Sounding on his way.'[9]

So Coleridge went on his. In digressing, in dilating, in passing from
subject to subject, he appeared to me to float in air, to slide on ice.
He told me in confidence (going along) that he should have
preached two sermons before he accepted the situation at Shrewsbury, one on Infant Baptism, the other on the Lord's Supper,
shewing that he could not administer either, which would effectively have disqualified him for the object in view.[10] I observed that
he continually crossed me on the way by shifting from one side of
the foot-path to the other. This struck me as an odd movement; but
I did not at that time connect it with any instability of purpose or
involuntary change of principle, as I have done since. He seemed
unable to keep on in a strait line. He spoke slightingly of Hume
(whose Essay on Miracles he said was stolen from an objection
started in one of South's Sermons—*Credat Judæus Apella!*).[11] I was
not very much pleased at this account of Hume, for I had just been
reading, with infinite relish, that completest of all metaphysical
choke-pears, his *Treatise on Human Nature*, to which the *Essays*, in
point of scholastic subtlety and close reasoning, are mere elegant
trifling, light summer-reading. Coleridge even denied the excel-

lence of Hume's general style, which I think betrayed a want of taste or candour. He however made me amends by the manner in which he spoke of Berkeley. He dwelt particularly on his *Essay on Vision* as a masterpiece of analytical reasoning. So it undoubtedly is. He was exceedingly angry with Dr. Johnson for striking the stone with his foot, in allusion to this author's Theory of Matter and Spirit, and saying, 'Thus I confute him, Sir.'[12] Coleridge drew a parallel (I don't know how he brought about the connection) between Bishop Berkeley and Tom Paine.[13] He said the one was an instance of a subtle, the other of an acute mind, than which no two things could be more distinct. The one was a shop-boy's quality, the other the characteristic of a philosopher. He considered Bishop Butler as a true philosopher, a profound and conscientious thinker, a genuine reader of nature and of his own mind. He did not speak of his *Analogy*, but of his *Sermons at the Rolls' Chapel*, of which I had never heard.[14] Coleridge somehow always contrived to prefer the *unknown* to the *known*. In this instance he was right. The *Analogy* is a tissue of sophistry, of wire-drawn, theological special-pleading; the *Sermons* (with the Preface to them) are in a fine vein of deep, matured reflection, a candid appeal to our observation of human nature, without pedantry and without bias. I told Coleridge I had written a few remarks, and was sometimes foolish enough to believe that I had made a discovery on the same subject (the *Natural Disinterestedness of the Human Mind*)[15]—and I tried to explain my view of it to Coleridge, who listened with great willingness, but I did not succeed in making myself understood. I sat down to the task shortly afterwards for the twentieth time, got new pens and paper, determined to make clear work of it, wrote a few meagre sentences in the skeleton-style of a mathematical demonstration, stopped half-way down the second page; and, after trying in vain to pump up any words, images, notions, apprehensions, facts, or observations, from that gulph of abstraction in which I had plunged myself for four or five years preceding, gave up the attempt as labour in vain, and shed tears of helpless despondency on the blank unfinished paper. I can write fast enough now. Am I better than I was then? Oh no! One truth discovered, one pang of regret at not being able to express it, is better than all the fluency and flippancy in the world. Would that I could go back to what I then was! Why can we not revive past times as we can revisit old places? If I had the quaint Muse of Sir Philip Sidney to assist me, I would write a *Sonnet to the Road between W-m and Shrewsbury*, and immortalise every step of it by some fond enigmatical conceit. I would swear that the very milestones had ears, and that Harmerhill stooped with all its pines, to listen to a poet, as he passed! I remember but one other topic of discourse in this walk. He mentioned Paley, praised the naturalness and clearness of his style, but condemned his sentiments, thought him a mere time-serving casuist, and said that 'the fact of his work on Moral and Political Philosophy being made a text-book in our Universities was a disgrace to the national character.'[16] We parted at the six-mile stone; and I returned homeward, pensive but much pleased. I had met with unexpected notice from a person, whom I believed to have been prejudiced against me. 'Kind and affable to me had been his condescension, and should be honoured ever with suitable regard.'[17] He was the first poet I had known, and he certainly answered to that inspired name. I had heard a great deal of his powers of conversation, and was not disappointed. In fact, I never met with any thing at all like them, either before or since. I could easily credit the accounts which were circulated of his holding forth to a large party of ladies and gentlemen, an evening or two before, on the Berkeleian Theory, when he made the whole material universe look like a transparency of fine words; and another story (which I believe he has somewhere told himself) of his being asked to a party at Birmingham, of his smoking tobacco and going to sleep after dinner on a sofa, where the company found him to their no small surprise, which was increased to wonder when he started up of a sudden, and rubbing his eyes, looked about him, and launched into a three-hours' description of the third heaven, of which he had had a dream, very different from Mr. Southey's Vision of Judgment, and also from that other Vision of Judgment, which Mr. Murray, the Secretary of the Bridge-street Junto, has taken into his especial keeping![18]

On my way back, I had a sound in my ears, it was the voice of Fancy: I had a light before me, it was the face of Poetry. The one still lingers there, the other has not quitted my side! Coleridge in truth met me half-way on the ground of philosophy, or I should not have been won over to his imaginative creed. I had an uneasy, pleasurable sensation all the time, till I was to visit him. During those months the chill breath of winter gave me a welcoming; the vernal air was balm and inspiration to me. The golden sun-sets, the silver-star of evening, lighted me on my way to new hopes and prospects. *I was to visit Coleridge in the Spring.* This circumstance was never absent from my thoughts, and mingled with all my feelings. I wrote to him at the time proposed, and received an answer postponing my intended visit for a week or two, but very cordially urging me to complete my promise then. This delay did not damp, but rather increase my ardour. In the mean time, I went to Llangollen Vale, by way of initiating myself in the mysteries of natural scenery; and I must say I was enchanted with it. I had been reading Coleridge's description of England, in his fine *Ode on the Departing Year*,[19] and I applied it, *con amore*, to the objects before me. That valley was to me (in a manner) the cradle of a new existence: in the river that winds through it, my spirit was baptised in the waters of Helicon!

Hazlitt pays his visit, and, with Coleridge, visits the Wordsworths at Alfoxden.

That morning, as soon as breakfast was over, we strolled out into the park, and seating ourselves on the trunk of an old ash-tree that stretched along the ground, Coleridge read aloud with a sonorous and musical voice, the ballad of *Betty Foy*. I was not critically or sceptically inclined. I saw touches of truth and nature, and took the rest for granted. But in the *Thorn*, the *Mad Mother*, and the *Complaint of a Poor Indian Woman*,[20] I felt that deeper power and pathos which have been since acknowledged,

'In spite of pride, in erring reason's spite,'[21]

as the characteristics of this author; and the sense of a new style and a new spirit in poetry came over me. It had to me something of the effect that arises from the turning up of the fresh soil, or of the fresh welcome breath of Spring,

'While yet the trembling year is unconfirmed.'[22]

Coleridge and myself walked back to Stowey that evening, and his voice sounded high

'Of Providence, foreknowledge, will, and fate,
Fix'd fate, free-will, foreknowledge absolute,'[23]

as we passed through echoing grove, by fairy stream or waterfall, gleaming in the summer moonlight! He lamented that Wordsworth was not prone enough to belief in the traditional superstitions of the place, and that there was a something corporeal, a *matter-of-fact-ness*, a clinging to the palpable, or often to the petty, in his poetry, in consequence.[24] His genius was not a spirit that descended to him through the air; it sprung out of the ground like a flower, or unfolded itself from a green spray, on which the gold-finch sang. He said, however (if I remember right) that this objection must be confined to his descriptive pieces, that his philosophic poetry had a grand and comprehensive spirit in it, so that his soul seemed to inhabit the universe like a palace, and to discover truth by intuition, rather than by deduction. [...]

We went over to All-Foxden again the day following, and Wordsworth read us the story of Peter Bell in the open air; and the comment made upon it by his face and voice was very different from that of some later critics![25] Whatever might be thought of the poem, 'his face was as a book where men might read strange matters,'[26] and he announced the fate of his hero in prophetic tones. There is a *chaunt* in the recitation both of Coleridge and Wordsworth, which acts as a spell upon the hearer, and disarms the judgment. Perhaps they have deceived themselves by making habitual use of this ambiguous accompaniment. Coleridge's manner is more full, animated, and varied; Wordsworth's more equable, sustained, and internal. The one might be termed more *dramatic*, the other more *lyrical*. Coleridge has told me that he himself liked to compose in walking over uneven ground, or breaking through the straggling branches of a copsewood; whereas Wordsworth always wrote (if he could) walking up and down a strait gravel-walk, or in some spot where the continuity of his verse met with no collateral interruption. Returning that same evening, I got into a metaphysical argument with Wordsworth, while Coleridge was explaining the different notes of the nightingale to his sister, in which we neither of us succeeded in making ourselves perfectly clear and intelligible. Thus I passed three weeks at Nether Stowey and in the neighbourhood, generally devoting the afternoons to a delightful chat in an arbour made of bark by the poet's friend Tom Poole, sitting under two fine elm-trees, and listening to the bees humming round us, while we quaffed our *flip*.[27] It was agreed, among other things, that we should make a jaunt down the Bristol-Channel, as far as Linton. We set off together on foot, Coleridge, John Chester,[28] and I. This Chester was a native of Nether Stowey, one of those who were attracted to Coleridge's discourse as flies are to honey, or bees in swarming-time to the sound of a brass pan. He 'followed in the chace, like a dog who hunts, not like one that

made up the cry.'[29] He had on a brown cloth coat, boots, and cor-
duroy breeches, was low in stature, bow-legged, had a drag in his
walk like a drover, which he assisted by a hazel switch, and kept
on a sort of trot by the side of Coleridge, like a running footman by
a state coach, that he might not lose a syllable or sound, that fell
from Coleridge's lips. He told me his private opinion, that
Coleridge was a wonderful man. He scarcely opened his lips, much
less offered an opinion the whole way: yet of the the three, had I to
chuse during that journey, I would be John Chester. He afterwards
followed Coleridge into Germany, where the Kantean philosophers
were puzzled how to bring him under any of their categories.
When he sat down at table with his idol, John's felicity was complete; Sir Walter Scott's, or Mr. Blackwood's, when they sat down
at the same table with the King,[30] was not more so. We passed
Dunster on our right, a small town between the brow of a hill and
the sea. I remember eying it wistfully as it lay below us: contrasted
with the woody scene around, it looked as clear, as pure, as *em-
browned* and ideal as any landscape I have seen since, of Gaspar
Poussin's or Domenichino's. We had a long day's march—(our feet
kept time to the echoes of Coleridge's tongue)—through Minehead
and by the Blue Anchor, and on to Linton, which we did not reach
till near midnight, and where we had some difficulty in making a
lodgment. We however knocked the people of the house up at last,
and we were repaid for our apprehensions and fatigue by some
excellent rashers of fried bacon and eggs. The view in coming
along had been splendid. We walked for miles and miles on dark
brown heaths overlooking the channel, with the Welsh hills beyond, and at times descended into little sheltered valleys close by
the sea-side, with a smuggler's face scowling by us, and then had
to ascend conical hills with a path winding up through a coppice to
a barren top, like a monk's shaven crown, from one of which I
pointed out to Coleridge's notice the bare masts of a vessel on the
very edge of the horizon and within the red-orbed disk of the setting sun, like his own spectre-ship in the *Ancient Mariner*.[31] At Linton the character of the sea-coast becomes more marked and rugged. There is a place called the *Valley of Rocks* (I suspect this was
only the poetical name for it) bedded among precipices overhanging the sea, with rocky caverns beneath, into which the waves
dash, and where the sea-gull for ever wheels its screaming flight.
On the tops of these are huge stones thrown transverse, as if an

earthquake had tossed them there, and behind these is a fretwork of perpendicular rocks, something like the *Giant's Causeway*. A thunder-storm came on while we were at the inn, and Coleridge was running out bareheaded to enjoy the commotion of the elements in the *Valley of Rocks*, but as if in spite, the clouds only muttered a few angry sounds, and let fall a few refreshing drops. Coleridge told me that he and Wordsworth were to have made this place the scene of a prose-tale, which was to have been in the manner of, but far superior to, the *Death of Abel*, but they had relinquished the design.[32] In the morning of the second day, we breakfasted luxuriously in an old-fashioned parlour, on tea, toast, eggs, and honey, in the very sight of the bee-hives from which it had been taken, and a garden full of thyme and wild-flowers that had produced it. On this occasion Coleridge spoke of Virgil's Georgics, but not well. I do not think he had much feeling for the classical or elegant. It was in this room that we found a little worn-out copy of the *Seasons*;[33] lying in a window-seat, on which Coleridge exclaimed, '*That* is true fame!' He said Thomson was a great poet, rather than a good one; his style was as meretricious as his thoughts were natural. He spoke of Cowper as the best modern poet. He said the *Lyrical Ballads* were an experiment about to be tried by him and Wordsworth, to see how far the public taste would endure poetry written in a more natural and simple style than had hitherto been attempted; totally discarding the artifices of poetical diction, and making use only of such words as had probably been common in the most ordinary language since the days of Henry II.[34] Some comparison was introduced between Shakespear and Milton.[35] He said 'he hardly knew which to prefer. Shakespear seemed to him a mere stripling in the art; he was as tall and as strong, with infinitely more activity than Milton, but he never appeared to have come to man's estate; or if he had, he would not have been a man, but a monster.' He spoke with contempt of Gray, and with intolerance of Pope. He did not like the versification of the latter. He observed that 'the ears of these couplet-writers might be charged with having short memories, that could not retain the harmony of whole passages.' He thought little of Junius as a writer;[36] he had a dislike of Dr. Johnson; and a much higher opinion of Burke as an orator and politician, than of Fox or Pitt. He however thought him very inferior in richness of style and imagery to some of our elder prose-writers, particularly Jeremy Taylor.[37] He liked Richardson, but not Fielding;[38] nor could I get him to enter into the merits of *Caleb Williams*.[39] In short, he was profound and discriminating with respect to those authors whom he liked, and where he gave his judgment fair play; capricious, perverse, and prejudiced in his antipathies and distastes. We loitered on the 'ribbed sea-sands,'[40] in such talk as this, a whole morning, and I recollect met with a curious sea-weed, of which John Chester told us the country name! A fisherman gave Coleridge an account of a boy that had been drowned the day before, and that they had tried to save him at the risk of their own lives. He said 'he did not know how it was that they ventured, but, Sir, we have a *nature* towards one another.' This expression, Coleridge remarked to me, was a fine illustration of that theory of disinterestedness which I (in common with Butler) had adopted. I broached to him an argument of mine to prove that *likeness* was not mere association of ideas. I said that the mark in the sand put one in mind of a man's foot, not because it was part of a former impression of a man's foot (for it was quite new) but because it was like the shape of a man's foot. He assented to the justness of this distinction (which I have explained at length elsewhere, for the benefit of the curious)[41] and John Chester listened; not from any interest in the subject, but because he was astonished that I should be able to suggest any thing to Coleridge that he did not already know. We returned on the third morning, and Coleridge remarked the silent cottage-smoke curling up the valleys where, a few evenings before, we had seen the lights gleaming through the dark.

In a day or two after we arrived at Stowey, we set out, I on my return home, and he for Germany. It was a Sunday morning, and he was to preach that day for Dr. Toulmin of Taunton. I asked him if he had prepared any thing for the occasion? He said he had not even thought of the text, but should as soon as we parted. I did not go to hear him, — this was a fault, — but we met in the evening at Bridgewater. The next day we had a long day's walk to Bristol, and sat down, I recollect, by a well-side on the road, to cool ourselves and satisfy our thirst, when Coleridge repeated to me some descriptive lines from his tragedy of Remorse; which I must say became his mouth and that occasion better than they, some years after, did Mr. Elliston's and the Drury-lane boards,[42] —

> 'Oh memory! shield me from the world's poor strife,
> And give those scenes thine everlasting life.'

From 'On Going a Journey'; in William Hazlitt, Table Talk; or, Original Essays *(2 vols.; 1821-22), II, 39-40.*

To give way to our feelings before company, seems extravagance or affectation; and on the other hand, to have to unravel this mystery of our being at every turn, and to make others take an equal interest in it (otherwise the end is not answered) is a task to which few are competent. We must 'give it an understanding, but no tongue.'[43] My old friend C——, however, could do both. He could go on in the most delightful explanatory way over hill and dale, a summer's day, and convert a landscape into a didactic poem or a Pindaric ode. 'He talked far above singing.'[44] If I could so clothe my ideas in sounding and flowing words, I might perhaps wish to have some one with me to admire the swelling theme; or I could be more content, were it possible for me still to hear his echoing voice in the woods of All-Foxden. They had 'that fine madness in them which our first poets had[.]'[45]

And finally, from William Hazlitt, Lectures on the English Poets. *Delivered at the Surrey Institution (1818), 329-30. Some of Hazlitt's first excitement suddenly re-emerges in the closing passage of the last lecture.*

But I may say of him here, that he is the only person I ever knew who answered to the idea of a man of genius. He is the only person from whom I ever learnt any thing. There is only one thing he could learn from me in return, but *that* he has not. He was the first poet I ever knew. His genius at that time had angelic wings, and fed on manna. He talked on for ever; and you wished him to talk on for ever. His thoughts did not seem to come with labour and effort; but as if borne on the gusts of genius, and as if the wings of his imagination lifted him from off his feet. His voice rolled on the ear like the pealing organ, and its sound alone was the music of thought. His mind was clothed with wings; and raised on them, he lifted philosophy to heaven. In his descriptions, you then saw the progress of human happiness and liberty in bright and never-ending succession, like the steps of Jacob's ladder, with airy shapes ascending and descending, and with the voice of God at the top of the ladder. And shall I, who heard him then, listen to him now? Not I! . . . . That spell is broke; that time is gone for ever; that voice is heard no more: but still the recollection comes rushing by with thoughts of long-past years, and rings in my ears with never-dying sound.

NOTES

[1] Cf. 'The Castle of Indolence', II.xxxiii, l.7.

[2] Cf. 'The Castle of Indolence', I.lvii, l.3.

[3] Cf. *Hamlet*, III.iv, l.153; V.ii, l.287.

[4] Sir James Mackintosh (1765-1832), lawyer and writer, and STC's rival as greatest conversationalist of the age. STC described him to Godwin as 'the great Dung-fly' (*CL*, I, 588), and suggested that one might 'write on his forehead, "Warehouse to let"' (*TT*, I, 42).

[5] Mackintosh's *Vindiciæ Gallicæ* (1791) was a liberal defence of the Revolution in France; by 1799, he had retracted. STC considered his lectures the embodiment of everything wrong with modern metaphysics (*CL*, II, 675).

[6] Thomas Holcroft (1745-1809), novelist and radical, indicted for high treason in 1794. STC met him soon after, and formed a dim view (*CL*, I, 138).

[7] Tom Wedgwood (1771-1805), a psychologist and chemist, and son of the potter. Tom and his brother each granted STC an annuity of £150 to enable him to devote himself to poetry and metaphysics (see *CL*, I, 370; *BL*, I, 205). For STC's portrait of Tom, see *F*, I, 146-7.

[8] The Dee: as used in 'Lycidas', l.55 and 'The Castle of Indolence', II.xxv, l.1.

[9] Cf. the 'General Prologue' to the *Canterbury Tales*, l.307.

[10] STC's mixed feelings about infant baptism were aroused by the possibility of his own children being baptised (*CL*, I, 624-5); see J. Robert Barth, S.J., *Coleridge and Christian Doctrine* (Cambridge, Mass., 1969), 172-3. STC often dwelt on the question of transubstantiation (*LS*, 88; *SWF*, I, 901-2, *etc.*). After Cambridge, he didn't take the sacrament himself until 1827.

[11] 'Let the Jew Apella believe it!' ('don't believe it!'): Horace, *Satires*, I.v, l.100.

[12] James Boswell, *The Life of Samuel Johnson* (Everyman edn.; 1949), I, 292.

[13] Tom Paine (1737-1809), author of *Common Sense* (1776) and *The Rights of Man* (1791-2). STC had always taken a low view of his philosophical competence (*L1795*, 149), and it grew dimmer ('that rude blunderer': *BL*, II, 167).

[14] Joseph Butler (1692-1752), philosopher and divine, author of *The Analogy of Religion, Natural and Revealed* (1736). STC thought him one of 'the three *great* Metaphysicians which this Country *has* produced' (*CL*, II, 703).

[15] Finally published as *An Essay on the Principles of Human Action* (1805).

[16] William Paley (1743-1805), author of *The Principles of Moral and Political Philosophy* (1785) and *Natural Theology* (1802). STC attacked him in the 1795 lectures (*L1795*, 310), and continued to deplore his influence (*TT*, II, 162).

[17] Cf. Adam's words to Raphael: *Paradise Lost*, VIII, ll.648-50.

[18] Southey's ill-judged *Vision of Judgement* (1821) depicted the dead George III entering heaven to applause; Byron's parody appeared in the first issue of *The Liberal* the following year. Charles Murray of Bridge Street, a member of the Constitutional Association, prosecuted John Hunt for publishing it.

[19] ll.121-158 (*CPW*, I, 167-8).

[20] Poems destined for *Lyrical Ballads*: 'The Idiot Boy', 'The Thorn', 'The Mad Mother', and 'The Complaint of a Forsaken Indian Woman'.

[21] Cf. Pope, 'Essay on Man', I, l.293.

[22] Cf. Thomson, 'Spring', l.18.

[23] *Paradise Lost*, II, ll.559-60. Cf. *BL*, I, 16.

[24] A 'defect' which STC returns to at length in *BL*, II, 126-35.

[25] *Peter Bell. A Tale in Verse* was written in Spring 1798.

[26] *Macbeth*, I.iv, ll.63-4.

[27] A sweet alcoholic drink made with spices and beaten egg.

[28] John Chester, later STC's travelling companion in Germany.

[29] Cf. *Othello*, III.iii, ll.369-70.

[30] William Blackwood (1776-1834), publisher of *Blackwood's Magazine*, and staunch Tory. Scott was largely responsible for the festivities (including a lavish banquet) marking George IV's visit to Scotland in August 1822.

[31] ll.171-80 (*CPW*, I, 193).

[32] The abandoned Wordsworth-Coleridge collaboration is 'The Wanderings of Cain', of which only STC's share ever existed (*CPW*, I, 288-92). *The Death of Abel* (1758) is a once-popular poem by Salomon Gessner (1730-88).

[33] Thomson's *The Seasons* (1726-30) — from which Hazlitt has already quoted.

[34] Wordsworth's 1802 'Appendix' to the 'Preface' to *Lyrical Ballads* had described the rejection of 'poetic diction'. No published text seems precisely to reproduce the argument Hazlitt remembers. The 1798 'Advertisement' had claimed of 'The Ancyent Marinere' that 'the language adopted in it has been equally intelligible for these last three centuries', and the 'Preface' had judged most of Chaucer still intelligible.

[35] A recurrent comparison: see, e.g., *BL*, II, 27-8.

[36] Author of the anonymous *Letters of Junius* (1769-71), a Whig satire.

[37] Jeremy Taylor (1613-67), one of STC's favourite divines (see *BL*, II, 55, etc.).

[38] Samuel Richardson (1689-1761), author of *Pamela* (1740) and *Clarissa* (1748); and Henry Fielding (1707-54), whose *Joseph Andrews* (1742) and *Tom Jones* (1749) react against Richardson. STC's later preference was for Fielding (*TT*, I, 496): he describes Richardson's 'oozy, hypocritical, praise-mad, canting, envious, concupiscent' mind in the notebook (*CN*, II, 2471).

[39] Godwin's novel, *Things as They Are; or, the Adventures of Caleb Williams* (1794).

[40] Cf. 'The Ancient Mariner', l.227 (*CPW*, I, 196).

[41] In the 'Remarks on the Systems of Hartley and Helvetius', appended to the *Essay on the Principles of Human Action*.

[42] *Remorse*, a revised version of the unperformed *Osorio* finally made it to the stage in 1813, with Robert William Elliston (1774-1831), leading Shakespearean and one of Lamb's favourites, as Don Alvar. The play ran for twenty nights.

[43] Cf. *Hamlet*, I.ii, l.249.

[44] Cf. Beaumont and Fletcher, *Philaster*, V.v, ll.166-7.

[45] Cf. Drayton's 'To My Most Dearely-loved Friend Henery Reynolds Esquire. Of Poets and Poesie', ll.105-9.

Two Cooler Views

(i) DANIEL STUART

From Daniel Stuart, 'Anecdotes of the Poet Coleridge', Gentleman's Magazine NS IX (1838) 485-92, 485-6. Stuart (1766-1846), journalist and editor, of the Morning Post and then of the Courier, employed Coleridge as a contributor. This account of Coleridge and Mackintosh (who was Stuart's brother-in-law) implies the mutual distrust which characterised the two greatest talkers of the age.

Mr. (after Sir James) Mackintosh was on a visit at Cote House, Bristol, the residence of Mr. Wedgewood [*sic*], passing the Christmas holidays in 1797. A large party of the Wedgewoods and Allans[1] was assembled, among whom were Coleridge and Mackintosh. Coleridge was not a mere holiday visitor: he had been an inmate for some time, and had so riveted, by his discourse, the attention of the gentlemen, particularly of Mr. Thomas Wedgewood, an infirm bachelor; he had so prevented all general conversation, that several of the party wished him out of the house. I believe the Wedgewoods were at the same time very liberal to him with their purse: he was said to be—his family, at least—starving, and that he had no means of employment. Mackintosh wrote to me, soliciting for him an engagement to write for the Morning Post pieces of poetry and such trifles. I agreed; and settled him at a small salary. Mackintosh, at the instance of some of the inmates, attacked Coleridge on all subjects, politics, poetry, religion, ethics, &c.[.] Mackintosh was by far the most dexterous disputer. Coleridge overwhelmed listeners in, as he said, with reference to Madame de Stäel [*sic*], a monologue;[2] but at sharp cut-and-thrust fencing, by a master like Mackintosh, he was speedily confused and subdued. He felt himself lowered in the eyes of the Wedgewoods: a salary, though small as it was, was provided for him; and Mackintosh drove him out of the house: an offence which Coleridge never forgave.[3] He sent to me three or four pieces of poetry; a Christmas carol, some lines on an unfortunate girl in the boxes of the theatre, and *'fire, famine, and slaughter.'*[4] [...] Among other poems, Coleridge sent one attacking Mackintosh, too obviously for me not to understand it, and of course it was not published. Mackintosh had had one of his front teeth broken and the stump was black. The poem described a hungry, pert Scotchman, with little learning but much brass, with a black tooth in front, indicative of the blackness of his heart.[5] Long afterwards, Coleridge told me how well Mackintosh maintained an argument about Locke, in these conflicts at Cote House, but Coleridge detecting his mistakes, Mackintosh privately owned he had never read Locke.

Coleridge did not send me much; not even, as I thought, to the value of his small salary. By a letter written to him more than twenty years ago, I calculated the whole, in eight months, at ten or twelve short pieces. But, conscious of the deficiency, Southey supplied a most satisfactory quantity, for I believe the small salary went to Mrs. Coleridge.

(ii) ROBERT HALL

From 'Fragments of a Conversation with the Late Rev. Robert Hall'; in Robert Balmer, Academical Lectures and Pulpit Discourses, ed. John Brown (2 vols.; Edinburgh, 1845), I, 95-6. Robert Hall (1764-1831), Baptist minister in Bristol, and (said Sara Coleridge) an 'intimate friend' of Mackintosh (TT, I, 553), would have been known to Coleridge since Cambridge days, when Hall was a celebrated preacher among the radicals. (Hall and Coleridge shared an acquaintance in Benjamin Flower (CL, I, 197; 247).) They crossed paths later in Bristol: Cottle, a great admirer of both, reports one meeting (Early Recollections, I, 98-106; 183-4). Coleridge's respect for Hall was long-lived (see CL, I, 197; III, 463).

I felt exceedingly desirous to know Mr. Hall's opinion of Coleridge the poet, as I had been somewhat interested by his writings, and had heard much of his eloquence in conversation. I was, therefore, disappointed to find that Mr. Hall seemed to feel so extremely indifferent about him, as not to speak of him but with apparent reluctance. [...] BALMER: 'I have heard much of Coleridge's conversational talents. May I ask, Sir, if you ever met with him; and, if so, whether you were struck with the eloquence of his discourse.' HALL: 'I met with him once or twice in Bristol, some years ago. He has great talents for talk; not for conversation; for that implies an interchange of sentiments. With Mr. Coleridge there can be no such interchange. He will talk for half an hour; then make a short pause, to allow you to offer a remark; then run on for another half hour, but what he says is no answer to you. He is a man from whom one can learn nothing. Sometimes you have a glimpse of an important idea, or a magnificent image, but he presents nothing fully and distinctly. His talk in company is just like his writings. He is a will of the wisp. In listening to him, or reading him, you see a light flickering and dancing before you, but it leads only over moors and morasses.'

On my observing that Coleridge's writings gave me the impression that there was a great degree of perversity and self-conceit about him, Mr. Hall replied, 'Of that, Sir, there can be no doubt.' After this, there was either a brief pause, or the conversation had digressed to some other subject, when Mr. Hall resumed, exclaiming very abruptly, and with great vehemence of manner, 'The time will come when mankind will be ashamed of having admired Virgil. I mean, Sir, that is what Mr. Coleridge says. Does not that prove him to be a man of infinite perversity and self-conceit? If he had a particle of humility or common sense, he would lament it as a grievous calamity, that he is incapable of seeing the beauty of Virgil's poetry, which all the world admires. Were it a question of *truth*, to be determined by reasoning, the case would be different; but it is a question of *taste*; and what other standard is there of taste than general consent?'

From the writings and opinions of Coleridge, the conversation not unnaturally passed to his want of success as an author, to his personal character and habits, and particularly to his habit of intemperance in the use of opium. After some remarks on these topics, Mr. Hall said, 'Sir, I saw, some time ago, a letter from Coleridge, complaining most bitterly of his disappointments and misfortunes, and regretting that he had not been a shoemaker or a tailor, rather than a poet. I never saw such another production. It was more like the confessions of a lost spirit from the bottomless pit, than like any thing earthly. It had all the conscious degradation and chagrin, all the remorse and wretchedness of a man utterly ruined, without a single expression of penitence or hope.'

NOTES

[1] The Allens: a family into which the Wedgwoods had severally married.

[2] Stuart has the story backwards: for de Staël's comment, see below.

[3] Mackintosh knew STC's view of him. Denying (truly) his involvement in STC's 'Letters to Mr. Fox', Mackintosh said: 'Coleridge is well known to have (capriciously enough) disliked me. He is also known to be a man not well disposed to receive suggestions, or materials, from any one' (*Memoirs of the Life of Sir James Mackintosh*, ed. Robert James Mackintosh (2 vols.; 1835), I, 326).

[4] Stuart's dates are muddled, and he misremembers the amount of STC's verse he published (cf. *EOT*, III, 285-99). The poems mentioned are: 'A Christmas Carol', 'To an Unfortunate Woman at the Theatre', and 'Fire, Famine, and Slaughter. A War Eclogue' (*CPW*, I, 338; 171-2; 237-40).

[5] 'The Two Round Spaces on the Tombstone', ll.13-20 (*CPW*, I, 354-5).

Germany: Student and Traveller

(i) CLEMENT CARLYON

From Clement Carlyon, Early Years and Late Reflections (4 vols.; 1843-58), I, 29-30; 32-4; 44-5; 50-51; 67-8; 68-9; 91; 92; 92-3; 100-102; 137-8; 161-2; 173; 193-4. As Lyrical Ballads appeared, Coleridge, John Chester, and the Wordsworths left for Germany. After some travelling, the Wordsworths moved to Goslar, Coleridge and Chester to Ratzeburg, and then, in February, arrived in Göttingen, where they met Carlyon (1777-1864). Carlyon had been at Pembroke, Cambridge; he later settled in Truro, a dignitary and physician. His memoirs are digressive and sometimes comically verbose, but contain some valuable glimpses.

When in company, his vehemence of manner and wonderful flow of words and ideas, drew all eyes towards him, and gave him pre-eminence, despite his costume, which he affected to treat with great indifference. He even boasted of the facility with which he was able to overcome to disadvantage of negligent dress; and I have heard him say, fixing his prominent eyes upon himself (as he was wont to do, whenever there was a mirror in the room), with a singularly coxcomical expression of countenance, that his dress was sure to be lost sight of the moment he began to talk; an assertion which, whatever may be thought of its modesty, was not without truth. [...]

After close application to our academic pursuits for about six weeks, it was proposed and agreed that the following part; viz. Coleridge, the two Parrys,[1] Chester, ——, a son of Professor Blumenbach,[2] and myself, should make a pedestrian tour over the Harz Mountains, to the summit of the Brocken.[3] The spring had made such slow progress that the month of May had this year but small pretensions to the glowing praises of the poets. Still, whether lingering in the lap of winter, or unfolding all the charms with which Buchanan has arrayed its calends, May is always, to the young especially, more or less joyous, and to all more or less the

'Flos renascentis juventæ
In senium properantis ævi'[4]

Nevertheless, backward as was the spring of 1799, its beauties were beginning to expand in bud and leaf and many a modest blossom, when, on Saturday, the 11th of May, we sallied forth from Göttingen.

Frederick Parry led the way on horseback, for, being subject to attacks of asthma, and the youngest, by several years, of the party, this indulgence was allowed him, not without an understanding that the pony on which he rode was, in some measure, common property. Our whole appearance was grotesque enough. Coleridge, whose own costume, as usual, was by no means studied, seemed struck with the great comfort and convenience of a jacket which I had ordered to be made for the occasion, and finding that I perceived on what part of my dress his eyes were fixed, he exclaimed, *'Haud equidem invideo, miror magis,'*[5] and trudged on. ——'s boots were tight, and caused him no small pain, and in fact it soon appeared that we were, none of us, exactly equipped as we ought to have been for a pedestrian tour.

The first part of our road lay chiefly though forests of beech, and Coleridge's muse presented us with nothing better for our journals, than the following couplet: —

> 'We went, the younger Parry bore our goods
> O'er d— bad roads through d— delightful woods.'

But if his muse was dull, the genius of metaphysics was in full activity, and he endeavoured to enlighten the minds of his companions by a long discussion, among other things, in favour of an opinion which he maintained, in opposition to ——, that, throughout nature, pleasurable sensations greatly predominate over painful. He said, that it must be so, for as the tendency of pain is to disorganize, the disorganization of the whole living system must ensue if the balance lay on its side. Exquisite pleasure becomes pain; does exquisite pain, he asked, ever become pleasure? There was another point which he could not settle so entirely to his satisfaction, and that was the nature or essential quality of happiness. He seemed to think that it might be defined 'a consciousness of an excess of pleasurable sensations, direct or reflex.' [...]

In my haste to proceed up the Brocken, I perceive that I have omitted to mention, what indeed is not very important, that we halted the first night at Satzfeld, or a romantic village bearing some such name, in the electorate of Hanover, which we had re-entered.[6] Here we arrived tired and sore enough, about ten o'clock, yet the latter part of our walk had lain through a picturesque and highly-interesting country, much of which Coleridge likened to the scenery near Dulverton;[7] whilst our sense of increasing fatigue was likewise not a little relieved by the exhilarating effect of the first view we caught of the Harz mountains, which burst upon us this afternoon in all their grandeur. And, as the day further declined, a bright moonlight shed a varied interest over wood and dale and murmuring stream; but the wind was bitterly cold; the frogs were beginning to drown the voice of the nightingale by their croaking; and Coleridge, who had already designated our tour the Carlyon-Parry-Green-ation,[8] and who was never above a pun when it crossed his mind opportunely, informed us that the dissonance proceeded from a species of crocadile (croak-a-deal) so extremely common in the north of Germany, that he considered Lessing's Fable of the Frogs, as given by Gifford,[9] almost unintelligible to one who had not travelled out of England. Upon the whole, however, we could not be more glad than we were to enter our little inn, where we found but a comfortless supper, and a still more comfortless lodging; but hunger was our sauce, and fatigue our night-cap; so that after appeasing the former by the aid of coffee, ham, and metwurst (a sort of German sausage usually eaten raw), we threw ourselves down, in perfect reliance on the latter for sleep, on beds of straw, for such only could we procure. Coleridge strongly recommended us to take off the whole or the greater part of our dress, assuring us, on the authority of Professor Blumenbach, whose lectures on physiology he had attended, that our warmth would depend on the removal of all pressure from our limbs. He and —— accordingly tried the experiment fully, but in this, as in other cases, it was found that extremes had better be avoided. [...]

Coleridge made the profound, although seemingly trivial, remark that no animal but man appears ever to be struck with wonder. He was fond of amusing himself and his fellow tourists by asking the definition of some particular word, closing the inquiry, after each had exercised his ingenuity, with his own, which we seldom failed, with due submission to him, to consider the best.

When we were ascending the Brocken, and ever and anon stopping to take breath, as well as to survey the magnificent scene, a long discussion took place upon the sublime and beautiful. We had much of Burke,[10] but more of Coleridge. Of beauty much, but more of sublimity, which was in accordance with the grandeur of surrounding objects. Many were the fruitless attempts made to define sublimity satisfactorily, when Coleridge, at length, pronounced it to consist in a suspension of the power of comparison.[11] [...]

The Germans, of all mortals the most imaginative, take extraordinary delight in their albums; and Coleridge being a NOTICEABLE ENGLANDER, and a poet withal, was not unfrequently requested to favour with a scrap of verse persons who had no very particular claims upon his muse. As a specimen of the playful scintillations of this gifted man upon such occasions, I subjoin the following quatrain, which he wrote when about to leave the university, in the stammbuch of a Göttingen student, who had studied the same course of lectures (Collegium) with him: —

> 'We both attended the same college,
> Where sheets of paper we did blur many,
> And now we're going to sport our knowledge,
> In England, I, and you in Germany.' [...]

He had a great wish to make us metaphysicians, and the perseverance with which he would occasionally re-word the same train of thought, for the edification of his pupils, was quite extraordinary. It was in fact far from an easy matter for any unpractised person to keep pace with him in threading his metaphysical labyrinths. The impressions made upon the minds of his hearers often gave an abundant consciousness of new light: but they were too like the impressions of a seal upon wax, when the seal adheres; there the impressions were, but where was the capacity of communicating them to others?

We frequently, however, trod on much safer ground than the *terra incognita* of metaphysics. In the course of one of our afternoons' walks, the conversation ran almost exclusively on English Poetry. Coleridge was more especially critical; whilst Parry, who in belles lettres and the arts was great authority, tempered our severer lessons with numberless illustrative remarks and recitations. [...]

In the conversation to which I have just alluded, Coleridge dwelt a good deal on the circumstances which, in his opinion, must have largely contributed to the developement of Shakspeare's dramatic powers, which, great as they were by nature, owed their vast expansion, he maintained, to the cheering breath of popular applause, or the enthusiatic gale, rather, of admiration, to which there was no check in the habits or literature of society at that period. There were no writhings, moreover, he added, in those days from the stings of a trafficking criticism, against which he has elsewhere so feelingly inveighed;[12] and I am not at all sure that it seemed to himself a thing impossible to attain the same eminence with Shakspeare, the same opportunity being afforded. But this was indeed applying to himself flattering unction. [...]

Coleridge was certainly far from being, even at this time, an enemy to revealed religion.[13] It might be going too far to affirm that his faith was settled. Yet he seemed duly to appreciate the subtle scepticism of the German Universities, and, devoted as he was to metaphysical disquisitions, he was likewise fond of repeating that 'an old woman's grain of faith was worth them all.' [...]

Fond as Coleridge was of raising our views to the sublimest truths, he never, to my knowledge, either by example or precept, made any effort to check the abominable neglect of religious worship which prevailed among the English, equally with the German students, at Göttingen. No one ever thought of going to church. And yet as a proof that he did not like the Lord's Day to be desecrated, I must tell a tale against myself. It happened that my friend —— and I were on a rambling visit at Keswick, in the summer of 1801, during the time that Coleridge resided there with his family.[14] He came to dine with us at the inn on a Sunday afternoon, and expressed his disapprobation very strongly of a breach of the Sabbath, which we had that day committed, in spending the forenoon in perch-fishing, from a boat, on the lake of Derwent Water. It was my first and last offence of this kind, and the stamp of Coleridge's disapprobation will never be effaced from my recollection. And yet I do not believe that he had been at church himself that day; or that he was, at any time, much in the habit of going to church. A gentleman who lived near him at Highgate, informed me, that during his long residence there, he did not recollect having seen him at church more than once, and that upon some, I forget what, public occasion, which he mentioned. [...]

The view which we commanded from the Hübichen-Stein delighted us, and whilst we were contemplating its beauty and grandeur, —— observed, 'that the charms of nature were relished by man alone; no other animal, however great its sagacity, appearing to feel any pleasure from lakes, or forests, or mountains[']. True, replied Coleridge, and yet how short-lived is man, for whose pleasure and benefit these, as far as we see, are in great measure formed! Eighty-four years is almost his farthest limit, whilst the rocks and mountains are, many of them, undoubtedly pre-Adamitical. Hence he drew an argument for the immortality of the soul; since, that being admitted, the means will be no more than adequate to the end.

Coleridge was in good spirits, very amusing, and as talkative as ever, throughout this little excursion. He frequently recited his own poetry, and not unfrequently led us rather farther into the labyrinth of his metaphysical elucidations, either of particular passages, or of the original conception of any of his productions, than we were able to follow him.

> "Tis the middle of night by the castle clock,
> And the owls have awakened the crowing cock;
> > Tu whit! — Tu whoo!
> > And hark again! The crowing cock,
> > How drowsily it crew.'[15]

At the conclusion of this, the first stanza of Christabel, he would perhaps comment at full length upon such a line as

> Tu whit! — Tu whoo!

that we might not fall into the mistake of supposing originality to be its sole merit. In fact, he very seldom went right on to the end of any piece of poetry — to pause and analyze was his delight. [...]

Monday, the 24th of June, having been fixed upon for his final departure from Göttingen, I had the pleasure of spending a most entertaining take-leave evening with him at Professor Blumenbach's. Our party, at supper, consisted, in addition to the professor's own family, of young Blumenbach's fellow tourists only; and the conversation, which was chiefly in German, was particularly sprightly and amusing on the part of the professor and Coleridge, who even then, after nine months' residence in Germany, thought it no undue precaution to carry with him a pocket dictionary, to which he hesitated not to apply, if he happened to be at a loss for a word; but this was seldom the case; and there was something inexpressibly comic in the manner in which he dashed on, with fluent diction, but with the very worst German accent imaginable, through the thick and thin of his subject. Mrs. and Miss Blumenbach, the ladies of the party, were as much astonished as they were highly delighted with him; and I do not think that their enjoyment was once interrupted, by any allusion whatever to Miss Matilda Pottingen; for it was well understood by us, that 'Sweet Matilda,' false or true, and all the rest about the 'U—niversity of Gottingen,'[16] was far from being a favourite topic of conversation with the Göttingen ladies.

Carlyon and a friend accompany Coleridge and Chester to Brunswick.

Our walk was one of great difficulty to ——, who suffered severely from the effects of the alternate cold and heat to which he had been exposed the preceding night. On our arrival at Elbingerode, he immediately retired to a bed-room, and getting between two immense feather-beds, according to the custom of the country, first shivered for a certain time, then fell into a burning fever, and, lastly, into profuse perspiration, which relieved him, but it took him several days thoroughly to recover.

On the following morning, he thought it necessary to apologize for having taken possession, *sans ceremonie*, of the best bed; whereupon an amusing argumentation arose between him and Coleridge, upon the question whether his conduct, in so doing, did not fairly subject him to the charge of great selfishness. He thought, himself, that it did. On the other hand, Coleridge contended, that so far was this from being the case, that he would really have manifested selfishness if, instead of going quietly to bed, he had made a *sputter*, in order to excite compassion and induce one of us to remain and watch by him. Chester and I sided with Coleridge, and the argument ended, in giving our scrupulous convalescent an unanimous verdict of acquittal.

At one point, Carlyon recalls being told that most German literati are Spinozists (I, 185). This prompts reminiscences of Coleridge on 'the doctrines of Spinoza'.

His concentrated definition of Spinozism was, 'Each thing has a life of its own, and we are all one life;'[17] but the expanded doctrine amounts to this, 'That there is but one substance in nature; that this one substance is endued with an infinite number of attributes, among which are extension and cogitation; that all the bodies in the universe are modifications of the former, and all the souls of the latter; that God is a self-existent and infinitely perfect Being, the cause of all things which exist, but yet not a different Being from them, since there is but one Being and one Nature, which Nature produces within itself, by an immanent act, all those which we call creatures, and which Being is at the same time both agent and patient, efficient cause and subject, yet producing nothing but modifications of Himself.'

According to another version: —

'The great principle of Spinozism is, that there is nothing properly and absolutely existing but matter, and the modifications of matter; among which are even comprehended thought, abstract and general ideas, comparisons, relations, combinations of relations, &c.[.]

'Or it has been defined to be a "A species of Naturalism, or Pantheism, or Hylotheism," as it is sometimes called, that is, the dogma which allows of no other God but Nature or the Universe, and therefore makes matter to be God.

> '*Estne Dei sedes nisi terra et pontus et aer*
> *Et cœlum et virtus? Superos quid quærimus ultra?*
> *Jupiter est quodcunque vides, quodcunque videris.*'[18]

(ii) CHARLES PARRY

From Carlyon, Early Life and Late Reflections, *I, 100-101n.. The Parry brothers, both medical students, travelled with Carlyon and Coleridge in the Harz mountains; Charles illustrated one of Coleridge's letters home (facing CL, I, 496).*

Göttingen, May 25, 1799 [...] Pure Christianity is, unhappily, at a very low ebb on the Continent. Pütter (Professor of History) is the only person of consideration here who openly professes it, and he has firmness to despise the ridicule which attaches to him on that account. It is an agreeable anecdote, as regards both parties, that when Coleridge, who was acquainted with this part of his character, accidentally met him for the first time, on the ramparts, he pulled off his hat, and made him a respectful bow; the only mark of esteem which he had it in his power to show. Eichorn,[19] one of the principal theologists in Germany, and a lecturer here, seems, from all accounts, to be doing his utmost to destroy the evidences on which we ground our belief. He is a good man and extremely charitable, but this attempt speaks neither for his head nor for his heart. Coleridge, an able vindicator of these important truths, is well acquainted with Eichorn,[20] but this latter is a coward, who dreads his arguments and his presence. [...] I have twice mentioned Coleridge, and much wish you were acquainted with him. It is very delightful to hear him sometimes discourse on religious topics for an hour together. His fervour is particularly agreeable when contrasted with the chilling speculations of the German philosophers. I have had occasion to see these successively abandon all their strong holds when he brought to the attack his arguments and his philosophy. Coleridge is much liked, notwithstanding many peculiarities. He is very liberal towards all doctrines and opinions, and cannot be put out of temper. These circumstances give him the advantage of his opponents here, who are always bigotted, and often irascible. Coleridge is an enthusiast on many subjects, and must, therefore, appear to many to possess faults—and no doubt he has faults—but he has a good heart, and a large mass of information, with superior talents. The great fault which his friends may lament, is the variety of subjects which he adopts, and the too abstruse nature of his ordinary speculations, *extra homines positas*.[21] They can easily excuse his devoted attachment to his country, and his reasoning as to the means of producing the greatest sum of human happiness; but they do not universally approve the mysticism of his metaphysics, nor the remoteness of his topics from human affairs and human comprehension. As a poet, he severely criticises his own productions. His best poems have, perhaps, not yet appeared in print. He is, at present, engaged on a work, which will be no less interesting in Germany than in England—a History of German Poetry, from the earliest times to the present day, including a particular review of Lessing's Works.[22] It will probably extend to two quarto volumes. Coleridge was twenty-six last October.

(iii) GEORGE BELLAS GREENOUGH

From Edith J. Morley, 'Coleridge in Germany (1799). As portrayed in the Journal of George Bellas Greenough and in some unpublished letters of the poet', London Mercury XXIII (1930-31) 554-65, 560; 561-2. Greenough, later President of the Geological Society, was another companion on tour. His journal confirms much in Carlyon—including Coleridge's reassurances that a member of the party (Greenough himself, we learn) had not acted selfishly in taking the bed when ill, a characteristic improvisation on a favourite Coleridgean theme ('not to have been selfish would have been the greatest selfishness': p. 560).

While my eye ranged with delight over so many scenes of grandeur and of beauty, it occurred very forcibly to my mind that as far as human observation has been able to go, the charms of nature are relished by man alone . . . and I could scarcely suppose that man was a being of so much consequence as that all these objects should have been formed simply and solely for his gratification. This I mentioned afterwards to Coleridge, who directed me to observe still farther that men were less durable than their works, which, as far as we see, are formed for their pleasure only . . . from hence he wished to draw a new argument for the immortality of the soul: for if this be admitted, the means will be only adequate to the end. [...]

Coleridge had one day been abusing Mrs. T. Robinson's poetry[23] more than he thought it deserved—he therefore agreed with his friends that by way of atonement he should publish a sonnet in praise of that lady in the public papers. He filled his sonnet with the most extravagant eulogy. A few days later he received a most highly complimentary letter from Mrs. Robinson in which she begged his acceptance of all her works, handsomely bound and printed on wire-woven paper.

(iv) GEORG FRIEDRICH BENECKE

From 'Göttingen in 1824', Putnam's Monthly Magazine *VIII (1856) 595-607, 599; 600. Benecke (1762-1844), Professor at Göttingen, is here recollected by George Henry Calvert, a student in 1824. (The memoir was later collected in Calvert's* First Years in Europe *(1866).)*

Benecke was a strongly-marked character, energetic, decisive, one-sided—a man of the world, who conversed well and dressed well, and who piqued himself on his breeding; punctiliously polite to his equals, but curt and indifferent to those whose equality with himself was questionable [...]

Benecke told me that Coleridge, when at Göttingen towards the close of the last century, was an idler, and did not learn the language thoroughly, and that he got a long ode of Klopstock by heart and declaimed without understanding it, playfully mystifying his countrymen with the apparent rapidity of his progress.[24] When the 'Opium-Eater' appeared,[25] Benecke at once attributed it to Coleridge, from knowing, he said, that Coleridge took opium when at Göttingen.

NOTES

[1] Fellow Göttingen students, Charles Henry Parry (1779-1860) and Frederick, sons of the physician Caleb Hillier Parry, and themselves training in medicine.

[2] Johann Friedrich Blumenbach (1752-1840), Professor at Göttingen, physiologist and comparative anatomist. STC praised him in *The Friend* (I, 154-5n.).

[3] The Brocken, highest of the Harz mountains, is famous for an optical illusion (the 'Brocken Spectre' or 'Brocken') in which an enlarged shadow of the climber appears before him, surrounded by prismatic colours.

[4] 'And the flower of reborn youth hurrying towards old age's decline': George Buchanan, 'Calendae Maiae', ll.7-8.

[5] i.e. 'Well, I grudge you not—rather I marvel': Virgil, *Eclogues*, I, l.11.

[6] Presumably Schmatzfeld, about ten miles from the Brocken.

[7] In Somerset. STC and the Wordsworths walked there (*CPW*, I, 196n.1).

[8] The 'Green' in STC's pun comes from Greenough: see below.

[9] Gotthold Ephraim Lessing (1729-81), dramatist and aesthetician, author of *Laokoon* (1766). William Gifford (1756-1826), satirist, editor of the *Quarterly*.

[10] Edmund Burke (1729-1797), *A Philosophical Enquiry into the Origin of our Ideas of the Sublime and Beautiful* (1757). In *Table Talk*, STC judges the 'Essay on Taste', added (1759) as a preface to the *Enquiry*, 'a poor thing' (*TT*, I, 85).

[11] Carlyon quotes *The Friend* (II, 257), a passage describing sounds 'more sublime than any sight *can* be, more absolutely *suspending the power of comparison*, and more utterly absorbing the mind's self-consciousness'.

[12] For STC on journalistic criticism (and especially Jeffrey's), see *BL*, I, 107-18.

[13] The place of revelation was evident in his early lectures (see *L1795*, lv-lviii).

[14] STC at this stage lived in Greta Hall, in Crosthwaite, just outside Keswick.

[15] 'Christabel', ll.1-5 (*CPW*, I, 215).

[16] In the celebrated *Anti-Jacobin* parody, our imprisoned hero laments his 'companions true / Who studied with me at the U—/—niversity of Göttingen': *Poetry of the Anti-Jacobin*, ed. L. Rice-Oxley (Oxford, 1924), 141-2.

[17] The definition of 'Spinozism' is close to STC's own position, as stated to Sotheby in a letter of 1802: he praised the 'Hebrew Poets' for their '*Imagination, or the modifying*, and *co-adunating* Faculty', thanks to which, in their poetry, 'each Thing has a Life of it's [*sic*] own, & yet they are all one Life' (*CL*, II, 866).

[18] Cf. Lucan, *De Bello Civile*, IX, ll.578-80 ('Estque dei sedes, nini terra et pontus et aer / Et caelum et virtus? superos quid quaerimus ultra? / Iuppiter est, quodcumque vides, quodcumque moveris': 'Has the Creator any dwelling-place save earth and sea, the air of heaven and virtuous hearts? Why do we seek further for deities? All that we see is God; and every motion we make is God'). The text features in *On the Prometheus of Aeschylus* (*SWF*, II, 1278).

[19] Johann Gottfried Eichorn (1752-1827), Professor of Philosophy at Göttingen.

[20] Carlyon (I, 191) says that STC either attended Eichorn's lectures himself or had access to notes of another student (which last is what STC says: *BL*, I, 207).

[21] i.e. 'beyond men's reach'.

[22] STC began work on Lessing, but the *Life* never materialised (see *CN*, I, 377).

[23] i.e. Mary Robinson (see below). No sonnet survives; 'A Stranger Minstrel' (*CPW*, I, 350-2), not a sonnet, was written to her, but appeared in 1801.

[24] Thomas Lovell Beddoes (1803-49), the poet, studied under Benecke a little after Calvert. This unlikely opinion is reported in a letter home of 1 April 1826:

> Benecke who taught Coleridge German here, says that he has a very superficial knowledge of it. From what I know of Kant, i.e. his Anthropology—a very sensible acute man-of-the-world book—I suspect C. has never read him, at all events he has given the English a totally absurd opinion of him. (*The Letters of Thomas Lovell Beddoes*, ed. Edmund Gosse (1894), 105)

[25] Thomas De Quincey's *Confessions of an English Opium Eater* (1822).

Journalist and Celebrity

(i) DANIEL STUART

From Daniel Stuart, 'Anecdotes of the Poet Coleridge', 486-7; 488. Stuart writes here in disgruntled self-defence: Coleridge had implied in Biographia that he was largely responsible for the success of the Morning Post, and had gone unrewarded (BL, I, 214-5) – a view adopted by the loyal Gillman (Life, 152-4). At the time, Stuart too had attributed a boost in sales to Coleridge's contributions (EOT, III, 169), so distance seems to have lent disenchantment to the view.

In September 1798, Coleridge went to Germany, and returned about Christmas 1799. He came to me, and offered to give his whole time and services to the Morning Post. Whether he made any stipulations about the politics or tone of the paper, I cannot now say; but it would be unnecessary for him to do so, as these were already to his mind, and it was not likely I would make great changes to please any one, or wholly give the conduct of the paper out of my own power. I agreed to allow him my largest salary. I took a first floor for him in King Street, Covent Garden, at my tailor's, Howell's, whose wife was a cheerful good housewife, of middle age, who I knew would nurse Coleridge as kindly as if he were her son; and he owned he was comfortably taken care of. My practice was to call on him in the middle of the day, talk over the news, and project a leading paragraph for the next morning. In conversation he would make a brilliant display. This reminds me of a story he often told with glee: — At a dinner party, Sir Richard Phillips the bookseller being present, Coleridge held forth with his usual splendour, when Sir Richard, who had been listening with delight, came round behind his chair and, tapping him on the shoulder, said, 'I wish I had you in a garret without a coat to your back.'[1] In something like this state I had Coleridge; but though he would talk over everything so well, I soon found he could not write daily on the occurrences of the day.[2]

Having arranged with him the matter of a leading paragraph one day, I went about six o'clock for it; I found him stretched on the sofa groaning with pain. He had not written a word; nor could he write. The subject was one of a temporary, an important, and a pressing nature. I returned to the Morning Post Office, wrote it out myself, and then I went to Coleridge at Howell's, read it over, begged he would correct it, and decorate it a little with some of his graceful touches. When I had done reading, he exclaimed, 'Me cor-

rect that? It is as well written as I or any other man could write it.'
And so I was obliged to content myself with my own works [sic].

I did not suppose Coleridge's illness to be of the permanently
disabling kind which it proved years afterwards to be; I expected
his health to be restored soon, and that I should have an ample
supply, on paper, of the brilliant things he said in conversation. I
did not complain, or in any way betray impatience or discontent. I
took him to the gallery of the House of Commons, in hopes he
would assist me in parliamentary reporting, and that a near view
of men and things would bring up new topics in his mind. But he
never could write a thing that was immediately required of him.
The thought of compulsion disarmed him. I could name other able
literary men in this unfortunate plight. The only occasions, I recollect, on which this general rule was contradicted, were his observations as a leading paragraph in the Morning Post on Lord Grenville's state paper, haughtily rejecting Bonaparte's overtures of
peace in January 1800. I remember Coleridge's sneers at his lordship's using the double phrase, 'the result of experience and the
evidence of facts.'[3] [...]

He wrote nothing that I remember, and consequently nothing
that is worth remembering in the Morning Post during the first six
or eight months of his engagement, except the paragraph on Lord
Grenville's state paper already mentioned, and the Character of
Pitt.[4] I may add, the poem of 'The Devil's Thoughts,' which I think
came by post from Dorsetshire.[5] I never knew two pieces of writing, so wholly disconnected with daily occurrences, produce so
lively a sensation. Several hundred sheets extra were sold by them,
and the paper was in demand for days and weeks afterwards. Mr.
Gillman has republished in his volume the Character of Pitt; and as
a masterly production, the perusal will delight any and every class
of men. Coleridge promised a pair of portraits, Pitt and Bonaparte.
He gave Pitt; but to this day Bonaparte has not appeared. I could
not walk a hundred yards in the streets but I was stopped by inquiries, 'when shall we have Bonaparte?' One of the most eager of
these inquirers, daily, was Doctor Moore (Zelucco);[6] and, for ten or
twelve years afterwards, whenever Coleridge required a favour
from me, he promised Bonaparte, though then it would have been
for the Courier, as I sold and finally left the Morning Post in
August 1803.

(ii) MARY ROBINSON

'To the Poet Coleridge', from The Poetical Works of the Late Mrs. Mary Robinson *(3 vols.; 1806), I, 226-9. Mary Robinson (1758-1800), 'Perdita', was a famous beauty and actress, a novelist and poet; her poem to Coleridge (written October 1800) is a vivid evocation of his performing style. Coleridge often recited his poems, especially 'Christabel' and 'Kubla Khan' ('which said vision,' as Lamb later wrote, 'he repeats so enchantingly that it irradiates and brings heaven and elysian bowers into my parlour while he sings or says it').*[7]

Rapt in the visionary theme!
   SPIRIT DIVINE! with THEE I'll wander,
Where the blue, wavy, lucid stream,
   'Mid forest glooms, shall slow meander!
With THEE I'll trace the circling bounds
   Of thy NEW PARADISE extended;
And listen to the varying sounds
   Of winds, and foamy torrents blended.

Now by the source, which lab'ring heaves
   The mystic fountain, bubbling, panting,
While Gossamer its net-work weaves,
   Adown the blue lawn, slanting!
I'll mark thy *sunny dome*, and view
Thy *Caves of Ice*,[8] thy fields of dew!
Thy ever-blooming mead, whose flow'r
Waves to the cold breath of the moonlight hour!
Or when the day-star, peering bright
On the grey wing of parting night;
While more than vegetating pow'r
Throbs grateful to the burning hour,
As summer's whisper'd sighs unfold
Her million, million buds of gold;
Then will I climb the breezy bounds,
   Of thy NEW PARADISE extended,
And listen to the distant sounds
   Of winds, and foamy torrents blended!

SPIRIT DIVINE! with THEE I'll trace
Imagination's boundless space!
With thee, beneath thy *sunny dome*,
   I'll listen to the minstrel's lay,
   Hymning the gradual close of day;
In *Caves of Ice* enchanted roam,
Where on the glitt'ring entrance plays

The moon's-beam with its silv'ry rays;
Or, when the glassy stream
That thro' the deep dell flows,
Flashes the noon's hot beam;
The noon's hot beam, that midway shows
Thy flaming Temple, studded o'er
With all PERUVIA'S lustrous store!
There will I trace the circling bounds
Of thy NEW PARADISE, extended!
And listen to the awful sounds,
Of winds, and foamy torrents blended!

And now I'll pause to catch the moan
Of distant breezes, cavern-pent;
Now, ere the twilight tints are flown,
Purpling the landscape, far and wide,
On the dark promontory's side
I'll gather wild flow'rs, dew besprent,
And weave a crown for THEE,
GENIUS OF HEAV'N-TAUGHT POESY!
While, op'ning to my wond'ring eyes,
Thou bid'st a new creation rise,
I'll raptur'd trace the circling bounds
Of thy RICH PARADISE extended,
And listen to the varying sounds
Of winds, and foamy torrents blended.

And now, with lofty tones inviting,
Thy NYMPH, her dulcimer swift smiting,
Shall wake me in ecstatic measures!
Far, far removed from mortal pleasures!
In cadence rich, in cadence strong,
Proving the wondrous witcheries of song!
I hear thy voice! thy *sunny dome*,
Thy *caves of ice*, loud repeat,
Vibrations, madd'ning sweet,
Calling the visionary wand'rer home.
She sings of THEE, O favour'd child
Of *Minstrelsy*, SUBLIMELY WILD!
Of thee, whose soul can feel the tone
Which gives to airy dreams *a magic* ALL THY OWN!

(iii) RICHARD WARNER

*From Richard Warner, A Tour through the Northern Counties of England,
and the Borders of Scotland (2 vols.; 1802), II, 100-101. Despite his growing
celebrity in literary London, Coleridge's desire to be in Wordsworth's company
led him, in July 1800, to move his family north, settling at Greta Hall near
Keswick, thirteen miles from Grasmere. In 1802, Richard Warner (1763-1857), a
Bath curate and miscellaneous author, is counting Coleridge among Lakeland's
picturesque spectacles. (Coleridge wasn't impressed: 'O Lord! what a lie!' he protested to Sara Hutchinson, quoting from the passage below (CL, II, 827).)*

Penetrating into the awful recesses of Borrodale at the southern
extremity of the lake, we took a view of the *Bowther stone*,[9] a vast
mass of rock, torn by some natural convulsion from the aërial brow
of the adjoining mountain, and rolled into the flat below. [...] Beyond this a most pleasing walk, through peaceful hamlets, embos-
omed by the rudest mountains, brought us to the black-lead mines,
the most famous of the kind in the world. Amongst the crags and
precipices which tower on every side, the effects of a loud sound
suddenly emitted are truly astonishing, and it is utterly impossible
for a lively imagination unused to the delusion, to experience it
without a momentary belief that he is surrounded by the unseen
spirits of the mountain, reproving his intrusion into their *adyta*,[10] in
vocal thunder.

The animated, enthusiastic, and accomplished Coleridge, whose
residence at Keswick gives additional charms and interest to its
impressive scenery, inspired us with terror, whilst he described the
universal uproar that was awakened through the mountains by a
sudden burst of involuntary laughter in the heart of their precipices; an incident which a kindred intellect, his friend and neighbour at Grasmere, Wordsworth, (whose 'Lyrical Ballads,' exclusively almost of all modern compositions, breathe the true, nervous, and simple spirit of poetry) has worked up into the following
admirable effusion[.][11]

In his later Literary Recollections *(1830), 155-6n., Warner recalled again his
meeting Coleridge in the Lakes, and added some vignettes of him reciting:*

I must not forget to mention a remarkable instance of the tena-
ciousness of Mr. Coleridge's memory, which occurred to my observation, during the time we were together in Cumberland. I
mentioned the pleasure I had received from his poems. He spoke
of them, not merely modestly, but, as I considered, disparagingly. I
ventured to differ from him widely: and quoted some passages of

high merit. Among others, I repeated the opening of his 'Ode to the Departing Year;' and remarked on the felicitous use of the epithet, 'beautiful,' in that well-known line:—

> 'And stood up, *beautiful*, before the cloudy seat.'[12]

He demurr'd as to the merit of the line, but said, he had introduced the same epithet more happily into another poem.[13] I demanded 'which?' 'It was not printed, nor a word of it committed to paper.' —'Could he repeat the line?' He recited a stanza.—'Did he recollect more of it?' He repeated a long poem: about a year after this, Mr. Coleridge dined with me at my house near Bath. In the evening I reminded him of the pleasure which he had afforded to myself and friend, by the repetition of a poem among the mountains of Cumberland. 'Had he printed it?'—'No.'—'Would he give me a copy of it?'—'It was not written down.'—'Could he oblige the ladies by reciting it?' This he very readily and obligingly did. It met with great applause; and, in about two years, appeared in print, under the title, I believe, of 'Cristabel' [*sic*].

(iv) WILLIAM WORDSWORTH

*From 'Stanzas Written in my Pocket-Copy of Thomson's "Castle of Indolence"',
in William Wordsworth, Poems (2 vols.; 1815) I, 123–4. Wordsworth's poem
(written May 1802) contains a portrait of Coleridge. Wordsworth said late in life:
'his son Hartley has said that his father's character and habits are here preserved
in a livelier way than in anything that has been written about him'.*[14]

> With him there often walked in friendly guise
> Or lay upon the moss by brook or tree
> A noticeable Man with large grey eyes,
> And a pale face that seemed undoubtedly
> As if a blooming face it ought to be;
> Heavy his low-hung lip did oft appear,
> Deprest by weight of musing Phantasy;[15]
> Profound his forehead was, though not severe;
> Yet some did think that he had little business here:
>
> Sweet heaven forefend! his was a lawful right;
> Noisy he was, and gamesome as a boy;
> His limbs would toss about him with delight
> Like branches when strong winds the trees annoy.
> Nor lacked his calmer hours device or toy
> To banish listlessness and irksome care;
> He would have taught you how you might employ

Yourself; and many did to him repair, —
And, certes, not in vain; he had inventions rare.

Expedients, too, of simplest sort he tried:
Long blades of grass, plucked round him as he lay,
Made — to his ear attentively applied —
A Pipe on which the wind would deftly play;
Glasses he had, that little things display,
The beetle with his radiance manifold,
A mailed angel on a battle day;
And cups of flowers, and herbage green and gold;
And all the gorgeous sights which fairies do behold.

He would entice that other Man to hear
His music, and to view his imagery:
And, sooth, these two did love each other dear,
As far as love in such a place could be:
There did they dwell — from earthly labour free,
As happy spirits as were ever seen;
If but a bird, to keep them company,
Or butterfly sate down, they were, I ween,
As pleased as if the same had been a Maiden Queen.

(v) FRANCES ALLEN

From Richard Buckley Litchfield, Tom Wedgwood, the First Photographer *(1903), 125; 125-6. In late November 1802, Coleridge and Tom Wedgwood visited Cresselly, staying at the house of John Bartlett Allen, father of Tom's sisters-in-law. Coleridge delighted in 'plenty of music & plenty of Cream' (CL, II, 900) — a reproof to Poole (Sandford,* Thomas Poole, *I, 101.) Frances was the youngest Allen daughter; in old age, she recalled Coleridge for her niece.*

One day at Cresselly Mr. Coleridge was saying something about the Ten Commandments which T.W. thought would shock Mr. Allen, and he tapped him [Coleridge] on the arm and took him out of the room and stopped him. [...]

Another day at Cresselly, Coleridge, who was fond of reading MS. poems of Wordsworth's, asked Fanny whether she liked poetry, and when she said she did, came and sat by her on the sofa, and began to read the *Leechgatherer*.[16] When he came to the passage, now I believe omitted, about his skin being so old and dry that the leeches wouldn't stick,[17] it set Fanny a-laughing. That frightened her, and she got into a convulsive fit of laughter that shook Coleridge, who was sitting close to her, looking very angry. He put up his MS., saying he ought to ask her pardon, for perhaps to a person who had not genius (Fanny cannot exactly remember the expression) the poem might seem absurd. F. sat in a dreadful fright, everybody looking amazed, Sarah[18] looking angry; and she almost expected her father would turn her out of the room, but Uncle Tom came to her rescue. 'Well, Coleridge, one must confess that it is not quite a subject for a poem.' Coleridge did not forgive Fanny for some days, putting by his reading aloud if she came in. But afterwards he was very good friends with her, and one day in particular gave her all his history, saying, amongst other things, 'and there I had the misfortune to meet with my wife.'

(vi) KATHERINE THOMSON

From 'Literary Retrospect of the Departed Great. By a Middle-Aged Man [sic]', in Bentley's Miscellany *XVII (1845) 83-88, 83 (and reprinted in* Recollections of Literary Characters *(1854), 58-9.) Thomson (1797-1862) was the daughter of the nephew and partner of Josiah Wedgwood.*

My earliest recollections are of Coleridge, taking me upon his knee, and telling me, with a plaintive voice, and with an emphasis that I can never forget, the story of Mary of Buttermere, then a recent subject of popular discourse.[19] His pallid face, his long black hair, suffered, with the characteristic affectation of Coleridge's younger days, to fall about his neck, – the appealing tones of his voice – the earnest gaze which he fastened upon my puzzled countenance, and the simple eloquence with which he told the story, are still present with me. Tears ran down his cheeks – for his were feelings that could be conjured up instantaneously. I must not omit to say, that this little scene was enacted before a large circle of admiring and sympathetic young women, – my elder sisters amongst the most approving, – and whilst philosophers and literati looked on.

(vii) HUMPHRY DAVY

From Cottle, Early Recollections, *II, 72. Sandford quotes the letter (Thomas Poole, II, 286-7), and dates the sighting to the eve of departure for Malta (March 1804). Cottle's fuller text suggests a year earlier, when Coleridge returned North.*

Coleridge has left London for Keswick. During his stay in town, I saw him seldomer than usual: when I did see him, it was generally in the midst of large companies, where he is the image of power and activity. His eloquence is unimpaired; perhaps it is softer and stronger. His will is less than ever commensurate with his ability. Brilliant images of greatness float upon his mind, like images of the morning clouds on the waters. Their forms are changed by the motion of the waves, they are agitated by every breeze, and modified by every sun-beam. He talked in the course of an hour, of beginning three works; and he recited the poem of Christabel unfinished, and as I had before heard it. What talent does he not waste in forming visions, sublime, but unconnected with the real world! I have looked to his efforts, as to the efforts of a creating being; but as yet he has not laid the foundation for the new world of intellectual forms.

(viii) SIR GEORGE BEAUMONT

From Tom Mayberry, 'A Newly-Discovered Letter of Sir George Beaumont, 1803', in The Coleridge Bulletin *NS 1 (Winter 1992-3) 5-7, 6. (The letter is in the Hampshire Record Office: ref. 38M49/C6/25/2.) Beaumont (1753-1827), patron and painter, sent this breathless letter to Anne Bowles (6 August 1803) from Greta Hall, where the Beaumonts were staying, initially unaware that the Coleridges occupied part of it. Beaumont had met Coleridge in London in March.*

When we arrived here we found Coleridge whose poems you have heard of if not read in possession of part of the house, I will confess to you this was not pleasant news to me at first for I had met him once at Sothebys,[20] & was by no means prejudiced in his favor, I had moreover a Great objection to his political opinions—but I hope in future I shall be more cautious in forming my opinions of men—for whatever may have been his former errors he has utterly renounced them, & as far as I can judge a more amiable man with a more affectionate & kind heart does not exist, his information is boundless, & he seems to have elevated his mind above every mean & selfish passion—his friend Wordsworth, the author of the Thorn (which I read to you in London) & various poems lives about 13 miles off at Grasmere, & paid him a visit lately, so that I saw them both every day—he has a mind truly poetical & will I am sure produce something 'which will not die'. It is most pleasing to see the pure affection which subsists between the two bards, free from all bias of jealousy or weakness they correct the errors of each other with manly freedom, & to their mutual advantage. Wordsworth is now employed on a work called the Recluse, I believe it is (for I have not seen it) a history of his own feelings,[21] & will probably take up years in the completion, for his health will not permit him to work upon it at all times, he says it prevents his sleeping & he is obliged to quit all thoughts of it for months together. Coleridge has written part of a poem called Cristobel [—]

he repeated some of it the other day & it seems full of imagination he is a great metaphicician [*sic*] & sometimes soars a little above my comprehension but he soon descends & is truly instructive and entertaining — I could write on about these two genius's till you would be tired to death.

(ix) DOROTHY WORDSWORTH

From Dorothy Wordsworth, Recollections of a Tour Made in Scotland, *ed. J.C. Shairp (Edinburgh, 1894), 15; 17; 37. On 9 August, the poet Samuel Rogers and his sister took tea at Grasmere, depressing Coleridge (CL, II, 964): his lowered spirits affected his health, and threatened the Scottish trip they had planned; but he rallied, and on 15 August 1803, he and the Wordsworths set out.*

After some time our road took us upwards towards the end of the valley. Now the steeps were heathy all around. Just as we began to climb the hill we saw three boys who came down the cleft of a brow on our left; one carried a fishing-rod, and the hats of all were braided with honeysuckles; they ran after one another as wanton as the wind. I cannot express what a character of beauty those few honeysuckles in the hats of the three boys gave to the place: what bower could they have come from? We walked up the hill, met two well-dressed travellers, the woman barefoot. Our little lads before they had gone far were joined by some half-dozen of their companions, all without shoes and stockings. They told us they lived at Wanlockhead, the village above, pointing to the top of the hill; they went to school and learned Latin, Virgil, and some of them Greek, Homer, but when Coleridge began to inquire further, off they ran, poor things! I suppose afraid of being examined. [...]

Our road turned to the right, and we saw, at the distance of less than a mile, a tall upright building of grey stone, with several men standing upon the roof, as if they were looking out over battlements. It stood beyond the village, upon higher ground, as if presiding over it, — a kind of enchanter's castle, which it might have been, a place where Don Quixote would have gloried in. When we drew nearer we saw, coming out of the side of the building, a large machine or lever, in appearance like a great forge-hammer, as we supposed for raising water out of the mines. It heaved upwards once in half a minute with a slow motion, and seemed to rest to take breath at the bottom, its motion being accompanied with a sound between a groan and 'jike'.[22] There would have been something in this object very striking in any place, as it was impossible not to invest the machine with some faculty of intellect; it seemed to have made the first step from brute matter to life and purpose, showing its progress by great power. William made a remark to this effect, and Coleridge observed that it was like a giant with one idea.[23] [...]

They finally reach the Falls of Clyde.

We sat upon a bench, placed for the sake of one of these views, whence we looked down upon the waterfall, and over the open country, and saw a ruined tower, called Wallace's Tower, which stands at a very little distance from the fall, and is an interesting object. A lady and gentleman, more expeditious tourists than ourselves, came to the spot; they left us at the seat, and we found them again at another station above the Falls. Coleridge, who is always good-natured enough to enter into conversation with anybody whom he meets in his way, began to talk with the gentleman, who observed that it was a *majestic* waterfall. Coleridge was delighted with the accuracy of the epithet, particularly as he had been settling in his own mind the precise meaning of the words grand, majestic, sublime, etc., and had discussed the subject with William at some length the day before. 'Yes, sir,' says Coleridge, 'it *is* a majestic waterfall.' 'Sublime and beautiful,' replied his friend. Poor Coleridge could make no answer, and, not very desirous to continue the conversation, came to us and related the story, laughing heartily.[24]

(x) SAMUEL ROGERS

From Recollections of the Table-Talk of Samuel Rogers, *to which is added* Porsoniana *(1856), 205-6. Rogers (1763-1855), poet (*The Pleasures of Memory *and* Italy*), and his sister had met Coleridge earlier in the month (see above). Now, on their own Scottish tour, they found themselves staying in the same inn (DWJ, I, 197-8). Coleridge and the Wordsworths parted company on 29 August.*

Early in the present century, I set out on a tour in Scotland, accompanied by my sister; but an accident which happened to her prevented us from going as far as we had intended. During our excursion we fell in with Wordsworth, Miss Wordsworth, and Coleridge, who were, at the same time, making a tour in a vehicle that looked very like a cart. Wordsworth and Coleridge were entirely occupied in talking about poetry; and the whole care of looking out for cottages where they might get refreshment and pass the night, as well as of seeing their poor horse fed and littered, devolved upon Miss Wordsworth. She was a most delightful person, — so full of talent, so simple-minded, and so modest! If I am not mistaken, Coleridge proved so impracticable a travelling-companion, that Wordsworth and his sister were at last obliged to separate from him.

(xi) JOSEPH FARINGTON

From Joseph Farington, The Farington Diary, ed. James Greig (8 vols.; 1922-8), II, 209-10; 210-11. Farington (1747-1821) was a landscape painter, a power in the Royal Academy, and a diner. Beaumont remained excited by his encounter with Coleridge: 'great genius, — a Poet, — prodigious command of words, — has read everything', Farington reported him saying on 29 November 1803 (II, 172) — an example of why one should not succumb to 'first prejudices' (21 March 1804: II, 207). On 25 March, Farington dined at the Beaumonts, where Coleridge was present, in full spate. (I omit the editor's subtitles.)

[George] Dance[25] called on me & I went with him to dinner at Sir George Beaumonts. — The conversation after dinner & throughout the evening was very metaphysical in which Coleridge had the leading & by far the greatest part of it. His habit seems to be to analyse every subject. A comparison was made between the powers required, or rather what was requisite for painting & Sculpture. Sir George was decidedly of the opinion that it required much more to make a complete work in Painting than to arrive at perfection in Sculpture. He instanced *colouring* which alone had occupied the greatest talents to arrive at excellence yet it was but a part of what was necessary to make a picture.

Coleridge concurred with him. Upon it being observed that in Sculpture to make a *perfect form* it was necessary not to copy any individual figure for nothing human is perfect, but to make a selection of perfect parts from various figures & assemble them together & thereby constitute a perfect whole[,] Coleridge observed that it was the same in good poetry, — nature was the basis or original from which all should proceed. He said that perhaps there was not in any poem a line which separately might not have been expressed by somebody, it was the assembling so many expressions of the feelings of the mind and uniting them consistently together that delighted the imagination. [...] Coleridge sd. Dr Darwin was a great *plagiarist*.[26] 'He was like a pigeon picking up peas, and afterwards voiding them with excrementitious additions.'

Novels were mentioned. Coleridge objected to them altogether; even the best of them did harm[:] 'they afforded amusement to the mind without requiring exertion.' At Lady Beaumont's desire I related the story of the *Apparition* of His Brother [John] appearing to Captn. Wynyard.[27] It was told at the private instigation of Lady Beaumont who was desirous to hear Coleridge's opinion upon it. — He gave a decided opinion upon it 'That it [was] an *Ocular Spectrum*,' a deception created by the disordered imagination of Captn. Wynyard when in a nervous, languid state, & that Coll. Sherbroke who also professed to have seen the apparition had the notion of it excited by the sudden assertion of the other.

The evening was passed not in conversation but in listening to a succession of opinions, & explanations delivered by Coleridge, to which I attended from a desire to form a judgment of his ability. It was all metaphysical, frequently perplexed, and certainly at times without understanding His subject. Occasionally there was some brilliance, but I particularly noticed that His *illustrations* generally disappointed me, & rather weakened than enforced what He had before said. He read some lines written by Wordsworth upon 'The Maid of Loch Lomond,' a pretty girl they found residing there; and also some lines upon Westminster Bridge [...] & the scenery from it.[28] His Dialect particularly when reading, is what I shd. call *broad Devonshire*, for a gentleman. — His manner was good-natured & civil, & He went on like one who was accustomed to take the lead in the company He goes into. He sd. His mother is 80 years of age, from which I judge Him to be 35. —

On coming away I expressed to Dance how much I was fatigued by that sort of confinement we had been under. He sympathised in it.

The following day, Farington dined with the painter James Northcote (1746-1831), who was finishing a portrait of Coleridge for Beaumont.

Northcotes I dined at. Before dinner Northcote shewed us a Head of Coleridge which He began yesterday & finished today, It is for Sir G.: Beaumont, & is very like. Coleridge is going to Malta for his health. He and *Southey* married 2 sisters. — When Sir George first mentioned Coleridge to Northcote the latter expressed His surprise observing that He was '*a great Democrat.*' Sir George sd. His opinions were altered. Opie[29] mentioned that William Godwin has a high idea of the powers of Coleridge and 'of *the riches of his mind.*' [Prince] Hoare sd. some Sonnets published by Him are very good. — Fuseli[30] had met him at Johnsons[31] and thought little of him.—Northcote & Coleridge had differed abt. the *disposition of Milton.*—Coleridge sd. He was next to *our Saviour* in *humility.* Northcote on the contrary thought that ambition was the prevailing quality in his mind. That He was arrogant and tyrannical.— Opie sd. that Don Quixotte was nearer to that pattern of humility than Milton.—Coleridge noticed to Northcote the *high family* of Sir George Beaumont. The latter [Northcote] replied that He was surprised *that* shd. seem to him (Coleridge) to be any consideration, He who held all distinctions so cheap. [...]

Northcote heard Coleridge read a long poem of his own composing. He said His manner & tone put him in mind of 'the drone of a presbyterian parson.'—Lady Beaumont and a Sister of Mr. Addington,[32] (the Premier) appeared to be delighted.—

NOTES

[1] Phillips—whom STC thought a 'gross flatterer' (*TT*, II, 386)—in generous mood. Cf.:

> Before he went to Germany I passed a long afternoon in his company at a dinner party at Dr. Estlin's, at Bristol. Mr. Benjamin, afterwards Sir B. Benjamin, Dr. Beddoes, Mr. and Mrs. Barbauld, and some others were there. Coleridge sat next me, and he deafened me by set harangues on many trite subjects, treated in a scholastic and dogmatic way. In five or six hours the rest of the company edged in economically for a few minutes, but only when Coleridge took breath. He certainly was eloquent and very ingenious in quibbling. Though I tried the next morning to recollect something that he had said, yet the whole resembled smoke, and I could grapple with no point whatever. (Quoted in William E.A. Axon, 'Lancelot Sharpe, Sir R. Phillips, and S.T. Coleridge' (continued), *N&Q*, 9th ser., XI (1903) 381-2, 381)

[2] A harsh way of putting a genuine truth: as H.N. Coleridge recalled,

> More than once has Mr. Coleridge said, that with pen in hand he felt a thousand checks and difficulties in the expression of his meaning; but that— authorship aside—he never found the smallest hitch or impediment in the fullest utterance of his most subtle fancies by word of mouth. His abstrusest thoughts became rhythmical and clear when chaunted to their own music. ('The Poetical Works of S.T. Coleridge', *Quarterly Review* LII (1834) 1-38, 5)

[3] *EOT*, I, 115-16. Grenville (1759-1834) was foreign secretary from 1791. STC reported French offers of peace negotiations, rejected by the cabinet on 4 January (*EOT*, I, 64; 72-3). Discussing the possibility of a change in French policy, Grenville had said 'the conviction of such a change, however agreeable to His Majesty's wishes, can result only from experience, and from the evidence of facts': quoted in *Essays on His Own Times*, ed. Sara Coleridge (3 vols.; 1850), I, 211. STC often mocked untroubled appeals to 'fact' (cf. *CN*, II, 2043; 2122).
[4] *EOT*, I, 219-26.

5 Published in the *Morning Post*, 6 September 1799 (*CPW*, I, 319-23).

6 John Moore (1729-1802), author of *Zelucco. Various Views of Human Nature*.

7 To Wordsworth, 26 April, 1816 [*sic*] (*Final Memorials of Charles Lamb*, I, 221).

8 Cf. 'Kubla Khan', l.36 (*CPW*, I, 298).

9 A huge rock, apparently precariously balanced, near Derwent-Water.

10 The innermost part of the temple; a sanctum (*OED*).

11 Warner here quotes Wordsworth's 'To Joanna', ll.38ff..

12 l.73 (*CPW*, I, 164).

13 ll.223-4? ('The lofty lady stood upright: / She was most beautiful to see': *CPW*, I, 223). The dates are muddled: 'Christabel' was not published until 1816.

14 Fenwick Notes: Wordsworth, *Prose Works*, ed. Grosart, III, 23.

15 An earlier version had 'A face divine of heaven born idiotcy'.

16 The early title of 'Resolution and Independence' (published 1807).

17 A lost draft? No such lines appear in the texts that survive.

18 Sarah Wedgwood, Tom's sister, who accompanied him and STC into Wales.

19 The story of Mary Robinson, the 'Beauty of Buttermere' was told as it unfolded by STC in the *Morning Post* in the last months of 1802. Mary was duped into a bigamous marriage by one John Hatfield, posing as an M.P.. Hatfield was hanged in September 1803; STC visited him in Carlisle prison. Mary's story caused a great stir: a melodrama ran at Sadler's Wells in Spring 1803.

20 William Sotheby (1757-1833), poet and translator.

21 Beaumont elides (or heard elided) *The Recluse* and the autobiographical poem accompanying it, known posthumously as *The Prelude*.

22 A Cumbrianism for 'creak'.

23 An often-repeated joke. Wordsworth also recalled the story (*Prose Works*, ed. Grosart, III, 445), and Scott knew it too (to Rogers, 12 [June?] 1815: *Letters of Sir Walter Scott*, ed. H.J.C. Grierson (12 vols.; 1932-9), IV, 73). STC himself recycled the phrase, using it of Thomas Clarkson (11 June 1811; Henry Crabb Robinson, *On Books and their Writers*, ed. Edith J. Morley (3 vols.; 1938), I, 35).

24 A story that endured much improved re-telling: cf. *LL*, I, 34; 188; *SWF*, I, 362.

25 George Dance (1741-1825), architect and R.A.. He drew STC for Beaumont in March 1804.

26 For STC's low view of Darwin's poetry see, e.g., *BL*, I, 19-20, and 19n.3.

27 A celebrated incident: Wynyard and a fellow officer, stationed in America (c.1785), saw an apparition of Wynyard's brother—at exactly the time (it transpired) that he died in Britain. (See Frederick George Lee, *The Other World; or, Glimpses of the Supernatural* (2 vols.; 1875), II, 26-33.)

28 'To a Highland Girl' and 'Composed Upon Westminster Bridge'.

29 Opie (1761-1807), Professor of Painting at the Royal Academy.

30 Prince Hoare (1755-1834), dramatist, honorary foreign secretary of the R.A.; and Henry Fuesli (1741-1825), a Professor from 1801.

31 Presumably, Joseph Johnson (1739-1809), radical publisher and bookseller.

32 Henry Addington, Viscount Sidmouth (1757-1844), prime minister, 1801-4.

Malta: Civil Servant

By 1803 opium addiction was giving Coleridge terrible nightmares, his health was deteriorating, relations with his wife were worsening, and he was hopelessly in love with Sara Hutchinson, Wordsworth's sister-in-law. As early as August 1803, he had considered travelling 'to Malta with Stoddart, or to Madeira' (*CL*, II, 965) to convalesce away from damp weather. (Stoddart, a friend of Lamb's, had recently been appointed an Advocate in Malta.) Later, following the advice of Greenough, he settled on 'Malta & thence to Sicily', in part thanks to Greenough's account of Etna (*CL*, II, 1050). The Southeys had moved into Greta Hall (as they thought temporarily) which meant that the children and Mrs. Coleridge could be safely abandoned to a brother-in-law's sturdy 'Vice-fathership' (*CL*, II, 1062); and, on 9 April 1804, ignoring French dangers, Coleridge set sail from Portsmouth on the *Speedwell*, arriving on Malta on 18 May, and presenting himself without warning at Stoddart's house. A couple of days later, he introduced himself to Sir Alexander Ball, Governor of the island. Although initially unenthusiastic, Ball soon employed Coleridge: he was appointed under-secretary, and then Public Secretary, which brought with it a comfortable apartment attached to the Treasury.[1] He met the American naval hero Stephen Decatur;[2] he visited Sicily, and climbed Etna.

MR. UNDERWOOD

From the 'Memoir' prefacing Charles Wentworth Dilke, The Papers of a Critic [...] *with a biographical sketch by his grandson, Sir Charles Wentworth Dilke (2 vols.; 1875), I, 32-3. After Coleridge's death, Dilke, editor of* The Athenæum, *sent an investigator to Paris to sort out some details for a biographical account. Two points made by De Quincey in his memoir were found to be inaccurate: Coleridge was not Sir Alexander Ball's 'treasurer' but his secretary; and Coleridge was not 'forced' to marry his wife (erroneously referred to by Dilke's agent here as 'Miss Taylor'). On the contrary, wisdom was that he was very fond of her.[3] The source for all this, and more, was one Underwood, a former member of Ball's staff. The moral offered by Dilke's grandson seems the right one.*

In October, 1834, Mr. Dilke sent a messenger to Paris on behalf of the *Athenæum* in reference to two matters, of which the first was the Life of Coleridge. This agent writes:—'I have seen the Mr. Underwood to whom Sir E. Bull referred. The letter of Coleridge does not refer to the Regiment, but is about his early "wives." He says that Quincey's account is uncommonly true, with two exceptions. 1. About his being *Treasurer* to Sir A. (*sic*)[4] Ball, and 2. About his being *forced* to marry Miss Taylor. He was only secretary, and was exceedingly enamoured of his wife. His appointment of secretary was thus: — Coleridge got hold of a sum of money (Mr. Underwood thinks it was his allowance from the Wedgewoods [*sic*]), and with that he ran off to Malta. There Sir J. Holland, then Mr. Holland and Attorney-General, was at a ball at the Governor's, when he was told a gentleman from England wished to see him. He went out, and saw Coleridge. "My God! what has brought you here." "To see you." "Well, as you *are* here, one must be glad to see you. Come and have some supper." This was the meeting. Coleridge was soon introduced to Sir E. Ball [*sic*] and appointed Secretary, but was so totally inefficient that they could not get on. Colin Mackenzie had at that time (the height of the war), got a ship to bring him home, and arrangements were made that Coleridge should accompany him. Underwood and Mackenzie say that there was more humbug in Coleridge than in any man that was ever heard of. Underwood was one day transcribing something for Coleridge when a visitor appeared. After the common-places, Coleridge took up a little book lying upon the table and said, "By the bye, I casually took up this book this morning, and was quite enchanted with a little sonnet I found there." He then read off a blank verse translation, and entered into a long critique upon its merits. The same story, the same translation, and the same critique were repeated five times in that day to different visitors, without one word being altered. Mr. Underwood says that every one of his famous evening conversations was got up.' Truly a hero is not a hero to his valet.[5]

NOTES

[1] Donald Sultana, *Samuel Taylor Coleridge in Malta and Italy* (1969), 52; 144; 163; 269.

[2] See Alexander Slidell Mackenzie, *Life of Stephen Decatur, A Commodore in the Navy of the United States* (Boston, 1848), 123-4.

[3] Sultana (*Malta and Italy*, 243) says this means STC was fond of Ball's wife.

[4] The original editor's 'sic'.

[5] Another Malta story. The poet Thomson, it was said, was so indolent that he ate fruit from the tree without bothering to pick it. Cary (for whom, see below) told STC the story, who wasn't surprised:

> On my once speaking of this with Mr. Coleridge, he observed that there was nothing remarkable in it, for that it was no more than he used to do himself at Malta. But I doubted whether this was so much an apology for Thomson as a proof that my admirable friend, who resembled him in his higher qualities, partook also of this infirmity. ('Biographical Notice of James Thomson'; in *Poetical Works of John Milton, James Thomson, and Edward Young*, ed. Rev. H.F. Cary (1841), v-vi)

Coleridge in Rome

Coleridge was Public Secretary pending the return of one Chapman, who, in September 1805, turned up—to Coleridge's relief (Sultana, *Malta and Italy*, 360). Coleridge left the island on 24 September to travel, finally arriving in Rome at the end of the year. There, he settled quickly into the city's flourishing intellectual life, which included the German writer Ludwig Tieck, and Washington Allston.

(i) WASHINGTON ALLSTON

From The Life and Letters of Washington Allston, *ed. Jared B. Flagg (1893), 64; 65-6; 355-56; 357; 359; 366; 104. Allston (1779-1843) was best known for his large paintings of Biblical subjects. He also painted one of the best portraits of Coleridge. The two men came to know each other well during Coleridge's stay in Rome, and they remained friends in Highgate days. Coleridge's impact on Allston is clearly detectable in his* Lectures *on* Art *and in some of Allston's 'Aphorisms' ('Originality in Art is the individualizing the Universal').[1] Allston influenced Coleridge too, especially by prompting his interest in visual art, which came to fruition in the 'Essays on the Principles of Genial Criticism' (1814) written (partly) to accompany an exhibition of Allston's paintings. This account comes from the* Life and Letters *worked up by Flagg from material gathered by Richard H. Dana, the brother of Allston's second wife.*

Allston said: 'To no other man do I owe so much intellectually as to Mr. Coleridge, with whom I became acquainted in Rome, and who has honored me with his friendship for more than five and twenty years. He used to call Rome "the silent city," but I could never think of it as such while with him, for meet him when and where I would, the fountain of his mind was never dry, but, like the far-reaching aqueducts that once supplied this mistress of the world, its living stream seemed specially to flow for every classic ruin over which we wandered; and when I recall some of our walks under the pines of the Villa Borghese, I am almost tempted to dream that I have once listened to Plato in the groves of the Academy.' [...]

The charge that Coleridge endeavored to drawn Allston from his love of Greek art has, we think, no sufficient foundation, though in conversation upon the comparative beauties of Greek and Gothic styles, he once said to Allston: 'Grecian architecture is a thing, but the Gothic is an idea.'[2] And then added: 'I can make a Grecian temple of two brick-bats and a cocked hat.'

Flagg quotes R.H. Dana, Jr., whose father was Allston's brother-in-law.

Allston became intimately acquainted with Coleridge, and they were continually together during a residence of several months in Rome. When Coleridge was at Highgate he was often there for days together. He had the highest admiration, nay, reverence, for Coleridge's powers of mind, and he loved him as a man and a friend; and, what was still more, he looked up to him as a sincere and humble Christian. He often spoke of Coleridge as having been of the greatest advantage to his mind in every way — in his art, in poetry, and in his opinions and habits of thought generally — and also to his religious character. [...]

When Mr. Allston and Coleridge were travelling in Italy they stopped at a miserable inn, where Mr. Allston, for want of something better to do, took up an execrable book and was reading it when Coleridge came in. He showed it to him and said that he had been much amused with the exceeding badness of the style; but Coleridge advised him to put it down, saying:

'You may think that it amuses you, but you had better be doing nothing. You cannot touch pitch without being defiled.' [...]

When Allston was in Italy there was an English artist there who had lived abroad more than in England, and affected to hate his own country, and was a man of rather bad character. Allston painted a picture which was much admired for its clouds. This artist asked him how he produced his effect, and Mr. Allston told him freely how he managed his colors.

The English artist then began a picture and endeavored to paint clouds in the same manner. Allston went into his studio, and finding that he been partly misunderstood, took the brush into his own hands and painted for him until he had made him master of the mode. Coleridge said to Allston, 'You are doing yourself no good, and him a favor for which he will not thank you.' Allston doubted the man's ingratitude, and said that at all events he was not sorry he had done him a kindness. Coleridge, to try the man, went to his studio and praised the picture, especially the clouds. The man made no explanation. Coleridge then went further and said, 'You've got Allston's clouds, or Allston's method of painting clouds.' 'Oh,' said the man, 'we knew all that before.'

Dana recollects some snippets of Allston's conversation:

'Coleridge told me that he could introduce me to the acquaintance of nearly all the authors in London, but he would not do it, for he would be sorry to have me know them. He told me seriously that he did not know so entirely worthless and despicable a set of men as the authors by profession in London, and warned me solemnly to avoid any intercourse with them.' [...]

'So far as I can judge of my own production the likeness of Coleridge is a true one, but it is Coleridge in repose; and, though not unstirred by the perpetual ground-swell of his ever-working intellect, and shadowing forth something of the deep philosopher, it is not Coleridge in his highest mood, the poetic state, when the divine afflatus of the poet possessed him. When in that state, no face that I ever saw was like his; it seemed almost spirit made visible without a shadow of the physical upon it. Could I then have fixed it upon canvas! but it was beyond the reach of my art. He was the greatest man I have ever known, and one of the best; as his nephew, Henry Nelson, truly said, "a thousand times more sinned against than sinning!".'[3]

(ii) JOSEPH COTTLE

From Cottle, Early Recollections, II, 77-82. Coleridge heard on the first day of 1806 that the French were due to arrive in Rome: 'To stay or not to stay', he asked himself (CN, II, 2785), curiously unaware of the danger he was in. In March, Bonaparte demanded the expulsion of British subjects from Papal territories; the Pope refused; in April, French troops closed the ports. Coleridge was later to claim that Bonaparte nursed a particular grudge against him (BL, I, 216); the truth is more likely that he was one of a large number of Britons anxious to get out. The following is (according to Cottle) the story Coleridge gave of his escape. He left Rome for Florence, thence for Pisa (CN, II, 2848; 2856), finally finding passage on the Gosport, an American ship.

Shortly after Mr. Coleridge had arrived in this city, he attracted some notice amongst the literati, as an English 'Man of Letters.' Cardinal Fesch, in particular, was civil, and sought his company;[4] but that which was more remarkable, Jerome Buonaparte (the best of the Buonaparte family) was then a resident at Rome, and Mr. C.'s reputation becoming known to him, he sent for Mr. Coleridge, and after showing him his palace, pictures, &c. thus generously addressed him. 'Sir, I have sent for you to give you a little candid advice. I do not know that you have said, or written any thing against my brother Napoleon, but, as an Englishman, the supposition is not unreasonable. If you have, my advice is, that you leave Italy as soon as you possibly can!'

This hint was gratefully received, and Mr. Coleridge soon after quitted Rome, in the suite of Cardinal Fesch.[5] From his anxiety to reach England, he proceeded to Leghorn, where an occurrence attended Mr. C. which will excite every reader's sympathy. Mr. Coleridge had journeyed to this port, where he hoped, rather than expected, to find some conveyance, through the medium of a neutral, that should waft him to the land, 'more prized than ever.' The hope proved delusive. The war was now raging between England and France, and Buonaparte being lord of the ascendant in Italy, Mr. Coleridge's situation became insecure, and even perilous. To obtain a passport was impossible; and as Mr. C. had formerly rendered himself obnoxious to the great Captain, by some political papers, he was in daily and hourly expectation of being incarcerated in an Italian prison, which would have been the infallible road to death![6]

In half despair of ever again seeing his family and friends, and under the constant dread of apprehension by the emissaries of the Tuscan government, or French spies; Mr. Coleridge said, he went out one morning, to look at some ruins in the neighbourhood of Leghorn, in a state of despondency, where certainty, however terrible, would have been almost preferable to suspense. While musing on the ravages of time, he turned his eye, and observed, at a little distance, a sea-faring looking man, musing, like himself, in silence, on the waste around. Mr. Coleridge advanced toward him, supposing, or, at least, deeming it possible, that he also might be mourning his captivity, and commenced a discourse with him; when he found that the stranger was an American captain, whose ship was then in the harbour, and on the point of sailing for England.[7]

This information sent joy into Mr. C.'s heart; but he testified no emotion, determined, he said, to obtain the captain's good will, by showing him all the civilities in his power, as a preliminary to any future service the captain might be disposed to render him, whether the power were united with the disposition or not. This showed adroitness, with great knowledge of human nature; (and more winning and captivating manners than those of Mr. C. when called forth, were never posssessed by mortal!) In conformity with this almost forlorn hope, Mr. Coleridge explained to the American captain the history of the ruin; read to him some of the half defaced Latin and Italian inscriptions, and concluded with extolling General Washington, and predicting the stability of the Union. The right keys, treble and tenor, were touched at the same moment. 'Pray, young man,' said the captain, 'who are you?' Mr. C. replied, 'I am a poor unfortunate Englishman, with a wife and family at home; but I am afraid I shall never see them more! I have no *passport,* nor means of escape; and, to increase my sorrow, I am in daily dread of being thrown into jail, when those I love will not have the last pleasure of *knowing* that I am dead!' The captain's heart was touched. He had a wife and family at a distance. 'My young man,' said he, 'what is your name?' The reply was, 'Samuel Taylor Coleridge.' 'Poor young man,' answered the captain. 'You meet me at this place to-morrow morning, exactly at ten o'clock.' So saying, the captain withdrew. Mr. C. stood musing on the singular occurrence, in which there was something *inexplicable.* His discernment of the stranger's character, however, convinced him that there existed no *under plot,* but still there was a wide space between *probability* and *certainty.* On a balance of circumstances, he still thought *all fair,* and, at the appointed hour, repaired to the interior of the ruins.

No captain was there; but, in a few minutes he appeared, and, hastening up to Mr. Coleridge, exclaimed, exultingly, 'I have got your passport!' 'How! What!' said Mr. C. almost overpowered by his feelings. 'Ask me no questions,' replied the captain; 'you are my *steward,* and you shall sail away with me to-morrow morning!' He continued, (giving him his address) 'You come to my house, to-morrow, early, when I will provide you with a *jacket* and *trowsers,* and you shall follow me to the ship with a *basket of vegetables.*' In short, thus accoutred, he *did* follow the captain to the ship, the next morning; and in three hours, he fairly sailed out of Leghorn harbour, triumphantly, on his course to England!

As soon as the ship had cleared the port, Mr. Coleridge hastened down to the cabin, and cried, 'my dear captain, tell me how you obtained my passport?' Said the captain, very gravely, 'Why, I went to the authorities, and *swore* that you were an *American,* and my steward! I *swore,* also, that I knew your father and mother; that they lived in a red-brick house, about half a mile out of New York, on the road to Boston!'

It is gratifying to add, that this benevolent little-scrupulous captain refused to accept any thing from Mr. C. for his passage to England; and behaved, in many other respects, with the same uniform kindness. During the voyage, Mr. Coleridge told me, he was attacked with a dangerous illness, when, he said, he thought he should have *died,* but for the '*good captain,*' who attended him with the solicitude of a father. Mr. C. also said, had he known what the captain was going to *swear*, whatever the consequences might have been, he would have prevented him.

NOTES

[1] Washington Allston, *Lectures on Art, and Poems*, ed. Richard Henry Dana, Jr. (N.Y., 1850), 172. Many of Allston's thoughts about artistic unity, harmony, and the 'Living Principle' (p.104), have a distinctly Coleridgean timbre.

[2] STC makes the comparison elsewhere: e.g., *LL*, II, 49; 62; and *CN*, III, 4021.

[3] Samuel Morse (1791-1872), inventor of the Morse code, also studied with Allston in Rome, and recalled STC's visits:

> When Leslie and I were studying under Allston, Coleridge was a frequent, almost daily, visitor to our studio. For our entertainment while painting, we used to arrange in advance some question in which we were interested, and propound it to Coleridge upon his coming in. This was quite sufficient, and never failed to start him off on a monologue to which we could listen with pleasure and profit throughout the entire sitting. (Flagg, *Life and Letters of Allston*, 63)

The painter Gottlieb Schick (1779-1812) also came across STC, lodging with the Scottish painter Wallis (who was accompanied by his prodigious son Trajan: see *CN*, II, 2816 & n.). In a letter of 5 July 1806, Schick complained about STC:

> This gentleman was very poorly; he slept mostly during the day, and was awake during the whole night. He was the cause that the whole house got out of its proper every-day order, and I did not dine on that account at Wallis', as this Englishman (who, however, is a celebrated poet and scholar) made me lose too much of my time. (Quoted in Hermann Kindt, 'Coleridge at Rome in 1806', *Notes and Queries* 3rd ser., XII (1867), 281)

[4] Fesch was Napoleon's uncle and his minister in Rome (Sultana, *Malta and Italy*, 8).

[5] Certainly an embellishment: Sultana, *Malta and Italy*, 394.

[6] Caroline Fox heard a garbled version of the story from John Sterling (for whom, see below): *Journal of Caroline Fox*, ed. Horace N. Pym (3rd.edn.; 2 vols.; 1882), I, 122-3.

[7] Captain Derkheim of the *Gosport* (see *CL*, II, 1184-5).

Four
Lecturer and Man of Letters 1806-16

Coleridge arrived in England on 17 August 1806. He lodged in the *Courier* offices, and negotiated a lecture-series at the Royal Institution (*CL*, II, 1187-8). He headed north in October, hoping to meet Sara Hutchinson.

'utterly changed'

(i) DOROTHY WORDSWORTH

From Letters of the Wordsworth Family, *ed. Knight, I, 251-2. Sir George Beaumont offered the Wordsworths use of a house on his estate in Leicestershire. When Coleridge finally met up with them on their way there, they were shocked by his appearance, as Dorothy told Catherine Clarkson (5-6 November 1806).*

Alas! what can I say? I know not what to hope for, or what to expect. My wishes are plain and fair, that he may have strength of mind to abide by his resolution of separating from Mrs. C., and hereafter may continue unshaken; but his misery has made him so weak, and he has been so dismally irresolute in all things since his return to England, that I have more of fear than hope. He is utterly changed; and yet sometimes, when he was animated in conversation concerning things removed from him, I saw something of his former self; but never when we were alone with him. He then scarcely ever spoke of anything that concerned him, or us, or our common friends, except we forced him to it; and immediately he changed the conversation to Malta, Sir Alexander Ball, the corruptions of government, anything but what we were yearning after. All we could gather from him was that he must part from her, or die and leave his children destitute, and that to part he was resolved.

We would have gone back to Grasmere, or taken a house near Hawkshead (Belmont), but this he was against, and indeed it would have been worse than useless, for he gave us a promise to come to us here in a month; and, if he do part, the further the better. So matters stood when we left him, and we are now in anxious expectation of a letter from him. He did not complain of his health, and his appetite appeared to be not bad; but that he is ill I am well assured, and that he must sink if he does not grow more happy. His fatness has quite changed him. It is more like the flesh of a person in a dropsy than one in health; his eyes are lost in it — but why talk of this? you must have seen and felt all. I often thought of Patty Smith's remark.[1] It showed true feeling of the divine expression of his countenance. Alas! I never saw it, as it used to be — a shadow, a gleam there was at times, but how faint and transitory!

(ii) WILLIAM WORDSWORTH

'A Complaint'; from William Wordsworth, Poems, in Two Volumes (2 vols.; 1807), II, 117-18. Coleridge joined the Wordsworths at Coleorton in December 1806. At first, Dorothy was pleased to see him more his old self (MY, I, 121); but a permanent change in his manner gradually became more apparent.[2]

> There is a change — and I am poor;
> Your Love hath been, nor long ago,
> A Fountain at my fond Heart's door,
> Whose only business was to flow;
> And flow it did; not taking heed
> Of its own bounty, or my need.
>
> What happy moments did I count!
> Bless'd was I then all bliss above!
> Now, for this consecrated Fount
> Of murmuring, sparkling, living love,
> What have I? shall I dare to tell?
> A comfortless and hidden WELL.
>
> A Well of love — it may be deep —
> I trust it is, and never dry:
> What matter? if the Waters sleep
> In silence and obscurity.
> — Such change, and at the very door
> Of my fond Heart, hath made me poor.

NOTES

[1] Presumably the remark mentioned by Clarkson in a letter to Crabb Robinson (5 December 1811): '"To know him," she said, "all he is, and to see him with such lively childish spirits, one need not say, 'God bless him!' — he seems already in the fulness of every earthly gift"' (*Diary, Reminiscences, and Correspondence of Henry Crabb Robinson*, ed. Thomas Sadler (3 vols.; 1869), I, 348).

[2] Fenwick confirms STC is the subject of the poem (*Prose Works*, ed. Grosart, III, 23).

In the West Country

(i) JOSEPH COTTLE

From Cottle, Early Recollections, II, 74-5; 75-6. Coleridge, with Hartley, set off in May for Bristol, where Sara had been waiting for them. He had planned to visit Ottery St. Mary, but stayed in Stowey with Poole for most of the summer.

In the year 1807, I accidentally learnt that Mr. C. had returned to England, from the Mediterranean, very ill, and that he was then on a visit to his friend Mr. Poole, at Stowey. On receiving this information, I addressed to him a letter of condolence, and expressed a hope that his health would soon allow him to pay me a visit, in Bristol. [...]

Some weeks later, Mr. Coleridge called on me; when, in the course of conversation, he entered into some observations on his own character, that made him appear unusually amiable. He said that, naturally, he was very arrogant; that it was his easily beseting sin; a state of mind which he said, he ascribed to the severe subjection to which he had been exposed, till he was fourteen years of age, and from which, his own consciousness of superiority made him revolt. He then stated that he had renounced all his Socinian sentiments;[1] that he considered Socinianism as a heresy of the worst description; attempting, in vain, to reconcile sin and holiness; the world and heaven; opposing the whole spirit of the Bible: and he further said, that Socinianism was subversive of all that truly constituted Christianity. At this interview he professed his deepest conviction of the truth of Revelation; of the Fall of Man; of the Divinity of Christ, and redemption alone through his blood. To hear these sentiments so explicitly avowed, gave me unspeakable pleasure, and formed a new, and unexpected, and stronger bond of union.

(ii) THOMAS DE QUINCEY

From 'Samuel Taylor Coleridge. By the English Opium Eater', Tait's Edinburgh Magazine NS I (1834) 509-20, 509; 512-13; 513-14; 515; 517. De Quincey (1785-1859), journalist and autobiographer, was famous for Confessions of an English Opium-Eater *(1822). His memoirs broke the news of Coleridge's plagiarisms; but De Quincey was far from unsympathetic – unsurprisingly, since Coleridge was (De Quincey said) 'in a literary sense, our brother'.[2]*

It was, I think, in the month of August, but certainly in the summer season, and certainly in the year 1807, that I first saw this illustrious man, the largest and most spacious intellect, the subtlest and the most comprehensive, in my judgment, that has yet existed amongst men. My knowledge of him as a man of most original genius began about the year 1799. A little before that time Mr. Wordsworth had published the first edition (in a single volume) of the 'Lyrical Ballads,' at the end or the beginning of which was placed Mr. Coleridge's poem of the *Ancient Mariner*, as the contribution of an anonymous friend. It would be directing the reader's attention too much to myself, if I were to linger upon this, the greatest event in the unfolding of my own mind. Let me say in one word, that, at a period when neither the one nor the other writer was valued by the public, — both having a long warfare to accomplish of contumely and ridicule before they could rise into their present estimation, — I found in these poems 'the ray of a new morning,' and an absolute revelation of untrodden worlds, teeming with power and beauty, as yet unsuspected amongst men.

In Stowey, De Quincey learns that Coleridge has been expected for some days.

From the sort of laugh with which Lord Egmont taxed his own simplicity, in having confided at all in the stability of any Coleridgian plan, I now gathered that procrastination in excess, was, or had become, a marking feature in Coleridge's daily life. Nobody who knew him ever thought of depending on any appointment he might make: spite of his uniformly honourable intentions, nobody attached any weight to his assurances *in re futura:* those who asked him to dinner or any other party, as a matter of course, sent a carriage for him, and went personally or by proxy to fetch him; and, as to letters, unless the address were in some female hand that commanded his affectionate esteem, he tossed them all into one general *dead-letter bureau*, and rarely, I believe, opened them at all. Bourrienne mentions a mode of abridging the trouble attached to a very extensive correspondence, by which infinite labour was saved to himself and to Bonaparte, when commanding in Italy. Nine out of ten letters, supposing them letters of business with official applications of a special kind, he contends, answer themselves: in other words, time alone must soon produce events which virtually contain the answer. On this principle the letters were opened periodically, after intervals, suppose of six weeks: and, at the end of that time, it was found that not many remained to require any further more particular answer. Coleridge's plan, however, was shorter: he opened none, I understood, and answered none. At least such was his habit at that time. But on that same day, all this, which I heard now for the first time, and with much concern, was fully explained: for already he was under the full dominion of opium, as he himself revealed to me, and with a deep expression of horror at the hideous bondage, in a private walk of some length, which I took with him about sun-set.

Lord Egmont's information, and the knowledge now gained of Coleridge's habits, making it very uncertain when I might see him in my present hospitable quarters, I immediately took my leave of Mr. Poole, and went over to Bridgewater. I had received directions for finding out the house where Coleridge was visiting; and, in riding down a main street of Bridgewater, I noticed a gateway corresponding to the description given me. Under this was standing, and gazing about him, a man whom I shall describe. In height he might seem to be about five feet eight; (he was, in reality, about an inch and a half taller, but his figure was of an order which drowns the height;) his person was broad and full, and tended even to corpulence; his complexion was fair, though not what painters technically style fair, because it was associated with black hair; his eyes were large and soft in their expression; and it was from the peculiar appearance of haze or dreaminess, which mixed with their light, that I recognized my object. This was Coleridge. I examined him steadfastly for a minute or more; and it struck me that he saw neither myself nor any other object in the street. He was in a deep reverie; for I had dismounted, made two or three trifling arrangements at an inn door, and advanced close to him, before he had apparently become conscious of my presence. The sound of my voice, announcing my own name, first awoke him: he started, and, for a moment, seemed at a loss to understand my purpose or his own situation; for he repeated rapidly a number of words which had no relation to either of us. There was no *mauvaise honte* in his manner, but simple perplexity, and an apparent difficulty in recovering his position amongst day-light realities. This little scene over, he received me with a kindness of manner so marked that it might be called gracious. The hospitable family, with whom he was domesticated, were distinguished for their amiable manners and enlightened understandings: they were descendants from Chubb, the philosophic writer, and bore the same name.[3] For Coleridge, they all testified deep affection and esteem—sentiments in which the whole town of Bridgewater seemed to share; for in the evening, when the heat of the day had declined, I walked out with him; and rarely, perhaps never, have I seen a person so much interrupted in one hour's space as Coleridge, on this occasion, by the courteous attentions of young and old. All the people of station and weight in the place, and apparently all the ladies, were abroad to enjoy the lovely summer evening; and not a party passed without some mark of smiling recognition; and the majority stopping to make personal inquiries about his health, and to express their anxiety that he should make a lengthened stay amongst them. [...]

Coleridge led me to a drawing-room, rang the bell for refreshments, and omitted no point of a courteous reception. He told me that there would be a very large dinner party on that day, which perhaps might be disagreeable to a perfect stranger; but, if not, he could assure me of a most hospitable welcome from the family. I was too anxious to see him under all aspects, to think of declining this invitation. And these little points of business being settled, — Coleridge, like some great river, the Orellana, or the St. Lawrence, that had been checked and fretted by rocks or thwarting islands, and suddenly recovers its volume of waters, and its mighty music, — swept at once, as if returning to his natural business, into a continuous strain of eloquent dissertation, certainly the most novel, the most finely illustrated, and traversing the most spacious fields of thought, by transitions the most just and logical, that it was possible to conceive. What I mean by saying that his transitions were 'just,' is by way of contradistinction to that mode of conversation which courts variety by means of *verbal* connexions. Coleridge, to many people, and often I have heard the complaint, seemed to wander; and he seemed then to wander the most, when in fact his resistance to the wandering instinct was the greatest, — viz. when the compass, and huge circuit, by which his illustrations moved, travelled farthest into remote regions, before they began to revolve. Long before this coming-round commenced, most people had lost him, and naturally enough supposed that he had lost himself. They continued to admire the separate beauty of the thoughts, but did not see their relations to the dominant theme. Had the conversation been thrown upon paper, it might have been easy to trace the continuity of the links; just as in Bishop Berkeley's Siris, from a pedestal so low and abject, so culinary, as Tar Water, the method of preparing it, and its medicinal effects, the dissertation ascends, like Jacob's ladder, by just gradations, into the Heaven of

Heavens, and the thrones of the Trinity.[4] But Heaven is there connected with earth by the Homeric chain of gold; and being subject to steady examination, it is easy to trace the links. Whereas, in conversation, the loss of a single word may cause the whole cohesion to disappear from view. However, I can assert, upon my long and intimate knowledge of Coleridge's mind, that logic, the most severe, was as inalienable from his modes of thinking, as grammar from his language. On the present occasion, the original theme, started by myself, was Hartley, and the Hartleian theory. [...] It is known to most literary people that Coleridge was, in early life, so passionate an admirer of the Hartleian philosophy that 'Hartley' was the sole baptismal name which he gave to his eldest child; and in an early poem, entitled 'Religious Musings,' he has characterised Hartley as —

—— 'Him,
Wisest of men, who saw the mimic trains
Pass in fine surges to the sentient brain.'[5]

But at present, (August 1807,) all this was a forgotten thing. Coleridge was so profoundly ashamed of the shallow Unitarianism of Hartley, and so disgusted to think that he could at any time have countenanced that creed, that he would scarcely allow to Hartley the reverence which is undoubtedly his due[.] [...]

For about three hours he had continued to talk, and in the course of this performance he had delivered many most striking aphorisms, embalming more weight of truth, and separately more deserving to be themselves embalmed than any that are on record. In the midst of our conversation, if that can be called conversation which I so seldom sought to interrupt, and which did not often leave openings for contribution, the door opened, and a lady entered. She was in person full and rather below the common height; whilst her face showed, to my eye, some prettiness of rather a commonplace order. Coleridge turned, upon her entrance: his features, however, announced no particular complacency, and did not relax into a smile. In a frigid tone he said, whilst turning to me, 'Mrs. Coleridge:' in some slight way he then presented me to her: I bowed; and the lady almost immediately retired. From this short, but ungenial scene, I gathered, what I afterward learned redundantly, that Coleridge's marriage had not been a very happy one. [...]

The gloom, however, and the weight of dejection which sat upon Coleridge's countenance and deportment at this time, could not be accounted for by a disappointment, (if such it were,) to which time must, long ago have reconciled him. Mrs. Coleridge, if not turning to him the most amiable aspects of her character, was, at any rate, a respectable partner. And the season of youth was now passed. They had been married about ten years; had had four children, of whom three survived; and the interests of a father were now replacing those of a husband. Yet never had I beheld so profound an expression of cheerless despondency. And the restless activity of Coleridge's mind in chasing abstract truths, and burying himself in the dark places of human speculation, seemed to me, in a great measure, an attempt to escape out of his own personal wretchedness. At dinner, when a very numerous party had assembled, he knew that he was expected to talk, and exerted himself to meet the expectation. But he was evidently struggling with gloomy thoughts that prompted him to silence, and perhaps to solitude; he talked with effort; and passively resigned himself to the repeated misrepresentations of several amongst his hearers. [...] At night he entered into a spontaneous explanation of this unhappy over-clouding of his life, on occasion of my saying accidentally that a toothache had obliged me to take a few drops of laudanum. At what time or on what motive he had commenced the use of opium, he did not say; but the peculiar emphasis of horror with which he warned me against forming a habit of the same kind, impressed upon my mind a feeling that he never hoped to liberate himself from the bondage. About ten o'clock at night I took leave of him; and feeling that I could not easily go to sleep after the excitement of the day, and fresh from the sad spectacle of powers so majestic already besieged by decay, I determined to return to Bristol through the coolness of the night.

NOTES

[1] The doctrines of Laelius and Faustus Socinus (1525-62, 1539-1604), who denied the Trinity (and so the divinity of Christ). 'Socinian' became STC's pejorative term for the Unitarianism to which he had himself held as a young man.

[2] 'Coleridge and Opium-Eating', *Blackwood's* LVII (1845) 117-32, 117.

[3] Thomas Chubb (1679-1747), Deist philosopher; STC had known John Chubb, of Bridgewater, at least since Stowey days (*CL*, I, 341-3).

[4] Berkeley's *Siris* (1744) indeed follows such a path (as STC says: *BL*, I, 303).

[5] ll.368-70 *var.* (*CPW*, I, 123).

London Life, 1807-8

(i) WILLIAM HAZLITT

From 'Table-Talk. No.III. On the Conversation of Authors', London Magazine
II (1820) 250-62, 256-7; 258. *Coleridge returned to London in November 1807,
staying till the following June. Hazlitt's account of lively evenings at Lamb's
probably draws on memories of this period.*[1]

C—— is the only person who can talk to all sorts of people, on all
sorts of subjects, without caring a farthing for their understanding
one word he says — and *he* talks only for admiration and to be
listened to, and accordingly the least interruption puts him out.[2] I
firmly believe he would make just the same impression on half his
audiences, if he purposely repeated absolute nonsense with the
same voice and manner, and inexhaustible flow of undulating
speech! In general, wit shines only by reflection. You must take
your cue from your company — must rise as they rise, and sink as
they fall. You must see that your good things, your knowing
allusions, are not flung away, like the pearls in the adage. What a
check it is to be asked a foolish question; to find that the first
principles are not understood! You are thrown on your back
immediately, the conversation is stopped like a country-dance by
those who do not know the figure. But when a set of adepts, of
illuminati, get about a question, it is worth while to hear them talk.
They may snarl and quarrel over it, like dogs; but they pick it bare
to the bone, they masticate it thoroughly.

This was the case at L——'s formerly where we used to have
many lively skirmishes at their Thursday evening parties. I doubt
whether the small-coal man's musical parties could exceed them.
Oh! for the pen of John Buncle to consecrate a *petit souvenir* to their
memory![3] There was L—— himself, the most delightful, the most
provoking, the most witty and sensible of men. He always made
the best pun, and the best remark, in the course of the evening. His
serious conversation, like his serious writing, is his best. No one
ever stammered out such fine, piquant, deep, eloquent things in
half a dozen half sentences, as he does. His jests scald like tears:
and he probes a question with a play upon words. What a keen,
laughing, hair-brained vein of home-felt truth! What choice
venom! How often did we cut into the haunch of letters, while we
discussed the haunch of mutton on the table! How we skimmed
the cream of criticism! How we got into the heart of controversy!

How we picked out the marrow of authors! 'And, in our flowing cups, many a good name and true was freshly remembered.'[4] [...]

Once, and once only, the literary interest overcame the general. For C—— was riding the high German horse, and demonstrating the Categories of the Transcendental philosophy to the author of the *Road to Ruin;* who insisted on his knowledge of German, and German metaphysics, having read the *Critique of Pure Reason* in the original. 'My dear Holcroft,' said C——, in a tone of infinitely provoking conciliation, 'you really put me in mind of a sweet pretty German girl, about fifteen, that I met with in the Hartz forest in Germany—and who one day, as I was reading the Limits of the Knowable and the Unknowable, the profoundest of all his works, with great attention, came behind my chair, and, leaning over said, What, *you* read Kant? Why, *I* that am a German born, don't understand him!' This was too much to bear, and Holcroft starting up, called out in no measured tone, 'Mr. C——, you are the most eloquent man I ever met with, and the most troublesome with your eloquence!' P—— held the cribbage-peg that was to mark him game, suspended in his hand; and the whist table was silent for a moment. I saw Holcroft down stairs, and, on coming to the landing-place in Mitre-court, he stopped me to observe that 'he thought Mr. C—— a very clever man with a great command of language, but that he feared he did not always affix very precise ideas to the words he used.' After he was gone, we had our laugh out, and went on with the argument on the nature of Reason, the Imagination, and the Will. I wish I could find a publisher for it: it would make a supplement to the *Biographia Literaria* in a volume and a half octavo.

(ii) THOMAS FROGNALL DIBDIN

From Reminiscences of a Literary Life *(2 vols.; 1836), I, 253-57. Dibdin became editor of* The Director, *a literary and bibliographical periodical, in 1807; Sir Thomas Bernard was its proprietor (I, 249-50).*

It was during my constant and familiar intercourse with Sir T. Bernard, while 'The Director' was going on, that I met the celebrated Mr. COLERIDGE—himself a Lecturer at the Royal Institution—at the table of the baronet. I shall never forget the effect his conversation made upon me at the first meeting. It struck me as something not only quite out of the ordinary course of things, but as an intellectual exhibition altogether matchless. The party was usually large, but the presence of Coleridge concentrated all attention towards himself. The viands were usually costly, and the banquet was at once rich and varied; but there seemed to be no dish like Coleridge's conversation to feed upon—and no information so varied and instructive as his own. The orator rolled himself up, as it were, in his chair, and gave the most unrestrained indulgence to his speech—and how fraught with acuteness and originality was that speech, and in what copious and eloquent periods did it flow! The auditors seemed to be rapt in wonder and delight, as one observation, more profound or clothed in more forcible language than another, fell from his tongue. A great part of the subject discussed at the time of my meeting Mr. Coleridge, was the connexion between Lord Nelson and Lady Hamilton. The speaker had been secretary to Sir Alexander Ball, governor of Malta—and a copious field was here afforded for the exercise of his colloquial eloquence. For nearly two hours he spoke with unhesitating and uninterrupted fluency.

As I retired homeward (to Kensington) I thought a SECOND JOHNSON had visited the earth to make wise the sons of men; and regretted that I could not exercise the powers of a second BOSWELL, to record the wisdom and eloquence which had that evening flown from the orator's lips. It haunted me as I retired to rest. It drove away slumber: or if I lapsed into sleep, there was Coleridge—his snuff-box and his 'kerchief before my eyes!—his mildly beaming looks—his occasionally deep tone of voice—the excited features of his physiognomy—the secret conviction that his auditors seemed to be entranced with his powers of discourse! The speaker, however, it must be fairly admitted, did not 'give and take.' His generosity was illimitable, for he would receive nothing in return. It was true, there were very few who could *give* as they had *received;* but still, as an irritated hearer once observed by the side of me, 'fair play was a jewel.' The manner of Coleridge was rather *emphatic* than *dogmatic,* and thus he was generally and satisfactorily listened to. There was neither the *bow-wow* nor the *growl* which seemed usually to characterise Johnson's method of speaking; and his periods were more lengthened and continuous; but they were sometimes 'richly dight' in splendid imagery and resistless argument:— not, however, betraying such a range of reading, or fraught with so much personal anecdote, as were those of Mackintosh. In fact, it might be said of Coleridge, as Cowper has so happily said of Sir P. Sidney, that he was

> ... 'the warbler of poetic prose.'[5]

A love of truth, however, obliges me to remark that Coleridge was a *mannerist*. It was always the same tone—in the same style of expression—not quick and bounding enough to diffuse instant and general vivacity; and the *chair* would sometimes assume the solemn gravity of the *pulpit*. In consequence, when heard repeatedly, this would have, and *did* have, the effect of tiring. But there was such rhapsody, originality, and marked emphasis, in almost every thing which fell from him, that the hearer would, three times out of four, endure the manner for the matter. There was always *this* characteristic feature in his multifarious conversation—it was delicate, reverend, and courteous. The chastest ear could drink in no startling sound; the most serious believer never had his bosom ruffled by one sceptical or reckless assertion. Coleridge was eminently simple in his manner. Thinking and speaking were his delight; and he would sometimes seem, during the more fervid moments of discourse, to be abstracted from all and every thing around and about him, and to be basking in the sunny warmth of his own radiant imagination.

NOTES

[1] Lucas suggests 1814 as a likely date (*Life of Charles Lamb* (2nd. edn.; 2 vols.; 1905), I, 378); but STC spent 1814 in the West Country; Holcroft died in 1809; and the Lambs left Mitre Court in the Inner Temple in 1809. CT suggests 1807 (p. 252). Hazlitt's grandson records a larky anecdote (told to him by George Daniel) of the time: 'It was while Lamb was in his rooms at Mitre Court Buildings that he insisted one evening, when Coleridge was there, on carrying the latter upstairs, and then on Coleridge carrying him down again' (*Lamb and Hazlitt. Further Letters and Records [...]*, ed. William Carew Hazlitt (1900), xvi).

[2] Later in the essay, Hazlitt includes an example of it happening. Horne Tooke (1736-1812) was a radical and a philologist, whom Coleridge admired as 'ready-witted' while distrusting his 'shallowness' (*TT*, I, 117; see *CL*, I, 559). Hazlitt recalled him putting 'a full stop to one of C——'s long-winded prefatory apologies for his youth and in experience [*sic*], by saying abruptly,—'Speak up, young man!' (p. 260)

[3] Thomas Amory, *The Life of John Buncle, Esq.* (1756-66), a digressive fictional autobiography, praised by Hazlitt in *The Round Table*.

[4] *Henry V*, IV.iii, l.55.

[5] Willam Cowper, *The Task*, IV, l.516.

The 1808 Lectures

(i) KATHERINE THOMSON

From 'Literary Retrospect of the Departed Great', 83-4. Coleridge's first series of lectures, on 'the principles of poetry', began on 14 January 1808. Coleridge was to become one of the great lecturers of his day;[1] but his career had a rocky start.[2]

The next occasion on which I beheld Coleridge was, when lecturing to a fashionable audience at the Royal Insitution. He came unprepared to lecture. The subject was a literary one, and the poet had either forgotten to write, or left what he had written at home. His locks were now trimmed, and a conscious importance gleamed in his eloquent eyes, as he turned them towards the fair and noble heads which bent down to receive his apology. Every whisper—and there were some hundreds of ladies present—was hushed, and the poet began. I remember there was a stateliness in his language, and the measured tones did not fall so pleasantly upon my ear, as the half-whispered accents in which 'Mary of Buttermere' was described to my childish understanding. 'He must acknowledge,' he said, 'his error—the lecture was *not*; but the assembly before him must recollect, that the Muses would not have been old maids, except for want of a dowry.' The witticism was received with as much applause as a refined audience could decorously manifest, and the harangue proceeded. I began to think, as Coleridge went on, that the lecture had been left at home on purpose; he was *so* eloquent—there was such a combination of wit and poetry in his similes—such fancy, such a finish in his illustrations: yet, as we walked home after the lecture, I remember that we could not call to mind any real instruction, distinct impression, or new fact imparted to us by the great theorist. It was all fancy, flourish, sentiment, that we had heard.

(ii) EDWARD JERNINGHAM

From The Jerningham Letters (1780-1843). Being Excerpts from the Correspondence and Diaries of the Honourable Lady Jerningham and of her Daughter Lady Bedingfeld, *ed. Egerton Castle (2 vols.; 1896), I, 315-17. This is from a letter sent by Jerningham (1727-1812), poet and dramatist, to Lady Bedingfield in the autumn of 1808.*

I attended at the Royal Institution the Lectures of Colleridge [sic] upon Shakespear and Milton: I need not observe to you that He is Southey's Friend—My opinion as to the Lecturer is that He possesses a great reach of mind; That He is a wild Enthusiast respecting the objects of his Elogium; That He is sometimes very eloquent, sometimes paradoxical, sometimes absurd. His voice has something in it particularly plaintive and interesting. His person is short, Thick, his countenance not inspirited with any Animation. He spoke without any Assistance from a manuscript, and Therefore said several Things suddenly, struck off from the Anvil, some of which were entitled to high Applause and others Incurred mental disapprobation. He too often Interwove Himself into the Texture of his Lecture. I formed an Acquaintance with Him: that is, I generally spoke to Him at the End of the Lecture—with which He appeared much pleased. He was in some respect, I told Him one day, like Abelard:[3] His Lectures were attended by Ladies of the first fashion, by Judges, and Bishops; and I could have added since another Resemblance to Abelard, by the Disgrace his course of Lectures concluded with. In one of his Lectures upon Milton, who wrote a short Treatise upon Education, He Abandoned the Treatise of Milton to abuse the plan of Education Instituted by Lancaster, of which plan He spoke in Terms of the utmost Asperity.[4]

Being Ignorant of Lancaster's mode of Education I went along with the Lecturer and silently Approved. On the day, however, of the next Lecture He appeared much dejected; his voice assumed a more plaintive sound while he told us That his last had given great offence in speaking Truth. He cou'd hardly at Times refrain from Tears: long pauses sometimes Intervened—and he seemed as if He did not know well how to proceed.

I hastened to him immediately after the Lecture. He said that some of the proprietors of the Institution were much Displeased with his previous discourse; That Sir Henry Englefield had made an attack upon Him in company, without any preparation, and had said so many harsh Things, That He was obliged to Leave the room.[5] Great Expectations were raised for the Day of the next Lecture and a crowd attended; but He had sent a Letter to the secretary to Inform him That coming out a Boat the Day before He fell back and hurt his head, and the Continuance of the Pain obliged Him to defer his Lecture. A common personage would have been satisfied with this Information that He had convey'd to the Secretary; But Mr. Colleridge goes on in this manner (I read the Letter—and These are the very words):

'The pain however will soon subside, for it does not rise from so recent an Event as yesterday, but from a more distant period. It was when I was at Malta, Two years ago: a person rushed into my Apartment and abruptly announced to me the Death of a dear Friend, this occasioned my falling backwards and gave a contusion on my head which Brings back the pain occasionally upon any Exertion or Accident.'[6]

To continue the History of this Lecturer: He appeared among us again in about three weeks after [sic] — He looked sullen and told us that He previously had prepared and written down Quotations from different Authors to illustrate the present Lecture. These Quotations he had put among the Leaves of his Pocket Book which was stol'n as He was coming to the Institution.[7] This narrative was not indulgently received, and He went thro' his Lecture heavily and without advancing any Thing that was spirited and animated — The next Day He received an Intimation from the Managers that his Lectures were no longer Expected. —

I did not Think the royal Institution would have Taken up so much of my Paper —

(iii) JOSEPH FARINGTON
From The Farington Diary, V, 62. The entry for 16 May 1808.

Haydon[8] dined lately at Sir G. Beaumonts with *Coleridge* & *Wilkie* — Coleridge spoke of Dr. Johnson with little respect, said He had '*verbiage*' meaning words & little more; Lady Beaumont acknowledged she had been impressed with a high idea of Johnson but now thought differently. This Haydon told to Prince Hoare, — who estimated it duly. —

Prince Hoare attended one of Coleridge's Lectures at the Royal Institution. When Coleridge came into the Box there were several Books laying. He opened two or three of them silently and shut them again after a short inspection. He then paused, & leaned His head on His hand, and at last said, He had been thinking for a word to express the distinct character of Milton as a Poet, but not finding one that wd. express it, He should make one '*Ideality*.' He spoke extempore. —

NOTES

[1] And not only a lecturer himself, but the cause that lectures were in others. Aaron Burr suffered 'the weekly lecture' of Godwin's nine-year old son: 'having heard how Coleridge and others lectured, he would also lecture' (*The*

Private Journal of Aaron Burr, ed. Matthew L. Davis (2 vols.; N.Y., 1828), II, 307). The full text reveals that Burr heard STC himself lecturing, and found it 'a tissue of very flat attempts at wit' (quoted H&C, II, 207).

[2] S.C. Hall, later a fervent admirer (see below), was also disappointed:

> I attended one of his lectures at the Royal Institution, and I strive to recall him as he stood before his audience there. There was but little animation; his theme did not seem to stir him into life; the ordinary repose of his countenance was rarely broken up; he used little or no action; and his voice, though mellifluous, was monotonous. He lacked, indeed, that earnestness without which no man is truly eloquent. (S.C. Hall, *A Book of Memories of Great Men and Women of the Age, from Personal Acquaintance* (1871), 43)

[3] Peter Abelard (1079-1142), philosopher and famous teacher.

[4] STC found himself in the midst of a fierce dispute raging between the supporters of Andrew Bell (1753-1832), founder of the monitorial 'Madras-system' for teaching large classes, and those of Joseph Lancaster (1778-1838), whose alternative 'Lancastrian method' relied more upon punishment in a way that STC deplored. STC had written admiring letters to Bell (*CL*, III, 86-7; 88-9), and attacked Lancaster in his lecture on 3 May. A few days later, he was doorstepped by Lancaster and an intimidating sidekick (*CL*, III, 105).

[5] Englefield (1752-1822) was a power in the Royal Institution. STC complained to Bell about his attack (*CL*, III, 106-7).

[6] Griggs dates the letter 11 May 1808 (*CL*, III, 100). The 'dear Friend' must be John Wordsworth, whose death STC learnt of while on Malta (*CN*, II, 2517).

[7] De Quincey (20 June 1808) repeats the story; but De Quincey thought STC nevertheless 'managed to get through very well' (H.A. Page, *Thomas De Quincey: His Life and Writings* (2 vols.; 1877), I, 141).

[8] Benjamin Robert Haydon, for whom, see below.

The Friend: Back in the Lakes, 1808-10

(i) ROBERT SOUTHEY

From Selections from the Letters of Robert Southey, *ed. John Wood Warter (4 vols.; 1856), II, 16-17 (from a letter to his brother, 9 September 1808). Southey, now master of Greta Hall, regarded his brother-in-law with some exasperation.*

Coleridge is arrived at last, about half as big as the house. He came over with Wordsworth on Monday, and returned with him on Wednesday. His present scheme is to put the boys to school at Ambleside, and reside at Grasmere himself. Some good is likely to result from his coming, for Wordsworth declares that if he does not write an essay upon the pleasure produced by bad poetry, he will do it himself. You have heard him talk upon the subject; — whoever does this, the effect will be to flay —— alive[.]

(ii) ELIZA NEVINS

From Theodore Compton, 'Recollections of the Poet Coleridge', in the New Church Magazine CXVI *(1891) 356-60, 358-9. Compton repeats some memories of his mother, Eliza Nevins, who visited the Coleridges in 1808 (and quotes a letter sent to her by Coleridge: CL, III, 123-4).*

The young lady [...] had just completed her nineteenth year. She was a daughter of Mr. Pim Nevins, a member of the Society of Friends, and well known for his hospitality and benevolence. [...] Coleridge, hearing that Miss Eliza Nevins was about to visit some relations at Kendal, invited her to extend her visit to Keswick, where, at Greta Hall, the families of Coleridge and Southey and another sister, Mrs. Lovell, were living together. Coleridge himself was often from home, 'domesticated,' as his daughter says, with the Wordsworths at Grasmere. But they were all at home during my mother's visit at Greta Hall, and a merry household they were, as she used to describe them. Both Coleridge and Southey were full of fun, answering to Wordsworth's description of the former.

Noisy he was, and gamesome as a boy.[1]

But it was difficult to get him down to breakfast, and his ways justified Sir Humphrey [*sic*] Davy's opinion that 'Coleridge, with the most exalted genius, enlarged views, sensitive heart, and enlightened mind, will be the victim of want of order, precision, and regularity.' My mother used to imitate his intonation, as he recited, pacing up and down, his then unpublished poem of *Christabel* [...]

Coleridge accompanied Miss Nevins on her return to Kendal, introducing her, on the way, to the Wordsworths at Allan Bank, where she spent some days and was present at the christening of the little Catherine, to whom Coleridge stood god-father. The priest was deaf and did not notice the poet's response to his question, 'Dost thou believe, etc.?' but my mother heard him say, 'Part of it.' The naming of the child was not so easily got over. Coleridge's articulation was not very clear, and he pronounced the name Catherwine. 'Cataline!' said the priest: 'Catha-wine' repeated the poet. She was duly 'made a child of God;' and was taken to heaven in her infancy; an event alluded to in a letter from Wordsworth to Haydon the painter, sympathizing with him in a similar bereavement.[2]

(iii) CHARLES LLOYD

From Charles Lamb and the Lloyds, *ed. E.V. Lucas (1898), 240; 244. Lloyd was now living in the Lakes, near Ambleside. He renewed acquaintance; and was to remain a member of Coleridge's circle ('poor Charles Lloyd': CL, V, 446). These passages come from letters to his brother (late 1808, and 12 June 1809).*

Coleridge has made us several visits lately. We are very much interested with his society—indeed I can set no bounds to my astonishment at his talents. Coleridge is talking of publishing a weekly paper which he calls The Friend[3]—it is to resemble in its plan the Spectator, Guardian, &c.—The prospectus of the work is now printing at Kendal.—It is to treat of subjects moral, and in connection with taste and general literature—and indeed it is to extend to all topics except those of politics and religion.— [...]

Coleridge has such a lamentable want of voluntary power. If he is excited by a remark in company, he will pour forth, in an evening, without the least apparent effort, what would furnish matter for a hundred essays—but the moment that he is to write—not from present impulse but from pre-ordained deliberation—his powers fail him; and I believe that there are times when he could not pen the commonest notes. He is one of those minds who, except in inspired moods, can do nothing—and his inspirations are all *oral*, and not *scriptural*. And when he is inspired he surpasses, in my opinion, all that could be thought or imagined of a human being . . . . But I have more *fears* than *hopes* about this publication.

(iv) AGATHA LLOYD

From Charles Lamb and the Lloyds, *241-2. Agatha, Charles's sister, was staying in January 1809 when Coleridge visited, and wrote to her sister-in-law.*

Coleridge has been our guest since sixth day;[4] he intends going to Grasmere to-day. He is too interesting a man to live comfortably with a long time—he has very strong affections, but in his domestic habits I do not wonder at his being a very trying husband, unless his wife could be so entirely *absorbed* in his *mind* as not to think of the inconvenience of being put out of her way in every day occurences, which after all make up the great sum of our lives; and I believe little inattentions of that sort are and must be felt. He is truly a wonderful man—his powers of conversation and the richness and extent of his mind are indeed extraordinary, and I only wish, by a little more attention to *system* than to *impulse*, he were more calculated to shine as a domestic character. He has two interesting boys for whom he has a most fatherly affection. Hartley is a child to me *painfully* out of the common way both in *mind* and constitution—should he live, poor fellow, he will be a most interesting character, and I wish, as related his *parents*, he were in more happy circumstances. I have been going on without *appearing* to consider thee, but thou must excuse me. Southey was here for an hour on sixth day, and Wordsworth called; so the three northern poets were all here that day. This seems the land of genius[.]

(v) ROBERT SOUTHEY

From Selections from the Letters, *II, 188-90. A letter (29 January 1810) to Mary Barker, a friend of the Southeys and the Wordsworths (see* MY, *II, 133-4).*

I have, as you may suppose, had many things said to me concerning the 'Friend,' but nothing so much to the purpose as what you have remarked. It is not a little extraordinary that Coleridge, who is fond of logic, and who has an actual love and passion for close, hard thinking, should write in so rambling and inconclusive a manner; while I, who am utterly incapable of that toil of thought in which he delights, never fail to express myself perspicuously, and to the point. I owe, perhaps, something of this to the circumstance of having lived with him during that year in my life which was most likely to give my mind its lasting character. Disliking his inordinate love of talking, I was naturally led to avoid the same fault; when we were alone, and he talked his best (which was always at those times), I was pleased to listen; and when we were in company, and I heard the same things repeated,—repeated to every fresh company, seven times in the week if we were in seven parties,—still I was silent, in great measure from depression of spirits at perceiving those vices in his nature which soon appeared to be incurable. When he provoked me into an argument, I made the most of my time; and, as it was not easy to get in more than a few words, took care to make up in weight for what they wanted in measure. His habits have continued, and so have mine. Coleridge requested me to write him such a letter upon the faults of the 'Friend' as he might insert and reply to. I did so; but it was not inserted, and therefore I am sorry I did not copy it. It described the fault you have remarked as existing in Burke, and having prevented him from ever persuading anybody to his opinions,—for Burke made no proselytes except such as wanted an excuse for professing to change their party. You read his book, you saw what his opinions were; but they were given in such a way, evolving the causes of everything, and involving the consequences, that you never knew from whence he set out, nor where he was going. So it is with C.; he goes to work like a hound, nosing his way, turning, and twisting, and winding, and doubling, till you get weary with following the mazy movements. My way is, when I see my object, to dart at it like a greyhound.

Never was anything so grievously mismanaged as the 'Friend.' Because he would have all the profit (having taken it in his head that I was cheated by my publisher), he would publish for himself; thus has he the whole trouble of collecting his money, the whole responsibility, instead of having a publisher to look to; and the expense of postage will far, very far, exceed any publisher's percentage. Then he writes to the public about all his difficulties and his projects, as if they wanted to know anything about them,—not perceiving that this lowers him in the eyes of the foolish, and certainly does not raise him in the judgment of the wise. And certainly of all modes of publication that could be devised, nothing could be so ill adapted for such materials as a weekly form. Had he brought out these same papers in a body, either as a system, or as so many essays, they would have commanded more attention, he would have been saved the whole anxiety of periodical exertion, and people would have had no reason to complain because they found something altogether different from what they expected. However, we must be glad to get some part of what is in him out of him in any way. Satyrane is himself, though, if you are versed in Spenser, you will think the name marvellously inappropriate.[5]

(vi) SARA (FRICKER) COLERIDGE

From Minnow Among Tritons. Mrs. S.T. Coleridge's Letters to Thomas Poole 1799-1834, *ed. Stephen Potter (1934), 11-12. From a letter of 3 August 1810.*

S.T.C. has been here the last four or five months, and I am sorry to add that in all that time he has not *appeared* to be employed in composition, although he has repeatedly assured me he was. The latest N° of the 'Friend' lies on his Desk, the sight of which fills my heart with grief, and my Eyes with tears; but am obliged to conceal my trouble as much as possible, as the slightest expression of regret never fails to excite resentment—Poor Man!—I have not the least doubt but he is the most unhappy of the two; and the reason is too obvious to need any explanation. — It must, however, be confessed, he has been in almost uniform kind disposition towards us all his residence here; and all Southey's friends who have been here this Summer have thought his presence a great addition to the society here; and have all been uniformly great admirers of his conversation; his spirits too, are in general better than I have known them for years, and I cannot divine the reason of his passing his hours in so unprofitable [a] manner. Yet, I must not say that his abode here has been without some advantages to us, for as soon as he came, finding his daughter was desirous of learning Latin, which she had begun, he thought it a good opportunity of teaching both her and her Mother the Italian Language while he staid: I was rejoiced at this offer but was afraid he would not persevere, and I am convinced he would very often have put off the child, when he could not find an excuse to send us *both* away when our tasks were ready. —

(vii) FRANCIS JEFFREY

From the review of Biographia Literaria, Edinburgh Review *XXVIII (1817) 488-515, 509-10n.. Jeffrey, the editor, adds a lengthy footnote to the review of* Biographia, *disputing the book's allegations of double-handedness. Coleridge complained that Jeffrey perpetuated the idea of a 'Lake School' despite Coleridge's rebuttals; and, furthermore, that Jeffrey's antagonism towards 'Christabel' was hypocritical, as he had warmly praised it to Coleridge's face (BL, I, 50-2n.).*

It was in 1810, I think, that I went with some of my near relations to Cumberland. I had previously been in some correspondence of a literary nature with Mr. C., though I had never seen him personally. Mr. Southey I had seen in the company of some common friends, both at Edinburgh and Keswick, a year or two before; and though he then knew me to be the reviewer of his Thalaba and Madoc, he undoubtedly treated me with much courtesy and politeness.[6] I had heard, however, in the *interim*, that he had expressed himself on the subject of the Edinburgh Review with so 2much bitterness, that I certainly should not have thought of intruding myself spontaneously into his company. When I came to Keswick, I had not the least idea that Mr. C. lived in Mr. Southey's house; and sent a note from the inn, saying, I should be glad to wait on him. He returned for answer, that he *and Mr. Southey*, would be glad to see me. I thought it would be pitiful to decline this invitation; and went immediately. Mr. Southey received me with cold civility — and, being engaged with other visiters [*sic*], I had very little conversation with him. With Mr. C. I had a great deal; and was very much amused and interested. I believe coffee was offered me — and I came away in an hour or two. I did not see Mr. Southey afterwards. Next day, Mr. C. and I spent all the morning together in the fields, — he did me the honour to dine with me at the inn, — and next morning I left Keswick, and have not seen him since.

At this distance of time I do not pretend to recollect all that passed between us. I perfectly recollect, however, that I was much struck with the eloquence and poetical warmth of his conversation; of which all my friends can testify that I have ever since been in the habit of speaking with admiration.[7] I dare say I may have expressed that sentiment to him. Indeed, I remember, that when dissuading him from publishing on metaphysical subjects, I exhorted him rather to give us more poetry, and, upon his replying that it cost him more labour, I observed, that his whole talk to me that morning was poetry. I think I said also, that the verses entitled 'Love' were the best in the Lyrical Ballads, and had always appeared to me extremely beautiful. These are the only compliments I can remember paying him; and they were paid with perfect sincerity. But it rather appeared to me that Mr. C. liked to receive compliments; and I may have been led to gratify him in other instances. I cannot say I recollect of his telling me that he and his friends were of no school but that of good sense, &c.; but I remember perfectly that he complained a good deal of my coupling his name with theirs in the Review, saying, that he had published no verses for a long time, and that his own style was very unlike theirs. I promised that I would take his name out of the firm for the future; and I kept my promise. We spoke too of Christabel, and I advised him to publish it; but I did not say it was either the finest poem of the kind, or a fine poem at all; and I am sure of this, for the best of all reasons, that at this time, and indeed till after it was published, I never saw or heard more than four or five lines of it, which my friend Mr. Scott once repeated to me. That eminent person, indeed, spoke favourably of it; and I rather think I told Mr. C. that I had heard him say, that it was to it he was indebted for the first idea of that romantic narrative in irregular verse, which he afterwards exemplified in his Lay of the Last Minstrel, and other works.[8] In these circumstances, I felt a natural curiosity to see this great original; and I can sincerely say, that no admirer of Mr. C. could be more disappointed or astonished than I was, when it did make its appearance.

NOTES

[1] 'Stanzas Written in my Pocket Copy of Thomson's "Castle of Indolence"', l.47.

[2] Presumably *MY*, II, 361.

[3] STC's long-meditated plan for a weekly periodical finally emerged as *The Friend*, first published, from Grasmere, in 1809-10, and having as its declared ambition 'to uphold those Truths and those Merits, which are founded in the nobler and permanent Parts of our Nature' (*F*, II, 18).

[4] i.e. Friday: a Quaker usage.

[5] Satyrane appears in *The Faerie Queene*, I.vi.. STC adopted the title for a self-portrait in issue 14, interpreting it as 'Idoloclast, or breaker of Idols' (*F*, I, 185); 'You will grin at my *modest* account of Satyrane, the Idoloclast, in No.14', he wrote to Southey, 'but what can I do? — I must wear a mask' (*CL*, III, 261).

[6] Jeffrey wrote hostile reviews of *Thalaba* and of *Madoc* (*Edinburgh Review* I (1802), 63-83; and VII (1805), 1-28).

[7] Samuel Rogers wrote to Thomas Moore (21 October 1810):

> Jeffrey has been lately in town, though I missed him. In his way hither he stopped at Keswick, and saw Southey and Coleridge. He seems to have been dazzled by the rhetoric of Coleridge, whom he had never met before. (*Memoirs, Journal, and Correspondence of Thomas Moore*, ed. Lord John Russell (8 vols.; 1853-6), VIII, 89).

[8] Scott's metrical romance, *The Lay of the Last Minstrel* (1805).

London Life, 1810-13

Coleridge returned to London in late October 1810, in the company of Basil Montagu.[1] Just after arriving, Montagu tactlessly repeated what he claimed was Wordsworth's verdict on his old friend — that 'he had no Hope of me!' (*CN*, III, 3991): Coleridge was privately distraught (*CN*, III, 3991-7); but threw himself into London literary life.

(i) HENRY CRABB ROBINSON

From Diary, Reminiscences, and Correspondence of Henry Crabb Robinson, *ed. Thomas Sadler (3 vols.; 1869), I, 304-5; 306; 307-8; 309; 310; 312; 324-5; 333; 369-70. Crabb Robinson (1775-1867), a barrister, man of letters, and Germanist, as well as a dedicated follower of London literary life, was later to prove instrumental in smoothing relations between the poets. He first met*

Coleridge in late 1810; by his accounts, Coleridge's performance was apparently unimpaired by the recent shock of the Montagu debacle.

Nov. 14th. – Saw Coleridge for the first time in private, at Charles Lamb's. A short interview, which allowed of little opportunity for the display of his peculiar powers.

He related to us that Jeffrey, the editor of the *Edinburgh Review*, had lately called on him, and assured him that he was a great admirer of Wordsworth's poetry, that the Lyrical Ballads were always on his table, and that Wordsworth had been attacked in the *Review* simply because the errors of men of genius ought to be exposed. Towards me, Coleridge added, Jeffrey was even flattering. He was like a schoolboy, who, having tried his man and been thrashed, becomes contentedly a fag.

Nov. 15th. – A very delightful evening at Charles Lamb's; Coleridge, Morgan, Mr. Burney,[2] &c., there. Coleridge very eloquent on German metaphysics and poetry, Wordsworth, and Spanish politics.

Of Wordsworth he spoke with great warmth of praise, but objected to some of his poems. Wishing to avoid an undue regard to the high and genteel in society, Wordsworth had unreasonably attached himself to the low, so that he himself erred at last. He should have recollected that verse being the language of passion, and passion dictating energetic expressions, it became him to make his subjects and style accord. One asks why tales so simple were not in prose. With 'malice prepense' he fixes on objects of reflection, which do not naturally excite it. Coleridge censured the disproportion in the machinery of the poem on the Gipsies. Had the whole world been standing idle, more powerful arguments to expose the evil could not have been brought forward.[3] Of Kant he spoke in terms of high admiration. In his 'Himmel's System' he appeared to unite the genius of Burnet and Newton. He praised the 'Träume eines Geistersehers,' and intimated that he should one day translate the work on the Sublime and Beautiful. The 'Kritik der Urtheilskraft' he considered the most astonishing of Kant's works.[4] Both Fichte and Schelling he thought would be found at last to have erred where they deviated from Kant; but he considered Fichte a great logician, and Schelling perhaps a still greater man. In both he thought the want of gratitude towards their master a sign of the absence of the highest excellence.

Schelling's system resolves itself into fanaticism, not better than that of Jacob Boehme.[5] [...]

He made an elaborate distinction between fancy and imagination.[6] The excess of fancy is delirium, of imagination mania. Fancy is the arbitrarily bringing together of things that lie remote, and forming them into a unity. The materials lie ready for the fancy, which acts by a sort of juxtaposition. On the other hand, the imagination under excitement generates and produces a form of its own. The 'seas of milk and ships of amber' he quoted as fanciful delirium.[7] He related, as a sort of disease of imagination, what occurred to himself. He had been watching intently the motions of a kite among the mountains of Westmoreland, when on a sudden he saw two kites in an opposite direction. This delusion lasted some time. At last he discovered that the two kites were the fluttering branches of a tree beyond a wall. [...]

Dec 20th. – Met Coleridge by accident with Charles and Mary Lamb. As I entered he was apparently speaking of Christianity. He went on to say that miracles are not an essential in the Christian system. He insisted that they were not brought forward *as* proofs; that they were acknowledged to have been performed by others as well as the true believers. Pharaoh's magicians wrought miracles, though those of Moses were more powerful. In the New Testament, the appeal is made to the knowledge which the believer has of the truths of his religion, not to the wonders wrought to make him believe. Of Jesus Christ he asserted that he was a Platonic philosopher. And when Christ spoke of his identity with the Father, he spoke in a Spinozistic or Pantheistic sense, according to which he could truly say that his transcendental sense was *one* with God, while his empirical sense retained its finite nature. On my making the remark that in a certain sense every one who utters a truth may be said to be inspired, Coleridge assented, and afterwards named Fox and others among the Quakers, Madame Guyon, St. Theresa, &c., as being also inspired. [...]

Dec. 23rd. – Coleridge dined with the Colliers, talked a vast deal, and delighted every one. Politics, Kantian philosophy, and Shakespeare successively – and at last a playful exposure of some bad poets. His remarks on Shakespeare were singularly ingenious. Shakespeare, he said, delighted in portraying characters in which the intellectual powers are found in a pre-eminent degree, while the moral faculties are wanting, at the same time that he taught the superiority of moral greatness. [...]

Hamlet he considered in a point of view which seems to agree very well with the representation given in 'Wilhelm Meister'.[8] Hamlet is a man whose ideal and internal images are so vivid that all real objects are faint and dead to him. This we see in his soliloquies on the nature of man and his disregard of life: hence also his vacillation, and the purely convulsive energies he displayed. He acts only by fits and snatches. He manifests a strong inclination to suicide. On my observing that it appeared strange Shakespeare did not make suicide the termination to his piece, Coleridge replied that Shakespeare wished to show how even such a character is at last obliged to be the sport of chance—a salutary moral doctrine. [...]

In the course of his metaphysical conversation, Coleridge remarked on Hartley's theory of association. This doctrine is as old as Aristotle, and Hartley himself, after publishing his system, when he wrote his second volume on religion, built his proofs, not on the maxims of his first volume, which he had already learnt to appreciate better, but on the principles of other schools. Coleridge quoted (I forget from whom) a description of association as the 'law of our imagination.' Thought, he observed, is a laborious breaking though the law of association; the natural train of fancy is violently repressed; the free yielding to its power produces dreaming or delirium. The great absurdity committed by those who would build everything on association is that they forget the things associated: these are left out of the account. [...]

March 30th. [1811] – At C. Lamb's. Found Coleridge and Hazlitt there, and had a half-hour's chat. Coleridge spoke feelingly of Godwin and the unjust treatment he had met with. [...] Coleridge used strong language against those who were once the extravagant admirers of Godwin, and afterwards became his most bitter opponents. [...] Coleridge said there was more in Godwin, after all, than he was once willing to admit, though not so much as his enthusiastic admirers fancied. He had openly opposed him, but nevertheless visited him. Southey's severity he attributed to the habit of reviewing. Southey had said of Coleridge's poetry that he was a Dutch imitator of the Germans.[9] Coleridge quoted this, not to express any displeasure at it, but to show in what way Southey could speak of him. [...]

Later in the year, they encounter one another at the Royal Academy exhibition.

June 6th. – Met Coleridge at the Exhibition. He drew my attention to the 'vigorous impotence' of Fuseli, especially in his 'Macbeth'. 'The prominent witch,' said Coleridge, 'is smelling a stink.' He spoke of painting as one of the lost arts. [...]

Jan. 17th [1812]. – [...] Coleridge was less profound than usual, but exceedingly agreeable. He related anecdotes of himself. Once he was arrested as a spy at Fort St. George.[10] The Governor, as soon as he saw him, muttered, 'an ill-looking fellow.' At first everything that Coleridge could say for himself was ingeniously perverted and applied against him; but at length a card he accidentally had by him, from a person of quality, convinced the Governor that he was a gentleman, and procured for him an invitation to breakfast next morning. Coleridge then took an opportunity of asking the Governor what it was in his appearance that induced him to say 'an ill-looking fellow.' 'My dear sir,' said the Governor, squeezing him by the hand, 'I nearly lost my sight in the West Indies, and cannot see a yard before me.' At Bristol, Coleridge delivered lectures in conjunction with Southey. A fellow who was present hissed him, and an altercation ensued. The man sneered at him for professing public principle, and asked, 'Why, if you have so much public spirit, do you take money at the door?' – 'For a reason,' said Coleridge, 'which I am sorry in the present instance has not been quite successful – to keep out blackguards.' In reference to the schools of Lancaster and Bell – a delicate subject in such a society – Coleridge contented himself with urging that it is unsafe to leave religion untaught while *anything* is taught. Reading and writing must not be supposed to be in themselves education.

(ii) LADY JERNINGHAM

From The Jerningham Letters, *II, 7-8. Lady Jerningham's letter, 16 March 1811.*

On Sunday I made a different sort of a new acquaintance. Miss Betham,[11] at my desire, invited Mr. Coleridge to dine with me. He Came and displayed a superabundance of words; and, tho Certainly Clever, I think His ideas Lack behind, which makes Him in the space of an Hour give several Contradictory opinions. He deemed Himself obliged to Play first Violin, and was much fatigued with the violent exertion He made, as He Communicates to Miss Betham in a most extraordinary epistle. Miss Lamb is, it seems, again out of Her Head, and Mr. Coleridge says (at the end of a Long excuse to Miss Betham for not Coming to Her):

'I had just time to have half an hours mournful Conversation with Charles Lamb. He displayed such fortitude in His manner, and such a ravage of mental Suffering in His Countenance, that I walked off, my Head throbbing with Long weeping. And the Haste I made, in the fear of being too Late on Sunday and the having to act before the Curtain, as it were, afterwards—for the more I force my attention from any inward distress, the worse it becomes after, and what I keep out of my mind or rather *keep down* in a state of under Consciousness, is sure to act meanwhile with its whole power of Poise on my Body—this is the History of my Breach of Engagement, my dear Miss B., of its Cause and of the occasions of that Cause.'[12]

This is the end of a Letter she has sent me, three previous sides are a detail of the illness He was taken with, after the fatigue of his Presentation here, and from its finding Him under the pressure of that original uneasiness. I am afraid he will go out of his head also. You will think, my dear, that I am going out of mine. But I thought these details might amuse you.

(iii) SIR JOHN TAYLOR COLERIDGE

From Specimens of the Table Talk of the late Samuel Taylor Coleridge *(2 vols.; 1835), II, 343-57. In April 1811, Coleridge visited John May, a wine merchant and friend of Southey's living in Richmond, where, on 20 April 1811, he met his nephews, sons of his brother James: Henry Nelson Coleridge (1798-1843), later to marry Coleridge's daughter Sara and to edit several of his works (including* Table Talk*), and John Taylor Coleridge (1790-1876), later a lawyer and biographer of Keble, and presently a dazzling undergraduate at Corpus Christi, Oxford. 'He spent two days at Richmond,' John wrote to another brother, James, 'and so delightful and astonishing a man I have never met with. [...] When he saw us first he was affected distressingly, and through the whole time he was affectionate in the highest degree. He made a conquest of all the men and women at Richmond, gave us analyses of long works which are to come out, recited songs and odes of his own, told stories of his youth and travels, never sparing himself at all, and altogether made the most powerful impression on my mind of any man I ever saw. Yet I saw and heard some things which I did not quite like.'[13]*

We got on politics, and he related some curious facts of the Prince and Perceval.[14] Then, adverting to the present state of affairs in Portugal, he said that he rejoiced not so much in the mere favourable turn, as in the end that must now be put to the base reign of opinion respecting the superiority and invincible skill of the French generals. Brave as Sir John Moore was, he thought him deficient in that greater and more essential manliness of soul which should have made him not hold his enemy in such fearful respect, and which should have taught him to care less for the opinion of the world at home.[15]

We then got, I know not how, to German topics. He said that the language of their literature was entirely factitious, and had been formed by Luther from the two dialects, High and Low German; that he had made it, grammatically, most correct, more so, perhaps, than any other language: it was equal to the Greek, except in harmony and sweetness. And yet the Germans themselves thought it sweet;—Klopstock had repeated to him an ode of his own to prove it, and really had deceived himself, by the force of the association, into a belief that the harsh sounds, conveying, indeed, or being significant of, sweet images or thoughts, were themselves sweet. Mr. C. was asked what he thought of Klopstock. He answered, that his fame was rapidly declining in Germany; that an Englishman might form a correct notion of him by uniting the moral epigram of Young, the bombast of Hervey, and the minute description of Richardson. As to sublimity, he had, with all Germans, one rule for producing it;—it was, to take something very great, and make it very small in comparison with that which you wish to elevate. Thus, for example, Klopstock says,—'As the gardener goes forth, and scatters from his basket seed into the garden; so does the Creator scatter worlds with his right hand.'[16] Here *worlds*, a large object, are made small in the hands of the Creator; consequently, the Creator is very great. In short, the Germans were not a poetical nation in the very highest sense. Wieland was their best poet: his subject was bad, and his thoughts often impure;[17] but his language was rich and harmonious, and his fancy luxuriant. Sotheby's translation had not at all caught the manner of the original. But the Germans were good metaphysicians and critics: they criticized on principles previously laid down; thus, though they might be wrong, they were in no danger of being self-contradictory, which was too often the case with English critics.

Young, he said, was not a poet to be read through at once.[18] His love of point and wit had often put an end to his pathos and sublimity; but there were parts in him which must be immortal. He (Mr. C.) loved to read a page of Young, and walk out to think of him.

Returning to the Germans, he said that the state of their religion, when he was in Germany, was really shocking. He had never met one clergyman a Christian; and he found professors in the universities lecturing against the most material points in the Gospel. He instanced, I think, Paulus, whose lectures he had attended. The object was to resolve the miracles into natural operations; and such a disposition evinced was the best road to preferment. He severely censured Mr. Taylor's book, in which the principles of Paulus were explained and insisted on with much gratuitous indelicacy.[19] He then entered into the question of Socinianism, and noticed, as I recollect, the passage in the Old Testament; 'The people bowed their faces, and *worshipped* God and the king.'[20] He said, that all worship implied the presence of the object worshipped: the people worshipped, bowing to the sensuous presence of the one, and the conceived omnipresence of the other. He talked of his having constantly to defend the Church against the Socinian Bishop of Llandaff, Watson.[21] The subject then varied to Roman Catholicism, and he gave us an account of a controversy he had had with a very sensible priest in Sicily on the worship of saints. He had driven the priest from one post to another, till the latter took up the ground, that, though the saints were not omnipresent, yet God, who was so, imparted to them the prayers offered up, and then they used their interference with Him to grant them. 'That is, father, (said C. in reply), — excuse my seeming levity, for I mean no impiety — that is; I have a deaf and dumb wife, who yet understands me, and I her, by signs. You have a favour to ask of me, and want my wife's interference; so you communicate your request to me, who impart it to her, and she, by signs back again, begs me to grant it.' The good priest laughed, and said, '*Populus vult decipi, et decipiatur!*'[22]

We then got upon the Oxford controversy, and he was decidedly of opinion that there could be no doubt of Copleston's complete victory.[23] He thought the Review had chosen its points of attack ill, as there must doubtless be in every institution so old much to reprehend and carp at. On the other hand, he thought that Copleston had not been so severe or hard upon them as he might have been; but he admired the critical part of his work, which he thought very highly valuable, independently of the controversy. He wished some portion of mathematics was more essential to a degree at Oxford, as he thought a gentleman's education incomplete without it, and had himself found the necessity of getting up a little, when he could ill spare the time. He every day more and more lamented his neglect of them when at Cambridge.

Then glancing off to Aristotle, he gave a very high character of him. He said that Bacon objected to Aristotle the grossness of his examples, and Davy now did precisely the same to Bacon: both were wrong; for each of those philosophers wished to confine the attention of the mind in their works to the *form* of reasoning only by which other truths might be established or elicited, and therefore the most trite and common-place examples were in fact the best. He said that during a long confinement to his room, he had taken up the Schoolmen, and was astonished at the immense and acute knowledge displayed by them; that there was scarcely any thing which modern philosophers had proudly brought forward as their own, which might not be found clearly and systematically laid down by them in some or other of their writings. Locke had sneered at the Schoolmen unfairly, and had raised a foolish laugh against them by citations from their *Quid libet* questions, which were discussed on the eves of holidays, and in which the greatest latitude was allowed, being considered mere exercises of ingenuity. We had ridiculed their *quiddities*, and why? Had we not borrowed their *quantity* and their *quality*, and why then reject their *quiddity*, when every schoolboy in logic must know, that of every thing may be asked, *Quantum est? Quale est?* and *Quid est?* the last bringing you to the most material of all points, its individual being. He afterwards stated, that in a History of Speculative Philosophy which he was endeavouring to prepare for publication, he had proved, and to the satisfaction of Sir James Mackintosh, that there was nothing in Locke which his best admirers most admired, that might not be found more clearly and better laid down in Descartes or the old Schoolmen; not that he was himself an implicit disciple of Descartes, though he thought that Descartes had been much misinterpreted.

When we got on the subject of poetry and Southey, he gave us a critique of the Curse of Kehama,[24] the fault of which he thought consisted in the association of a plot and a machinery so very wild with feelings so sober and tender: but he gave the poem high commendation, admired the art displayed in the employment of the Hindu monstrosities, and begged us to observe the noble feeling excited of the superiority of virtue over vice; that Kehama went on, from the beginning to the end of the poem, increasing in power, whilst Kailyal gradually lost her hopes and her protectors; and yet by the time we got to the end, we had arrived at an utter contempt and even carelessness of the power of evil, as exemplified in the almighty Rajah, and felt a complete confidence in the safety of the unprotected virtue of the maiden. This he thought the very great merit of the poem.

When we walked home with him to the inn, he got on the subject of the Latin Essay for the year at Oxford,[25] and thought some consideration of the corruption of language should be introduced into it. It originated, he thought, in a desire to abbreviate all expression as much as possible; and no doubt, if in one word, without violating idiom, I can express what others have done in more, and yet be as fully and easily understood, I have manifestly made an improvement; but if, on the other hand, it becomes harder, and takes more time to comprehend a thought or image put in one word by Apuleius than when expressed in a whole sentence by Cicero, the saving is merely of pen and ink, and the alteration is evidently a corruption. [...]

Before breakfast we went into Mr. May's delightful book-room, where he was again silent in admiration of the prospect. After breakfast, we walked to church. He seemed full of calm piety, and said he always felt the most delightful sensations in a Sunday church-yard, — that it struck him as if God had given to man fifty-two springs in every year. After the service, he was vehement against the sermon, as common-place, and invidious in its tone towards the poor. Then he gave many texts from the lessons and gospel of the day, as affording fit subjects for discourses. He ridiculed the absurdity of refusing to believe every thing that you could not understand; and mentioned a rebuke of Dr. Parr's[26] to a man of the name of Frith, and that of another clergyman to a young man, who said he would believe nothing which he could not understand: — 'Then, young man, your creed will be the shortest of any man's I know.'

As we walked up Mr. Cambridge's meadows towards Twickenham, he criticized Johnson and Gray as poets, and did not seem to allow them high merit. The excellence of verse, he said, was to be untranslatable into any other words without detriment to the beauty of the passage;[27] — the position of a single word could not be altered in Milton without injury. Gray's personifications, he said, were mere printer's devils' personifications — persons with a capital letter, abstract qualities with a small one. He thought Collins had more genius than Gray, who was a singular instance of a man of taste, poetic feeling, and fancy, without imagination. He contrasted Dryden's opening of the 10th satire of Juvenal with Johnson's: —

> 'Let observation, with extensive view,
> Survey mankind from Ganges to Peru.'[28]

which was as much as to say, —

> 'Let observation with extensive observation observe mankind.'

After dinner he told us a humorous story of his enthusiastic fondness for Quakerism, when he was at Cambridge, and his attending one of their meetings, which had entirely cured him. When the little children came in, he was in raptures with them, and descanted upon the delightful mode of treating them now, in comparison with what he had experienced in childhood. He lamented the haughtiness with which Englishmen treated all foreigners abroad, and the facility with which our government had always given up any people which had allied itself to us, at the end of a war; and he particularly remarked upon our abandonment of Minorca.[29] These two things, he said, made us universally disliked on the Continent; though, as a people, most highly respected. He thought a war with America inevitable; and expressed his opinion, that the United States were unfortunate in the prematureness of their separation from this country, before they had in themselves the materials of moral society — before they had a gentry and a learned class, — the former looking backwards, and giving the sense of stability — the latter looking forwards, and regulating the feelings of the people.

Afterwards, in the drawing-room, he sat down by Professor Rigaud,[30] with whom he entered into a discussion of Kant's System of Metaphysics. The little knots of the company were speedily silent: Mr. C.'s voice grew louder; and abstruse as the subject was, yet his language was so ready, so energetic, and so eloquent, and his illustrations so very neat and apposite, that the ladies even paid him the most solicitous and respectful attention. They were really entertained with Kant's Metaphysics! At last I took one of them, a very sweet singer, to the piano-forte; and, when there was a pause, she began an Italian air. She was anxious to please him, and he was enraptured. His frame quivered with emotion, and there was a titter of uncommon delight on his countenance. When it was over, he praised the singer warmly, and prayed she might finish those strains in heaven!

This is nearly all, excepting some anecdotes, which I recollect of our meeting with this most interesting, most wonderful man. Some of his topics and arguments I have enumerated; but the connection and the words are lost. And nothing that I can say can give any notion of his eloquence and manner, — of the hold which he soon got on his audience — of the variety of his stores of information — or, finally, of the artlessness of his habits, or the modesty and temper with which he listened to, and answered arguments, contradictory to his own.

(iv) JOHN PAYNE COLLIER

From Seven Lectures on Shakespeare and Milton by the late S.T. Coleridge *(1856), xiv-xv; xx-xxii; xxvi-xxvii; xxxvi; xxxviii-xxxix; liv, n.. John Payne Collier (1789-1883), Shakespearean critic and editor, took shorthand notes of Coleridge's 1811-12 lectures.[31] He first met Coleridge in the autumn of 1811.*

Sunday, 13th Oct. — [...] Two or three months ago I was in Coleridge's company for the first time: I have seen him on various occasions since, to my great delight and surprise. I was delighted with his gentle manners and unaffected good humour, and especially with his kindness and considerateness for young people:[32] I was surprised by the variety and extent of his knowledge, displayed and enlivened by so much natural eloquence. All he says is without effort, but not unfrequently with a sort of musical hum, and a catching of his breath at the end, and sometimes in the middle, of a sentence, enough to make a slight pause, but not so much as to interrupt the flow of his language. He never disdains to talk on the most familiar topics, if they seem pleasing to others. [...]

Thursday, 17th Oct. — Yesterday, at Lamb's, I met Coleridge again. I expected to see him there, and I made up my mind that I would remember as much as possible of what he said. I went into the apartment, where he and others were assembled, at 8, and before 9 my recollection was so burdened that I was obliged to leave the room for some time, that I might lighten the weight. However, I could not prevail upon myself to stay away long, and returned to the company with a resolution to take the matter more easily. Few others talked, although Hazlitt, Lloyd, Rickman,[33] Dyer, and Burney, with Lamb and his sister, now and then interposed a remark, and gave Coleridge, as it were, a bottom to spin upon: they all seemed disposed to allow him sea-room enough, and he availed himself of it, and, spreading canvas, sailed away majestically. The following is the bare skeleton, and mere bone of what fell from him. He was speaking of Shakespeare when I entered the room:

'He said that Shakespeare was almost the only dramatic poet, who by his characters represented a class, and not an individual: other writers for the stage, and in other respects good ones too, had aimed their satire and ridicule at particular foibles and particular persons, while Shakespeare at one stroke lashed thousands: Shakespeare struck at a crowd; Jonson picked out an especial object for his attack. Coleridge drew a parallel between Shakespeare and a geometrician: the latter, when tracing a circle, had his eye upon the centre as the important point, but included also in his vision a wide circumference; so Shakespeare, while his eye rested upon an individual character, always embraced a wide circumference of others, without diminishing the separate interest he intended to attach to the being he pourtrayed. Othello was a personage of this description; but all Shakespeare's chief characters possessed, in a greater or less degree, this claim to our admiration. He was not a mere painter of portraits, with the dress, features, and peculiarities of the sitter; but a painter of likenesses so true that, although nobody could perhaps say they knew the very person represented, all saw at once that it was faithful, and that it must be a likeness. [...]

'The conversation (my Diary continues) then turned upon Walter Scott, whose 'Lady of the Lake' has recently been published, and I own that there appeared on the part of Coleridge some disposition, if not to disparage, at least not to recognise the merits of Scott. He professed himself comparatively ignorant of Scott's productions, and stated that 'The Lady of the Lake' had been lying upon his table for more than a month, and that he had only been able to get through two divisions of the poem, and had there found many grammatical blunders, and expressions that were not English on this side of the Tweed—nor, indeed, on the other. If (added he) I were called upon to form an opinion of Mr. Scott's poetry, the first thing I should do would be to take away all his names of old castles, which rhyme very prettily, and read very picturesquely; then, I would remove out of the poem all the old armour and weapons; next I would exclude the mention of all nunneries, abbeys, and priories, and I should then see what would be the residuum—how much poetry would remain. At present, having read so little of what he has produced, I can form no competent opinion; but I should then be able to ascertain what was the story or fable (for which I give him full credit, because, I dare say, it is very interesting), what degree of imagination was displayed in narrating it, and how far he was to be admired for propriety and felicity of expression. Of these, at present, others must judge, but I would rather have written one simile by Burns,

> Like snow that falls upon a river,
> A moment white, then gone for ever—[34]

than all the poetry that his countryman Scott—as far as I am yet able to form an estimate—is likely to produce.' [...]

My next note with a date is the 1st November [...] Again I saw Coleridge, and again I was an attentive listener. He once more quoted his favourite simile from Burns, in order to establish the position, that one of the purposes and tests of true poetry was the employment of common objects in uncommon ways—the felicitous and novel uses of images of daily occurrence. Everybody had seen snow falling upon a river, and vanishing instantly, but who had applied this result of ordinary experience with such novelty and beauty? My note goes on thus, under the date of—

1st November.—'Shakespeare,' said Coleridge, 'is full of these familiar images and illustrations: Milton has them too, but they do not occur so frequently, because his subject does not so naturally call for them. He is the truest poet who can apply to a new purpose the oldest occurrences, and most usual appearances: the justice of the images can then always be felt and appreciated.' [...]

'"For my part (said Coleridge) I freely own that I have no title to the name of a poet, according to my own definition of poetry. (He did not state his definition.) Many years ago a small volume of verses came out with my name: it was not my doing, but Cottle offered me £20, when I much wanted it, for some short pieces I had written at Cambridge, and I sold the manuscripts to him, but I declare that I had no notion, at the time, that they were meant for publication; my poverty, and not my will, consented. Cottle paid my poverty, and I was dubbed poet, almost before I knew whether I was in Bristol or in London. I met people in the streets who congratulated me upon being a poet, and that was the first notice I had of my new rank and dignity. I was to have had £20 for what Cottle bought, but I never received more than £15, and for this paltry sum I was styled poet by the reviewers, who fell foul of me for what they termed my bombast and buckram. Nevertheless, 500 copies were sold, and a new edition being called for, I pleaded guilty to the charge of inflation and grandiloquence. But now, only see the contrast! Wordsworth has printed two poems of mine,[35] but without my name, and again the reviewers have laid their claws upon me, and for what? Not for bombast and buckram—not for inflation and grandiloquence, but for mock simplicity; and now I am put down as the master of a school for the instruction of grown children in nursery rhymes."'

A reminiscence of Coleridge's face when he was in full spate.

I always thought his mouth beautiful: the lips were full, and a little drawn down at the corners, and when he was speaking the attention (at least my attention) was quite as much directed to his mouth as to his eyes, the expression of it was so eloquent. In the energy of talking, 'the rose-leaves' were at times 'a little bedewed,' but his words seemed to flow the easier for the additional lubricity. I did not especially admire Coleridge's 'large grey eyes,' for, now and then, they assumed a dead, dull look, almost as if he were not seeing out of them; and I doubt if external objects made much impression upon his sight, when he was animated in discourse.

(v) SARA (FRICKER) COLERIDGE

From Minnow Among Tritons, *17 (a letter of 30 October 1812). Coleridge paid a flying visit north in early 1812; he did not call on the Wordsworths.*

When C. was here in Febr[uar]y he was cheerful & good natured & full of fair promises—he talked of our setling [sic] finally in London, that is, when he had gone on for a year or so giving me, and all his friends satisfaction as to the possibility of making a livelihood by his writings so as to enable us to live in great credit there—I listened, I own, with incredulous ears, while he was building these 'airy castles' and calmly told him that I thought it was much better that I and the children should remain in the country until the Boys had finished their School-education and then, if he found himself in circumstances that would admit of it, & would engage not to leave us all alone in that wide city, I would cheerfully take leave of *dear Keswick*, and follow his amended fortunes; he agreed to this, & in the meantime, a regular correspondence *was* to be kept up between himself, and me, and the children; and *never more* was he to keep a letter of mine, or the Boys', or Southey's *un*opened—his promises, poor fellow, are like his Castles,—airy nothings!

(vi) LADY BEAUMONT

From the Farington Diary, *VII, 164. The entry for 1 April 1813.*

Lady Beaumont gave me an account of an interview which Coleridge, the Poet, had with Mr. Samuel Whitbread[36] previous to the bringing forward of Coleridge's play which was acted last winter. Mr. Whitbread appointed that Coleridge shd. call upon him at half past 8 oClock in the morning, and received the Poet while He was shaving in order to save time to both. Whitbread talked of dramatick poetry & as Coleridge said very foolishly, and after sometime by a motion of his hand signified that Coleridge might depart, which He did much disatisfied [*sic*] with the hauteur and self importance of Whitbread.[37]

(vii) CHARLES ROBERT LESLIE

From Autobiographical Recollections (2 *vols.;* 1860), *I, 33-5; 50-1. Leslie (1794-1859), friend of Allston and Constable (of whom he wrote a memoir), was himself a successful illustrator and painter, especially of literary — and particularly Shakespearean — subjects. This encounter with Coleridge was in 1813.*

I think it was during the second year of my residence in London that Allston's health became seriously affected; and, as change of air was recommended, he determined to visit Bristol, where he had an uncle living, who hearing of his state had advised him to try the air of Clifton. Mr. and Mrs. Allston left London, accompanied by Morse and myself; but, when we reached Salt Hill, Allston became too ill to proceed, and it was determined that Morse should return to town and acquaint Coleridge with the circumstance. He was affectionately attached to Allston, and came to Salt Hill the same afternoon, accompanied by his friend Dr. Tathill. He stayed at the Inn for the few days that Allston was confined there. The house was so full that the poet was obliged to share a double-bedded room with me. We were kept up late in consequence of the critical condition of Allston, and, when we retired, Coleridge seeing a copy of 'Knickerbocker's History of New York'[38] (which I had brought with me) lying on the table, took it up and began reading. I went to bed, and I think he must have sate up the greater part of the night, for the next day I found he had nearly got through Knickerbocker. This was many years before it was published in England, and the work was of course entirely new to him. He was delighted with it.

I had seen Coleridge before, but it was on this occasion that my acquaintance commenced with this most extraordinary man, of whom it might be said as truly as of Burke, that 'his stream of mind was perpetual.' His eloquence threw a new and beautiful light on most subjects, and when he was beyond my comprehension, the melody of his voice, and the impressiveness of his manner held me a willing listener, and I was flattered at being supposed capable of understanding him. Indeed, men far advanced beyond myself in education might have felt as children in his presence.

Luckily for me he could not help talking, be he where or with whom he might, and I shall ever regret that I did not take notes, imperfect as they must have been, of what he said. I can only now remember, that besides speaking much of Allston, whom he loved dearly, he gave an admirable analysis of the character of Don Quixote. He said, 'there are two kinds of madness; in the one, the object pursued is a sane one, the madness discovering itself only in the means by which it is to be gained. In the other, an insane intention is aimed at or compassed by means that the soundest mind would employ, as in cases of murder, suicide, &c.[.] The madness of Don Quixote is of the first class, his intention being always to do good, and his delusion only as to the mode of accomplishing his object.'

It was said of Coleridge by one who knew him intimately, and was indeed one of his most active friends, that 'he was a good man, but whenever anything presented itself to him in the shape of a moral duty he was utterly incapable of performing it.' He had, no doubt, great faults and weaknesses, but this was unquestionably a sweeping exaggeration, uttered perhaps in a moment of irritation. At Salt Hill, and on some other occasions, I witnessed his performance of the duties of friendship in a manner which few men of his constitutional indolence could have roused themselves to equal. [...]

Coleridge's want of success in all worldly matters may be attributed to the mastery possessed over him by his own wonderful mind. Common men as often succeed by the qualities they want, as great men fail by those they have. Coleridge could not direct his extraordinary powers to the immediately useful occupations of life, or to those exercises of them likely to procure him bread, unless he was perpetually urged on by some kind friend. The tragedy of 'Remorse' was written whilst he lived with Mr. Morgan, and I believe would never have been completed but for the importunities of Mrs. Morgan.[39] A few days after the appearance of his piece, he was sitting in the coffee-room of a hotel, and heard his name coupled with a coroner's inquest, by a gentleman who was reading a newspaper to a friend. He asked to see the paper, which was handed to him with the remark that, 'It was very extraordinary that Coleridge, the poet, should have hanged himself just after the success of his play; but he was always a strange mad fellow.' 'Indeed, sir,' said Coleridge, 'it is a *most extraordinary* thing that he should have hanged himself, be the subject of an inquest, and yet that he should at this moment be speaking to you.' The astonished stranger hoped he had 'said nothing to hurt his feelings,' and was made easy on that point. The newspaper related that a gentleman in black had been cut down from a tree in Hyde Park, without money or papers in his pockets, his shirt being marked 'S.T. Coleridge;' and Coleridge was at no loss to understand how this might have happened, since he seldom travelled without losing a shirt or two.

(viii) MADAME DE STAËL

From Crabb Robinson, Diary, I, 313-14. Madame de Staël (1766-1817), author of Corinne (1807) and On Germany (1810), presided over a celebrated salon. Her comment is probably the single most famous assessment of Coleridge's style of talking, and it recurs throughout the history of Coleridgean memoir. Crabb Robinson mentions it in the course of re-assessing his own earlier opinion.

[']Though an incomparable declaimer and speech-maker, he has neither the readiness nor the acuteness required by a colloquial disputant; so that, with a sense of inferiority which makes me feel humble in his presence, I do not feel in the least afraid of him. Rough said yesterday, that he is sure Coleridge would never have succeeded at the Bar even as a speaker.'

This I wrote when I knew little of him; I used afterwards to compare him as a disputant to a serpent—easy to kill, if you assume the offensive, but if you let him attack, his bite is mortal.

Some years after this, when I saw Madame de Staël in London, I asked her what she thought of him: she replied, 'He is very great in monologue, but he has no idea of dialogue.' This I repeated, and it appeared in the *Quarterly Review*.[40]

NOTES

[1] Basil Montagu (1770-1851), legal writer, scholar, and early friend of STC and Wordsworth. (There is a late glimpse of STC at Keswick (15 October 1810) in Louis Simond's anonymous *Journal of a Tour and Residence in Great Britain* (2 vols.; Edinburgh, 1815), I, 349-50; but the account is mostly about Southey.)

[2] John James Morgan (17??-1820), a friend of STC's since school; Martin Burney (1788-1852), barrister, and a regular at the Lambs'.

[3] Wordsworth's 'Gipsies' deplores their fixity and idleness (cf. *BL*, II, 137).

[4] *Universal Natural History and Theory of the Heavens* (1755); *Dreams of a Spirit-Seer* (1766); *Observations on the Feelings of the Beautiful and the Sublime* (1764); and the *Critique of Judgement* (1790). Thomas Burnet (?1635-1715), author of *The Sacred Theory of the Earth* (1684-90), a Coleridgean favourite.

[5] J.G. Fichte (1762-1814), author of *Science of Knowledge* (1794), and F.W.J. von Schelling (1775-1854), author of *System of Transcendental Idealism* (1800), were important influences on STC. Jakob Böhme (1575-1624), mystic, author of *Aurora* (1612). Schelling and Böhme are also said to coincide in *BL* (I, 161).

[6] A crucial Coleridgean distinction: cf. *BL*, I, 304-5.

[7] Thomas Otway, *Venice Preserved*, V.ii, 1.243 — a Coleridgean touchstone for fancy (e.g., *BL*, I, 84, where delirium and mania are also distinguished).

[8] The analysis of Hamlet appears in *Wilhelm Meister's Apprenticeship* (1795-6).

[9] Southey called 'The Ancient Mariner' 'a Dutch attempt at German sublimity' in his review of *Lyrical Ballads* (*Critical Review*, 2nd ser., XXIV (1798), 197-204).

[10] Fort Augustus. The incident occurred in September 1803 (*CL*, II, 982; 984).

[11] Mary Matilda Betham (1776-1852), poet and painter. In 1802 STC wrote her a poem 'from a stranger' (*CPW*, I, 374-6), having admired her 'On a Cloud'. (He told her 'it would have been faultless if I had not used the word *Phoebus* in it, which he thought inadmissable in modern poetry': *CPW*, I, 374.)

[12] Cf. *CL*, III, 310.

[13] Bernard, Lord Coleridge, *The Story of a Devonshire House* (1905), 190-1.

[14] Spencer Perceval (1762-1812), Prime Minister from 1809; assassinated, 1812.

[15] Moore defeated the French at Coruna in 1809, and was fatally wounded.

[16] Only Klopstock-esque, according to *TT* (I, 6n.9). STC often contrasted *Der Messias* (1748-73) by Friedrich Gottlieb Klopstock (1724-1803) — whom he and Wordsworth met in 1798 (*BL*, II, 194-205) — with *Paradise Lost* (e.g., *LL*, II, 425).

[17] Christoph Martin Wieland (1733-1813), author of 'Oberon' (1780); Sotheby's translation appeared in 1798.

[18] Edward Young (1683-1765), author of the popular *Night Thoughts* (1742-6).

[19] After reviewing Paulus's *Kommentar* in the *Critical Review*, William Taylor published *Who Was the Father of Jesus Christ?* (1810). (The answer is Zacharias, father of John the Baptist: see Merton Christensen, 'Taylor of Norwich and the

Higher Criticism', *Journal of the History of Ideas* XX (1959), 179-94, esp. 189-92). Heinrich Eberhard Paulus (1761-1851) was an editor of Spinoza; STC describes him in the notebook as one of the 'German Unitarians' (*CN*, III, 3906).

[20] I Chronicles 29.20, *var.*.

[21] Richard Watson (1737-1816), 'that beastly Bishop, that blustering Fool' (*CL*, II, 740).

[22] i.e. 'The people want to be deceived; let them be deceived!'

[23] Edward Copleston (1776-1849) had published *A Reply to the Calumnies of the Edinburgh Review against Oxford* (1810), answering a piece by Sydney Smith which had objected to the universities' emphasis upon classical learning. (Smith himself noted that Cambridge diluted the classics with mathematics.)

[24] Southey's exotic epic *The Curse of Kehama* was published in 1810.

[25] It was on etymology.

[26] Samuel Parr (1747-1825), curate and Whig.

[27] A lasting criterion: e.g., *BL*, II, 142.

[28] Johnson, 'The Vanity of Human Wishes', ll.1-2 *var.*; cf., e.g., *LL*, I, 292.

[29] Minorca was returned to Spain as part of the Treaty of Amiens (1802).

[30] Stephen Peter Rigaud (1774-1839), Professor of Geometry at Oxford.

[31] No easy task. H.N. Coleridge's story bears witness to the difficulties (the Gurneys were a dynasty of celebrated shorthand-writers):

> A very experienced short-hand writer was employed to take down Mr. Coleridge's lectures on Shakspeare, but the manuscript was almost entirely unintelligible. Yet the lecturer was, as he always is, slow and measured. The writer—we have some notion it was no worse an artist than Mr. Gurney himself—gave this account of the difficulty: that with regard to every other speaker whom he had ever heard, however rapid or involved, he could almost always, by long experience in his art, guess the form of the latter part, or apodosis, of the sentence by the form of the beginning; but that the conclusion of every one of Coleridge's sentences was a *surprise* upon him. He was obliged to listen to the last word. ('The Poetical Works of S.T. Coleridge', *Quarterly Review* LII (1834) 1-38, 4)

[32] One memoirist recorded that 'no distinguished man, no eminent veteran in literature, could be kinder to the young, struggling aspirant, and none could take more diligent interest in putting young men in the right way in matters of belief' (Charles MacFarlane, *Reminiscences of a Literary Life* (1917), 51). Another watched STC after a lecture: 'I was especially struck with the kindness of Coleridge's manner, and the consideration which he showed to the remarks of the young men by whom he was surrounded' ('Ethee', 'Recollections of Coleridge', *Mirror for Magistrates* I (16 April 1836), 3).

[33] John Rickman (1771-1840), secretary to the Speaker of the House.

[34] Robert Burns, 'Tam o'Shanter', ll.61-2, *var.*. A favourite: e.g., *BL*, I, 81.

[35] STC apologises for 'general turgidity' in his 1797 *Poems* (*CPW*, II, 1145). From 1800, several of Coleridge's poems, including 'The Ancient Mariner', appeared in *Lyrical Ballads*, with Wordsworth's name alone on the title-page.

[36] Whitbread (1758-1815), politician and brewer, and a power at Drury Lane.

[37] William Jerdan tells a story which looks like a variation:

> This same evening was memorable for his account of reading the tragedy of "Remorse" to Douglas Kinnaird (then one of the regents of Drury Lane) in his apartments in Pall Mall. It was most graphic and descriptive. Kinnaird made his toilet whilst Coleridge read, perhaps a whole act; but having finished teeth-brushing, &c. he said, 'Come now, we've had enough of that nonsense; you shall hear part of an opera which I have written, and give me your opinion of *that!*' ('Coleridge's Table Talk', *London Literary Gazette* 958 (30 May 1835), 342)

[38] Leslie illustrated Irving's *Knickerbocker's History of New York*.

[39] After the Montagu debacle, STC lodged in a Covent Garden hotel until Morgan rescued him. Morgan, his wife Mary, and her sister Charlotte Brent were, STC said, 'my Saviours, Body and Soul' (*CL*, III, 399).

[40] STC was taken to see de Staël by Southey (letter, 8 October 1813: *Selections from the Letters*, II, 332 and n.); Crabb Robinson dined with her on the 18th (*Diary*, I, 419-21). Leslie repeated a version to Haydon (whose response is telling):

> Leslie said Coleridge and Madame de Staël met—each furious talkers; Coleridge would talk. The next day she was asked how she liked Coleridge. 'For a mono-logue,' said she, 'excellent, but as to a dialogue—good heavens!'
>
> She would have been better pleased if Coleridge could have said this of her. For that evening never were two people so likely to hate each other. (18 September 1831; *Autobiography and Memoirs of Benjamin Robert Haydon 1786-1846*, ed. Alexander P.D. Penrose (1927), 405)

H.N. Coleridge also glosses the remark, commenting on STC's contrast between 'discursive and continuous' Burke and the 'short sharp things' of Johnson:

> Burke, I am persuaded, was not so continuous a talker as Coleridge. Madame de Staël told a nephew of the latter, at Coppet, that Mr. C. was a master of mono-logue, *mais qu'il ne savait pas le dialogue*. There was a spice of vindictiveness in this, the exact history of which is not worth explaining. And if dialogue must be cut down in its meaning to small talk, I, for one, will admit that Coleridge, amongst his numberless qualifications, possessed it not. But I am sure that he could, when it suited him, converse as well as any one else, and with women he frequently did converse in a very winning and popular style, confining them, however, as well as he could, to the detail of facts or of their spontaneous emotions. In general, it was certainly otherwise. 'You must not be surprised,' he said to me, 'at my talk-ing so long to you—I pass so much of my time in pain and solitude, yet everlast-ingly thinking, that, when you or any other persons call on me, I can hardly help easing my mind by pouring forth some of the accumulated mass of reflection and feeling, upon an apparently interested recipient.' But the principal reason, no doubt, was the habit of his intellect, which was under a law of discoursing upon all subjects with reference to ideas or ultimate ends. You might interrupt him when you pleased, and he was patient of every sort of conversation except mere personality, which he absolutely hated. (*Specimens of the Table Talk*, II, 216-17n.)

The Lecturer, 1811-13

(i) HENRY CRABB ROBINSON

From Crabb Robinson, Diary, I, 347-8; 348-9; 350-1. Coleridge's lectures 'on Shakespeare and Milton in Illustration of the Principles of Poetry' were delivered in 1811-12, in Scot's Corporation Hall, off Fleet Street.

December 5th. – Accompanied Mrs. Rutt to Coleridge's lecture. In this he surpassed himself in the art of talking in a very interesting way, without speaking at all on the subject announced. According to advertisement, he was to lecture on 'Romeo and Juliet,' and Shakespeare's female characters. Instead of this he began with a defence of school-flogging, in preference at least to Lancaster's mode of punishing, without pretending to find the least connection between that topic and poetry. Afterwards he remarked on the character of the age of Elizabeth and James I., as compared with that of Charles I; distinguished not very clearly between wit and fancy; referred to the different languages of Europe; attacked the fashionable notion concerning poetic diction; ridiculed the tautology of Johnson's line, 'If Observation, with extensive view,' &c.; and warmly defended Shakespeare against the charge of impurity. While Coleridge was commenting on Lancaster's mode of punishing boys, Lamb whispered: 'It is a pity he did not leave this till he got to "Henry VI.," for then he might say he could not help taking part against the Lancastrians.' Afterwards, when Coleridge was running from topic to topic, Lamb said, 'This is not much amiss. He promised a lecture on the Nurse in 'Romeo and Juliet,' and in its place he has given us one in the *manner* of the Nurse.' [...]

December 9th. – Accompanied Mrs. Rough to Coleridge's seventh and incomparably best lecture. He declaimed with great eloquence about love, without wandering from his subject, 'Romeo and Juliet.' He was spirited, methodical, and, for the greater part, intelligible, though profound. [...]

December 12th. – Tea with Mrs. Flaxman, who accompanied me to Coleridge's lecture. He unhappily relapsed into his desultory habit, and delivered, I think, his worst lecture. He began with identifying religion with love, delivered a rhapsody on brotherly and sisterly love, which seduced him into a dissertation on incest. I at last lost all power of attending to him.

(ii) JAMES AMPHLETT

From The Rifleman *(1812); and reprinted in James Amphlett's* The
Newspaper Press *(1860), 13-15. Amphlett was a journalist and editor (see
W.E.A. Axon, 'James Amphlett and Samuel Taylor Coleridge', The Library, 3rd.
ser., II (1911), 34-9). He wrote up Coleridge's lectures for his Rifleman.*

This gentleman's course of lectures on Shakespeare is drawing
towards a close, and the town will be speedily deprived of one of
the most intellectual treats which it has experienced for a number
of years. These lectures, though, in a select circle, well supported,
have not been attended with that degree of success which ought,
perhaps, to have been expected from so enlightened a city as the
capital of Great Britain. But there are some considerations which
will qualify any charge of apparent deficiency of the public taste.
The present course is given in *the city*, and in *the winter*; a time
when snow, and rain, and dirt, and fogs, muster such an advanced
guard of uncomfortable enemies to London life, that the citizen is
content to encounter the privations of mind, with the fire-side
weapons of cards and tobacco. 'Fetter Lane,' where, during the
winter months, the sun is 'invisible, or dimly seen,' has no inviting
sound to the delicate ears of the west end of the town. The *literati*
there, considered, perhaps, that the lecturer ought to have come
'betwixt the *smoke* and their nobility.'

We have always been aware that a man of Mr. Coleridge's
peculiar powers of mind, could never in a lecture, do himself
anything like justice. So refining and multifarious are his habits of
thought, that he cannot subject even his pen to any order or
arrangement in his subject. In his writings we find him constantly
changing his course, to catch the interesting impulse of some new
thought, elicited from, or crossing his subject. There is only one
thing in him that is certain, and that is, though his subject should
be *physics*, a *metaphysical* conclusion. It is his governing tendency,
and beats him out of that which is simple into that which is
complex; from individualities to generalities, in defiance of
himself.

There is another peculiarity in him which ought to be
particularised, and which seems to be an illustration of the affinity
that is said to exist in extremes. If he begins on any one particular
passion or principle, he commonly works about it, from some
strange and incomprehensible impetus, till he involves himself in a
mass of nebulous matter, that is as remote from the nature of his

text as possible! A great portion of one of his lectures, on the nature of love (as exemplified in *Juliet*) consisted of a decomposition of the character of the nurse; a most masterly delineation of the characteristics of garrulous age; and of contrasted powers and habits of memory, in educated and uneducated minds. He pursued this mining enquiry till love was lost in the boundless wilds of thought; and Shakespeare himself disappeared in the ocean of human nature. But all these things are rather a proof of Mr. Coleridge's powers of mind than any thing else. If the female part of his audience be sometimes disappointed, they are sometimes as agreeably surprised. For a cross wind and current of thought and feeling, will frequently drive the lecturer from the most rugged and masculine philosophy, into the calm and captivating confines of the circle of the affections, and the influences of the heart.

(iii) W.H. HARRISON

From 'Notes and Reminiscences', The University Magazine I (1878) 537-47, 537-8.

The first man of any note in literature whom I ever saw was Samuel Taylor Coleridge. He was giving a series of lectures on the Belles Lettres in a large room on the first floor of a sixth-rate tavern at the end of a blind alley on the right hand side of Fetter Lane, not far from Fleet Street. The admission fee was five shillings, and I, a boy of some sixteen or seventeen, was taken by an uncle. I was struck by his wonderful forehead — full of power. He began with a few short sentences, but when he warmed to his subject his eloquence was almost overpowering in its volume and brilliancy. I well remember his remarking of one of the Greek poets, with reference to the simplicity of his language, that it was 'such as a lamenting mother in a cottage might be supposed to have used.' In classifying the various kinds of readers, he said some were like jelly bags — they let pass away all that is pure and good, and retained only what is impure and refuse. Another class he typified by a sponge; these were they whose minds sucked all up, and gave it back again, only a little dirtier. Others, again, he likened to an hour-glass, and their reading to the sand which runs in and runs out, and leaves no trace behind. I forget the fourth class, but the fifth and last he compared to the slaves in the Golconda mines, who retained the gold and the gem, and cast aside the dirt and the dross.

Among the auditors in that low tavern there were Daw, the painter, who afterwards went to Russia, and William Godwin, the author of 'St Leon' and 'Caleb Williams' — one, I forget which, of them had a hooked nose, and though it was Christmas, wore nankeen pantaloons. There was also Edward Erasmus Phillips, who was clerk to Rickman, secretary to the Speaker, to which office he succeeded, and served Abbott (afterwards Lord Colchester), and Manners Sutton, son of the Archbishop, and afterwards Lord Canterbury.[1] Phillips took his B.A. degree at Oxford at eighteen, and his M.A. before he was twenty-one. He associated very much with the Lake school of poets, and used to say that Coleridge was wont to talk long and eloquently in society, but if he was interrupted, or, as he thought, not sufficiently attended to, he would go into a corner and turn his back to the company. Phillips told me that before Coleridge parted from his wife, he took her round to his most intimate friends, and bearing the highest testimony to her virtues as a wife and a woman, explained that there was between them a want of sympathy which rendered it impossible that they could live happily together. I heard Coleridge lecture the same winter at the Surrey Institution, formerly the Leverean Museum, on the Surrey side of Blackfriars Bridge, where there was a very pretty theatre adapted to the purpose. I remember that he came on the stage eating an apple; and appeared a little hazy. He however quickly recovered himself.

(iv) MARY RUSSELL MITFORD

From The Life of Mary Russell Mitford, Related in a Selection from her Letters to her Friends, *ed. A.G. L'Estrange (3 vols.; 1870), I, 162–3. This comes from a letter to Sir William Elford, banker and politician, 15 December 1811.*

Your most kind letter followed me to London, where I have been staying for the last ten days. I went thither for a purpose which, I think, was extremely soberminded and praiseworthy; albeit I never mentioned it to any one that did not laugh in my face. I went thither to improve in my vocation (just as country milliners and mantua-makers go to *finish* and learn fashions) by hearing divers lectures — on Milton and Shakespeare, and criticism and poetry, and poets and critics, and whipping little boys, and love and philosophy, and every subject that ever entered the head of man — from my good friend Mr. Coleridge. And here I am returned quite Coleridgified; much in the same way, I suppose, as Boswell was after a visit to Johnson; sprinkling, but not mixing, his brilliancy with my dulness, 'like sprigs of embroidery on a ground of linsey-woolsey.'[2]

What a simpleton I am to tell you all this! I shall not say a pretty thing to you for these six months, but you will give the credit of it to my dearly-beloved lecturer. I wish you had heard him. You would certainly have been enchanted; for, though his lectures are desultory in the highest degree, and though his pronunciation is an odd mixture of all that is bad in the two worst dialects of England, the Somersetshire and the Westmoreland, with an addition, which I believe to be exclusively his own, namely giving to the *a* long as in 'wave' and 'bane,' a sound exactly resembling that which children make in imitating the bleating of a sheep, 'ba-a-a;' yet in spite of all these defects, he has so much of the electric power of genius—that power which fixes the attention by rousing at once the fancy and the heart—that the ear has scarcely the wish to condemn that which so strongly delights the intellect.

I must tell you a misadventure which happened to me at one of these lectures. I had set my heart on taking my friend Mrs. Rowden with me.[3] Now, she is about as difficult to draw as a road waggon (not personally, but mentally, I mean), and had no fancy for the expedition; but as she had to do with one quite as obstinate, and a thousand times more enthusiastic than herself, I carried my point, and had the satisfaction of seating her close by my side in the lecture-room. It was very full. The orator was more than usually brilliant; and I had just got Mrs. R. to confess that 'he really was tolerable' (a wonderful confession, considering she was *a lady*, and determined to dislike him), when to my utter dismay he began a period as follows: 'There are certain poems—or things called poems—which have obtained considerable fame—or that which is called fame—in the world; I mean the Pleasures of Tea-drinking, and the Pleasures of Wine-drinking, and the Pleasures of Love, and the Pleasures of Nonsense, and the Pleasures of Hope.'[4] There, thank God, the list ended, for his censure was only aimed at Campbell, whom he proceeded to abuse. But think what I felt while he was going on with his 'Pleasures,' and I expected the 'Pleasures of Friendship' to come out every moment. Mr. Rogers[5] was just by, so that Mrs. Rowden had the comfort of company in

her sensations, whatever they might be; but they had both the wit
to keep them to themselves.

(v) HENRY CRABB ROBINSON

*From Crabb Robinson, Diary, I, 399-401; 407. Coleridge began another series of
lectures in late 1812, on 'belles lettres', held at the Surrey Institution in the
Blackfriar's Road. At the same time, his tragedy 'Remorse' was on at Drury
Lane. (Crabb Robinson went to see it on 23 January: Diary, I, 406-7.)*

Oct. 3rd. — Coleridge walked with me to A. Robinson's for my Spinoza, which I lent him. While standing in the room he kissed Spinoza's face in the title-page, and said, 'This book is a gospel to me.'
But in less than a minute he added, 'his philosophy is nevertheless
false. Spinoza's system has been demonstrated to be false, but only
by that philosophy which has demonstrated the falsehood of all
other philosophies. Did philosophy commence with an *it is* instead
of an *I am*, Spinoza would be altogether true.' And without allow-
ing a breathing time, Coleridge parenthetically asserted, 'I, however, believe in all the doctrines of Christianity, even the Trinity.'
[...]

January 26th. — Heard Coleridge's concluding lecture. He was received with three rounds of applause on entering the room, and
very loudly applauded during the lecture and at its close. That
Coleridge should ever become a popular man would at one time
have been thought a very vain hope. It depends on himself; and if
he would make a sacrifice of some peculiarities of taste (his enemies assert that he has made many on essential points of religion
and politics), he has talents to command success. His political
opinions will suit a large portion of the public; and, though not yet
a favourite with the million, the appreciation of his genius is
spreading.

(vi) CHARLES ROBERT LESLIE

From Autobiographical Recollections, 36-7. *Once Allston had recovered (see
above) his party went on to Clifton, where Leslie encountered Coleridge again,
engaged in a new lecture series, advertised as about Milton and Cervantes.*

While I was at Clifton, Coleridge very unexpectedly arrived and
engaged to give a course of lectures on Milton and Shakespeare. I
heard three of them, and here again the regret arises that I took no
notes. In a letter I wrote at the time, and which has since been
returned to me, I find the following passage: — 'His object, he says,
is not to show, what everybody acknowledges, that Shakespeare

and Milton were men of great genius, but to efface the impression, that because their genius was great, they must *necessarily* have great faults, and to prove that their judgment was equal to their genius; — in other words, that neither of them was *an inspired idiot.*' 'He has given me,' I added, 'a much more distinct and satisfactory view of the nature and ends of poetry, and of painting, than I ever had before.'

(vii) JOHN FOSTER

From J.E. Rylands, Life and Correspondence of John Foster *(2 vols.; 1846), I, 444-5. Foster (1770-1843), Baptist minister, essayist, friend of Cottle. 'In Coleridge', he wrote, 'you saw one of the highest class of human beings' (I, 349).*

I could not conveniently hear more than one of his lectures (on Shakespeare), but it was a still higher luxury to hear him talk as much as would have been two or three lectures. I use the word *luxury*, however, not without some very considerable qualification of its usual meaning, since it may not seem exactly descriptive of a thing involving much severe labour, — and this one is forced often to undergo in the endeavour to understand him, his thinking is of so surpassingly original and abstracted a kind. This is the case often even in his recitals of facts, as that recital is continually mixed with some subtle speculation. It was perfectly wonderful, in looking back on a few hours of his conversation, to think what a quantity of perfectly original speculation he had uttered, in language incomparably rich in ornament and new combinations. In point of theological opinion, he is become, indeed has now a number of years been, it is said, highly orthodox. He wages victorious war with the Socinians, if they are not, which I believe they now generally are, very careful to keep the peace in his company. His mind contains an astonishing mass of all sorts of knowledge, while in his power and manner of putting it to use, he displays more of what we mean by the term genius than any mortal I ever saw or ever expect to see. He is still living in a wandering, precarious, and comfortless way, perpetually forming projects which he has not the steady resolution to prosecute long enough to accomplish. His appearance indicates much too evidently, that there is too much truth in the imputation of intemperance. It is very likely he beguiles his judgment and conscience by the notion of an exciting effect to be produced on his faculties by strong fluids. I have not heard that he ever goes the length of disabling himself for the clearest mental operation, but certainly he indulges to a degree that, if not for-borne, will gradually injure his faculties and health. It is probable that he is haunted by an incurable restlessness, a constant, perma-nent sense of infelicity. This has been augmented, doubtless, by the total deficiency of domestic satisfactions.[6]

NOTES

[1] George Dawe, RA, (1781-1829) spent nine years in Russia painting senior officers. Edward Phillips (1771-1844) succeeded John Rickman (1771-1840) as secretary to Charles Abbot [sic] (1757-1829), Speaker of the House 1802-17; and he remained secretary under Abbot's successor, Charles Manners-Sutton (1780-1845), son of the Archbishop of Canterbury, and later created Viscount Canterbury. (See W.R. McKay, *Secretaries to Mr. Speaker* (1986).) Both secretar-ies were known to STC: he thought Rickman 'a wonderful man' (*CL*, II, 1058). Phillips was in Lamb's card-playing circle. Harrison's account of his prodi-gious university career is quite right: see *Alumni Oxoniensis 1715-1886*, ed. Joseph Foster (2 vols.; Oxford, 1888), II, 1107.

[2] Sheridan, *The Critic*, I.i, *var.*.

[3] Frances Arabella Rowden wrote *The Pleasures of Friendship* (1810).

[4] Some at least are genuine: John Stewart's *The Pleasures of Love* (1806) and Thomas Campbell's *The Pleasures of Hope* (1799). (Campbell heard STC and judged him 'all preaching—no interchange—nothing like conversation' (*Life and Letters of Thomas Campbell*, ed. William Beattie (3 vols.; 1849), III, 329).)

[5] Samuel Rogers wrote *The Pleasures of Memory* (1792).

[6] Foster's journal recorded rather a different impression:

> The eloquent Coleridge sometimes retires into a sublime mysticism of thought; he robes himself in moonlight, and moves among images of which we can not be assured for a while whether they are substantial forms of sense or fantastic visions. (I, 223)

Divers Encounters, 1813-16

(i) JOSEPH COTTLE

From 'S.T. Coleridge in Company with Socinians and Atheists', Con-gregational Magazine XI (1835) 486-90, 486; 487; 488-9; 489-90. Back in Bristol, Coleridge renewed acquaintance with Cottle. (The article purports to be made up of notes taken from Cottle's recent On the Predictions and Miracles of Jesus Christ—which seems, in fact, never to have been published.)

The writer, many years ago, was invited to meet an old friend (that extraordinary genius, the late *Samuel Taylor Coleridge*,) with a zealous *Socinian Minister*. It was natural to conclude, that such uncongenial, and, at the same time, such inflammable materials, would soon ignite. The subject of *Socinianism* being introduced, by a third party, Mr. Coleridge, from having received something that was construed as a *challenge*, advanced at once to the charge. 'Sir,' said he, 'you give up so much that the little you retain of Christianity is not worth keeping.' The thunder was expected immediately to follow the flash; but, after a manifest internal conflict, the disciple of Socinus very *prudently* allowed the gauntlet to remain undisturbed.

Cottle quotes Coleridge from a fraught letter, alleging a campaign against him by a Unitarian minister. (The letter is CL, III, 476-8, so we know the minister to be Coleridge's old friend John Prior Estlin, and we can date the episode to 1814.)

Mr. C. said, he had recently had a long conversation with Dr. ——, (a Socinian minister) who declared that, 'He could discover nothing in the New Testament which in the *least* favoured the *Divinity of Christ.*' Mr. C. replied, that 'It appeared to him *impossible* for any man to read the New Testament, with the common exercise of his understanding, without being convinced of the *Divinity of Christ*, from the testimony of *every page.*'

He said, 'it was evident that different persons might look at the same object with very opposite feelings. For instance,' he remarked, 'If Sir Isaac Newton looked at the planet Jupiter, he would view him, with his revolving moons, and would be led to the contemplation of his being inhabited, which thought would open a boundless field to his imagination: whilst another person, standing perhaps at the side of the great philosopher, would look at Jupiter, with the same set of feelings that he would at a silver sixpence. So, he said, some persons were wilfully blind, and did not seek for that change, that preparation of the heart, and understanding, which would enable them to see clearly the Gospel Truth.' [...]

He then referred to the dreadful state of the *Literati* in London, as it respects religion, and of their having laughed at him, and believed him to be in jest, when he professed his belief in the Bible.[1]

The writer having introduced to Mr. C. some years before, Mr. Davy, (afterwards Sir Humphry) he inquired, with some anxiety, for Mr. D. and expressed a hope, that he, since his removal from Bristol to London, was not tinctured with the prevailing scepticism. Mr. C. assured him that he was *not*: that *his* heart and understanding were not the *soil* for infidelity. The writer then remarked, During your stay in London, you doubtless saw a great many of what are called 'the cleverest men,' how do you estimate *Davy*, in comparison with these? Mr. C.'s reply was strong, but expressive. 'Why!' said he, 'Davy could *eat* them all! There is an energy, an elasticity in his mind, which enables him to seize on, and analyze, all questions, pushing them to their legitimate consequences. Every subject in Davy's mind had the principle of *vitality*. Living thoughts spring up, like the turf under his feet.' With equal justice, Mr. Davy entertained the same exalted opinion of Mr. Coleridge.

Mr. C. now changed the subject and spoke of ——, and Holcroft. (The former gentleman being living, delicacy requires that he should be passed over.)[2] He stated that Holcroft was a man of small powers, with superficial, rather than solid talents, and possessing principles of the *most horrible description:* a man who at the very moment he denied the existence of a *Deity*, in his heart, believed and trembled. He said that Holcroft, and other Atheists, reasoned with so much *fierceness* and *vehemence* against a GOD, that it plainly showed they were inwardly conscious, there *was* a GOD, to reason against; for he remarked, a *nonentity* would never excite passion.

An easy transition having been made to the Bible, Mr. C. spoke of our Saviour, with an utterance so sublime and reverential, that none could have heard him without experiencing an accession of love, gratitude, and adoration to the *Great Author of our Salvation*. The suffusion of his own eyes showed it to be the genuine feelings of his heart. He referred to the *Divinity of Christ*, as a Truth, incontestible to all who admitted the Inspiration, and consequent authority of Scripture. He particularly alluded to the 6th of John, v.15. 'When Jesus perceived that they would come and take him by force to make him a king, he departed again into a mountain, *"alone["]*.'

Coleridge recalls several run-ins with Holcroft, dating from 1794 (see CL, I, 138-9). Coleridge evidently told these stories with relish. (Carlyon (I, 244-47) repeats the following paragraphs, attributing them to an 'intimate friend of Coleridge'.)

He said that in his visit to London, he accidentally met, in a public office, the atheist, *Holcroft*, without knowing his name, when H. began, stranger as he was, the enforcement of some of his *diabolical sentiments!* (which, it appears, he was in the habit of doing, at all seasons, and in all companies, and thereby he often corrupted the principles of those simple persons whom he could get to listen to his shallow, and worn-out impieties.) Mr. C. declared himself to have been *indignant* at a conduct *so infamous*, and at once closed with the *'prating Atheist'*, when they had a sharp encounter. *Holcroft* then abruptly addressed Mr. C. 'I perceive you have *mind*, and know what you are talking about. It will be worth while to make a convert of *you*. I am engaged at present, but if you will call on me to-morrow morning (giving him his card) I will engage, *in half an hour*, to *convince* you, *there is no God!'* (He little knew the strength of the *fortress* he was inconsiderately attacking.)

Mr. Coleridge called on Holcroft the next morning, when the discussion was renewed, but none being present except the disputants, no account is preserved of this important conversation; but Mr. C. affirmed that *he beat all his arguments to atoms;* a result that none who knew him could doubt. He also stated, that instead of *his* being converted to Atheism, the *Atheist himself*, (after his manner) was converted; for the same day he sent Mr. C. a letter, saying, his reasoning was so clear, and satisfactory, that he had changed his views, and was now *'a Theist.'*[3] The next sun beheld him an Atheist again: but whether he *called* himself this or that, his character was the same.

Soon after the foregoing incident, Mr. Coleridge found himself in a large party, at the house of a man of letters,[4] amongst whom, to his surprise, were *Mr.* and *Mrs. Holcroft*, when to incite to a *renewal* of their late dispute, and *before witnesses* (in the full consciousness of *strength*) Mr. C. enforced the propriety of teaching children, as soon as they could articulate, to lisp the praises of their *Maker*, 'for,' said he, 'though they can form no correct idea of God, yet they entertain a high opinion of their *father*, and it is an easy introduction to the truth, to tell them that their *Heavenly Father* is stronger, and wiser, and better, than their *earthly father.'*

The whole company looked at *Mr. Holcroft*, implying that *now* was the time for him to meet a *competent* opponent, and justify sentiments which he had so often triumphantly advanced. They looked in vain. Mr. Holcroft maintained, to their surprise, *a total silence*, well remembering *the severe castigation he had so recently received.* But a very different effect was produced on *Mrs. Holcroft*. She *indignantly heard*, when, giving vent to her *passion*, and her *tears*, she said, 'She was quite surprised at Mr. Coleridge talking in that way before *her*, when he knew that both herself and Mr. Holcroft were *Atheists!*'

Mr. C. spoke of the unutterable *horror* he felt, when Holcroft's son, a boy, *eight years of age*, came up to him and said, '*There is no God!*' so that these wretched parents, alike father and *mother!* were as earnest in teaching *Atheism* to their children, as Christian parents are in inspiring their offspring with respect for *religious truth.*

(ii) RICHARD WARNER

From Warner, Literary Recollections, *153-4n.. An encounter of 1814 or so.*

The last time I had the pleasure of seeing Mr. Coleridge, was during the year previous to the peace. The excellent poet parted from me with a *pun.* I observed that his *diameter* was increased since we met, and that he bore before him a striking prognostic of future obesity. — 'True,' said he, stroking the ample rotundity: 'but, you must recollect, my dear sir, that these are *belligèrent* times.'

(iii) THOMAS A. METHUEN

From 'Retrospect of Friendly Communications with the Poet Coleridge', The Christian Observer *NS 89 (May 1845) 257-63, 257-63. In August 1813 Morgan went bankrupt, and fled to Ireland. In his absence, Coleridge snapped into activity, sorting out the creditors, and moving the two Morgan women to Ashley, near Box, in Wiltshire (where De Quincey visited them);[5] Coleridge meanwhile was working, despite bad health, in Bath and Bristol. In December 1814 he moved with the (reunited) Morgan family to Calne, and spent a highly productive year, dictating* Biographia *to Morgan, and preparing his poems for publication. In October 1814 he visited Corsham House, where Paul Cobb Methuen (1752-1816) had a fine art collection; the surviving letters show Coleridge became a regular visitor. Thomas, Methuen's son, was rector of All Cannings.*

In the autumn of 1815, I unexpectedly met him at my late father's house, and ventured to introduce myself to him. He treated me with great politeness, and was presently made known to my father, and invited to pass a few days under his roof. He did so, and amazement and delight seemed to take possession of the minds of all persons present. They appeared to themselves to gaze on as bright an intellectual comet as ever visited our moral system. To describe with any justness his conversational fluency, his imaginative powers, his classical wealth, his gigantic memory, his varied and occasionally very pointed wit, his theological and

Scriptural attainments, his familiarity with Leighton[6] and kindred religious authors, his readiness to enter at all times upon any topic, and his ability to suit himself to any taste,—were an undertaking too vast for my own competency, and certainly far too extended for your own limits. Yet, in accordance with your wishes, I will submit to you some sketchy observations on his character, and present you with such of his sayings as to this day I distinctly recollect.

First, as to *his conversational fluency*. As I listened to him day after day, both in my father's house and my own, (for he was my guest for nearly a week) it struck me that he could converse with as much facility for an hour on any given subject, as another man for five minutes. He generally chose some one important topic, whether literary, moral or political, and on that he employed, with not less concentration than effect, his interminable stores of appropriate and striking language. Not to listen to him was impossible. Not to hear him with delight was (as I have already intimated) no every-day occurence; for though Madame de Staël once took occasion to observe, with no slight severity, that 'he excelled greatly in monologue,' and though the commencement of his remarks was usually a signal to lower intelligences to be silent, I can with truth testify to his willingness to hear, as well as speak— and that with such modesty and patience, as reflected no slight credit on a man of his extraordinary talents. The fact was, that his words, as well as his ideas, had so much of that majestic flow which characterizes certain rivers in the western world, that (to say nothing of the difficulty of restraining a mind so productive as his) he was generally heard with that degree of silent admiration, that 'the art of stopping' must have been to him singularly difficult, and his volubility of speech, to a considerable extent, pardonable.

A few facts may illustrate the foregoing observations. A nobleman, distinguished both by his mental powers and classical proficiency, was invited to meet Mr. Coleridge at my father's table. His Lordship evidently listened with profound attention to him both on political and scientific subjects; and, before he left the house, invited him to his Lordship's residence in Wilts.[7] There he passed two days. Some time afterwards it was remarked, and with great good humour, by a member of the noble family, 'Mr. Coleridge has been talking to us for two whole days.' What were his prevailing topics during that memorable visit, I have no means of ascertaining. But wherever he partook of the hospitality of friends or neighbours, he rarely, if ever, failed to excite that appetite for his discourse which was not quickly satiated, and to leave upon their minds a delightful impression of astonishment. Such unquestionably was the result of his eloquence, both literary and political, at my own table. One of the company then present, and who was sitting opposite to him, made one or two attempts to set him right on some question relating to European politics; saying with considerable emphasis, 'But, Mr. Coleridge.' Instead of replying to my guest, he proceeded with his masterly harangue (if I may so describe it); and that in spite of the remonstrant's sufficiently audible remark to the gentleman by his side, 'Mr. Coleridge is decidedly wrong in that political opinion.' That he *ought* to have listened, and even replied to the remonstrance, I readily admit. Yet so prodigious were the movements of his intellect, as well as of his tongue, and such were the effects produced by each upon the party present; that to pause till he had delivered himself of his thoughts and arguments on the occasion, seemed to be a moral impossibility. Well do I remember his conversation (in 1815, I think) with a visitor and myself, soon after breakfast, on some deeply interesting topic, when, to our mutual surprise, the luncheon was brought in; the intermediate time having glided imperceptibly away, as we listened to the gifted speaker.

Candour compels me to acknowledge an occasional obscurity in his conversation. The cause was sufficiently apparent. He was not so constituted as easily to confine himself to a beaten path of intellect; and he accordingly sought out such strange, if not untrodden, tracks, as seemed to be peculiarly suited to his great powers to afford them a necessary range, and to promise much gain as well as gratification to his hearers. Yet in these bold and original excursions, he had sometimes to encounter an unexpected and impenetrable mist. The result (by no means frequent during my own intercourse with him) was that, however splendid his phraseology, others could not understand him; and, in sober truth, I suspect that he could scarcely understand himself. His lamentable use of opium (of which I shall presently say more) had not a little to do with the cloudy conceptions of his genius; nor was such an observation of a friend of mine less just than pointed, with reference to such conceptions: 'Coleridge has layers of mud as well as layers of gold.' On the whole, perhaps, his vast conversational powers were too little exercised in *dialogue*.

Let me next speak of his *sprightly*, and *occasionally severe*, *sayings*. Soon after I became acquainted with him, I was induced to ask him why he had so suddenly given up his residence at Box. His reply, accompanied with no slight playfulness of manner, was, 'My dear Sir, I was actually driven from my lodgings.' I naturally enquired as to the cause of his expulsion: 'Oh,' said he, 'I was informed, to my surprise and horror, that a barrel of gunpowder was regularly kept in the cellar over which I then lodged; and on begging that it might be immediately removed, the servant maid significantly observed to me, "Why, Sir, I thought it was the *shot* that killed, and not the *powder*." I rejoined, "Yes, and if I was a little bird, I should think so too."'

On another occasion, when he was residing in a certain town, being asked by an acquaintance, 'What society do you find there, either of an intellectual or interesting kind?' he replied, 'Alas, I find little of either sort; and, as to the *brains* of the inhabitants, a —— (naming an insect not unacquainted with the superficies of human craniology) might easily walk through them without being up to his ancles.' Not less caustic was an allusion, which he made in my own hearing, to the Athenæum, a periodical publication of that day, and, if I greatly mistake not, of an Unitarian order, and then chiefly conducted by Dr. Aikin. 'Here is an *aching void* and a *void Aikin*.'[8] The pun is of less value than the testimony of his opinion of the character of that melancholy system. The severity of his remarks relative to the Socinian body, from which he had happily seceded, was generally great. Once, for instance, he said to my father, taking up a large conch and applying it to his own ear, 'This shell may fitly represent the whole body of the Unitarians; for though it is dead and hollow, it still makes a great appearance, and no inconsiderable noise.' So, when writing, at my request, some notes on *Waterlands's* well-known queries with the Deists,[9] (a work which I fear I have lost, enriched as it was with the numerous annotations of my guest), he remarked, at the conclusion of the Preface, 'On the whole, Socinianism may fitly be considered as a dance, in which self-complacent blank-headedness and blank-heartedness are the two blind-fiddlers.' The edge of his animadversions on the Socinian party was, no doubt, considerably increased by the recollection of his former association with them, and by his consequent familiarity with their favourite opinions and delusive arguments. This I collected from the tone of his occasional references to the subject. Nor did it strike me that the severity of his strictures extended beyond the *system*, to its admirers and abettors.

But who shall depict even a shadow of that *imagination* which so pre-eminently belonged to *Mr. Coleridge?* Well might it be compared to some inexhaustibly productive region, some interminable mine, or (shall I be extravagant if I add?) to the lights and constellations of the heavens. Whether I listened to his prose or poetry, I seldom failed to observe some play of fantastic images in the former, and a singular exuberance of them in the latter. I will mention a few instances. Referring one day to a leaf that had just been gathered from a tulip tree, he said to one of my sisters, 'This leaf terminates so strangely, it almost seems as if nature had not been satisfied with the formation of it, and by suddenly cutting off the end, reduced it to this straight line.' The philosophy of Hobbes being alluded to, he exclaimed, (pointing, of course, to the unsoundness of his first principle), 'Ah! poor Hobbes, he possessed fine talents: in forming his theories, however, he fancied that the first link of his chain was fastened to a rock of *adamant;* but it proved to be a rock of *ice.*' On the mention of Archbishop Leighton, and his invaluable writings, he remarked, 'If we could conceive a region of intellect between reason and revelation to have been previously unoccupied, we might say that the Archbishop had taken possession of that region.' Again, when admiring Carlo Dolce's inimitable picture of Christ consecrating the elements,[10] he thus addressed me, 'Other painters have represented the humility of our blessed Saviour; but it was not (as in the masterpiece before us) the humility of one who could have called on the Father, and he would presently have sent him more than twelve legions of angels.' These are some of his conversational images which I have, imperfectly indeed, yet faithfully, rescued from oblivion. Had I preserved a larger store of them, their production would have been quite unnecessary, so well known was the playfulness, the power, the felicity of his vast imagination. Even Lord Byron (in a letter addressed to him in 1815, and of which I then had a copy) ultimately admitted his transcendent merits as a poet, and expressed great regret at having formerly denied them; that is, in his 'English Bards and Scottish [*sic*] Reviewers.'[11]

Of the *classical wealth* of Mr. Coleridge, I need not speak at any length. He was once described in my hearing, and by a man sufficiently qualified to estimate his merits, as 'a ripe and pregnant scholar.' Such unquestionably he was. Without attempting to call to mind any instance of his scholarship, both Greek and Latin, I may say, without fear of contradiction, that, like a subtile spirit, it pervaded all his discourse as well as his compositions, and gave to them that peculiar character which could not but gratify the taste of every classical hearer. With the Grecian dramas, poems, orations, and history, he was confessedly familiar. This added much to the weight and interest of his conversation. It was evidently that of a man who had devoted days and nights to the enthusiastic study of the classics; who had deeply imbibed their spirit, and who had happily imitated their models. To say thus much (and far more might justly be recorded to the same effect) is but to transcribe, however imperfectly, the opinions generally entertained of him in the literary world.

Nor is his *gigantic memory* to be overlooked. This quality was the more remarkable, being found in close alliance with his rarely rivalled imagination; for (as *Pope* has graphically told us, in his 'Essay on Criticism,')

> 'Where beams of warm imagination play,
> The memory's soft figures melt away.'[12]

But to this rule Mr. Coleridge was an undeniable exception. Yet on what part of the unbounded province which I have now entered it may be advisable to dwell, is a question of no common difficulty. One thing, however, I may truly as well as confidently aver— namely, that whatever subject was started, during my own intercourse with him, he appeared to be thoroughly at home upon it. History, biography, travels, science, events recent as well as remote, were all marvellously held in his mighty grasp; and, in all their most interesting shapes and important associations, were generally subject to his use. More than once did I make trial of the extent and accuracy of his recollection, and that by referring to matters of a very varied character. On no one of these did he plead, or ever betray, ignorance. It was, therefore, no ordinary treat to get him on some specific subject, and to find him stored, like an Encyclopædia, with such ample information regarding it, that one was naturally led to reflect, 'How vast must be those cells of memory which contain such a variety of solid and valuable matter.' Here again I am only testifying to a fact that will readily be admitted by all who were intimate with him.

His quotations from books, whether ancient or modern, poetical or in prose, were witnesses to the amazing capacity and rich treasures of his memory. From the pages of Christian theology and vital piety, he could freely and profitably quote. One example may be sufficient. He once asked me if I recollected what Dr. Donne had said respecting the conversion of St. Paul. On my replying in the negative, my friend delighted me with the following invaluable extract from his writings: 'Christ was the lightning flash that melted him, Christ was the mould that formed him.'[13] From the rich and, spiritually speaking, jewelled pages of Leighton, he would repeat ample passages. On such occasions the delighted attention of his hearers was a natural tribute to the extraordinary endowments of the speaker; and to that fascinating natural eloquence which characterized his conversation.

His *theological views* were not the least remarkable part of his great intellectual attainments. Well was I acquainted with those views, having had many opportunities of ascertaining them during his residence in my own abode. Theology appeared to have great attractions for his mind, and therefore became the theme of much friendly discussion between my gifted visitor and myself. The genuine doctrines of the glorious Reformation were his; unrefracted by any Popish, or (what would now be called) Puseyistic medium. From Romanism and all its affiliations he was immeasurably distant. He traced, with unfeigned satisfaction, the stream of Gospel light from the Apostles to the Fathers, from the Fathers to the Reformers, and from the Reformers to the more modern vindicators of the truth as it is in Jesus—especially of the fundamental verity of Justification by faith only. Unhappily I have mislaid his 'Thoughts on the Church,' written on a sheet of note-paper, before he took his leave of me. One point, however, I distinctly recollect: namely, that, though Jeremy Taylor, among the moderns, was, in some respects, 'the os et lyra Ecclesiæ,' he was in others doctrinally unsound; especially as to the depravity of human nature, and the value of a death-bed repentance. 'Over that part of his theology' (said Mr. Coleridge) 'Bishop Sanderson, and others of his dear friends, dropped a tear.'[14] And (Mr. Coleridge added) 'that part of Bishop Taylor's writings was evidently the most prolix, without splendour, without unction.' Nor did my guest hesitate to affirm, 'I exclude from the list of sound theologians your Syncretists, Prettymen, Aliassers, and *Isthmus* divines.' In conclusion, he emphatically pressed the observance of the sacred rule in all theological discussion, the supreme authority of *Scripture*; admitting, at the same time, the importance of consulting truly enlightened commentators, especially those of 'the first three centuries.'

Mr. Coleridge's letter to myself, lately published in your own pages, on Baptismal Regeneration, may prove, to no small extent, the soundness of his theological opinions.[15] But as I am not his biographer, but an unpretending recorder of certain 'memorabilia' respecting him, I must not venture further into this part of the poet's character, than to refer to a conference, (not to say collision) at which I myself was present, between himself and a nameless individual in 1815, on the great and consolitary [*sic*] doctrine of salvation by Christ only. Upon that point the parties considerably differed; each arguing, with no slight ability and spirit, in support of his own hypothesis. At length Mr. Coleridge, entering more fully and fervently into the mighty argument, contended and concluded thus: 'Why, Sir, Christ is as necessary to my spiritual, as bread is to my natural, existence; and, as my body must perish if deprived of food, so must my soul "perish everlastingly," if I had no Saviour.' No rejoinder followed.

The *religious character* of Mr. Coleridge is the last and most interesting topic on which I would detain your readers. To asseverate that he was a devoted and consistent Christian at the period when I received him as my guest, would not accord with those evidences which were then presented to my mind; yet, while truth compels me to acknowledge certain parts of his history, which were at variance with his exalted views of vital Christianity — such as his repeated absence, and without any apparent cause, from the sanctuary on the Lord's-day, and his too free use of stimulants at one time, and of opium at another — there were circumstances that even then (1815) came upon me with the force of presumptive testimony in favour of his serious, however fitful, determination to devote himself to his Redeemer's service; and this in spite of his publications (such, alas! were some of his poems, edited, I would hope, *by some other person*, in the last year of his existence) which in parts manifested an unchastised and unchristian wit on deeply important subjects. I now allude to his manner, that frequently betokened some strong religious feelings, or I should rather say, some terrible internal conflict with his own corruptions. Even then it was remarked by some members of my own household, that, as they passed, with a gentle tread, by the bed-chamber of Mr. Coleridge, they distinctly heard him praying, and apparently with great earnestness; and it is but justice to him to add, that, about the period in question, on a medical friend advising him to relinquish the use of opium, and occasionally ardent spirits, as greatly detrimental to his health, and in the end destructive of his life, Mr. Coleridge solemnly replied, 'I will relinquish it, though I should *die* in the attempt.' And I am informed by those who knew him, that, on leaving my own neighbourhood for that of the metropolis, he happily succeeded in that attempt; and consequently reaped the benefit of improved health.

Judging by such indirect evidences as I had then within my reach, I indulge the hope that the grace of Jesus at length changed the character, and so crowned the accomplishments, of my departed friend. The well-known letter, (dated July 13, 1834), addressed to his godson, Adam Kinnaird, shortly before his death, manifests a spirituality of views which would do honour to the most advanced Christian.[16] Nor can I forget some admirable remarks, once made by him, at my own table, on communion with God. He thus expressed himself on that high and holy topic: 'Sir, it is my fixed persuasion that no man ever yet prayed in earnest, who never felt the misery of being unable to pray. For when the soul feels that she is sinking, as it were, from Him who is the author of all happiness, she beseeches Him to stretch out his hand and suffer her to sink no further.' A gentleman, of a worldly character, once remarked that Mr. Coleridge, who had just closed some splendidly eloquent observations of a religious kind, 'spoke almost like a *Methodist preacher.*' The charge was so far just that he had admirably touched upon some of those Christian verities which, in the worldly nomenclature, were then identified with Methodism, as now they more commonly are with Calvinism and saintship.

From Methuen's Autobiography *(1870), 308-10; 310-11. This account comes from the memoir by Methuen's son, Thomas Plumptre Methuen.*

It was the practice at Corsham House that the visitors who arrived on the public day to see the pictures, wrote their names in a book, which was carried to my grandfather. Once upon a time the name of Mr. Coleridge appeared among them; and my father, always rather given to hunt 'lions', though not in the same sense as his son Henry, begged to be allowed to go and speak to Mr. Coleridge, and offer him the hospitalities of the house. Permission was willingly given, Coleridge was 'bagged,' brought into the library, and persuaded to stay for a couple of nights. What the rest thought of his astonishing monologues I know not, but my father's tendency to hero-worship was brought out strongly. He was wrapt in admiration, and fascinated into a spell of silence before the great thinker's words. I believe he admitted that he did not always understand what it was all about; but he was greatly pleased, and, when he became rector of All Cannings, Coleridge accepted an invitation to visit him.

By this time my father's views of religion had undergone that revolution of which he himself has told us, and he suspected that Coleridge did not quite relish the atmosphere in which he found himself; but the poet made himself agreeable, played with the children, brought out the heavy artillery of his conversation at a dinner-party of the neighbours, out-thundered a very vigorous little clergyman, (who had never been matched before, and did not understand it, but whose words seemed in comparison as poor as pop-guns), and, lastly, took himself off to Devizes, on a Sunday, after the morning service.

This, of course, my father did not approve. Coleridge, however, had made him happy just before by a speech which we always thought had a tinge of flattery in it, but which my father remembered and often told us of. The great man had been to church in the morning, and said to my father, in allusion to his text and sermon, 'Sir, I never knew the *wealth* of that passage before.'

When Coleridge was staying at Corsham, the Lord Lansdowne of the period was invited to meet him, and from thence he passed on as a visitor to Bowood, where Lady Lansdowne said of him, 'Coleridge has been talking for two whole days.'

Methuen, Jr.,repeats a handful of anecdotes of Coleridge's Wiltshire period.

I believe it was on the Sunday afternoon, when Coleridge bid my father good-bye, that he called at Mr. Anstey's manufactory at Devizes, to buy some snuff; but, as might be supposed, the rules of the house were against Sunday trade, and the particular case was not held to justify any exception; so that the poet had to do without snuff, for that day at least. He was very angry at the refusal, and gave vent to his displeasure in these words: 'A plague on that man's religion who would starve his neighbour's nose in order to save his soul!'

My father used to speak with regret and disapproval of the way in which Coleridge, as *he* thought, neglected his wife. He used to say of her, 'Sarah Coleridge has no soul.'

My father once induced Coleridge to attend a Bible-meeting and speak, but the performance was not thought satisfactory.

(iv) THOMAS DE QUINCEY

From 'Samuel Taylor Coleridge (continued). By the English Opium-Eater', Tait's Magazine *NS II (1835) 3-10, 4.*

Coleridge, during this part of his London life, I saw constantly — generally once a-day, during my own stay in London; and sometimes we were jointly engaged to dinner parties. In particular, I remember one party at which we met Lady Hamilton — Lord Nelson's Lady Hamilton — the beautiful, the accomplished, the enchantress![17] Coleridge admired her, as who would not have done, prodigiously; and she, in her turn, was fascinated with Coleridge. He was unusually effective in his display; and she, by way of expressing her acknowledgments appropriately, performed a scene in Lady Macbeth — how splendidly, I cannot better express, than by saying that all of us who then witnessed her performance, were familiar with Mrs Siddons's matchless execution of that scene;[18] and yet, with such a model filling our imaginations, we could not but acknowledge the possibility of another, and a different perfection, without a trace of imitation, equally original, and equally astonishing.

NOTES

[1] The story resembles Priestley's experience in Revolutionary Paris — a story repeated by Rogers (P.W. Clayden, *The Early Life of Samuel Rogers* (1887), 266).
[2] Godwin, presumably (who died in 1836).

[3] The story resembles STC's later conversion of Godwin to theism (in 1800):

> In my forty-fourth year I ceased to regard the name of Atheist with the same complacency I had done for several preceding years, at the same time retaining the utmost repugnance of understanding for the idea of an intelligent Creator and Governor of the universe, which strikes my mind as the most irrational and ridiculous anthropomorphism. My theism, if such I may be permitted to call it, consists in a reverent and soothing contemplation of all that is beautiful, grand, or mysterious in the system of the universe, and in a certain conscious intercourse and correspondence with the principles of these attributes, without attempting the idle task of developing and defining it—into this train of thinking I was first led by the conversations of S.T. Coleridge. (C. Kegan Paul, *William Godwin: His Friends and Contemporaries* (2 vols.; 1876), I, 357-8)

[4] If this is the occasion elsewhere described by STC (17 December 1794; *CL*, I, 138), the hosts were Perry and Grey, proprietor and editor of the *Morning Chronicle*.

[5] 'Samuel Taylor Coleridge', *Tait's Edinburgh Magazine* NS II (1835) 3-10, 4.

[6] *Aids to Reflection* (1825) was based upon aphorisms of Robert Leighton (1611-84), Archbishop of Glasgow, 'that *"wonderful man"'* (*CL*, V, 197).

[7] STC was puffed by the invitation: 'the Marquis of Lansdown[e] expressed [...] a Wish to meet me—I accordingly went again—met the Marquis—& rather suppose that he was not displeased with me—for he invited me home to Bow Wood—I went—& was prest to stay for a week or more' (*CL*, III, 536).

[8] *The Athenæum* began in 1828; Methuen may have misremembered STC speaking of the *Annual Review*, edited by (Dr.) John Aikin's son, Arthur between 1803 and 1808, which was full of contributions from Unitarians.

[9] Daniel Waterland (1683-1740); his *Scripture Vindicated* (1730-2) answered Matthew Tindal's Deistical *Christianity as Old as the Creation*.

[10] Carlo Dolci (1616-87), whose 'Christ Consecrating the Elements of the Mass' hung in Corsham Court.

[11] See *CL*, IV, 563. STC is a target in 'English Bards and Scotch Reviewers' (1809).

[12] Pope, 'Essay on Criticism', ll.58-9.

[13] A striking conflation of passages from the sermon on Acts 9.4: 'S. *Paul* was borne a man, not an Apostle, not carved out, as the rest in time; but a fusil Apostle, an Apostle powred out, and cast in a Mold' and 'It was a light that struck him blinde [*etc.*]' (*Sermons of John Donne*, ed. Evelyn M. Simpson and George R. Potter (10 vols.; Berkeley, 1953-62), VI, 207; 215). Cf. *CM*, II, 252n..

[14] Robert Sanderson (1587-1663), Bishop of Lincoln.

[15] *CL*, IV, 580-3; published in the *Christian Observer* in February and March 1845.

[16] *CL*, VI, 989-90.

[17] Emma Hamilton (?1761-1851), Nelson's celebrated mistress.

[18] Sarah Siddons (1755-1831), a famous Lady Macbeth.

Five
Highgate
1816-34

On 13 April 1816, Coleridge arrived at Moreton House on Highgate Hill, referred to the medical care of Dr. James Gillman. Gillman later recalled how a visitor present at their first meeting discreetly withdrew, mistaking them for old friends. The following Monday (according to Gillman), Coleridge returned, carrying the proofs of 'Christabel' (Gillman, *Life*, 272; 276; but the proofs are a nice invention (see *CL*, IV, 631n.)). Coleridge was never to leave the household. In November 1823, he moved with his hosts to 3, The Grove, where he established his attic study-bedroom. Coleridge was now (as Sara was surprised to learn) *'quite grey haired'*;[1] but Lamb was not the only one to find 'his essentials not touched; he is very bad, but then he wonderfully picks up another day, and his face, when he repeats his verses, hath its ancient glory; an archangel a little damaged'.[2]

Encounters at Highgate, 1816-18

(i) JAMES GILLMAN
From Gillman, Life, *314-15. A variant of the shell routine Methuen witnessed.*

During the first week of his residence at Highgate, he conversed frequently on the Trinity and on Unitarianism, and in one of these conversations, his eye being attracted by a large cowry, very handsomely spotted: 'Observe,' said he, 'this shell, and the beauty of its exterior here pourtrayed. Reverse it and place it to your ear, and you will find it empty, and a hollow murmuring sound issuing from the cavity in which the animal once resided. This shell, with all its beautiful spots, was secreted by the creature when living within it, but being plucked out, nothing remains save the hollow sound for the ear. Such is Unitarianism; it owes any beauty it may have left to the Christianity from which it separated itself. The teachers of Unitarianism have severed from *their* Christianity its *Life,* by removing the doctrine of St. John; and thus mutilated, *they* call the residue the religion of Christ, implying the whole of the system, but omitting in their teaching the doctrine of redemption.'

(ii) HENRY CRABB ROBINSON

From Crabb Robinson, Diary, II, 11-12; Henry Crabb Robinson, On Books and Their Writers, *ed. Edith J. Morley (3 vols.; 1938), I, 215-16. 'I made one attempt to visit him (a morning call) at Highgate,' Lamb told Wordsworth, 'but there was something in him or his apothecary which I found so unattractively-repulsing- from any temptation to call again, that I stay away as naturally as a Lover visits'.[3] (Not an opinion he held long.)*

July 14th. [1816] – I walked to Becher, and he accompanied me to Gilman's [*sic*], an apothecary at Highgate, with whom Coleridge is now staying. And he seems to have profited already by the abstinence from opium, &c., for I never saw him look so well. He talked very sensibly, but less eloquently and vehemently than usual. He asked me to lend him some books, &c., and related a history of the great injustice done him in the reports circulated about his losing books. And certainly I ought not to join in the reproach, for he gave me to-day Kant's works, three vols., miscellaneous. Coleridge talked about Goethe's work on the theory of colours,[4] and said he had some years back discovered the same theory, and would certainly have reduced it to form, and published it, had not Southey diverted his attention from such studies to poetry. On my mentioning that I had heard that an English work had been published lately,[5] developing the same system, Coleridge answered, with great naïveté, that he was very free in communicating his thoughts on the subject wherever he went, and among literary people. <Becher was pleased with Coleridge. Lamb, who was to have joined me at Becher's, came to us here. He had not been long with us before Mr. Gillman entered the room very much with the air of a man who meant we should understand him to mean: 'Gentleman, it is time for you to go!' We took the hint and Lamb said he would never call again.>[6] [...]

30th Dec. [1817] ... I dined with the Colliers and spent the evening at Lamb's. I found a large party collected round the two poets, but Coleridge had the larger body. Talfourd[7] only had fixed himself by Wordsworth and remained by his side all the evening. There was, however, scarcely any conversation beyond a whisper. Coleridge was philosophising in his rambling way to Monkhouse, who listened attentively; to Manning, who sometimes smiled, as if he thought Coleridge had no right to metaphysicize on chemistry without any knowledge on the subject; to Martin Burney, who was eager to interpose, and Alsager, who was content to be a listener; while Wordsworth was for a great part of the time engaged *tête-à-tête* with Talfourd. I could catch scarcely anything of the conversation; but I heard at one time Coleridge quoting Wordsworth's verses, and Wordsworth quoting—*not* Coleridge's but his own. I chatted with the ladies.

(iii) JOHN R. DIX

From Pen and Ink Sketches of Poets, Preachers, and Politicians *(1846), 129-30; 132-3; 134-5 (recycled in Dix's* Lions: Living and Dead; or, Personal Recollections *(1852), 20-6.) Dix (?1800-?65), man of letters, was author of a controversial* Life of Chatterton. *At the time of this encounter, he had lately returned from meeting Wordsworth; the reference to* Biographia *dates it about 1816.*

I had just returned from my Lake visit [...] and was strolling in a beautiful meadow of romantic site, five miles from the metropolis, and outside of the village of Highgate, when I passed a rather corpulent, clerkly-looking man of the middle size, sauntering along, the autumn evening being a glorious one, when a courteous kind of voice said, 'Look to your pocket-handkerchief, sir,' which was, indeed, nearly trailing the ground behind. Turning to thank him, I saw a pale, rather heavy, phlegmatic-looking face, apparently of from fifty to sixty years' standing, with grey hairs, grey eyes, of a benign expression, yet somewhat inexpressive as a whole, marked with a peculiar languor, that might be a calm interval of pain, or profound pensiveness, or an absence of mind that often mimics deep thought, when perhaps the mind rests from thinking. His twinkling eyes seemed to enjoy the landscape. [...]

I shall throw together what I remember of the effects of his general deportment on my mind. Of course, I was more anxious to hear, than be heard. Yet I confess, I did fancy that the consciousness of what his friends told the public, and the public repeated, of his wondrous eloquence, was too visible, imparting a very little of what we dislike in a be-praised beauty's perpetual simper—an itch for admiration, prompting constant self-recollection. He seemed aware that strangers expected a treat from that eloquent mouth. [...] As to any interjected obstacle that his hearer might venture to edge in—a suggested flaw in his argument, or doubt to be resolved—it caused not a ripple. He smiled—gesticulated *seeming* assent, (with too much an air of adult indulgence to innocent child's prattle,) and pursued his 'high argument' just the same, never recurring to yours. [...]

Of the daily, almost hourly, arrivals of packets — letters with new works, imploring his obstetric aid in their struggles to avoid the fate of the still-born children of the press, — of religious debutants on a more sacred stage, all crowding under the wing of a public character, he complained almost with groaning; yet I did somehow conceit a — not 'roguish,' yet self-complacent 'twinkle in his eye,' that hinted some spice of comfort under the mountain of supplications, the penalty of 'finding oneself famous.' Indeed, I had proof of the fact, even on the few occasions of my seeing him at home.

He inquired about Edinburgh chit-chat with ostensible indifference, but ill-concealed eagerness, especially of the doings and sayings of the great little pole-star of the literary world — Jeffrey, whose battery of long range against him, as one of the 'knot of hypochondriacal and whining poets that haunt the Lakes,' as he wickedly described them, evidently broke through his habitually lofty elevation of thoughts, which kept, or seemed to keep, a calm for ever round him. He even anxiously hinted repeatedly his non-relationship to that family, in a manner which I fancied his friend Wordsworth (whose opinions of Coleridge I had listened to not a fortnight before,) would have deemed an 'unkind cut' at least, and Southey not less so. Of his friend Wordsworth, however, he spoke with admiration, though disclaiming for himself, as well as him, all pretension to being considered of any school, much less founders of one.

(iv) MARY RUSSELL MITFORD

From The Life of Mary Russell Mitford, *II, 11-12. From a letter to Sir William Elford, 13 September 1817.*

The best estimate I ever met with of Wordsworth's powers is in Coleridge's very out-of-the-way, but very amusing 'Biographia Literaria.' It is in the highest degree flattering, but it admits that he may have faults; and Mr. Lamb, who knows them both well, says he is sure Mr. Wordsworth will never speak to Mr. Coleridge again. Have you met with the 'Biographia Literaria'? It has, to be sure, rather more absurdities than ever were collected together in a printed book before; but there are passages written with sunbeams. The pleasantry throughout is as ungraceful as a dancing cow, and every page gives you reason to suspect that the author had forgotten the page that preceded it. I have lately heard a curious anecdote of Mr. Coleridge, which, at the risk—at the certainty—of spoiling it in the telling, I cannot forbear sending you. He had for some time relinquished his English mode of intoxication by brandy and water for the Turkish fashion of intoxication by opium; but at length the earnest remonstrances of his friends, aided by his own sense of right, prevailed on him to attempt to conquer this destructive habit. He put himself under watch and ward; went to lodge at an apothecary's at Highgate, whom he cautioned to lock up his opiates; gave his money to a friend to keep; and desired his druggist not to trust him. For some days all went well. Our poet was ready to hang himself; could not write, could not eat, could not—incredible as it may seem—could not talk. The stimulus was wanting, and the apothecary contented. Suddenly, however, he began to mend; he wrote, he read, he talked, he harangued; Coleridge was himself again! And the apothecary began to watch within doors and without. The next day the culprit was detected; for the next day came a second supply of laudanum from Murray's, well wrapped up in proof sheets of the 'Quarterly Review.'

(v) ANNA LETITIA LE BRETON

From Memories of Seventy Years. By One of a Literary Family *(1883), 77-78. Le Breton (1808-85) was a member of the Aikin dynasty, and grand-daughter of Gilbert Wakefield, Unitarian poet.*

My sister and myself, young girls, were on a visit to our good friends, Sir William and Lady Domville; they lived at Highgate, close to Mr. Gillman's, where Coleridge lived. One evening we were all asked to tea there. No one but the family were present. Mr. Coleridge was then giving a course of lectures on 'The female characters of Shakespeare.' He had delivered one that day, and his mind being full of the subject, he was easily led to it by Sir William, and began speaking without any break for more than an hour, giving us, I suppose, the whole of the lecture, all of us listening with wrapt attention to his wonderful eloquence.[8]

NOTES
[1] To Poole, June 1817: *Minnow Among Tritons*, 56.
[2] To Wordsworth, 26 April 1816: Talfourd, *Final Memorials of Lamb*, I, 221-2.

³ To Wordsworth, 23 September 1816: Lucas, *Life of Lamb*, I, 366.

⁴ Goethe's *Zur Farbenlehre* (1810) disputed Newton's theory of colours.

⁵ *TT* suggests (I, 288n.) that the English work is Richard Saumarez, *Principles of Physiological and Physical Science* (1812), praised in *BL* (I, 162n.).

⁶ Words in angle-brackets from *On Books and Their Writers*, ed. Morley, I, 185.

⁷ Thomas Noon Talfourd: for whom, see headnote below.

⁸ There was no 'course', but the first lecture of the 1818-19 series (*LL*, II, 269-70) dealt with the subject, and (as Leslie's report, following, suggests) STC returned to it more than once.

Last Lectures, 1818-19

(i) CHARLES ROBERT LESLIE

From Leslie, Autobiographical Recollections, I, 46-8.

A most interesting portion of Coleridge's lectures consisted in his pointing out the truth and refinement of Shakespeare's women, beyond those of all other dramatists; and how purified his imagination was from every thing gross, in comparison with those of his contemporaries.

Coleridge's lectures were, unfortunately, extemporaneous. He now and then took up scraps of paper on which he had noted the leading points of his subject, and he had books about him for quotation. On turning to one of these (a work of his own),[1] he said, 'As this is a secret which I confided to the public a year or two ago, and which, to do the public justice, has been very faithfully kept, I may be permitted to read you a passage from it.'

His voice was deep and musical, and his words followed each other in an unbroken flow, yet free from monotony. There was indeed a peculiar charm in his utterance. His pronunciation was remarkably correct: in some respects pedantically so. He gave the full sound of the *l* in *talk*, and *should* and *would*.[2]

Sir James Mackintosh attended the whole course of these lectures, and listened with the greatest interest. This was heaping coals of fire on the head of Coleridge, who had lampooned him with great severity for his political apostacy, as it was considered. I remember many years afterwards, when I had frequent opportunities of seeing Sir James, hearing him say that the best thing ever said of ghosts was by Coleridge, who, when asked by a lady if he believed in them, replied, 'No, Madam, I have seen too many to believe in them.'[3]

(ii) WILLIAM MUDFORD

From 'Geoffrey Oldcastle', 'The Late S.T. Coleridge, Esq.', Canterbury Magazine I (1834) 121-131, 127; 128. Mudford (1782-1848), of the Courier, came to know Coleridge, after he had praised Mudford's articles on the recently deceased Bishop of Llandaff (CL, IV, 813-14). Mudford attended Coleridge's next lectures.

These lectures, so eminently worthy of every encouragement, attracted but scanty audiences. If, instead of deep philosophy, various erudition, eloquent disquisition, and the stores of an exuberant imagination, Coleridge had invited the intellectual people of London to see a man swallow a sword, or toss about brass balls, he would have put money in his pocket. As it was, he gained nothing; if indeed he were not absolutely a loser by the experiment. His anxieties and disappointments formed the theme of most of the letters I received from him at that time [...]

I ventured to suggest to him, that he made his lectures too long for a mixed auditory, more especially as their matter was not of that flimsy, superficial character, that would admit of the attention being withdrawn and brought back at pleasure, without sustaining any intermediate loss. His reasonings were so close and subtle, and the series of his illustrations and demonstrations so beautifully connected, that like a problem in mathematics, if you missed any one of the propositions there was an end of the interest you felt in the deductions. But Coleridge, full of his subject, and his mind teeming with images, and facts, and illustrations, went on, without once considering, (though his delivery was not rapid,) how exhausting it was to those who really listened with a desire to follow him through the whole.[4]

(iii) JAMES GILLMAN

From Gillman, Life, 335-7; 354-7. Gillman formed rather a different impression.

These lectures, from his own account, were the most profitable of any he had before given, though delivered in an unfavorable situation; but being near the Temple, many of the students were his auditors. It was the first time I had ever heard him in public. He lectured from notes, which he had carefully made; yet it was obvious, that his audience was more delighted when, putting his notes aside, he spoke extempore;—many of these notes were preserved, and have lately been printed in the Literary Remains.[5] In his lectures he was brilliant, fluent, and rapid; his words seemed to flow as from a person repeating with grace and energy some delightful poem. If, however, he sometimes paused, it was not for the want of words, but that he was seeking the most appropriate, or their most logical arrangement.

The attempts to copy his lectures verbatim have failed, they are but comments. Scarcely in anything could he be said to be a mannerist, his mode of lecturing was his own. Coleridge's eloquence, when he gave utterance to his rich thoughts, flowing like some great river, which winds its way majestically at its own 'sweet will,' though occasionally slightly impeded by a dam formed from its crumbling banks, but over which the accumulated waters pass onward with increased force, so arrested his listeners, as at times to make them feel almost breathless. Such seemed the movement of Coleridge's words in lecture or in earnest discourse, and his countenance retained the same charms of benignity, gentleness, and intelligence, though this expression varied with the thoughts he uttered, and was much modified by his sensitive nature. His quotations from the poets, of high character, were most feelingly and most luminously given, as by one inspired with the subject. In my early intimacy with this great man, I was especially struck with the store of knowledge he possessed, and on which I ever found one might safely rely. I begged him to inform me by what means the human mind could retain so much, to which he always gave the following answer: 'The memory is of two kinds,' (a division I have ever found useful), 'the one kind I designate the passive memory, the other the creative, with the first I retain the names of *things*, *figures*, and *numbers*, &c. and this in myself I believe to be very defective. With the other I recall facts, and theories, &c. by means of their law or their principle, and in tracing these, the images or facts present themselves to me.' [...]

Early one morning he received two letters, which he sent me to read; one to inform him that he was *expected* that same evening to deliver a lecture at the rooms of the London Philosophical Society, where it was supposed that four or five hundred persons would be present: the other contained a list of the gentlemen who had already given a lecture in the course; to which was added, the subject on which each had addressed the audience. I well knew that Coleridge, not expecting this sudden appeal, would be agitated, as he was always excited before delivering a lecture, and that this would probably bring on a return of his inward suffering. After consulting together, we determined to go to town at seven o'clock in the evening to make some enquiries respecting this unexpected application, and arrived at the house of the gentleman who had written the letter. His servant informed us that he was not at home, but would return at eight o'clock, the hour fixed for the commencement of the lecture. We then proceeded to the society's room, which we found empty. It was a long one, partitioned off by a pole, the ends of which were fastened to the side-walls, and from this pole was nailed a length of baize which reached the floor, and in the centre was fixed a square piece of board to form a desk. We passed under this baize curtain to observe the other arrangements, from whence we could easily discern the audience as they entered. When we looked over the pole which formed the partition, we saw rows of benches across the room, prepared for about four or five hundred persons – on the side were some short ones, one above the other, intended for the committee. The preparations looked formidable – and Coleridge was anxiously waiting to be informed of the subject on which he was to lecture. At length the committee entered, taking their seats – from the centre of this party Mr. President arose, and put on a president's hat, which so disfigured him that we could scarcely refrain from laughter. He thus addressed the company: – 'This evening, Mr. Coleridge will deliver a lecture on the "Growth of the Individual Mind."' Coleridge at first seemed startled, and turning round to me whispered, 'a pretty stiff subject they have chosen for me.' He instantly mounted his standing place, and began without hesitation; previously requesting me to observe the effect of his lecture on the audience. It was agreed, that, should he appear to fail, I was to clasp his ancle, but that he was to continue for an hour if the countenances of his auditors indicated satisfaction. If I rightly remember his words, he thus began his address: – 'The lecture I am about to give this evening is purely extempore. Should you find a nominative case looking out for a verb – or a fatherless verb for a nominative case, you must excuse it. It is purely extempore, though I have thought and read much on this subject.' I could see the company begin to smile, and this at once seemed to inspire him with confidence. This beginning appeared to me a sort of mental curvetting, while preparing his thoughts for one of his eagle flights, as if with an eagle's eye he could steadily look at the mid-day sun. He was most brilliant, eloquent, and logically consecutive. The time moved on so swiftly, that on looking at my watch, I found an hour and a half had passed away, and therefore waiting only a desirable moment (to use his own playful words;) I prepared myself to 'punctuate his oration.' As previously agreed, I pressed his ancle, and thus gave him the hint he had requested — when bowing graciously, and with a benevolent and smiling countenance he presently descended.

NOTES

[1] Probably *Biographia* (published 1817), as Leslie says in a footnote.

[2] Henry Holgate Carwardine thought STC had 'a solemn and pompous mode of delivery, which he applies indiscriminately to the elevated and the familiar; and he reads poetry, I think, as ill as any man I ever heard' ('Rough Notes on Coleridge's Lectures', *N&Q* 4th. ser., V (1870) 335-6, 335).

[3] A response of which STC was clearly proud (e.g., *F*, I, 146). The anecdote did the rounds: Mackintosh repeated it in 1828 (*Memoirs of the Life of Sir James Mackintosh*, ed. Robert James Mackintosh (2 vols.; 1835), II, 436-7).

[4] STC's response to Mudford's advice survives (*CL*, IV, 912).

[5] H.N. Coleridge (ed.), *The Literary Remains of Samuel Taylor Coleridge* (4 vols.; 1836-9).

Scenes from Highgate Life

(i) S.C. HALL

From Samuel Carter Hall, A Book of Memories *(1871), 38; 42-3. Hall (1800-89) was editor (1826-36) of* The Amulet.

It was during his residence with the Gillmans that I knew Coleridge. He had arranged to write for the *Amulet*, and circumstances warranted my often seeing him — a privilege of which I gladly availed myself. In this home at Highgate, where all even of his whims were studied with affectionate and attentive care, he preferred the quiet of home influences to the excitements of society; and although I more than once met there his friend, Charles Lamb, and other noteworthy men of whom I shall have to say something, I usually found him, to my delight, alone. There he cultivated flowers, fed his pensioners, the birds, and wooed the little children who gamboled on the heath where he took his walks daily. [...]

I have listened to him more than once for above an hour, of course without putting in a single word; I would as soon have attempted a song while a nightingale was singing. There was rarely much change of countenance; his face, when I knew him, was overladen with flesh, and its expression impaired; yet to me it was so tender, and gentle, and gracious, and loving, that I could have knelt at the old man's feet almost in adoration. My own hair is white now; yet I have much the same feeling as I had then, whenever the form of the venerable man rises in memory before me. Yet I cannot recall — and I believe could not recall at the time, so as to preserve as a cherished thing in my remembrance — a single sentence of the many sentences I heard him utter. In his 'Table Talk' there is a world of wisdom, but that is only a collection of scraps, chance-gathered. If any left his presence unsatisfied, it resulted rather from the superabundance than the paucity of the feast. And probably there has never been an author who was less of an egotist: it was never of himself he talked; he was always under the influence of that divine precept, 'It is more blessed to give than to receive.'

(ii) WILLIAM HARNESS

From A.G. L'Estrange, The Literary Life of the Rev. William Harness, Vicar of All Saints, Knightsbridge, and Prebendary of St Paul's *(1871), 143-4. Harness (1790-1869), a visitor to Highgate, was an eminent preacher and a Shakespearean scholar, and the biographer of Mary Russell Mitford.*

Eminent literary men have often been remarkable for the fertility of their conversation, and their powers in this respect have not unfrequently been used without due restraint and discrimination. Coleridge was no exception to this rule; he would continue to talk on in an unbroken flow, and connect his arguments and observations so adroitly that until you had left him you could not detect their fallacy. Mr Harness called on him one day with Milman, on their return from paying a visit to Joanna Baillie. The poet seemed unus[u]ally inspired, and rambled on, raising his hands and his head in the manner which Charles Mathews so cleverly caricatured; and asserting, among other strange theories, that Shakespeare was a man of too pure a mind to be able to depict a really worthless character. 'All his villains,' he said, 'were bad upon good principles; even Caliban had something good in him.' Coleridge, in his old age, became a characteristic feature in Highgate. He was the terror and amusement of all the little children who bowled their hoops along the poplar avenue. Notwithstanding his fondness for them—he called them 'Kingdom-of-Heaven-ites'—his Cyclopean figure and learned language caused them indescribable alarm. Sometimes he would lay his hand on the shoulders of one of them and walk along discoursing metaphysics to the trembling captive, while the rest fled for refuge and peeped out with laughing faces from behind the trees. 'I never,' he exclaimed one day to the baker's boy—'I never knew a man good because he was religious, but I have known one religious because he was good.'[1]

(iii) THE LANDLADY OF THE LION AND SUN
From George Hodder, Memories of my Time *(1870), 102. Hodder is recalling the conversation of Joseph Kenny Meadows, illustrator and painter.*

Meadows, in these our pleasant perambulations, was wont to speak of an old lady who kept the Lion and Sun hotel in that neighbourhood. This was a favourite resort of Coleridge, and the communicative landlady used to remark that he was a great talker, and 'when he began there was no stopping him.' Whenever she returned to the room, she said, after leaving it for a short time, he would still be 'going on,' and sometimes he made such a noise that she wished him further.[2]

(iv) SEYMOUR TEULON PORTER
From 'Notes respecting the late S.T. Coleridge'; in Earl Leslie Griggs, 'Samuel Taylor Coleridge and Opium', Huntington Library Quarterly *XVII (1953-4) 357-78, 366; 368; 371-3; 373-4.[3] Porter worked for Dunn, the Highgate chemist who supplied Coleridge with opium until Gillman found out (in 1828, says Porter: p.376-7) and forbade him to continue. Coleridge visited only rarely thereafter.*

On the day on which I entered Dunn's house he spoke to me to the following effect:

'Porter, do you know the old gentleman who lives at Mr. Gillman's? Boys, you know, call him 'Gillman's Softie,' & such like; and many people who should know better speak of him as if he were only half-baked. I, however, think him the most wonderful man living; & though I have not read any of his books except a poem or two, I don't think there has been any one like him since the Apostle Paul.' (The Apostle was Mr Dunn's standard of human greatness.) 'Well, you'll see him here in a day or two. He will give you his bottle—one like this—and you'll fill it with laudanum from this big bottle, labelled 'Tinct. Opii'; and you'll say nothing to him unless he speaks to you, which, perhaps, he will do when you have seen him once or twice; and if he does, well, you'll never forget it. I have told him about you, so that, perhaps, he will talk to you very freely after a time; though at first he may look as if afraid of you. But mark! You must never tell anybody anything about him, not even that he takes laudanum. Never speak of him, if you can help it, unless to me; for if you do, I don't know what the consequences may be. He would be sure to die, to say the least; perhaps he would go out of his mind really, as some say he is now. But it is THEY, I think, who are silly; HE has got mind enough for any dozen of them.' [...]

I declare, without the slightest misgiving of any kind, that during my five years' residence at Mr. Dunn's I never heard from man, woman, or child, of the hundreds of people of whom I have spoken, & almost all of whom must have recognised Mr. Coleridge often on his errand to our house, a single word, either jocose or grave, to the dishonour of the august & venerable sage. He may have been called 'Gillman's Ward,' or 'Side Man,' or even 'Half-wit'; but such terms were used in pity rather than in reproach, & in mere familiar brevity rather than in either.

'So the old gentleman comes still for his dose!' 'What does such a good-looking old fellow want with so much physic!' 'Can't Gillman give him all the medicine he wants without sending him to you?' such words as these were the most unpleasant that I ever heard respecting Coleridge even from the worst-bred & the most ignorant of those who saw him come to our shop. He came about every five days; he never came but in full daylight; he came to the side-door, it is true, but he came openly, without disguise or false pretence; I do not suppose that he ever came without recognition by some one beside ourselves; he must have been seen often by several persons at once; if he came to the side-door not to the front, as this was only that he might not be obliged to lose time in conversation with friends & acquaintance whom he was liable to meet in the front-shop, it seems to have been understood by all about us without explanation. [...]

I went to Mr Dunn's in February, 1824; & we learn from various sources that in July of the same year Lord Byron's relics were conveyed through Highgate towards their final resting-place.[4] As I stood at our front-shop door, observing that small part of the funeral procession which had ascended the hill from St. Pancras, Mr. Coleridge who had been walking on the other side of the hearse, recognised me and presently crossed over & poured forth for some time to me, certainly not less than a quarter of an hour, a strain of marvellous eloquence on topics suggested by the scene of the hour, or rather by what we felt to be the great event of the day. I was too unwise, & had too little literary experience, to take notes of what he said; but I recal[l] distinctly the chief topics on which he spoke; such as Byron's unhappy youth; the extraordinary issue of it in his prodigious works & his numerous & great public merits; his great & special claims on his countrymen's generous if discriminative appreciation; the delightful fact that even then, at that so early period after his death, the funeral ceremonies indicated strong public action, or re-action in his favour; & the certainty that in the future, according to the noble wont of the English people, Byron's literary merits would seem continually to rise, while his personal errors, if not denied, or altogether forgotten, would be little noticed, & would be treated with ever softening gentleness. Let it be remembered, now, that when Mr. Coleridge honoured me with this choice discourse, I was only a white-aproned youth of fifteen years of age, of whom he knew nothing, or very little, beyond the facts that I was accustomed to fill his laudanum-bottle every five or six days, & that he had frequently, when calling for the medicine and seeing no bystander, talked with me on various topics, for the most part such topics as were part of 'the news of the day'. [...] Some of my longest & most pleasant interviews of the kind, however, having been enjoyed by me not in the back-shop, but in a green lane nearly parallel to the West Hill as it descended from Highgate to Kentish Town. For this lane, not much frequented, was a favourite resort of Coleridge's, particularly at certain hours; & as business took me at times to London I used to endeavour to time my journeys so as to meet him, who, whether he was reading or making notes, never, I believe, allowed me to pass without gratifying me with, at least, a passing remark or two, though more frequently with a few minutes' dissertation on whatever at the time engaged his thoughts. [...]

I do not wish to imply that in these later days Mr. Coleridge ever spoke at all, even to me, respecting the laudanum. He had spoken to me once or twice respecting it while I was alone, or only with Mr. Dunn, who could hear nothing: but there was no occasion for reverting to the topic, &, indeed, there was nothing to say about it. I cannot recal[l] his actual expressions in his earlier references to it; much less can I particularize times or occasions on which his language was unusually emphatic. But in the course of the few months during which I was virtually alone in the back-shop he had said enough to convince me unchangeably that laudanum was of vital importance to him. He admitted that he ought not to have prolonged his early use of it after recovery from acute disease; he admitted, too, that he had indulged himself very culpably in the subsequent use of it; & he spoke of his thankfulness that the quantity which he now took, was much less than his former. But he described his feelings, if from any cause debarred from it for a time, as those of a man sinking in various morbidity into the total collapse of death; he said that what he took now was only sufficient to sustain him in general health & vigour; & he more than once likened his case to that of a gouty man, who bore, indeed, consequences of sin or errors of youth, but who was not deprived of his guaiacum or his colchicum as a preventive or an alleviation of acute attacks. It should be borne in mind distinctly, too, that the utterer of all this self-defence, or explanation, was an elderly looking gentleman of most venerable & loveable aspect, & the simplest & most courteous manners; a man whom no person could have suspected of guile or social blame-worthiness of any nature; whose local reputation after long residence in Highgate was that of a saint-like & sinless sage who could do no wrong; & who certainly was incapable of trying to talk over an admiring & a trustful youth in order that the lad might spread a false report respecting him.

(v) MR. EAGLES

From Moses Coit Tyler, Glimpses of England, Social, Political, Literary (NY, 1898), 219-22. Tyler (1835-1900), ultimately Professor of American History at Cornell, was a keen Coleridgean. His book describes two visits to Highgate. The first, in 1863, found the Gillmans' house to let: 'William Howitt told me that an ardent American professor once tried to buy the door of the room which Coleridge used for his study. I confess that nothing but a very abject consideration prevented me from attempting to buy all the doors, and indeed the whole house with them, and packing them all off to America.' (pp. 218-19). In 1866, he returned to his site of pilgrimage.

I had seen in the papers that a chapel was then building in the churchyard, and that the graves of Coleridge and of his family were to be left untouched, in the middle of a crypt beneath the chapel. On arriving alone at the churchyard, I was unable to find the graves I sought. In reply to a question from me, the workmen on the new building stared at me curiously as a sentimental interloper; and all the more, when I made bold to ask them to show me the grave of

Coleridge. They knew nothing about Coleridge or his grave; but said rather compassionately that there was an old man in the village, one Eagles, a seedsman, who had lived here always, and knew every live man, and the grave of every dead one—and doubtless he could tell me what I wanted to know. I strolled along the street till I came to Mr. Eagles's little shop; and opening the sleepy door, with its bell jangling a shrill outcry at my invasion, I found a quiet, tall, elderly man, standing behind a little counter, and busy with papers of seeds. His appearance was, indeed, refined, benignant, even venerable; and to my questions he replied promptly, and with none of the pomposity or of the obsequiousness so common to petty English tradesmen. He told me how to find the grave; and as I turned to go, thanking him, I merely added: 'I come from a country a long way off—a country where Coleridge is greatly honored—from America.' Upon this he turned upon me with a brightened face and a manner surprised into cordiality, exclaiming: 'This is very extraordinary. I have had a great many American gentlemen here for the same errand, in former years, before the war; almost none for a long time now. I shall be most happy to go with you, and show you the place. I am going that way.'

As we went, he told me what he could remember about Coleridge. As a boy he had often seen and talked with the famous man; and he showed me the very path under the trees where Coleridge used to walk, and he pointed out one tree before which he had seen the poet stop perfectly still for a long time, and stare into vacancy. As an apprentice to a gardener, Eagles used to work near Mr. Gillman's house, and had hundreds of times stopped to gaze at the aged man, with his long, flowing white locks, his great eyes, his kind, wise face, as he paced slowly up and down beneath these elms, with a book in hand. The tones of the poet's voice, Eagles said, were very rich, beautiful, and friendly; and he was a great favorite with all the little boys and girls of the village, who used to rush up to him affectionately and hold merry talks with him. I asked the gardener if he remembered seeing any of Coleridge's friends coming to visit him.

'Oh, yes,' said he, 'I used to see many great folks; but I didn't know who they were. But at the house of my master there lodged a literary gentleman—I forget his name; and one evening he gave a dinner in his room to Coleridge, and to Charles Lamb, and others. Yes, I remember well Charles Lamb—he was so queer-looking and he came very often. I was in the next room, and heard them when they got very merry over their wine. Coleridge's voice I heard most of the time. Some one gave the toast, 'Here's to the lasses!' and some one else shouted 'With an offering of glasses!' and threw a large tray of them on the floor.'

NOTES

1 STC's encounters with bewildered children were a stock joke in the circle. Charles Mathews (see below) did a celebrated impersonation of STC way-laying an apothecary's boy: '"Boy, did you never reflect upon the magnificence and beauty of the external universe?" Boy. "No, sir, never," &c., &c.' (The Reminiscences of Alexander Dyce, ed. Richard J. Schrader (Columbus, OH, 1972), 179). Parents could be quite as bewildered: Sir T.H. Farrer recalled STC arriving early for dinner and walking 'up and down our pretty lawn with my mother, a handkerchief thrown over his white head, discoursing intently on all sorts of wonderful things, which were, no doubt, as unintelligible to her as they were to me' ('Recollections of Hampstead'; in Records of the Manor, Parish, and Borough of Hampstead, ed. F.E. Baines (1890), 503). People of all kinds might be caught:

> A friend of our's, who as he often observed, was the very antipodes of literature, paid a morning visit to some friends at Highgate, and afterwards returned to lunch at the Inn; here he discovered a gentleman in earnest conversation with a carrier, who was every moment lifting up his hand in ecstacy as the poet revealed some of the mysteries of his art. Our friend gradually approached the stranger, and was equally fascinated with the talismanic influence of his conversation; hour after hour passed imperceptibly, and still he found himself unable to quit the presence of this wizard. Five o'clock at last struck, and only on Mr. C—— rising to go away, was he able to follow the example. We asked him afterwards what he thought of the poet; 'by G-d,' he replied with enthusiasm, 'the fellow's either mad, or else he's the greatest genius that ever lived. I thought human ability could never have possessed such powers of fascination.' ('On the Conversation of Authors', The Déjeuné; or, Companion for the Breakfast Table XLI (7 December 1820) 323-28, 326)

2 The same 'old lady' reported in The Mirror, no doubt: 'An old lady was one day asked how far she approved of Mr. Coleridge's wonderful oratorical talents: "Don't tell me," replied she, (one who did not understand the fine un-ravellings of metaphysics,) "I would not give a fig for a man who wants all the talk to himself"' ('Enort', 'Coleridge', The Mirror XXIV (1834), 208).

3 Edmund Blunden met a 'gentleman of Highgate' who had known one of STC's former errand-boys. '"Everybody believed," the old man said, "that I was sent to get opium. But it was only snuff"' (TLS 1499 (23 October 1930), 866).

4 Byron's funeral procession climbed Highgate Hill on its way to the family burial site in Nottinghamshire: see Leslie A. Marchand, Byron: A Portrait (3 vols.; 1957), III, 1258-61.

Encounters at Highgate, 1819-25

(i) JOHN KEATS

From Letters of John Keats, *ed.* Sidney Colvin *(1891), 244; an excerpt from the long letter to George and Georgiana Keats, this part dated 15 April 1819. Keats (1795-1821) was in the midst of his great year, 'The Eve of St Agnes' behind him, and the great Odes to come, including, in May, 'Ode to a Nightingale'.*

Last Sunday I took a Walk towards Highgate and in the lane that winds by the side of Lord Mansfield's park I met Mr. Green[1] our Demonstrator at Guy's in conversation with Coleridge—I joined them, after enquiring by a look whether it would be agreeable—I walked with him at his alderman-after-dinner pace for near two miles I suppose. In those two Miles he broached a thousand things —let me see if I can give you a list—Nightingales—Poetry—on Poetical Sensation—Metaphysics—Different genera and species of Dreams—Nightmare—a dream accompanied by a sense of touch— single and double touch—a dream related—First and second consciousness—the difference explained between will and Volition —so say metaphysicians from a want of smoking the second consciousness—Monsters—the Kraken—Mermaids—Southey be- lieves in them—Southey's belief too much diluted—a Ghost story—Good morning—I heard his voice as he came towards me— I heard it as he moved away—I had heard it all the interval—if it may be called so. He was civil enough to ask me to call on him at Highgate.

(ii) CHARLES ROBERT LESLIE

From Leslie, Autobiographical Recollections, *48; 49; 50; 51-2.*

It was in company with Coleridge that I first heard the nightingale, that is, to know that I heard it. It was in a lane near Highgate where there were a number singing, and he easily distinguished and pointed out to me their full rich notes among those of other birds, for it was in the day time. He even told me how many were there. He took me to an eminence in the neighbourhood, commanding a view of Caen wood, and said the assemblage of objects, as seen from that point, reminded him of the passage in Milton, beginning—

> 'Strait mine eye hath caught new pleasures,
> Whilst the landskip round it measures.'[2]

—and running through the following eighteen or twenty lines.

Among the fragments of his conversation that I remember, are the following: —

'How natural is the exaggeration in the account the woman of Samaria carries to her friends of our Saviour. "Come, see a man which told me *all things that ever I did;*"[3] when, in reality, our Lord had only told her that she had had five husbands, and that he, whom she now had, was not her husband.' [...]

Speaking of the utilitarians, Coleridge said, 'The *penny saved penny got* utilitarians forget, or do not comprehend, *high moral utility,* – the utility of poetry and of painting, and of all that exalts and refines our nature.' He thought Lord Byron's misanthropy was affected, or partly so, and that it would wear off as he grew older. He said that Byron's perpetual quarrel with the world was as absurd as if the spoke of a wheel should quarrel with the movement of which it must of necessity partake. [...]

I once found Coleridge driving the balls on a bagatelle board for a kitten to run after them. He noticed that, as soon as the little thing turned its back to the balls it seemed to forget all about them, and played with its tail. 'I am amused,' he said, 'with their little short memories.' [...]

When Allston was suffering extreme depression of spirits, immediately after the loss of his wife, he was haunted, during sleepless nights, by horrid thoughts; and he told me that diabolical imprecations forced themselves into his mind. The distress of this to a man so sincerely religious as Allston, may be imagined. He wished to consult Coleridge, but could not summon resolution. He desired, therefore, that I would do it; and I went to Highgate, where Coleridge was at that time living with Mr. Gillman. I found him walking in the garden, his hat in his hand (as it generally was in the open air), for he told me that, having been one of the Blue-coat boys, among whom it is the fashion to go bare-headed, he had acquired a dislike to any covering of the head. I explained the cause of my visit, and he said, 'Allston should say to himself, "*Nothing is me but my will*. These thoughts, therefore, that force themselves on my mind are no part of *me*, and there can be no guilt in them." If he will make a strong effort to become indifferent to their recurrence they will either cease, or cease to trouble him.' He said much more, but this was the substance, and after it was repeated to Allston, I did not hear him again complain of the same kind of disturbance.

(iii) ANNE MATHEWS

From Mrs. [i.e. Anne] Mathews, Memoirs of Charles Mathews, Comedian *(4 vols.; 1838-9), III, 188-191; 193-5. Mathews (1776-1835) was a celebrated actor and a remarkable mimic. The Mathews family moved to Ivy Cottage, Kentish Town, in 1819, and came to know their new neighbour well.*

Many, many delightful hours did Mr. Coleridge's splendid conversation give us and our friends. His kind-heartedness, his beautiful simplicity of manner (for his familiar thoughts and expressions were as admirable as the higher attributes of his vast mind) we really loved, as much as we admired him. My flower-garden proved a very great attraction to him, and he visited it very often, being passionately fond of flowers. As he went he gathered them till his hands were full, repaying me for these floral treasures with the costly gems which fell from his mouth, as the pearls and diamonds were said to have poured from the lips of the good fairy, in the child's tale. He doted upon flowers, and discoursed so poetically upon them, that I frequently regretted my want of power to preserve the many-coloured beauties of his observations. He was so kind, too, whenever kindness was valuable. In illness his manner partook of the tender compassion of a woman; his pity was almost feminine. I remember, on one occasion, after a long confinement, his coming down the hill, one stormy and severe winter's night, to cheer me with an entertaining book—some periodical just published—and sitting with me and a friend, who resided with me, in my dressing-room, reading, and commenting upon what he read, until I forgot my indisposition. Indeed I do not know whether he was not a more charming companion when he stooped his magnificent mind to the understanding of the less informed and little gifted, than when he conversed with higher intellects. It is perhaps too bold an assertion, yet I will venture to say that he was not less delightful by such condescensions of his genius, or less esteemed for them. He was exceedingly attached to my husband, always writing and speaking of him as 'dear Mathews,' and he was equally partial to Charles.

The simplicity of Mr. Coleridge's character on familiar occasions, gave us infinite amusement; which, on his perceiving it, he allowed, with a smile against himself, while some charming remark would increase our enjoyment, and he would leave us with his benevolent features beaming with good-humour and kindness. One invariable result of his earnestly engaging in a long subject of discourse was a total abstraction of mind succeeding to it. In our drawing-room we had placed a large mirror, which reached from the ceiling to the floor, so inserted (without any visible frame) as to seem a continuation of the apartment. On taking leave, morning or night, he generally made an effort to pass through this glass; and it was our custom always to watch his first movement of departure, in order to be ready to guard against the consequences of an attempt to make his way out through this palpable impediment, and guide him to the door. To all this he would submit, talking and laughing upon the point which prevented his knowledge of outward things, until the entrance-gate was closed upon him.

During the first part of our acquaintance with him, Mr. Coleridge talked much to us of his friend 'Charles Lamb,' and expressed a strong desire that we should know him. His affectionate manner when speaking of Mr. Lamb, interested us as much for the *man* as for the *writer*, whose published works we had read; and it was at last arranged that we should dine on the fifth of May in this year [i.e. 1821], at Mr. and Mrs. Gilman's [*sic*] (the intellectual and excellent friends with whom Mr Coleridge resided), in order to meet this charming person and his amiable sister. [...]

My husband, who was punctuality itself, and all the little party, except the 'Elia' and his sister, were assembled. At last, Mr. and Miss Lamb appeared, and Mr. Coleridge led his friend up to my husband with a look which seemed to say, 'I pray you, like this fellow.' Mr. Lamb's first approach was not prepossessing. His figure was small and mean; and no man certainly was ever less beholden to his tailor. His 'bran' new *suit* of black cloth (in which he affected several times during the day to take great pride, and to cherish as a novelty that he had long looked for and wanted) was drolly contrasted with his very rusty silk stockings, shown from his knees, and his much too large *thick* shoes, without polish. His shirt rejoiced in a wide ill-plaited frill, and his very small, tight, white neckcloth was hemmed to a fine point at the ends that formed part of the little bow. His hair was black and sleek, but not formal, and his face the gravest I ever saw, but indicating great intellect, and resembling very much the portraits of King Charles I. Mr. Coleridge was very anxious about his *pet* Lamb's first impression upon my husband, which I believe his friend saw; and guessing that he had been extolled, he mischievously resolved to thwart his panegyrist, disappoint the strangers, and altogether to upset the suspected plan of showing him off. The *lamb*, in fact, would not consent to be made a *lion* of, and it followed that he became puerile and annoying all the day, to Mr. Coleridge's visible mortification. Before dinner he was suspicious and silent, as if he was taking the measure of the man he came to meet, and about whom he seemed very curious. Dinner, however, opened his lips for more than one purpose; and the first glass of wine (enough at all times, as we afterwards found, to touch if not shake his brain) set his spirit free, and he became quite impracticable. He made the most absurd puns and ridiculous jokes, and almost harassed Coleridge out of his self-complacency, though he managed to maintain a tolerable degree of evenness with his tormentor, now and then only rebuking him mildly for what he termed 'such unworthy trifling.' This only served to exasperate the perverse humour of him it was intended to subdue; and once Mr. Coleridge exclaimed meekly, after some very bad joke: 'Charles Lamb, I'm *ashamed* of you!' – a reproof which produced only an impatient 'You be hanged!' from the reproved; and another jest, 'more potent than the former,' was superadded to his punning enormities.

Mr. Lamb's last fire, however, was at length expended, and Mr. Coleridge took advantage of a pause to introduce some topic that might divert the party from his friend's determined foolery. He chose a subject which he deemed unlikely, if not impossible, for Lamb to interrupt with a jest. Mr. Coleridge stated, that he had originally been intended for the pulpit, and had taken orders; nay, had actually preached several times. At this moment fancying he saw something in Lamb's face that denoted a lucid interval, and wishing to turn him back from the nonsense which had so 'spoiled the pleasure of the time,' with a desire also to conciliate the 'pouting boy,' as he seemed, (who, to *our* observation, was only waiting for an opportunity to revenge himself upon his friend for all the grave checks he had given to his jocular vein during dinner,) Coleridge turned benignly towards him, and observed – 'Charles Lamb, I believe you never heard me *preach?*' As if concentrating his pent-up resentment and pique into one focus, and with less of his wonted hesitation, Lamb replied, with great emphasis, 'I *ne-ever* heard you do anything *else!*'[4]

(iv) CHARLES LLOYD

From 'Desultory Thoughts'; in Desultory Thoughts in London, Titus and
Gisippus, with Other Poems (1821), 25; 26-7; 31.

One near thee, London, dwells, to whom I fain
    Tribute would pay, or ere this lay I close;
Yet how can I — ungifted with a strain
    Fit to arrest the ear of him who knows
To build such verse as Seraphim might deign
    To listen to, nor break the deep repose
Of those immortal ardours that inspire
Spirit of inextinguishable fire —

How shall I fitly speak on such a theme?
    He is a treasure by the world neglected,
Because he hath not, with a prescience dim,
    Like those whose every aim is self-reflected,
Pil'd up some fastuous trophy, that of him
    Might tell, what mighty powers the age rejected,
But taught his lips the office of a *pen* —
By fools he's deem'd a being lost to men. [...]

No! with magnanimous self-sacrifice,
    And lofty inadvertency of fame,
He felt there is a bliss in *being* wise,
    Quite independent of the wise man's *name*.
Who now can say how many a soul may rise
    To a nobility of moral aim
It ne'er had known, but for that spirit brave,
Which, being freely gifted, freely gave?

Sometimes I think that I'm a blossom blighted;
    But this I ken, that should it not prove so,
If I am not inexorably spited
    Of all, that dignifies mankind below;
By him I speak of, I was so excited,
    While reason's scale was poising to and fro,
'To the better cause;' that him I have to bless
For that which it is comfort to possess.

In sickness both of body and of mind,
    Was he to me a friend in very deed;
When first I met him, you might likeness find,
    To that state from the which my heart he freed,
In fallow meadow, equally inclin'd,
    To be possess'd with good or evil seed:

Much toil he lavish'd on uncultur'd ground;
In that, if fruitless, must the fault be found. [...]

I have had comrades both for weal and *woe*;
I have had compeers both for good and *ill*;
But thou'rt the only one I e'er did know
Who sufferedst such a breeze life's sails to fill,
That all the *scath* I from the *last* did know,
Thou metamorphosedst, with wizard's skill,
Into a course more blithe, though not less sure:
And *Wisdom's* smile, in *thee*, had folly's lure.

(v) SIR JOHN TAYLOR COLERIDGE
From Bernard, Baron Coleridge, This for Remembrance *(1925), 34; 35; 36-9.*

January 1823. — On Thursday my Uncle Sam and Sara dined with us, and Rennell and Lyall came to meet him.[5] I have heard him more brilliant, but he was very fine, and delighted both Rennell and Lyall very much. It is impossible to carry off or commit to paper his long trains of argument, indeed it is not always possible to understand them, he lays the foundation so deep and views every question in so original a manner. Nothing can be finer than the principles he lays down in morals and religion; the wonder, the painful wonder, is that a man who can think and feel as he does — for I am convinced he feels as he speaks while he is speaking — should have acted and still act as he has done and does. [...]

We fell upon ghosts, and he exposed many of the stories metaphysically and physically. He seemed to think it impossible that you should really see with the bodily eye what was impalpable, unless it were a shadow; and what you fancied you saw with the bodily eye was in fact only an impression on the imagination; then you are seeing something 'out of your senses,' and your testimony is full of uncertainty. [...]

My uncle told us also at the same time the following striking story, which might well be dressed up and called 'The Phantom Portrait.'

A stranger came, recommended to a merchant's house at Lubeck. He was hospitably received, but the house being full, was lodged at night in an apartment handsomely furnished but not often used. There was nothing that struck him particularly in the room when left alone, till he happened to cast his eyes on a picture, which immediately arrested his attention. It was a single head, but there was something so uncommon, unearthly, and frightful in it, though by no means ugly, that he found himself irresistibly attracted to look at it; and he could not remove from it, until his whole imagination was so filled by it that it broke his rest.

He dreamed and continually awoke with the picture staring at him. In the morning his host saw by his looks he had slept ill, and inquired the cause, which he frankly told him. The master of the house was much vexed and said the picture ought to have been removed, that it was an oversight, and it always was removed when the chamber was used. The picture was indeed, he said, terrible to everyone, but it was so fine and had come into the family in so curious a way that he could not make up his mind to part with it or destroy it. The story of it was this:—

'My father,' said he, 'was at Hamburg on business, and dining at a coffee-house, when he observed a young man of a remarkable appearance enter, and seat himself alone in a corner, and commence a solitary meal. His countenance bespoke the extreme of mental distress, and he observed him every now and then turn his head quickly round, as if he heard something, shudder, grow pale, and then go on after an effort as before. He saw this same man at the same place for two or three successive days, and at length became so much interested about him that he spoke to him. His address was not repulsed, and the stranger seemed to find some comfort in the tone of sympathy and kindness which my father used. My father found him an Italian, well-informed, poor, but not desperate, living economically on the profits of his art as a painter. Their intimacy increased, and at length the Italian, seeing my father's involuntary emotion at his convulsive turns and shudders, which continued as before, interrupting their conversation, told him his story.

'He was a native of Rome who had lived in some familiarity with, and been much patronised by, a young nobleman. But upon some slight occasion they had fallen out, and the nobleman, besides many reproachful expressions, had struck him. The painter brooded over the disgrace of the blow. He could not challenge the nobleman on account of his rank. He watched his opportunity and assassinated him. Of course, he fled his country, and finally had reached Hamburg. He had not passed, however, many weeks from the day of the murder before one day, in the crowded street, he distinctly heard his name called by a voice familiar to him. He turned short round and saw the face of his victim looking at him with a fixed eye. From that time he had no interval of peace. At all hours and in all places, and amidst all companies, however engaged, he heard this voice, and could never help looking round when he saw always this same face staring at him. At last, in a mood of desperation, he had deliberately drawn the phantom as it looked at him, and this was the picture. He said he had struggled long, but life was a burthen which he could no longer bear, and he was resolved, when he had made money enough, to return to Rome to surrender himself to justice and expiate his crime on the scaffold. He gave the picture to my father in return for the kindness he had shown him.'

(vi) HENRY CRABB ROBINSON
From Crabb Robinson, Diary, *II, 250.*

May 2nd. [1823] — Having discharged some visits, I had barely time to return to dress for a party at Mr. Green's, Lincoln's Inn Fields. An agreeable party. Coleridge was the only talker, and he did not talk his best; he repeated one of his own jokes, by which he offended a Methodist at the whist-table; calling for her *last trump,* and confessing that, though he always thought her an angel he had not before known her to be an archangel.

(vii) GIOACCHINO DE'PRATI
From 'An Autobiography: The Medical Adviser's Life and Adventures. Part the Second — Chapter the Twelfth', Penny Satirist *II.77 (6 October 1838) 1-2, 2 (a revised version of 'S.T. Coleridge — Garden Talk',* The Shepherd *IV.ii (1 February 1837), 31-32). Prati (1790-1863), journalist and medical columnist, lived in exile in England from 1823 to 1852. His first visit to Coleridge was in April 1825, through Sir James Stuart (CL, V, 426-7; 452n.). (See M.H. Fisch, 'The Coleridges, Dr. Prati and Vico',* Modern Philology *XLI (1943-4), 111-22.)*

A few minutes after, the poet made his appearance. I never shall forget the impression which Coleridge made upon me. There is something indescribable in a man of genius, that reveals itself at the first glance to every one who has sympathy for that which is grand and beautiful; it inspires us both with confidence and admiration, and makes us feel as if we stood near one with whom we had been connected for years. [...]

As soon as the usual civilities were exchanged, the conversation became very lively, and the venerable poet soon began to pour out one of those torrents of eloquence which carry away the attention of the listener, and make him forget both time and space.

When Sir [J].S. looked at his watch he saw that we had remained there longer than we intended. We then arose from our seats and took leave both of Coleridge and the excellent couple, who, full aware of the worth of Coleridge, at an epoch when the fashionable world scarcely knew his very name, had received him as an inmate in their house, and taken that care of him which dutiful children only take of a respected aged parent. May the idea of having thus repaired the injustice, and indifference of our contemporaries, towards one of the most eminent geniuses of our age, fill their bosom with eternal bliss!

We did not leave the house without visiting the garden, which was a favourite place of our poet; here he took me under his arm, and we began to converse together in German. Coleridge spoke this language quite correctly, and with a soft Hanoverian accent. German literature stood highly in his favour; this sympathy for the German was only equalled by his aversion for the French. He seemed to take so much interest in me, that he made me promise to be with him the next day an hour or two before the company which was wont to visit him, did assemble. 'We shall,' said he 'have a private talk here in the garden if the weather be fine, otherwise you will excuse my taking you in my room, which is my place of rest, my study, and my library.'

On returning home, Mrs. W., the sister of the noble baronet, who introduced me to C., asked how I was satisfied with my new acquaintance. 'Satisfied,' answered I, 'I am delighted, enraptured; I find concentrated in him all the talents which I have left with regret on the continent. As a poet, he reminds me of Schiller, as a philosopher, he equals Schelling, and as a speaker, he excels Fichte. As far as I could judge of those different talents combined together, he stands between Göethe and Lessing. I shall see him to-morrow, and I expect a great treat from a private conversation which he promised me.'

From 'An Autobiography. The Medical Adviser's Life and Adventures. Part the Second – Chapter the Thirteenth', Penny Satirist, II.78 (13 October 1838), 4.

Whether he was speaking on metaphysics, theology, poetry, history, or the most trifling subjects of common occurrence, his genius threw a new light upon the object of his discourse, and compelled his company to think in their turn, and to examine the

question in a point of view, which, without his aid, would for ever
have escaped their minds. His friends assembled at Mr. Gillman's
towards tea time, and remained there till late in the evening.

I often spent the morning and afternoon with him, and had the
pleasure of conversing with him for whole hours, which I reckon
among the most agreeable and instructive ones I ever spent in my
life. For he was not only a deep philosopher and poet, but a man
possessed of great knowledge in many sciences, and was moreover
the most pleasant and humorous companion in the world. No day
elapsed in which he did not amuse me with some pleasant
anecdote, in which he or some of his friends cut the principal
figure.

I will relate one which afforded me great amusement. 'At one
time,' said Coleridge to me, 'I was obliged to write now an article,
now a squib for a morning paper; for you know as well as I do the
saying of the painter in Lessing's "Emilia Galotti," "Die kunst
gehet nach brot." Art craves after bread. It happened, that at the
same time I had published some work, which was condemned by
the public to perpetual oblivion. That vexed me, or as the Germans
graphically express it, "das warmte mich," which I could not better
translate than by periphrasis; it was like wormwood to me. To
draw the attention of the public upon this work, I wrote a most
pungent squib against its author, viz., against myself. Well, then,
so far so good. A few months later, when I was giving my lectures
on Shakspeare, a friend of mine wishing to introduce a gentleman
of his acquaintance, came to see me, and after some conversation
thus addressed me: — "S.C., there is a young gentleman who
wishes to make your acquaintance, yet he is afraid to approach
you, on account of his being conscious of having given you great
offence; but I, knowing you so well, told him that you were not the
man to resent any act of petulance or youthful imprudence." "But,
pray," asked I, "my friend, what has the young gentleman done
unto me?" "Well," replied he, "you have seen or heard of a most
impertinent squib, which appeared against you a few months ago
in a morning paper. He is the author of it. But having since heard
your lectures, he repents sincerely his foolish rhymes, and begs me
to apologise." I stood amazed. Such a piece of impudence I had
never heard before. Yet I did not wish to disgrace him before my
friend as a coxcomb, and replied: "Well, then, if the young

gentleman sincerely repents of his folly, you may introduce him to me, and I will say not a word about it."

Among the gentlemen and ladies who weekly assembled around Coleridge, were Basil Montagu,[6] his wife, Mrs. Jameson, Mr. Jameson, Lamb, Mr. Joseph Henry Green, his wife, and the Rev. Mr. Irving, the great preacher,[7] and several others, whose names have escaped my memory. Before and during tea, the conversation was promiscuous, but afterwards some subject was introduced, upon which Coleridge expanded himself in a torrent of eloquence. All around him were so taken up with his speech, that seldom a word or a whisper was heard during the whole time he was addressing the company. I remember with delight the instruction and pleasure I derived from these discourses, which cannot be better compared than with the dialogues of Plato. The finest loftiest ideas, pouring forth amidst the most blooming poetical phrases, allegories, and types, now spiced with Socratic irony, now strengthened by close and all-penetrating argumentation, afforded an intellectual banquet, nowhere to be met either here o[r] in any part of the continent. Goethe and Madame de Sta[ë]l were perhaps the only ones who could compete with Coleridge in fluency, depth, and originality of conversation. All three are gone. Who shall now dare to assume their station?

Once when walking with him in the garden, we wer[e] speaking about the difficulty of translating. 'Truly,' said he, 'no one knows how difficult it is to translate well, but he who has attempted to translate a masterwork. I have done all the justice I could to "Wallenstein," but I could not venture upon translating the "Camp," which is perhaps the most original part of the work. I would have attempted to translate your favourite "Faustus," but I must give it up in despair. To translate it so as to make the English readers acquainted with the plot, is a foolish task. The beauty of this work consists in the fine colour of the style, and in the tints, which are lost to one who is not thoroughly *au fait* with German life, German philosophy, and the whole literature of that country. The antithesis between the slang of Mephistophiles, the over-refined language of Faustus, and the pastoral simplicity of the child of Nature, Margaret, requires a man's whole life to be made self-evident in our language. And therein lies Goethe's peculiarity. I would have wished also to translate some of Goethe's minor poems, which I esteem not only as the best productions of Goethe, but among the best of the modern lyrics. I found equal difficulty. To show how hard it is for one who translates to give the true meaning of his author — take, for instance, our word clever and the German gemüthlich [*sic*]. Neither can the German convey, but by periphrasis, ideas which the single word "clever" signifies, nor that which the Germans understand under "gemüthlich."

'A clever man is not merely a man of talent — indeed, he may possess but moderate talents, little knowledge, and be clever.

'The clever man is a produce [*sic*] of a certain tact acquired by great practice. Yes, talent is a natural gift, cleverness an artificial one. The clever man does not what is the best, but that which is most to the purpose; his actions are not the offspring of principle, but of circumstances, to which he knows how to accommodate himself. If he is an artist, he produces that which fetches the greatest money; if a politician, he advises that which is most feasible for certain purposes; in morality, in religion, in every thing he is a latitudinarian. In fact, clever men are those which Tacitus calls *callidi temporum et sapientes*.[8] Now, what language can convey the ideas which we associate with the one word "clever"? and who can translate your "gemüthlich?" The very nature of the English, that which we call sterling English, is an antithesis to that which you call gemüthlich. In fact, our peculiarity is to be stern or humorous. In the whole gallery of Shakspeare's characters, there is no one trace of "gemüth" or "gemüthlich."'

(viii) HENRY CRABB ROBINSON
From Crabb Robinson, Diary, *II, 296-7.*

June 16th. [*1825*] — Finding myself released at an early hour from my professional duties, I took a cold dinner at the Athenæum, and then went to Basil Montagu. Mr. Edward Irving was there. He and his brother-in-law, Mr. Martin, and myself placed ourselves in a chariot. Basil Montagu took a seat on the outside, and we drove to Highgate, where we took tea at Mr. Gilman's [*sic*]. I think I never heard Coleridge so very eloquent as to-day, and yet it was painful to find myself unable to recall any part of what had so delighted me, — *i.e.* anything that seemed worthy to be noted down. So that I could not but suspect some illusion arising out of the impressive tone and the mystical language of the orator. He talked on for several hours without intermission. His subject the ever-recurring one of religion, but so blended with mythology, metaphysics, and psychology, that it required great attention sometimes to find the religious element. I observed that, when Coleridge quoted Scripture or used well-known religious phrases, Irving was constant in his exclamations of delight, but that he was silent at other times. Dr. Prati came in, and Coleridge treated him with marked attention. Indeed Prati talked better than I ever heard him. [...] Coleridge referred to an Italian, Vico, who is said to have anticipated Wolf's theory concerning Homer, which Coleridge says was his own at College.[9]

NOTES

[1] Joseph Henry Green (1791-1863), Professor of Anatomy at the Royal College of Surgeons, a devoted Coleridgean (and STC's literary executor). *Spiritual Philosophy* (1865) sought to systematise the master, without obvious success.

[2] 'L'Allegro', ll.69-70.

[3] John 4.29.

[4] A good story, with variations:

> William Coope tells us that he used often to see S.T. Coleridge till within a month of his death, and was an ardent admirer of his prominent blue eyes, reverend hair, and rapt expression. He has met Charles Lamb at his house. On one occasion Coleridge was holding forth on the effects produced by his preaching, and appealed to Lamb, 'You have heard me preach, I think?' 'I have never heard you do anything else,' was the urbane reply. (18 December 1836: *Journals of Caroline Fox*, ed. Horace N. Pym (3rd.edn.; 2 vols.; 1882), I, 23)

[5] Thomas Rennell (1754-1840), Dean of Winchester, and William Rowe Lyall (1788-1857), later Dean of Canterbury.

[6] Montagu was editing Bacon; Hatherley (with Wordsworth's old friend Francis Wrangham) was translating the Latin texts. STC left Montagu a lock of hair in his will (*CL*, VI, 1000); Montagu writes effusively about it in his odd little book, *The Funerals of the Quakers* (1840), 82-3.

[7] Edward Irving (1792-1834), divine and famously gifted orator, came to London from Glasgow in 1822, and soon became a celebrity at his chapel in Hatton Garden. STC heard him preach, and thought him 'the greatest *Orator*, I ever heard' (*CL*, V, 280; 286). Irving met STC through Montagu in 1823, and became a member of the intimate circle; though by 1826 STC was growing wary of the increasing audacity of Irving's Biblical interpretation. His career ended in disaster: dismissed from his Regent Square Church for heresy, and finally deprived of his status in the Church of Scotland (see *CL*, V, 280n.).

[8] *The Annals*, IV, §33; meaning here, perhaps, something like 'canny' or 'having nous'.

[9] Friedrich Wolf (1759-1824) argued, in his *Prolegomena in Homerum* (1795), for the multiple authorship of Homeric epic, a view that the Italian philosopher Giambattista Vico (1668-1744) had also held. Wolf didn't know Vico; but by the late eighteenth century, the idea of a collective 'Homer' was not unusual.

At the Seaside

(i) WILLIAM STEWART ROSE

From William Stewart Rose, Rhymes *(Brighton, 1837), 87; 92n.17. Coleridge regularly holidayed at the seaside, usually with the Gillmans. In 'Gundimore', Rose (1775-1843), poet and translator of Ariosto, describes his Brighton house, which was visited by Scott, Ugo Foscolo (the Italian poet and patriot), and Coleridge:*

> And these 'ribbed sands' was Coleridge pleased to pace,
> While ebbing seas have hummed a rolling bass
> To his rapt talk. Alas! all three are gone —
> 'And I and other creeping things live on.'

A note explains: Coleridge and Foscolo had each promised poems on Gundimore.

It is an odd coincidence that the same promise (and as well unexecuted) should have been volunteered to me by the person now commemorated, and an inmate then with his kind friends, Mr. and Mrs. Gilmore [*sic*], at Mudiford. It was confirmed in writing to one who has lived with me forty years, and has served me as faithfully as he has long. [...] It is contained in a fly-leaf of a corrected copy of Christabel: —

> Dear Hinves, — Till this book is concluded, and with it 'Gundimore, a poem by the same author,' accept of this *corrected* copy of Christabel, as a *small* token of regard; yet such a testimonial *as I would not* pay to one I did not esteem, tho' he were an emperor. Be assured, I will send you for your private library every work I have published (if there be be [*sic*] any to be had), and whatever I shall publish. Keep steady to the FAITH. If the fountain-head be always full, the stream cannot be long empty.
>
> Yours sincerely,
>
> S.T. COLERIDGE
>
> 11th Nov. 1816, Mudiford.[1]

With respect to the phrase 'keep steady to the faith, &c.,' I imagine he was cautioning him he was addressing, against Foscolo's supposed licence in religious opinions.

'Gundimore' was never completed, nor (I believe) ever begun. I will, however, stoop to pick up (as anxious to preserve whatever fell from Mr. Coleridge) one of the morsels that was destined to enter into its composition. Walking with him upon the beach, a long wave came rolling in, and broke at our feet. 'That wave (said he) seems to me *like a world's embrace*, and I shall introduce it into Gundimore.'

(ii) HENRY CARY

From Henry Cary, Memoir of the Rev. Henry Francis Cary *(2 vols.; 1847), II, 18-19. Cary (1772-1844) was a poet and editor, most famous for his translation of Dante (which Coleridge admired). This comes from the life written by his son.*

After a morning of toil over Greek and Latin composition it was our custom to walk on the sands and read Homer aloud, a practice adopted partly for the sake of the sea-breezes, and not a little, I believe, in order that the pupil might learn to read *ore rotundo,* having to raise his voice above the noise of the sea that was breaking at our feet. For several consecutive days Coleridge crossed us in our walk. The sound of the Greek, and especially the expressive countenance of the tutor, attracted his notice; so one day, as we met, he placed himself directly in my father's way and thus accosted him: 'Sir, yours is a face I *should* know: I am Samuel Taylor Coleridge.' His person was not unknown to my father, who had already pointed him out to me as the great genius of our age and country.

Our volume of Homer was shut up; but as it was ever Coleridge's custom to speak, it could not be called talking or conversing, on the subject that first offered itself, whatever it might be; the deep mysteries of the blind bard engaged our attention during the remainder of a long walk. I was too young at that time to carry away with me any but a very vague impression of his wondrous speech. All that I remember is, that I felt as one from whose eyes the scales were just removed, who could discern and enjoy the light, but had not strength of vision to bear its fulness. Till that day I had regarded Homer as merely a book in which boys were to learn Greek; the description of a single combat had occasionally power to interest me; but from this time, I was ever looking for pictures in the poem, endeavouring to realise them to my mind's eye, and especially to trace out virtues and vices as personified in the heroes and deities of the Homeric drama.

The close of our walk found Coleridge at our family dinner table. Amongst other topics of conversation Dante's 'divine' poem was mentioned: Coleridge had never heard of my father's translation, but took a copy home with him that night. On the following day when the two friends (for so they may from the first day of their meeting be called) met for the purpose of taking their daily stroll, Coleridge was able to recite whole pages of the version of Dante, and, though he had not the original with him, repeated passages of that also, and commented on the translation. Before leaving Littlehampton he expressed his determination to bring the version of Dante into public notice; and this, more than any other single person, he had the means of doing in his course of lectures delivered in London during the winter months.

(iii) CHARLES AND MARY COWDEN CLARKE

From Charles and Mary Cowden Clarke, Recollections of Writers (1878), 30-3; 35. Clarke (1787-1877) was an author, critic, musician, and lecturer, and friend of Keats; his wife Mary (1809-98) was an eminent Shakespearean.

It was in the summer of 1821 that I first beheld Samuel Taylor Coleridge. It was on the East Cliff at Ramsgate. He was contemplating the sea under its most attractive aspect: in a dazzling sun, with sailing clouds that drew their purple shadows over its bright green floor, and a merry breeze of sufficient prevalence to emboss each wave with a silvery foam. He might possibly have composed upon the occasion one of the most philosophical, and at the same time most enchanting, of his fugitive reflections, which he has entitled 'Youth and Age;' for in it he speaks of 'airy cliffs and glittering sands,' and —

> Of those trim skiffs, unknown of yore,
> On winding lakes and rivers wide,
> That ask no aid of sail or oar,
> That fear no spite of wind or tide.[2]

As he had no companion, I desired to pay my respects to one of the most extraordinary — and, indeed in his department of genius, *the* most extraordinary man of his age. And being possessed of a talisman for securing his consideration, I introduced myself as a friend and admirer of Charles Lamb. This pass-word was sufficient, and I found him immediately talking to me in the bland and frank tones of a standing acquaintance. A poor girl had that morning thrown herself from the pier-head in a pang of despair, from having been betrayed by a villain. He alluded to the event, and went on to denounce the morality of the age that will hound from the community the reputed weaker subject, and continue to receive him who has wronged her. He agreed with me that that question never will be adjusted but by the women themselves. Justice will continue in abeyance so long as they visit with severity the errors of their own sex and tolerate those of ours. He then diverged to the great mysteries of life and death, and branched away to the sublimer question—the immortality of the soul. Here he spread the sail-broad vans of his wonderful imagination, and soared away with an eagle-flight, and with an eagle-eye too, compassing the effulgence of his great argument, ever and anon stooping within my own sparrow's range, and then glancing away again, and careering through the trackless fields of etherial metaphysics. And thus he continued for an hour and a half, never pausing for an instant except to catch his breath (which, in the heat of his teeming mind, he did like a schoolboy repeating by rote his task), and gave utterance to some of the grandest thoughts I ever heard from the mouth of man. His ideas, embodied in words of purest eloquence, flew about my ears like drifts of snow. He was like a cataract filling and rushing over my penny-phial capacity. I could only gasp and bow my head in acknowledgment. He required from me nothing more than the simple recognition of his discourse; and so he went on like a steam-engine—I keeping the machine oiled with my looks of pleasure, while he supplied the fuel: and that, upon the same theme too, would have lasted till now. What would I have given for a short-hand report of that speech! And such was the habit of this wonderful man. Like the old peripatetic philosophers, he walked about, prodigally scattering widsom, and leaving it to the winds of chance to waft the seeds into a genial soil.

My first suspicion of his being at Ramsgate had arisen from my mother observing that she had heard an elderly gentleman in the public library, who looked like a Dissenting minister, talking as she never heard man talk. Like his own 'Ancient Mariner,' when he had once fixed your eye he held you spell-bound, and you were constrained to listen to his tale; you must have been more powerful than he to have broken the charm; and I know no man worthy to do that. He did indeed answer to my conception of a man of genius, for his mind flowed on 'like to the Pontick sea,' that 'ne'er feels retiring ebb.'[3] It was always ready for action; like the hare, it slept with its eyes open. He would at any given moment range from the subtlest and most abstruse question in metaphysics to the architectural beauty in contrivance of a flower of the field; and the gorgeousness of his imagery would increase and dilate and flash forth such coruscations of similies [sic] and startling theories that one was in a perpetual aurora borealis of fancy. As Hazlitt once said of him, 'He would talk on for ever, and you wished him to talk on for ever. His thoughts never seemed to come with labour or effort, but as if borne on the gust of Genius, and as if the wings of his imagination lifted him off his feet.' This is as truly as poetically described. He would not only illustrate a theory or an argument with a sustained and superb figure, but in pursuing the current of his thought he would bubble up with a sparkle of fancy so fleet and brilliant that the attention, though startled and arrested, was not broken. He would throw these into the stream of his argument, as waifs and strays. Notwithstanding his wealth of language and prodigious power in amplification, no one, I think (unless it were Shakespeare or Bacon), possessed with him equal power of condensation. He would frequently comprise the elements of a noble theorem in two or three words; and, like the genuine offspring of a poet's brain, it always came forth in a golden halo. I remember once, in discoursing upon the architecture of the Middle Ages, he reduced the Gothic structure into a magnificent abstraction—and in two words. 'A Gothic cathedral,' he said, 'is like a petrified religion.' [...]

The upper part of Coleridge's face was excessively fine. His eyes were large, light grey, prominent, and of liquid brilliancy, which some eyes of fine character may be observed to possess, as though the orb itself retreated to the innermost recesses of the brain. The lower part of his face was somewhat dragged, indicating the presence of habitual pain; but his forehead was prodigious, and like a smooth slab of alabaster. A grander head than his has not been seen in the grove at Highgate since his neighbour Lord Bacon lived there. From his physical conformation Coleridge ought to have attained an extreme old age, and he probably would have done so but for the fatal habit he had encouraged of resorting to the stimulus of opium. Not many months before his death, when alluding to his general health, he told me that he never in his life knew the sensation of head-ache; adding, in his own peculiarly vivid manner of illustration, that he had no more internal consciousness of possessing a head than he had of having an eye.

NOTES

[1] Cf. *CL*, IV, 691. Happily, we also have Hinves's view (as reported by Rose):

'"Master, you say this Mr. Coleridge is a wonderful man, and so says Mr. Frere, and so say all of you; but I can't make him out! I can understand Sir

Walter Scott perfectly; I can understand both the Mr. Freres; I have no difficulty in taking what Mr. Gally Knight says; Mr. Hallam talks plain common sense that a child may understand; I can even make you out, my master, pretty well, when you steer clear of Latin and Greek and foreign lingos, but I can make nothing, nothing at all, of Mr. Coleridge. Still, as you all say so, Mr. Coleridge must be a wonderfully clever man — but what a pity it is he talks such a deal of nonsense!"' (MacFarlane, *Reminiscences*, 37-8)

[2] ll.12-15, *var.* (*CPW*, I, 439).
[3] *Othello*, III.iii, ll.453; 455.

Coleridge at Table

(i) THOMAS NOON TALFOURD

From Letters of Charles Lamb, *ed.* Talfourd, II, 25-9; Final Memorials of Charles Lamb, *ed.* Talfourd, II, 195-6. *Sir Thomas Noon Talfourd (1795-1854) was serjeant-at-law, journalist, dramatist, and Lamb's biographer.*

The years which Lamb passed in his chambers in Inner Temple-lane were, perhaps, the happiest of his life. His salary was considerably augmented, his fame as an author was rapidly extending; he resided near the spot which he best loved; and was surrounded by a motley group of attached friends, some of them men of rarest parts, and all strongly attached to him and to his sister. Here the glory of his Wednesday nights shone forth in its greatest lustre [...] There Coleridge sometimes, though rarely, took his seat; — and then the genial hubbub of voices was still; critics, philosophers, and poets, were contented to listen; and toil-worn lawyers, clerks from the India House, and members of the Stock Exchange, grew romantic while he spoke. Lamb used to say that he was inferior then to what he had been in his youth; but I can scarcely believe it; at least there is nothing in his early writing which gives any idea of the richness of his mind so lavishly poured out at this time in his happiest moods. Although he looked much older than he was, his hair being silvered all over, and his person tending to corpulency, there was about him no trace of bodily sickness or mental decay, but rather an air of voluptuous repose. His benignity of manner placed his auditors entirely at their ease; and inclined them to listen delighted to the sweet, low tone in which he began to discourse on some high theme. Whether he had won for his greedy listener only some raw lad, or charmed a circle of beauty, rank, and wit, who hung breathless on his words, he talked with equal eloquence;

for his subject, not his audience, inspired him. At first his tones were conversational; he seemed to dally with the shallows of the subject and with fantastic images which bordered it; but gradually the thought grew deeper, and the voice deepened with the thought; the stream gathering strength, seemed to bear along with it all things which opposed its progress, and blended them with its current; and stretching away among regions tinted with etherial colours, was lost at airy distance in the horizon of fancy. His hearers were unable to grasp his theories, which were indeed too vast to be exhibited in the longest conversation; but they perceived noble images, generous suggestions, affecting pictures of virtue, which enriched their minds and nurtured their best affections. Coleridge was sometimes induced to recite portions of 'Christabel,' then enshrined in manuscript from eyes profane, and gave a bewitching effect to its wizard lines. But more peculiar in its beauty than this was his recitation of Kubla Khan. As he repeated the passage—

> A damsel with a dulcimer
> In a vision once I saw:
>   It was an Abyssinian maid
> And on her dulcimer she played,
> Singing of Mount Abora!

his voice seemed to mount, and melt into air, as the images grew more visionary, and the suggested associations more remote. He usually met opposition by conceding the point to the objector, and then went on with his high argument as if it had never been raised: thus satisfying his antagonist, himself, and all who heard him; none of whom desired to hear his discourse frittered into points, or displaced by the near encounter even of the most brilliant wits. The first time I met him, which was on one of those Wednesday evenings, we quitted the party together between one and two in the morning; Coleridge took my arm, and led me nothing loath, at a very gentle pace, to his lodgings, at the Gloucester Coffee-house, pouring into my ear the whole way an argument by which he sought to reconcile the doctrines of Necessity and Free-will, winding on through a golden maze of exquisite illustration; but finding no end, except with the termination of that (to me) enchanted walk. He was only then on the threshold of the Temple of Truth, into which his genius darted its quivering and uncertain rays, but which he promised shortly to light up with unbroken

lustre. 'I understood a beauty in the words, but not the words.'[1]
[...]

A visit of COLERIDGE was always regarded by Lamb, as an opportunity to afford a rare gratification to a few friends, who, he knew, would prize it; and I well remember the flush of prideful pleasure which came over his face as he would hurry, on his way to the India House, into the office in which I was a pupil, and stammer out the welcome invitation for the evening. This was true self-sacrifice; for Lamb would have infinitely preferred having his inspired friend to himself and his sister, for a brief renewal of the old Salutation delights; but, I believe, he never permitted himself to enjoy this exclusive treat. The pleasure he conferred was great; for of all celebrated persons I ever saw, Coleridge alone surpassed the expectation created by his writings; for he not only was, but appeared to be, greater than the noblest things he had written.

Lamb used to speak, sometimes with a moistened eye and quivering lip, of Coleridge when young, and wish that we could have seen him in the spring-time of his genius, at a supper in the little sanded parlour of the old Salutation hostel. The promise of those days was never realised, by the execution of any of the mighty works he planned; but the very failure gave a sort of mournful interest to the 'large discourse, looking before and after,' to which we were enchanted listeners; to the wisdom which lives only in our memories, and must perish with them.

(ii) THOMAS MOORE

From Memoirs, Journal, and Correspondence of Thomas Moore, *ed. Lord John Russell (8 vols.; 1853-6), IV, 49-50. Moore (1779-1852) was one of the age's most popular poets, author of* Irish Melodies *and* Lalla Rookh. *This is from his diary entry for 4 April 1823.*

Dined at Mr. Monkhouse's (a gentleman I had never seen before),[2] on Wordsworth's invitation, who lives there whenever he comes to town. A singular party: Coleridge, Rogers, Wordsworth and his wife, Charles Lamb (the hero, at present, of the 'London Magazine')[3] and his sister (the poor woman who went mad with him in the diligence on the way to Paris), and a Mr. Robinson, one of the *minora sidera* of this constellation of the Lakes, the host himself, a Mecænas of the school, contributing nothing but good dinners and silence. Charles Lamb, a clever fellow certainly; but full of villainous and abortive puns, which he miscarries of every minute. Some excellent things, however, have come from him; and his friend Robinson mentioned to me not a bad one. On Robinson's receiving his first brief, he called upon Lamb to tell him of it. 'I suppose,' said Lamb, 'you addressed that line of Milton's to it: "Thou *first* best *cause*, least understood."'[4] Coleridge told some tolerable things. One of a poor author, who, on receiving from his publisher an account of the proceeds (as he expected it to be) of a work he had published, saw among the items, 'Cellerage, 3*l*. 10*s*. 6*d*.,' and thought it was a charge for the trouble of *selling* the 700 copies, which he did not consider unreasonable; but on inquiry he found it was for the *cellar*-room occupied by his work, not a copy of which had stirred from thence. He told, too, of the servant-maid where he himself had lodged at Ramsgate, coming in to say that he was wanted, there being a person at the door inquiring for a poet; and on his going out, he found it was a pot-boy from the public house, whose cry, of 'any *pots* for the Angel,' the girl had mistaken for a demand for a *poet*. Improbable enough. In talking of Klopstock, he mentioned his description of the Deity's 'head spreading through space,' which, he said, gave one the idea of a hydrocephalous affection.

(iii) HENRY CRABB ROBINSON
From Robinson, Diary, *II, 246-7. The entry for 4 April, describing the same.*

Our party consisted of Wordsworth, Coleridge, Lamb, Moore, and Rogers. Five poets of very unequal worth and most disproportionate popularity, whom the public probably would arrange in a different order. During this afternoon, Coleridge alone displayed any of his peculiar talent. I have not for years seen him in such excellent health and with so fine a flow of spirits. His discourse was addressed chiefly to Wordsworth, on points of metaphysical criticism—Rogers occasionally interposing a remark. The only one of the poets who seemed not to enjoy himself was Moore. He was very attentive to Coleridge, but seemed to relish Lamb, next to whom he was placed.

(iv) CHARLES LAMB
From Letters of Charles Lamb, *ed. Talfourd, II, 95-6. A letter of 5 April 1823, to Lamb's friend Bernard Barton, describes the same dinner.*

I wished for you yesterday. I dined in Parnassus, with Wordsworth, Coleridge, Rogers, and Tom Moore—half the poetry of England constellated and clustered in Gloucester Place! It was a delightful evening! Coleridge was in his finest vein of talk—had all the talk; and let 'em talk as they will of the envy of poets, I am sure not one there but was content to be nothing but a listener. The Muses were dumb, while Apollo lectured, on his and their fine art. It is a lie that poets are envious; I have known the best of them, and can speak to it, that they give each other their merits, and are the kindest critics as well as the best authors. I am scribbling a muddy epistle with an aching head, for we did not quaff Hippocrene last night; marry, it was hippocrass⁵ rather.

(v) WILLIAM JERDAN
From Jerdan, 'Men I Have Known: Samuel Taylor Coleridge', 679-80.

A literary gentleman entertained a party of friends in a small suburban gardener's cottage, where he had hired lodgings for the summer. Of the party were Lockhart and Hook, the latter at the top of his most exuberant humour.⁶ Coleridge had never met Hook before, and seemed lost in wonder. Under Hook's instigation, he took part in a scene of boisterous merriment, the philosopher being for the nonce like a wild schoolboy at play. Presently he was diverted by a wonderful song, extemporised by Hook at the dictation of Captain Harris, who had suspected him of collusion and preparation in other instances, and gave the untoward subject of 'Cocoa-nut Oil.' On this theme the improvisatore descanted in the happiest vein, and brought the oil from the cocoa tree under which the negroes danced in the Mauritius, through various stages of importation and manufacture, till it ended (as it had in reality done on the dinner-table) by its refusing to burn in the lamp, and thus, by experiment, repudiating the patent then taken out for its enlightenment of mankind. It was certainly a marvellous display of the ready application of a remarkable talent. 'Well,' said Coleridge, 'I have met with many men of the readiest wit and resources, but of all the men I ever met, Mr. Hook is the most extraordinary; for none could ever, like him, bring the vast stores of quick intelligence to bear upon the mere incidents of the moment.'⁷

From Jerdan, Men I Have Known *(1866), 128-30. When Jerdan reprinted the anecdote in his volume of portraits from* Leisure Hour, *he wrote an addendum.*

The party was got together on a fine summer day by Mr. Mansell Reynolds, son of the dramatist, and a young gentleman of considerable literary talent, as shown in a remarkable romance entitled 'Miserimus,' and other productions of less questionable sobriety in taste and judgment. The meet was at a very small egg-shell of a gardener's abode on Highgate Hill, where he had taken lodgings for the benefit of fresh air; and consisted, besides those already signified, of three or four others, to about the prescribed number of the muses, including the inevitable 'Old Tom Hill' (Hook's favourite butt), and I am not quite certain, from recollection, Mr. Luttrell and Ingoldsby.[8] It was, however, a jovial set, and bent on holiday frolic. The host had provided excellent wines from his father's cellar in town, but port had been forgotten, and obtained on the spur of the moment from a tavern in Highgate. On Hook's motion it was voted execrable, and every one called to fill a bumper to toast the chair; which done, and the example set, every glass but one was rapt down and broken, as being too small for any gentlemanly wine. The rest were poised upon inverted tumblers, and smashed by missiles, after the fashion of Aunt Sally. But who can paint the astonished Auncient Mariner, with glasses broken everywhere, and not a drop to drink? I cannot tell by what process the master spirit of the revel prevailed upon him to demolish his, the last of the little glasses, by raising it on a tumbler, and with hand balancing and eye glistening, smashing it with a silver fork after several ineffectual 'shies.' It was a scene so grotesque and extraordinary as hardly to be imagined; and the after-potations were obliged to be drunk from the tumblers! It may be somewhat absurd to revive the memory of such a day, but it was long called to mind and spoken of as one for a white stone by all who were present. Hook's improvising was wonderful. Of one of half a dozen songs, Mrs. Macpherson, the gardener's wife and superintendent of the dinner, was the theme; and what with its uproarious mirth and the noise and hubbub of demolition, she flitted *pro tem.*, and afterwards told her lodger that she was so scared that she would not undergo a second edition, no, 'not for any consideration on earth.' But the worst of all was the reckoning when the feast was o'er. Next day Reynolds (still rejoicing in the highjinks outbreak) wrote to me with the particulars of twenty-seven bottles of wine and one of brandy, which had somehow been disposed of, and twenty-six small glasses and four tumblers breakage.[9]

(vi) ROBERT BENJAMIN HAYDON

From Benjamin Robert Haydon, Correspondence and Table-Talk *(2 vols.; 1876), II, 93; 94. Haydon (1786-1846), a member of Lamb's circle, was a painter and art critic. In this anecdote (from a letter to Mary Russell Mitford, 28 March 1825) Haydon encounters Coleridge at the house of Sir John Soane, architect and collector, where the newly-discovered Belzoni Sacrophagus is on display.*

I was at Soane's last night to see this sarcophagus by lamp-light. The first person I met, after seventeen years, was Coleridge, silver-haired! He looked at my bald front, and I at his hair, with mutual looks of sympathy and mutual head-shaking. It affected me very much, and so it seemed to affect him. I did not know what to say, nor did he; and then in his chanting way, half-poetical, half-inspired, half-idiotic, he began to console me by trying to prove that the only way for a man of genius to be happy was just to put forth no more power than was sufficient for the purposes of the age in which he lived, as if genius was a power one could fold up like a parasol! At this moment over came Spurzheim,[10] with his German simplicity, and shaking my hand: 'How doe you doe? Vy, your organs are more parfait den eàver. How luckee you lose your hair. Veel you pearmeet me to eîntrowdooze you to Mrs Spurzheim?' [...]

Upstairs stood Soane, spare, thin, caustic, and starched, 'mocking the thing he laughed at,' as he smiled approbation for the praises bestowed on his magnificent house. . . . Coleridge said, 'I have a great contempt for these Egyptians with all their learning. After all, what did it amount to, but a bad system of astronomy?'

(vii) THOMAS HOOD

From Thomas Hood and Charles Lamb. The Story of a Friendship. Being the Literary Reminiscences of Thomas Hood, *ed. Walter Jerrold (1930), 122-4. Hood (1799-1845), poet and novelist, editor of (among other things) the* Comic Annual, *and an Islington neighbour of Lamb's in the 1820s.*

Amongst other notable men who came to Colebrooke Cottage, I had twice the good fortune of meeting with S.T. Coleridge. The first time he came from Highgate with Mrs. Gillman, to dine with 'Charles and Mary.' What a contrast to Lamb was the full-bodied poet, with his waving white hair, and his face round, ruddy, and unfurrowed as a holy friar's! Apropos to which face he gave us a humorous description of an unfinished portrait, that served him for a sort of barometer, to indicate the state of his popularity. So sure as his name made any temporary stir, out came the canvas on the easel, and a request from the artist for another sitting: down sank the original in the public notice, and back went the copy into a corner, till some fresh publication or accident again brought forward the poet; and then forth came the picture for a few more touches. I sincerely hope it has been finished! What a benign, smiling face it was! What a comfortable, respectable figure! What a model, methought, as I watched and admired the 'Old Man eloquent,'[11] for a Christian bishop! But he was, perhaps, scarcely orthodox enough to be trusted with a mitre. At least, some of his voluntaries would have frightened a common everyday congregation from their propriety. Amongst other matters of discourse, he came to speak of the strange notions some literal-minded persons form of the joys of Heaven; joys they associated with mere temporal things, in which, for his own part, finding no delight in this world, he could find no bliss hereafter, without a change in his nature, tantamount to the loss of his personal identity. For instance, he said, there are persons who place the whole angelical beatitude in the possession of a pair of wings to flap about with, like '*a sort of celestial poultry.*'

After dinner he got up, and began pacing to and fro, with his hands behind his back, talking and walking, as Lamb laughingly hinted, as if qualifying for an itinerant preacher; now fetching a simile from Loddiges' garden, at Hackney; and then flying off for an illustration to the sugar-making in Jamaica. With his fine, flowing voice, it was glorious music, of the 'never-ending, still-beginning' kind; and you did not wish it to end. It was rare flying, as in the Nassau Balloon; you knew not whither, nor did you care. Like his own bright-eyed marinere; he had a spell in his voice that would not let you go. To attempt to describe my own feeling afterward, I had been carried, spiralling, up to heaven by a whirlwind intertwisted with sunbeams, giddy and dazzled, but not displeased, and had then been rained down again with a shower of mundane stocks and stones that battered out of me all recollection of what I had heard, and what I had seen!

On the second occasion, the author of 'Christabel' was accompanied by one of his sons. The poet, talking and walking as usual, chanced to pursue some argument, which drew from the son, who had not been introduced to me, the remark, 'Ah, that's just like your crying up those foolish Odes and Addresses!' Coleridge was highly amused with this *mal-àpropos*, and, without explaining, looked slily round at me, with the sort of suppressed laugh, one may suppose to belong to the Bey of *Tittery.* The truth was, he felt naturally partial to a book he had attributed in the first instance to the dearest of his friends.[12]

(viii) LEIGH HUNT

From Leigh Hunt, Lord Byron and Some of his Contemporaries *(1828; 2nd.edn.; 2 vols.; 1828), II, 46-7; 51-4. James Henry Leigh Hunt (1784-1859) was a prominent essayist, poet, and editor, and another Christ's Hospital boy.*

Mr. LAMB's friend, Mr. COLERIDGE, is as little fitted for action as he, but on a different account. His person is of a good height, but as sluggish and solid as the other's is light and fragile. He has, perhaps, suffered it to look old before its time, for want of exercise. His hair, too, is quite white (though he cannot much exceed fifty); and as he generally dresses in black, and has a very tranquil demeanour, his appearance is gentlemanly, and begins to be reverend. Nevertheless, there is something invincibly young in the look of his face: it is round and fresh-coloured, with agreeable features, and an open, indolent, good-natured mouth. This boy-like expression is very becoming to one who dreams as he did when he was a child, and who passes his life apart from the rest of the world, with a book, and his flowers. His forehead is prodigious, — a great piece of placid marble; and his fine eyes, in which all the activity of his mind seems to concentrate, move under it with a sprightly ease, as if it were pastime to them to carry all that thought. [...]

Mr. Coleridge is fat, and begins to lament, in very delightful verses, that he is getting infirm. There is no old age in his verses. I heard him the other day, under the grove at Highgate, repeat one of his melodious lamentations, as he walked up and down, his voice undulating in a stream of music, and his regrets of youth sparkling with visions ever young. At the same time, he did me the honour to show me, that he did not think so ill of all modern liberalism as some might suppose, denouncing the pretensions of the money-getting in a style which I should hardly venture upon, and never could equal; and asking, with a triumphant eloquence, what chastity itself were worth, if it were a casket, not to keep love in, but hate, and strife, and worldliness? On the same occasion, he built up a metaphor out of a flower, in a style surpassing the famous passage in Milton; deducing it from its root in religous mystery, and carrying it up into the bright-consummate flower, 'the bridal chamber of reproductiveness.'[13] Of all 'the Muse's mysteries,' he is as great a high-priest as Spenser; and Spenser himself might have gone to Highgate to hear him talk, and thank him for his 'Ancient Mariner.' His voice does not always sound very sincere; but perhaps the humble and deprecating tone of it, on those occasions, is out of consideration for his hearer's infirmities, rather than produced by his own. He recited his 'Kubla Khan,' one morning, to Lord Byron, in his Lordship's house in Piccadilly, when I happened to be in another room. I remember the other's coming away from him, highly struck with his poem, and saying how wonderfully he talked. This is the impression of every body who hears him.

It is no secret that Mr. Coleridge lives in the Grove at Highgate with a friendly family, who have sense and kindness enough to know that they do themselves an honour by looking after the comforts of such a man. His room looks upon a delicious prospect of wood and meadow, with coloured gardens under the window, like an embroidery to the mantle. I thought, when I first saw it, that he had taken up his dwelling-place like an abbot. Here he cultivates his flowers, and has a set of birds for his pensioners, who come to breakfast with him. He may be seen taking his daily stroll up and down, with his black coat and white locks, and a book in his hand; and is a great acquaintance of the little children. His main occupation, I believe, is reading. He loves to read old folios, and to make old voyages with Purchas and Marco Polo; the seas being in good visionary condition, and the vessel well-stocked with botargoes.

(ix) JAMES FENIMORE COOPER

From James Fenimore Cooper, England. With Sketches of Society in the Metropolis *(3 vols.; 1837), II, 31-4; 35. Many Americans visited: 'I am a poor poet in England', Coleridge told Arthur Hallam and Richard Monckton Milnes, 'but I am a great philosopher in America'.[14] The novelist Cooper (1789-1851) met him twice during his residence in 1828: once at Highgate, when Coleridge talked about phrenology (III, 80-85), and once dining at Sotheby's. Scott was also present.*

When the ladies had retired, the conversation turned on Homer, whom, it is understood, Mr. Sotheby is now engaged in translating. Some one remarked that Mr. Coleridge did not believe in his unity, or rather that there was any such man. This called him out, and certainly I never witnessed an exhibition as extraordinary as that which followed. It was not a discourse, but a dissertation. Scarcely any one spoke besides Mr. Coleridge, with the exception of a brief occasional remark from Mr. Sotheby, who held the contrary opinion, and I might say no one *could* speak. At moments he was surprisingly eloquent, though a little discursive, and the whole time he appeared to be perfectly the master of his subject and of his language. As near as I could judge, he was rather more than an hour in *possession of the floor*, almost without interruption. His utterance was slow, every sentence being distinctly given, and his pronunciation accurate. There seemed to be a constant struggling between an affluence of words and an affluence of ideas, without either hesitation or repetition. His voice was strong and clear, but not pitched above the usual key of conversation. The only peculiarity about it was a slight observable burring of the *r r rs*, but scarcely more than what the language properly requires.

Once or twice, when Mr. Sotheby would attempt to say a word on his side of the question, he was permitted to utter just enough to give a leading idea, but no argument, when the reasoning was taken out of his mouth by the essayist, and continued, pro and con, with the same redundant and eloquent fluency. I was less struck by the logic than by the beauty of the language, and the poetry of the images. Of the theme, in a learned sense, I knew too little to pretend to any verbal or critical knowledge, but he naturally endeavoured to fortify his argument by the application of his principles to familiar things; and here, I think, he often failed. In fact, the exhibition was much more wonderful than convincing.

At first I was so much struck with the affluent diction of the poet, as scarcely to think of anything else; but when I did look about me, I found every eye fastened on him. Scott sat immovable as a statue, with his little grey eyes looking inward and outward, and evidently considering the whole as an exhibition, rather than as an argument; though he occasionally muttered, 'eloquent!' — 'wonderful!' — 'very extraordinary!' Mr. Lockhart[15] caught my eye once, and he gave a very hearty laugh, without making the slightest noise, as if he enjoyed my astonishment. When we rose, however, he expressed his admiration of the speaker's eloquence. [...]

We were still at table, when the constant raps at the door gave notice that the drawing-room was filling above. Mr. Coleridge lectured on, through it all, for half an hour longer, when Mr. Sotheby rose. The house was full of company assembled to see Scott. He walked deliberately into a maze of petticoats, and, as he had told me at Paris, let them play with his mane as much as they pleased.

(x) SIR WALTER SCOTT

From The Journal of Sir Walter Scott *(2 vols.; Edinburgh, 1890), II, 164; his journal for 22 April 1828. Scott (1771-1832), poet, critic, editor, and biographer, greatest novelist of the age, recorded his impression of the same dinner.*

Lockhart and I dined with Sotheby, where we met a large dining party, the orator of which was that extraordinary man Coleridge. After eating a hearty dinner, during which he spoke not a word, he began a most learned harangue on the Samothracian Mysteries, which he considered as affording the germ of all tales about fairies past, present, and to come. He then diverged to Homer, whose Iliad he considered as a collection of poems by different authors, at different times during a century. There was, he said, the individuality of an age, but not of a country. Morritt,[16] a zealous worshipper of the old bard, was incensed at a system which would turn him into a polytheist, gave battle with keenness, and was joined by Sotheby, our host. Mr. Coleridge behaved with the utmost complaisance and temper, but relaxed not from his exertions. 'Zounds! I was never so bethumped with words.'[17] Morritt's impatience must have cost him an extra sixpence worth of snuff.[18]

(xi) EDWARD FITZGERALD

From Polonius: A Collection of Wise Saws and Modern Instances *(1852), p. XLVI, where it appears as 'Weight and Worth'. Fitzgerald (1809-83), most famous for 'The Rubaiyat of Omar Khayyam', included this anecdote in his engaging, anonymous collection of maxims and incidents.*

Coleridge used to relate how he formed a great notion of the understanding of a solid-looking man, who sat during dinner silent, and seemingly attentive to his discourse. Till suddenly, some baked potatoes being brought to table, Coleridge's disciple burst out, 'Them's the jockeys for me!'[19]

NOTES

[1] Cf. *Othello*, IV.ii, ll.32-3.

[2] Thomas Monkhouse (1783-1825), merchant, cousin of Wordsworth's wife, and celebrated host of literary dinners.

[3] Lamb's *Elia* was published at the beginning of 1823.

[4] The line being parodied is actually Pope's: 'Thou Great First Cause, least Understood!' ('The Universal Prayer', l.5).

5 A drink made of wine and spices (*OED*).

6 Theodore Hook (1788-1841), novelist, dramatist, wit, editor of *John Bull*.

7 Elsewhere, Jerdan has STC say, '"What surprises me the most [...] is that he can bring all the vast stores of his mind and imagination to bear upon the mere and sudden topics of the moment!"' ('Coleridge's Table Talk', *London Literary Gazette* 958 (30 May 1835) 340-2, 341). The story also appears in Jerdan's *Autobiography* (4 vols.; 1853-3), IV, 230-6.

8 Thomas Hill (1760-1840), bibliophile, gossip, and source of endless amusement to Hook: see J.G. Lockhart, *Theodore Hook: A Sketch* (1852), 24-5. Hill was STC's butt on at least one occasion: challenged by Hook to extemporise verse about their dining companion ('Look at him, and say what you think: Is he not like a Rose?'), STC made an epigram (*CPW*, II, 974). Henry Luttrell (?1765-1851) was author of the light verse 'Advice to Julia' (1820); 'Ingoldsby' was the pseudonym later adopted by R.H. Barham (1788-1845) for his verse tales.

9 In the version of the story (yet again by Jerdan?) that Lockhart repeats, the windows are smashed one by one, and the chandalier ruined, all of which Hook incorporates into his song. Walking home afterwards, STC gives 'a most excellent lecture on the distinction between talent and genius, and declared that Hook was as true a genius as Dante — *that* was his example' (*Hook*, 24).

10 Dr. Johann Spurzheim (1776-1832), the leading phrenologist.

11 Milton's description of Isocrates: 'Sonnet: To the Lady Margaret Ley', l.8.

12 Hood was author (with John Hamilton Reynolds) of the anonymous *Odes and Addresses to Great People* (1825). The encounter occurred after June 1825; for then, STC believed the book was by Lamb (*CL*, V, 472-3). Lamb replied: 'The Odes are 4-5ths done by Hood, a silentish young man you met at Islinton [*sic*] one day, an invalid [...] Hood has just come in; his sick eyes sparkled into health when he read your approbation' (2 July 1825; *Letters of Charles Lamb* [...], ed. E.V. Lucas (3 vols.; 1935), III, 7-8).

13 Cf. *Paradise Lost*, V, ll.479-82 (a passage quoted prominently in *BL*, I, 295).

14 T. Wemyss Reid, *The Life, Letters, and Friendships of Richard Monckton Milnes, First Lord Houghton* (2 vols.; 1891), II, 432. Peter Anthony Labouchère, who lived in Highgate in 1828, heard STC propose a toast 'To the continued good-understanding between England and America,' which he called 'Great Britain with elbow room.' ('The Drama at Hereford: Dramatic Costumes', *N&Q* 4th ser., I (1868) 464-5, 464).

15 John Gibson Lockhart (1794-1854), editor of the *Quarterly*; Scott's son-in-law and, later, biographer.

16 John Morritt (1772-1843), author of *A Vindication of Homer* (1798).

17 *King John*, I.ii, l.466.

18 Lord Ward (1781-1833), who enjoyed a reputation for animatedly talking to himself (he was eventually confined), was also an impatient auditor:

> The philosopher and bard arrived, with his laudanum bottle in his pocket, ate very little dinner, sipped a glass or two of wine, took another glass suspected to have been nearly all diluted laudanum, and then went off at score into a monologue which lasted the remainder of the dinner, the whole of the dessert,

and for nearly an hour after. Nobody interrupted him, as nobody could have cut across his torrent of talk without being washed away. Lord Dover, who had had former experience, seemed to enjoy it all; but not so the impatient, irritable Lord Ward; he liked to talk himself, and no man could better take his share at that exercise. As he took a hasty departure, he said: 'Well! I have heard of the *summum bonum* before, and now I know what is the *summum bore-em!*' (Quoted in MacFarlane, *Reminiscences*, 49-50)

[19] A story that reappears in the memoirs of Grantley F. Berkeley (1800-81), MP and man of leisure: *My Life and Recollections* (4 vols.; 1865-6), IV, 12-13.

Anecdotes of the Talker

(i) BRYAN WALLER PROCTER

From Bryan Waller Procter, An Autobiographical Fragment and Biographical Notes (1877), 144-7. Procter (1787-1874), who wrote as 'Barry Cornwall', was a poet and dramatist, and memoirist of Lamb.

Samuel Taylor Coleridge was like the Rhine,

> That exulting and abounding river.[1]

He was full of words, full of thought; yielding both in an unfailing flow, that delighted many, and perplexed a few of his hearers. He was a man of prodigious miscellaneous reading, always ready to communicate all he knew. From Alpha to Omega, all was familiar to him. He was deep in Jacob Behmen. He was intimate with Thomas Aquinas and Quevedo; with Bacon and Kant, with 'Peter Simple' and 'Tom Cringle's Log;'[2] and with all the old divines of both England and France. The pages of all the infidels had passed under his eye and made their legitimate (and not more than their legitimate) impression. He went from flower to flower, throughout the whole garden of learning, like the butterfly or the bee, — most like the bee. He talked with everybody, about anything. He was so full of information that it was a relief to him to part with some portion of it to others. It was like laying down part of his burden. He knew little or nothing of the art of painting; yet I have heard him discuss the merits and defects of a picture of the poorest class, as though it had sprung from the inspiration of Raffaelle. He would advert to certain parts, and surmise that it had been touched upon here and there; would pronounce upon its character and school, its *chiaroscuro*, the gradations, the handling, etc., when in fact it had no mark or merit or character about it. It became transfigured, sublimated, by the speaker's imagination, which far excelled both the picture and its author. Coleridge had a weighty head, dreaming grey eyes, full, sensual lips, and a look and manner which were entirely wanting in firmness and decision. His motions also appeared weak and undecided, and his voice had nothing of the sharpness or ring of a resolute man. When he spoke his words were thick and slow, and when he read poetry his utterance was altogether a chant.

One day, when dining with some lawyers, he had been more than usually eloquent and full of talk. His perpetual interruptions were resented by one of the guests, who said to his neighbour, 'I'll stop this fellow;' and thereupon addressed the master of the house with 'G——, I've not forgotten my promise to give you the extract from "The Pandects."[3] It was the ninth chapter that you were alluding to. It begins: "Ac veteres quidam philosophi."' 'Pardon me, sir,' interposed Coleridge, 'there I think you are in error. The ninth chapter begins in this way, "Incident sæpe causæ," etc.' It was in vain to refer to anything on the supposition that the poet was ignorant, for he really had some acquaintance with every subject. I imagine that no man had ever read so many books and at the same time had digested so much.

Coleridge was prodigal of his words, which in fact he could with difficulty suppress; but he seldom talked of himself or of his affairs. He was very speculative, very theological, very metaphysical, and not unfrequently threw in some little pungent sentence, characteristic of the defects of some of his acquaintance. In illustration of his unfailing talk, I will give an account of one of his days, when I was present. He had come from Highgate to London, for the sole purpose of consulting a friend about his son Hartley ('our dear Hartley'), towards whom he expressed, and I have no doubt felt, much anxiety. He arrived about one or two o'clock, in the midst of a conversation, which immediately began to interest him. He struck into the middle of the talk very soon, and held the 'ear of the house' until dinner made its appearance about four o'clock. He then talked all through the dinner, all the afternoon, all the evening, with scarcely a single interruption. He expatiated on this subject and on that; he drew fine distinctions; he made subtle criticisms. He descended to anecdotes, historical, logical, rhetorical; he dealt with law, medicine, and divinity, until, at last, five minutes before eight o'clock, the servant came in and announced that the Highgate stage was at the corner of the street, and was waiting to convey Mr. Coleridge home. Coleridge immediately started up oblivious of all time, and said, in a hurried voice, 'Mr dear Z——, I will come to you some other day, and talk to you about our dear Hartley.' He had quite forgotten his son and everybody else, in the delight of having such an enraptured audience.

(ii) SAMUEL ROGERS

From Table-Talk of Samuel Rogers, *150; 203-4.*

In Milton's description of the lazar-house there is a dreadful confusion of metaphor: —

> Sight so deform what *heart of rock* could long
> *Dry-ey'd* behold?[4]

I once observed this to Coleridge, who told Wordsworth that he could not sleep all the next night for thinking of it. [...]

Coleridge was a marvellous talker. One morning, when Hookham Frere also breakfasted with me, Coleridge talked for three hours without intermission about poetry, and so admirably, that I wish every word he uttered had been written down.

But sometimes his harangues were quite unintelligible, not only to myself, but to others. Wordsworth and I called upon him one forenoon, when he was in a lodging off Pall Mall. He talked uninterruptedly for about two hours, during which Wordsworth listened to him with profound attention, every now and then nodding his head as if in assent. On quitting the lodging, I said to Wordsworth, 'Well, for my own part, I could not make head or tail of Coleridge's oration: pray, did you understand it?' 'Not one syllable of it,' was Wordsworth's reply.[5]

Speaking of composition, Coleridge said most beautifully, 'What comes from the heart goes to the heart.'

(iii) PETER GEORGE PATMORE

From Victoire, Count de Soligny, Letters on England *(2 vols.; 1823), II, 83-5.* *Patmore (1786-1855) was author of* Rejected Articles *(1826), a volume of parodies. The pseudonymous* Letters on England *has a sighting (or a hearing).*

I have heard him talk! – and, when this has happened to any one, it seems to be an understood thing here that, from that time forth, he may be as enthusiastic as he pleases in his admiration of Coleridge's powers, without incurring the charge of extravagance.

In truth, the first evening passed with this person, if he happens to be in a talking mood, (and when is he not?) is an era in a man's life. I had no true notion of what is called the natural *gift* of eloquence, till I had been present at this extraordinary exhibition—for it is literally such. You do not go to converse, or to hear others converse; for it is the fault of Coleridge that, where he is, there can be no conversation. You go to hear *him* talk, and you expect and desire to hear nothing else. Between his prose writing and his talking there is no sort of comparison. If what he says in the course of one evening could be written down, it would probably be worth all the prose that he has ever published, in whatever light it were regarded; whether as to depth of thought, splendour of imagery, felicity of illustration, extent and variety of learning, or richness, purity, and elegance of diction. His talking is as extraordinary as the chess-playing of the mechanical figure that was exhibited some years ago in Paris. You sit, and witness it in silent admiration, and wonder how it can be. And, like that, there's no puzzling or putting him out. He seems wound up, and *must* go on to the end. But when that end will arrive no one can guess; so that the spectators are frequently obliged to get up and go away in the middle of the game—not being able to anticipate any finish to it. Like that celebrated figure, too, he always comes off triumphant. I never heard of any one having a chance with him. In fact, if there were not an evident appearance of his *feeling* all that he says, at the time he says it, he could be considered in no other light than as a wonderful talking machine, that talks on and on, because it can't help it.

But perhaps Coleridge's eloquence might, with more truth, be compared to Catalani's singing.[6] It is as rich, as brilliant, as dazzling, and as inexhaustible as that; and can as little be followed by the orchestra who are to accompany and fill up the pauses of it, or the audience who are listening to it. It may be full of inaccuracies and solecisms for what any one knows; and there are not wanting many to assert that this is the case in both instances; but in neither can any one detect and point them out. Perhaps the magical charm of both consists in the appearance of animated and fervent sincerity, which accompanies the *sentiment* of what they are delivering; which is not a little aided by the angelic, but somewhat vague and unmeaning smile, which is almost always playing about the lips of both. Finally, it must be confessed that we are apt soon to get satisfied, if not satiated, with the hearing of both. They surprise and delight for a time, but are too much beyond our reach, and perhaps interfere too much with our self-love, to create a permanent sympathy. Nothing but the exquisite simplicity, and appearance of good-nature and sincerity, accompanying both, has permitted them to be tolerated so long as they have.

(iv) SARAH FLOWER ADAMS

From 'S.Y.', 'An Evening with Charles Lamb and Coleridge', Monthly Repository *NS IX (1835) 162-8, 163-4; 166-8. Adams (1805-48) was a poet (she wrote 'Nearer, My God, to Thee'). She describes a meeting at Lamb's.*

How he came, or when he came, or whether they were there when we entered, is all forgotten; but I have them distinctly before me as if it were yesterday. Coleridge, with his clear, calm, blue eyes and expansive forehead, — his sweet, child-like, unruffled expression of face, — his painful voice, which, in spite of all the beauties and treasures it was the means of bringing to you, had yet such an expression in its tone of long suffering and patient endurance, as at first to prevent the sensation excited by his extraordinary power of conversation being one of perfect enjoyment. I had heard much of this power, but no description, however vivid, could give an idea of the uninterrupted outpouring of poetry in the spoken prose that streamed from his lips. It was a realization of the fairy tale of the enchanted child; he never opened his mouth but out came a precious gem, a pearl beyond all price, which all around gathered up to hoard in the cabinet of their memories. His figure was tall and somewhat inclined to corpulency; its expression was, like that of his voice, one of suffering borne long and patiently. There was a certain air of dissatisfaction — no, unsatisfiedness, — (how different are the two!) which set the mind busily to work to discover why, with all the choice gifts with which genius had blessed him, he should not be entirely happy. The mystery has been since unriddled; he had never known the reality of love; he had dreamt of it in his poems, but while seeking to make his dependence upon it in his own existence, it had failed him. He was a slave to the laws which doom a creature, who has mated mistakenly, either to live for ever in joyless companionship, or to live a solitary in the depths of his heart's affections, without hope of possessing that one sympathy which is essential to the developement of man's noblest, best, and most happiness-giving attributes. [...]

Coleridge, on the evening in question, spoke of death with fear; not from the dread of punishment, not from the shrinking from physical pain, but he said he had a horror lest, after the attempt to 'shuffle off this mortal coil,' he should yet 'be thrown back upon himself.' Charles Lamb kept silence, and looked sceptical; and, after a pause, said suddenly, 'One of the things that made me question the particular inspiration they ascribed to Jesus Christ, was his ignorance of the character of Judas Iscariot. Why did not he and his disciples kick him out for a rascal, instead of receiving him as a disciple?' Coleridge smiled very quietly, and then spoke of some person (name forgotten) who had been making a comparison between himself and Wordsworth as to their religious faith. 'They said, although I was an atheist, we were upon a par, for that Wordsworth's Christianity was very like Coleridge's atheism; and Coleridge's atheism was very like Wordsworth's Christianity.' After some time he moved round the room to read the different engravings that hung upon the walls. One, over the mantel-piece, especially interested his fancy. There were only two figures in the picture, both women. One was of a lofty, commanding stature, with a high intellectual brow, and of an abbess-like deportment. She was standing in grave majesty, with the finger uplifted, in the act of monition to a young girl beside her. The face was in profile, and somewhat severe in its expression; but this was relieved by the richness and grace of the draperies in which she was profusely enveloped. The girl was in the earliest and freshest spring of youth, lovely and bright, with a somewhat careless and inconsiderate air, and she seemed but half inclined to heed the sage advice of her elder companion. She held in her hand a rose, with which she was toying, and had she been alive you would have expected momentarily to see it taken between the taper fingers, and scattered in wilful profusion. Coleridge uttered an expression of admiration, and then, as if talking to himself, apostrophized in some such words as these: 'There she stands, with all the world before her: to her it is as a fairy dream, a vision of unmingled joy. To her it is as is that lovely flower, which woos her by its bright hue and fragrant perfume. Poor child! must thou too be reminded of the thorns that lurk beneath? Turn thee to thy monitress! she bids thee clasp not too closely pleasures that lure but to wound thee. Look into her eloquent eyes; listen to her pleading voice; her words are words of wisdom; garner them up in thy heart; and when the evil days come, the days in which thou shalt say "I find no pleasure in them," remember her as thus she stood, and, with uppointing finger, bade thee think of the delights of heaven—that heaven which is ever ready to receive the returning wanderer to its rest.'

He spoke of the effect of different sounds upon his sensations; said, of all the pains the sense of hearing ever brought to him, that of the effect made by a dog belonging to some German conujurer was the greatest. The man pretended that the dog would answer, 'Ich bedanke mein herr,' when anything was given to it; and the effort and contortion made by the dog to produce the required sound, proved that the scourge, or some similar punishment, had been applied to effect it. In contrast to this was the homage he rendered to the speaking voice of Mrs. Jordan, on which he expatiated in such rapturous terms, as if he had been indebted to it for a sixth sense. He said that it was the exquisite witchery of her tone that suggested an idea in his 'Remorse,' that if Lucifer had had permission to retain his angel voice, hell would have been hell no longer.[7] In the course of the evening the talented editor of the 'Comic Annual' made his appearance. He was then known only by his Hogarthian caricature of 'the Progress of Cant,' upon which Coleridge complimented him.[8] After some time he introduced many of his etchings, which were then unknown to the world, and they were the means of exciting in Coleridge the first genuinely hearty laugh I had seen. If one had not admired entirely, it would have been enough to have made him envied. Laugh after laugh followed as the square tablets (trump cards in the pack of the genius of caricature) were laid upon the table, and a merry game it was for all. The effect was not a little increased by the extreme quietude of their master, who stood by without uttering a word, except with the corners of his mouth, where the rich fund of humour which had furnished the treat we were enjoying, was speaking more intelligibly than any words. He went, and the time went, and the supper went; and at last it was time for Coleridge to go too, for he had the walk to Highgate all before him. His friend begged earnestly that he might walk with him, but without avail. There was an affectionate parting, as if they had been boys rather than men, and it seemed to concentrate their lives into that minute. It recalled the meetings and partings of other days; the wanderings by the lakes; the many minglings in social union; a whole host of recollections seemed to crowd around and enclose them in a magic circle. Coleridge lingered on the threshold, as if he were leaving what had been a part of his heart's home for many years; and again he who had been his companion in many a mountain ramble, many a stroll 'in dale, forest, and mead, by paved fountain and by rushy brook, and on the beached margent of the sea,'[9] would fain have kept up the old companionship even though it was night, and the way had no such temptations. Another grasp of the hand, and a kiss of affection on Mary's cheek, and he was gone.

(v) LEIGH HUNT

From The Autobiography of Leigh Hunt [...] with Thornton Hunt's Introduction and Postscript, *ed. Roger Ingpen (2 vols.; 1903), II, 53-4. This anecdote of Hunt and Lamb is repeated by Hunt's son, Thornton (1810-73).*

While Leigh Hunt was living at Highgate, he used sometimes to be visited by his old schoolfellow, and Coleridge, who, it will be remembered, was Lamb's contemporary at Christ's Hospital, would sometimes supervene, and join for a short space in the walk and the conversation, the talk being as usual chiefly appropriated by himself. One day the soliloquy thus poured into the ears of the two friends turned upon the blessings of faith, and it was both in tone and phraseology marked by the accepted dialect of the most 'regenerated' orthodoxy: in short, what uncourteous or invidious persons might call canting. After the illustrious poet had taken his leave, Leigh Hunt exclaimed, in a tone of perplexed vexation, 'What makes Coleridge talk in that way about heavenly grace, and the holy church, and that sort of thing?' 'Ah,' replied Lamb, with the hearty tone of a man uttering an obvious truism, but struggling with his habitual stammer, 'there is a g−g−reat deal of fun in Coleridge!'

(vi) CHARLES LAMB

From John R. Dix, Lions: Living and Dead; or, Personal Recollections of the Great and Gifted *(1852), 28-9. A famous and certainly mythical anecdote.*

I met Lamb at a party not long afterwards, and remember how he convulsed the company with an anecdote of Coleridge, which, without doubt, he hatched in his hoaxing-loving brain:−'I was,' he said, 'going from my house at Enfield to the India-house one morning, and was hurrying, for I was rather late, when I met Coleridge, on his way to pay me a visit; he was brimful of some new idea, and in spite of my assuring him that time was precious, he drew me within the door of an unoccupied garden by the road-side, and there, sheltered from observation by a hedge of ever-greens, he took me by the button of my coat, and closing his eyes commenced an eloquent discourse, waving his right hand gently, as the musical words flowed in an unbroken stream from his lips. I listened entranced; but the striking of a church-clock recalled me to a sense of duty. I saw it was of no use to attempt to break away, so taking advantage of his absorbtion in his subject, I, with my pen-knife, quietly severed the button from my coat and decamped. Five hours afterwards, in passing the same garden, on my way home, I heard Coleridge's voice, and on looking in there he was, with closed eyes, — the button in his fingers, — and his right hand grace-fully waving, just as when I left him. He had never missed me!'

NOTES

1 Byron, *Childe Harold's Pilgrimage*, II, l.442, *var.*.

2 'Tom Cringle's Log' appeared in *Blackwood's* (1829-33). *Peter Simple* (1834) is a sea-faring novel by Marryat which STC much enjoyed (see *CL*, VI, 980).

3 The *Pandects, or Digests*, of Justinian, a compendium of Roman civil law.

4 *Paradise Lost*, XI, ll.494-5.

5 The *Edinburgh Review* printed this allegedly better text of the exchange:

> Wordsworth and myself [...] had walked to Highgate to call on Coleridge, when he was living at Gillman's. We sat with him two hours, he talking the whole time without intermission. When we left the house, we walked for some time without speaking—'What a wonderful man he is!' exclaimed Wordsworth. 'Wonderful, indeed,' said I. 'What depth of thought, what richness of expression!' continued Wordsworth. 'There's nothing like him that ever I heard,' rejoined I, — another pause. 'Pray,' inquired Wordsworth, 'did you precisely understand what he said about the Kantian philosophy?' *R.* 'Not precisely.' *W.* 'Or about the plurality of worlds?' *R.* 'I can't say I did. In fact, if the truth must out, I did not understand a syllable from one end of his monologue to the other.' *W.* 'No more did I.' (*Edinburgh Review* CIV (1856) 73-122, 103)

6 Angelica Catalani (1780-1849), a celebrated Italian sporano with a famously pure voice, an immense hit during her stay in England (1806-13).

7 I.ii, ll.343-4 (*CPW*, II, 834). Dorothea Jordan (1762-1816) was a celebrated comic actress, best known for her Shakespearean heroines.

8 Hood edited *The Comic Annual* from 1830. Lamb praised his engraving, 'The Progress of Cant' (1825) in the *New Monthly*.

9 Cf. *Midsummer Night's Dream*, II.i, ll.83-5. Adams is fantasising: Lamb much preferred London, and most of his time with STC was spent there.

Three Portraits

(i) WILLIAM HAZLITT

From 'The Drama. No.XI', London Magazine II (1820) 685-690, 687-690. This brilliant impersonation appears in one of Hazlitt's theatre reviews. Faced with a set of uninspiring shows to notice, he imagines Coleridge's response.

'The French, my dear H——,' would he begin, 'are not a people of imagination. They have so little, that you cannot persuade them to conceive it possible that they have none. They have no poetry, no such thing as genius, from the age of Louis XIV. It was that, their boasted Augustan age, which stamped them French, which put the seal upon their character, and from that time nothing has grown up original or luxuriant, or spontaneous among them; the whole has been cast in a mould, and that a bad one. Montaigne and Rabelais (their two greatest men, the one for thought, and the other for imaginative humour, – for the distinction between imagination and fancy holds in ludicrous as well as serious composition) I consider as Francks rather than Frenchmen, for in their time the national literature was not *set*, was neither mounted on stilts, nor buckramed in stays. Wit they had too, if I could persuade myself that Moliere was a genuine Frenchman, but I cannot help suspecting that his mother played his reputed father false, and that an Englishman begot him. I am sure his genius is English; and his wit not of the Parisian cut. As a proof of this, see how his most extravagant farces, the Mock-doctor, Barnaby Brittle, &c.[1] take with us. What can be more to the taste of our *bourgeoisie*, more adapted to our native tooth, than his Country Wife, which Wycherly did little else than translate into English. What success a translator of Racine into our vernacular tongue would meet with, I leave you to guess. His tragedies are not poetry, are not passion, are not imagination: they are a parcel of set speeches, of epigrammatic conceits, of declamatory phrases, without any of the glow, and glancing rapidity, and principle of fusion in the mind of the poet, to agglomerate them into grandeur, or blend them into harmony. The principle of the imagination resembles the emblem of the serpent, by which the ancients typified wisdom and the universe, with undulating folds, for ever varying and for ever flowing into itself, – circular, and without beginning or end. The definite, the fixed, is death: the principle of life is the indefinite, the growing, the moving, the continuous. But every thing in French poetry is cut up into shreds and patches, little flowers of poetry, with tickets and labels to them, as when the daughters of Jason minced and hacked their old father into collops—we have the *disjecta membra poetæ*[2]—not the entire and living man. The spirit of genuine poetry should inform the whole work, should breathe through, and move, and agitate the complete mass, as the soul informs and moves the limbs of a man, or as the vital principle (whatever it be) permeates the veins of the loftiest trees, building up the trunk, and extending the branches to the sun and winds of heaven, and shooting out into fruit and flowers. This is the progress of nature and of genius. This is the true poetic faculty; or that which the Greeks literally call ποιησις. But a French play, (I think it is Schlegel, who somewhere makes the comparison, though I had myself, before I ever read Schlegel, made the same remark) is like a child's garden set with slips of branches and flowers, stuck in the ground, not growing in it. We may weave a gaudy garland in this manner, but it withers in an hour: while the products of genius and nature give out their odours to the gale, and spread their tints in the sun's eye, age after age—

> Outlast a thousand storms, a thousand winters,
> Free from the Sirian star, free from the thunder stroke,[3]

and flourish in immortal youth and beauty. Every thing French is, in the way of it, frittered into parts: every thing is therefore dead and ineffective. French poetry is just like chopped logic: nothing comes of it. There is no life of mind: neither the birth nor generation of knowledge. It is all patch-work, all sharp points and angles, all superficial. They receive, and give out sensation, too readily for it ever to amount to a sentiment. They cannot even dance, as you may see. There is, I am sure you will agree, no expression, no grace in their dancing. Littleness, point, is what damns them in all they do. With all their vivacity, and animal spirits, they dance not like men and women under the impression of certain emotions, but like puppets; they twirl round like *tourniquets*. Not to feel, and not to think, is all they know of this art or any other. You might swear that a nation that danced in that manner, would never produce a true poet or philosopher. They have it not in them. There is not the principle of cause and effect. They make a sudden turn because there is no reason for it: they stop short, or move fast, only because you expect something else.

Their style of dancing is difficult: would it were impossible.'* (By this time several persons in the pit had turned round to listen to this uninterrupted discourse, and our eloquent friend went on, rather raising his voice with a *Paulo majora canamus*.)[4] 'Look at that Mademoiselle Milanie with "the foot of fire," as she is called. You might contrive a paste-board figure with the help of strings or wires to do all, and more, than she does—to point the toe, to raise the leg, to jerk the body, to run like wild-fire. Antics are not grace: to dance is not to move against time. My dear H—— if you could see a dance by some Italian peasant-girls in the Campagna of Rome, as I have, I am sure your good taste and good sense would approve it. They came forward slow and smiling, but as if their limbs were steeped in luxury, and every motion seemed an echo of the music, and the heavens looked on serener as they trod. You are right about the Miss Dennetts, though you have all the cant-phrases against you. It is true, they break down in some of their steps, but is is like "the lily drooping on its stalk green," or like "the flowers Proserpina let fall from Dis's waggon."[5] Those who cannot see grace in the youth and inexperience of these charming girls, would see no beauty in a cluster of hyacinths, bent with the morning dew. To shew at once what is, and is not French, there is Mademoiselle Hullin, she is Dutch. Nay, she is just like a Dutch doll, as round-faced, as rosy, and looks for all the world as if her limbs were made of wax-work, and would take in pieces, but not as if she could move them of her own accord. Alas, poor tender thing! As to the men, I confess' (this was said to me in an audible whisper, lest it might be construed into a breach of confidence) 'I should like, as Southey says, to have them *hamstrung!*'—(At this moment Monsieur Hullin *Pere*, looked as if this charitable operation was about to be performed on him by an extra-official warrant from the poet-laureate.)

'Pray, H——, have you seen Macready's Zanga?'[6]

Yes.

'And what do you think of it?'

I did not like it much.

'Nor I.—Macready has talents and a magnificent voice, but he is, I fear, too improving an actor to be a man of genius. That little ill-looking vagabond Kean never improved in any thing. In some things he could not, and in others he would not. The only parts of M.'s Zanga that I liked (which of course I only half-liked) were some things in imitation of the *extremely natural manner* of Kean, and his address to Alonzo, urging him, as the greatest triumph of his self-denial, to sacrifice

A wife, a bride, a mistress unenjoyed —

where his voice rose exulting on the sentiment, like the thunder that clothes the neck of the war-horse. The person that pleased me most in this play was Mrs. Sterling: she did justice to her part — a thing not easy to do. I liked Macready's Wallace better than his Zanga, though the play is not a good one, and it is difficult for the actor to find out the author's meaning. I would not judge harshly of a first attempt, but the faults of youthful genius are exuberance, and a continual desire of novelty: now the faults of this play are tameness, common-place, and clap-traps. It is said to be written by young Walker, the son of the Westminster orator.[7] If so, his friend, Mr. Cobbett, will probably write a Theatrical Examiner of it in his next week's Political Register.[8] What, I would ask, can be worse, more out of character and costume, than to make Wallace drop his sword to have his throat cut by Menteith, merely because the latter has proved himself (what he suspected) a traitor and a villain, and then console himself for this voluntary martyrdom by a sentimental farewell to the rock and mountains of his native country! This effeminate softness and wretched cant did not belong to the age, the country, or the hero. In this scene, however, Mr. Macready shone much; and in the attitude in which he stood after letting his sword fall, he displayed extreme grace and feeling. It was as if he had let his best friend, his trusty sword, drop like a serpent from his hand. Macready's figure is awkward, but his attitudes are graceful and well composed. — Don't you think so?' —

I answered, yes; and he then ran on in his usual manner, by inquiring into the metaphysical distinction between the grace of form, and the grace that arises from motion (as for instance, you may move a square form in a circular or waving line), and illustrated this subtle observation at great length and with much happiness. He asked me how it was, that Mr. Farren in the farce of the Deaf Lover, played the old gentleman so well, and failed so entirely in the young gallant.[9] I said I could not tell. He then tried at a solution himself, in which I could not follow him so as to give the precise point of his argument. He afterwards defined to me, and those about us, the merits of Mr Cooper and Mr Wallack,

classing the first as a respectable, and the last as a second-rate
actor; with large grounds and learned definitions of his meaning
on both points; and, as the lights were by this time nearly out, and
the audience (except his immediate auditors) going away, he
reluctantly 'ended',

> But in Adam's ear so pleasing left his voice,[10]

that I quite forgot I had to write my article on the Drama the next
day; nor without his imaginary aid should I have been able to
wind up my accounts for the year, as Mr. Matthews [sic] gets
through his AT HOME by the help of a little awkward
ventriloquism.

* This expression is borrowed from Dr. Johnson. However, as Johnson is not a
German critic, Mr. C. need not be supposed to acknowledge it.[11]

(ii) THOMAS CARLYLE

From The Life of John Sterling *(1851), 70-1; 72-5. Carlyle (1795-1881),
essayist, lecturer, and biographer of Sterling (for whom, see below) – from which
work comes this brilliantly sardonic evocation of Coleridge in action.[12]*

The Gilmans [sic] did not encourage much company, or excitation
of any sort, round their sage; nevertheless access to him, if a youth
did reverently wish it, was not difficult. He would stroll about the
pleasant garden with you, sit in the pleasant rooms of the place, —
perhaps take you to his own peculiar room, high up, with a rear-
ward view, which was the chief view of all. A really charming
outlook, in fine weather. Close at hand, wide sweep of flowery
leafy gardens, their few houses mostly hidden, the very chim-
ney-pots veiled under blossomy umbrage, flowed gloriously down
hill; gloriously issuing in wide-tufted undulating plain-country,
rich in all charms of field and town. Waving blooming country of
the brightest green; dotted all over with handsome villas, handsome groves; crossed by roads and human traffic, here inaudible
or heard only as a musical hum: and behind all swam, under ol-
ive-tinted haze, the illimitable limitary ocean of London, with its
domes and steeples definite in the sun, big Paul's and the many
memories attached to it hanging high over all. Nowhere, of its
kind, could you see a grander prospect on a bright summer day,
with the set of the air going southward, — southward, and so
draping with the city-smoke not *you* but the city. Here for hours
would Coleridge talk, concerning all conceivable or inconceivable

things; and liked nothing better than to have an intelligent, or failing that, even a silent and patient human listener. He distinguished himself to all that ever heard him as at least the most surprising talker extant in this world, — and to some small minority, by no means to all, as the most excellent.

The good man, he was now getting old, towards sixty perhaps; and gave you the idea of a life that had been full of sufferings; a life heavy-laden, half-vanquished, still swimming painfully in seas of manifold physical and other bewilderment. Brow and head were round, and of massive weight, but the face was flabby and irresolute. The deep eyes, of a light hazel, were as full of sorrow as of inspiration; confused pain looked mildly from them, as in a kind of mild astonishment. The whole figure and air, good and amiable otherwise, might be called flabby and irresolute; expressive of weakness under possibility of strength. He hung loosely on his limbs, with knees bent, and stooping attitude; in walking, he rather shuffled than decisively stept; and a lady once remarked, he never could fix which side of the garden-walk would suit him best, but continually shifted, in corkscrew fashion, and kept trying both. A heavy-laden, high-aspiring and surely much-suffering man. His voice, naturally soft and good, had contracted itself into a plaintive snuffle and sing song; he spoke as if preaching, — you would have said, preaching earnestly and also hopelessly the weightiest things. I still recollect his 'object' and 'subject,' terms of continual recurrence in the Kantean province; and how he sung and snuffled them into 'om-m-mject' and 'sum-m-mject,' with a kind of solemn shake or quaver, as he rolled along. No talk, in his century or in any other, could be more surprising. [...]

Nothing could be more copious than his talk; and furthermore it was always, virtually or literally, of the nature of a monologue; suffering no interruption, however reverent; hastily putting aside all foreign additions, annotations, or most ingenuous desires for elucidation, as well-meant superfluities which would never do. Besides, it was talk not flowing anywhither like a river, but spreading everywhither in inextricable currents and regurgitations like a lake or sea; terribly deficient in definite goal or aim, nay often in logical intelligibility; *what* you were to believe or do, on any earthly or heavenly thing, obstinately refusing to appear from it. So that, most times, you felt logically lost; swamped near to

drowning in this tide of ingenious vocables, spreading out boundless as if to submerge the world.

To sit as a passive bucket and be pumped into, whether you
consent or not, can in the long-run be exhilarating to no creature;
how eloquent soever the flood of utterance that is descending. But
if it be withal a confused unintelligible flood of utterance, threat-
ening to submerge all known landmarks of thought, and drown
the world and you! — I have heard Coleridge talk, with eager musical energy, two stricken hours, his face radiant and moist, and
communicate no meaning whatsoever to any individual of his
hearers, — certain of whom, I for one, still kept eagerly listening in
hope; the most had long before given up, and formed (if the room
were large enough) secondary humming groups of their own. He
began anywhere: you put some question to him, made some sug-
gestive observation; instead of answering this, or decidedly setting
out towards answer of it, he would accumulate formidable appa-
ratus, logical swim-bladders, transcendental life-preservers and
other precautionary and vehiculatory gear, for setting out; perhaps
did at last get under way, — but was swiftly solicited, turned aside
by the glance of some radiant new game on this hand or that, into
new courses; and ever into new; and before long into all the Universe, where it was uncertain what game you would catch, or
whether any.

His talk, alas, was distinguished, like himself, by irresolution: it
disliked to be troubled with conditions, abstinences, definite ful-
filments; — loved to wander at its own sweet will, and make its
auditor and his claims and humble wishes a mere passive bucket
for itself! He had knowledge about many things and topics, much
curious reading; but generally all topics led him, after a pass or
two, into the high seas of theosophic philosophy, the hazy infini-
tude of Kantean transcendentalism, with its 'sum-m-mjects' and
'om-m-mjects.' Sad enough; for with such indolent impatience of
the claims and ignorances of others, he had not the least talent for
explaining this or anything unknown to them; and you swam and
fluttered in the mistiest wide unintelligible deluge of things, for
most part in a rather profitless uncomfortable manner.

Glorious islets, too, I have seen rise out of the haze; but they
were few, and soon swallowed in the general element again.
Balmy sunny islets, islets of the blest and the intelligible; — on
which occasions those secondary humming groups would all cease

humming, and hang breathless upon the eloquent words; till once your islet got wrapt in the mist again, and they could recommence humming. Eloquent artistically expressive words you always had; piercing radiances of a most subtle insight came at intervals; tones of noble pious sympathy, recognisable as pious though strangely coloured, were never wanting long: but in general you could not call this aimless, cloudcapt, cloud based, lawlessly meandering human discourse of reason by the name of 'excellent talk,' but only of 'surprising'; and were reminded bitterly of Hazlitt's account of it: 'Excellent talker, very,—if you let him start from no premises and come to no conclusion.' Coleridge was not without what talkers call wit, and there were touches of prickly sarcasm in him, contemptuous enough of the world and its idols and popular dignitaries; he had traits even of poetic humour: but in general he seemed deficient in laughter; or indeed in sympathy for concrete human things either on the sunny or on the stormy side. One right peal of concrete laughter at some convicted flesh-and-blood absurdity, one burst of noble indignation at some injustice or depravity, rubbing elbows with us on this solid Earth, how strange would it have been in that Kantean haze-world, and how infinitely cheering amid its vacant air-castles and dim-melting ghosts and shadows! None such ever came. His life had been an abstract thinking and dreaming, idealistic, passed amid the ghosts of defunct bodies and of unborn ones. The moaning singsong of that theosophico-metaphysical monotony left on you, at last, a very dreary feeling.

In close colloquy, flowing within narrower banks, I suppose he was more definite and apprehensible; Sterling in after times did not complain of his unintelligibility, or imputed it only to the abstruse high nature of the topics handled. Let us hope so, let us try to believe so! There is no doubt but Coleridge could speak plain words on things plain: his observations and responses on the trivial matters that occurred were as simple as the commonest man's, or were even distinguished by superior simplicity as well as pertinency. 'Ah, your tea is too cold, Mr. Coleridge!' mourned the good Mrs. Gilman [*sic*] once, in her kind, reverential and yet protective manner, handing him a very tolerable though belated cup.—'It's better than I deserve!' snuffled he, in a low hoarse murmur, partly courteous, chiefly pious, the tone of which still abides with me: 'It's better than I deserve!'[13]

(iii) THE ROUND TABLE AT *FRASER'S*

From 'The Fraserians; or the Commencement of the Year Thirty-Five. A Fragment', Fraser's Magazine XI (1835) 1-27, 15-17. Coleridge cuts rather a different figure at the Fraser's Round Table. William Maginn (1793-1842), journalist, rogue, and founder of Fraser's, fondly pictured him in one article 'drinking everlasting glasses of brandy and water in coffee-houses various, – or carousing potations pottle-deep, as of old, in the western world of Bristol, – or making orations to barmaids and landladies, and holding them by his glittering eye and suasive tongue' ('Gallery of Literary Characters. No.XXXVIII', Fraser's VII (1833), 64). Here, following Coleridge's death, the Fraserians swap tales.

'Yes,' said Hook, 'he would not only have aided in the discussion of questions literary and political, but in the discussion of any thing else that is before us. I confess I could not help laughing at the fuss made about the sobriety, and temperance, and so forth, of Coleridge, in the newspapers, immediately after his death, when I knew so much of his habits.

'Why,' said Jack Churchill, 'I have been informed by Barnett or Tarbor, I forget which, of the Spring Gardens' Coffee-house, that Coleridge's bill, when he stopped there, was something like that of Falstaff's, – a halfpenny worth of bread to a hogshead of sack. It was soda water and brandy, eighteenpence – glass of brandy, sixpence – roll of bread, twopence – glass of sherry, ninepence – brandy and water, cold, a shilling – roll of bread, twopence – pint of sherry, three shillings – mutton chop, a shilling – bottle of port, six shillings – glass of brandy, sixpence – pint of porter, threepence – roll of bread, twopence – paper, sixpence – brandy and water, seven shillings – anchovy toast, a shilling – glass of brandy, sixpence – small beer, twopence – and so forth, day after day. Coleridge was a wet customer.'

'I shall never forget,' remarked Hook, 'the first time he was introduced to me, or I to him, which you please. Mathews, who was always a great friend and admirer of his, promised to bring him down to dine with me, when I lived close by Putney Bridge; but he could not meet him in time. Old Cole, nevertheless, found out the way, but did not arrive until we had almost finished our wine.'

'By my soul, then,' interrupted Ainsworth, 'that must have been at rather a late hour, if I may judge by your present habits.'

'Never mind,' returned Theodore; 'I mean that he came about half-past nine o'clock, we having dined at six; so that we had

nearly arrived at our brandy and water, which was what I meant
when I said we had finished our wine; and into the room he
walked, with a countenance as solemn as a mustard-pot. Mathews
jumped up, and introduced his friend as rapidly as possible. "Mr.
Coleridge, Mr. Hook—Mr. Hook, Mr. Coleridge." I bowed; he
bowed. I offered him a chair; he accepted it. I asked him if he
would take any claret; he inclined his head in assent. I filled his
glass; I filled my own. I emptied mine; he emptied his. But not a
word did he speak. I made some observation about the heat or the
cold of the weather, but to no effect: he was silent. I filled him
another glass. He opened his mouth, it is true; but it was only to
swallow the claret. Can this, thought I, be the great speaker? Good
God, the man's dumb! The thought had scarcely passed through
my pericranium when our old friend, acting the part of Balaam's
ass, opened his mouth and spake. You all remember the chant of
his voice: I had never heard him speak before, and the first words
that saluted my ears were, "When we reflect upon the state of
Spain—" "Sir!" said I; but it was of no use, out flowed the gush of
eloquence. "When we reflect upon the state of Spain, the mind
naturally reverts—(your health, Mr. Hook!)—to the subjugation of
the Peninsula in the days of the Visigoths, when the Mahometan
hosts, introduced by the treachery of native grandees, having
succeeded in defeating the legitimate prince, broke down the force
of the Spanish nation for a moment, and made themselves masters
of tower, and town, and tented plain—(thank you, Mr. Hook; the
glass is full enough)—until the Goths were driven into the eternal
fastnesses of the everlasting mountains, thence to rebound, under
the conduct of the gallant Pelayo, destined to drive gradually, by
successive shocks, into the sea, the infidel invaders; and planting at
last the banners of Ferdinand and Isabella over the towers of
Granada, deserted by Boabdil, to regain for Christendom the land
of Spain. (Thank you; the claret is very good indeed.) So, when a
more godless army than that introduced by the treachery of Count
Julian crossed the Pyrenees under Napoleon Buonaparte—more
godless, I say, because the infidelity of Jacobinism is worse and
more unchristian in feeling and principle than that of the
Moslem—they, too, won tower, and town, and tented plain; but
the hills that lift up their heads into heaven, those they won not.
And from them came rebounding the might of Spain, supported by
the gallant army of the Duke of Wellington; and as the towers of

Granada saw the last of the Islam, so did Vittoria chase from
Iberian land the relics of the Frenchman. (Your health, Mr. Hook—
thank you.) Now you may inquire why I have thought it necessary
to institute this comparison between the Mahometan and
Jacobinical invaders of Spain. ['I declare to Heaven,' here
interjected Hook, 'I did not see the necessity; but as Coleridge did,
he proceeded.'] It was occasioned thus: I arose this morning
saddened and depressed by influences which I could not account
for, and I went to dissipate my chagrin in one of those green lanes
abounding about Highgate, and which are every where the
characteristic and the main ornament of the scenery of England.
And as I roved along, on lowly fancies bent, I saw seated across a
stile two of those gallant fellows whose dress denoted them to be
of the Guards of Britain, and from whose bosoms depended the
medal which proved that they had shared in the glorious day of
Waterloo. And I thought upon that day, and then upon him who
won it—and then upon his military career—and then upon his
deeds in freeing the Peninsula from the insolent foe; and while
thus musing, there came into my head the parallel which I have
been in some measure endeavouring to make out for the
information of the company. (Your health, Mr. Hook.") Such,'
continued Theodore, 'were the first words I heard from Coleridge.
I thought myself exceedingly lucky that he had seen only two
Guardsmen lounging over a hedge; for if he had seen a troop, the
oration would not have been over until the present moment. I can
bear testimony, however, to the fact, that he never lost a glass of
wine while he was pouring forth his sentences. If he was getting
rid of words *ore rotundo*, he was beyond doubt swallowing claret
ore aperto at the same moment.'

'Certainly,' said Barry Byran Cornwall Procter, 'there were
times when it was quite impossible to refrain from laughing at the
ultra eloquence of my friend Coleridge. I was a regular member of
his Thursday night's *conversazioni*, as were Mr. Irving, of whom we
have been speaking, and Mr. Basil Montagu, with whom I
generally went. And the drollest part of the thing was that it had
infected, as if by contagion, all the establishment of Gillman, with
whom he resided. I recollect calling one day with Basil Montagu to
visit Coleridge, who happened at the time to be in London. The
servant-maid who opened the door replied to our question, that
she did—not—know—but—that—if—we—were—so—kind—as—

to wait—for—the—shortest portion—of—time—she—would—inquire—of—the—lady—of—the—house. Every other inquiry we
made was answered in the same fashion; and at last, when out of
the infinite verbiage we had discovered that he was staying at
Blandford Place, Pall Mall, a little fellow about ten years of age
was consulted as to the particular address, and he answered, as
oracularly as Coleridge himself, "He— dwells— at— Blandford
Place—close—by—the—street—called—Pall Mall—as—to—the—
precise—number—I cannot—inform—you—but—there—being—
only—two—houses—in—the—place—if—you—do— not— find—
that— he—lives—at— number—one—you—may— apply—with—
the—certainty—of—discovering—him—at—number—two." And
this was from a gaffer not higher than the table.'

NOTES

[1] Fielding's *The Mock-Doctor, or the Dumb Lady Cur'd* (1732). *Barnaby Brittle; or, a Wife at her Wit's End* (1781), derived from Molière's *George Dandin.*

[2] 'The dismembered limbs of a poet'. Cf. Horace, *Satires*, I.iv, l.62.

[3] Beaumont and Fletcher, *Philaster*, V.iii—a conflation of ll.12 and 29-30.

[4] 'Let us sing a loftier strain': Virgil, *Eclogues*, IV, l.1.

[5] Chaucer, *The Knight's Tale*, l.1036.

[6] William Charles Macready (1793-1873), famous tragedian, played Zanga in Edward Young's *The Revenge.*

[7] Charles Edward Walker, *Wallace: an Historical Tragedy* (1820).

[8] William Cobbett (1763-1835), whose *Weekly Political Register* began in 1802.

[9] Frederick Pilon, *The Deaf Lover* (1780).

[10] *Paradise Lost*, VIII, ll.1-2.

[11] A swipe at plagiarism. (In Hawkins's *Life*, Johnson, hearing a piece of music described 'very difficult', remarks '"I would it had been impossible."')

[12] Carlyle's portrait was based upon his own abortive meetings with STC:

> Coleridge, a puffy, anxious, obstructed-looking, fattish old man, hobbled about with us, talking with a kind of solemn emphasis on matters which were of no interest (and even *reading* pieces in proof of his opinions thereon). I had him to myself once or twice, in various parts of the garden walks, and tried hard to get something about *Kant* and Co. from him, about 'reason' versus 'understanding' and the like, but in vain. Nothing came from him that was of use to me that day, or in fact any day. The sight and sound of a sage who was so venerated by those about me, and whom I too would willingly have vener- ated, but could not—this was all. Several times afterwards, Montagu, on Coleridge's 'Thursday evenings,' carried Irving and me out, and returned blessing Heaven (I not) for what he had received. Irving and I walked out more than once on mornings too, and found the Dodona oracle humanly ready to act, but never to me, or Irving either I suspect, explanatory of the question

put. Good Irving strove always to think that he was getting priceless wisdom out of this great man, but must have had his misgivings [...] Early in 1825 was my last sight of him; a print of Porson brought some trifling utterances: 'Sensuality such a *dissolution* of the features of a man's face;' and I remember nothing more. On my second visit to London (autumn 1830) Irving and I had appointed a day for a pilgrimage to Highgate, but the day was one rain deluge, and we couldn't even try. (*Reminiscences*, ed. James Anthony Froude (2 vols.; 1881), I, 230-1)

[13] John Galt was no more impressed: 'I think he was a *daft* man, a metaphysical *havrel* [...] I went to visit him with a very intelligent mutual friend. Oh, mon dieu! what a *spate* of clatter!' (*Diary Illustrative of the Times of George the Fourth*, ed. John Galt (4 vols.; 1838-9), IV, 179; 180). And a final example of a Scot unimpressed—Lady Elizabeth Grant Smith, who met STC in 1823: 'that poor, mad poet, Coleridge, who never held his tongue, stood pouring out a deluge of words meaning nothing, with eyes on fire, and his silver hair streaming down to his waist' (*Memoirs of a Highland Lady*, ed. Lady Strachey (2nd.edn.; 1898), 385).

Thursday Evenings at Highgate

The Thursday evenings referred to by Cornwall were a regular feature of Highgate life: these 'conversazioni' — or '*One*versazioni', as Coleridge self-mockingly called them (*CL*, VI, 790)—could make an immense impression. 'Certainly the most extraordinary evening I ever passed', Sir Henry Taylor told his diary.[1] Others, like Carlyle, were more sceptical.

(i) L.M. CRAWFORD

From L.M. Crawford, 'Thoughts on the Poet Coleridge', Metropolitan Magazine XI (1834) 142-6, 144; 145.

Here Coleridge was the centre and admiration of the circle that gathered round him. He could not be otherwise than aware of the intellectual homage, of which he was the object; yet there he sate, talking and looking all sweet and simple and divine things, the very personification of meekness and humility. Now he spoke of passing occurrences, or of surrounding objects, — the flowers on the table, or the dog on the hearth; and enlarged in most familiar-wise on the beauty of the one, the attachment, the almost moral nature of the other, and the wonders that were involved in each. And now, soaring upward with amazing majesty, into those sublimer regions in which his soul delighted, and abstracting himself from the things of time and sense, the strength of his wing soon carried him out of sight. And here, even in these his eagle flights, although the eye in gazing after him was dazzled and blinded, yet ever and anon a sunbeam would make its way through the loopholes of the mind, giving it to discern that beautiful amalgamation of heart and spirit, that could equally raise him above his fellow men, or bring him down again to the softest level of humanity. [...]

I remember Coleridge reading some passages from the old poets, with such a look and tone of enjoyment, that his whole soul seemed poured out in the flood of melody that fell from his lips. Nor was it surprising to find one of his most original turn giving the palm to those early writers, who, as he justly observed, were the parent streams of all those channels of thought, that diffuse themselves through modern poetry; which has chiefly the merit of dressing up old ideas in a new and more elegant costume, or, in other words, re-setting the jewels of antiquity in the filigree of the day. Talking of Shakspeare, he gave it as his opinion that both *Titus Andronicus*, and *Troilus and Cressida*, were the works of that mighty Archimage, and bore the impress of his genius too strongly, (despite their faults,) to give sanction to the idea entertained by some critics, that they were the compositions of an inferior hand.

Coleridge's manner of adducing his arguments was very pleasing. While he led you through a labyrinth, too long, perhaps, and intricate for you to thread of yourself, you have supposed that you held all the while the silken clue in your own hand. With all his learning, — and he was deeply learned, — with all his wisdom, and he was truly wise, — no satire, no pride, no unbecoming contempt of others less gifted than himself, threw even a passing shadow over the brightness of his nature, a nature the most *regenerate*, perhaps, that ever put on the inspiring mantle of *genius*.

(ii) JOHN HERMAN MERIVALE

From Leaves from the Diary of a Literary Amateur. John Herman Merivale *1819-1844, by Edward H.A. Koch (Hampstead, 1911), 27-30. Merivale (1779-1844), a friend of Byron, was a classical scholar, a poet and translator.*

1825. August 20. On Thursday I went to Hampstead, took an early dinner with Rogers,[2] and at six o'clock in the evening went with him and Mrs. Rogers to Coleridge's soirée at Highgate. [...] The first report on our arrival was that the philosopher was so ill as to make it doubtful whether he would be able to join us; and we spent nearly an hour (during which we were joined by the learned Basil, his lady, and Irving) before he made his appearance, which he did at last (as Mrs. Rogers told me), in consequence of her having informed him that I had come purposely to be introduced to him. Nothing could be more courteous than his manner of welcoming, and his hopes that I should renew my visit. He soon took his chair, and began to hold forth *ex cathedra*. He brought downstairs with him the folio edition of Baxter's *History of his Life and Times*, as a sort of text to preach from, and at first began to eulogize the book and its author. The former bore witness to the value he appears to set upon it from the number of registers inserted in almost every page. The author he designated as the most eminently entitled of any character he knows to the blessings of the peacemaker. From Baxter the strain of his argument flowed almost imperceptibly into metaphysics and the most abstruse mysteries of religion. . . . From the Unitarians he changed his battery to the Scotch Presbyterian Church; and so resolved were all present to do nothing but listen, that even this attack failed to rouse the Caledonian apostle, who (except by the interposition of one solitary attempt at illustration) was a silent hearer during the whole evening. For myself, I was certainly very much struck with his wonderful powers both of speech and thought, with the flow of his imagery and happiness of his illustrations; but I was often unable to follow him, and concur fully in the observation I have heard made on the *cloudy brilliancy* of his discourse. My curiosity is not by any means satisfied; on the contrary, I feel strongly urged to repeat my visit and endeavour to form a more distinct idea of his real powers than I have at present.

Sept. 4 (Sunday). [...] After church Herman[3] and I called at Coleridge's, which was the main object of our going to Highgate, and we had an hour of most interesting conversation with (or rather holding forth of) that most singular and highly gifted man. He began with Religion and Metaphysics. . . . We then talked (or rather *he* talked) of Predestination and Coplestone, whom he called a worthy good man, but seemed to value very little as a metaphysician! I could not follow him in this part of his discourse, which appeared to me abundantly mystical. Referring to our friend Rogers, he maintained that a man may be too thoroughly *good* to become distinguished, that to be so (i.e. *distinguished,*) a man should have some spice of the Devil in his composition, nay — that a portion of the devilish may stand a man in stead of all actual talents and acquirements—e.g. Bonaparte, whom he holds to be infinitely over-rated. Thence we slid into Grammar—Matthiae's Greek—Philosophical Grammar. . . . Thence to Webster on Witchcraft, and writers on Witchcraft generally. Baxter, (another instance of a man being too unmixedly good)—Jacob Behmen, etc.[.] I left him, still unconvinced both of the soundness and clearness of his perceptions, but astonished at his vast flow of words, retentiveness of memory, fecundity of illustration, and exalted powers of eloquence, and with a determination not to throw away the privilege he seems disposed to grant me of a more intimate acquaintance.

(iii) JOHN ABRAHAM HERAUD

From An Oration on the Death of Samuel Taylor Coleridge, Esq., delivered at the Russell Institution on Friday, August 8, 1834 *(2nd. edn., 1834), 4-7. Heraud (1799-1887) was a poet and essayist, an important mediator of modern German thought. He was one of Coleridge's most devoted champions. This comes from the section of his* Oration, *devoted to 'Personal Experience of "the Man"'.*

It was on the fourth day of February, 1827, that, fortified with a letter from Serjeant John Taylor Coleridge, then Editor of the Quarterly Review, I first visited the 'Old Man eloquent.' The venerable sage received me with great urbanity—at once ingenuous and engaging. He then spake profusely on the subject of his Philosophy, and of some late chemical experiments that had corroborated certain *a priori* reasonings. He contended that 'systems of philosophy, to be true, must be constructed on *a priori* grounds, and that experience could only confirm them. The process of right reasoning,' he said, 'was cathartic; a cleansing-away of all matter derived through sensuous media, and a proceeding in the Light of Ideas without regarding phenomenal facts—in a word, upon premises altogether and purely ideal, arriving at the appropriate conclusion. Having arrived at which, we should hold our system up, and ask, Does Nature echo this? And Nature will echo it, if care has been taken that all the premises should be included in the deduction. If only half the truth be taken, the conclusion must be erroneous. This was the case with Spinosa. While Spinosa supposed that phenomena were Objects only, and not Subjects also, not all the powers of heaven and earth,' said the eloquent and venerable man, 'could invalidate his argument. But some time before his death, Spinosa began to suspect that they were Subjects as well, which half of the truth added to the other half, will lead to a correct result. The things of experience and sense are Subject-Objects.'

In these few words I have abridged a conversation of two hours.[4] He then read to me some manuscript poems, and invited me to his Thursday evening Colloquies, at which more than once I was anxiously present. It so chanced, however, that the discourse on these occasions turned on subjects rather theological than philosophical, and which, for obvious reasons, I think it fit now to pass over.

One splendid passage, nevertheless, I may not pretermit. Speaking of Nature and Will—in reply to some remark made by the Rev. Edward Irving—'Will,' he said, 'is a higher Faculty than Reason, but a Will is none that does not act; and the highest act of a Will, which is the highest form of Being, is to beget Being. There must, therefore, have ever been the voice that said, "I AM" – and the Response, "Ay, Father, thou art, and I in thee!" It is the existence of a Will that constitutes Individuality.

'Nature,' he continued, 'is rather an appentence to be, than Being itself. Nature is essentially imperfect, and all her tendencies are, (so to speak,) "to supersede herself." Thus the fin of a fish is a hand, but without the uses, it only serves as a fan; but there it shews that an imperfection has begun to be *felt*; and which imperfection is removed, more or less, in a higher scale of creatures. Nature is the Opposite to God, and accordingly God can not be seen *in* Nature;[5] but all things are distinguishable by contrast only; and, therefore, by means of Nature, the idea of its Opposite may be evolved, which is God. Now God is a Spirit. It is between these two opposites of Spirit and Nature that there is an antagonism, and which, existing in man, explains the principles of his structure.'

Mr. Coleridge was next asked, What, then, was the nature of man before the Fall:—how could that be perfect? He answered, 'it was good, not perfect. What its state was, however, before the Fall, he would not decide. The state before the Fall,' he continued, 'is that of Ideas, which is antecedent to History, that deals with a period of facts. Will being always essentially active, there was an eternal possibility of Creation, and of all states of Being—there was also the possibility of a state of comparative perfection—there was one of man's standing, and one of his falling. Hence, in the world of Ideas, there is a continual process of Being—and an appetence for Being—Spirit—and Nature—which was necessary. For no Being is absolute Being, but that of the Absolute Will, or God. The existence of other Being, therefore, could be only relative. Nothing can be known to exist, but in consequence of some other thing, with which it is contrasted or compared. But its similitude supposes also a dissimilitude. There must, therefore, have everlastingly been an anguish, and an agony, and an eternal baffling, between True Being and that which was not True Being, but was striving to become so. Thus it is said of Satan, "He was a Liar from the beginning." All Theology' (concluded Coleridge) 'depends on mastering the term, Nature.'

(iv) LORD HATHERLEY

From A Memoir of the Right Hon. William Page Wood Baron Hatherley *[...], ed. W.R.W. Stephens (2 vols.; 1883), I, 157; 160-1; 175; 177-8. Hatherley (1801-81), later Lord Chancellor, was taken to Thursday evenings by Basil Montagu (I, 51), Coleridge's long-time friend, and a devoted participant.*

December 11 [1828]. – [...] We found a large party at Highgate, and Coleridge was very entertaining. He read us a fine passage from a manuscript on the foolish objection to theory and demand for facts. 'Such men,' he observed, are 'preparing their souls for the office of turnspit at the next metempsychosis.' [...]

December 18. – In the evening with the Montagus and Irving to Highgate. Coleridge was in full vigour of intellect, and his conversation, which took a theological turn, as is generally the case when Irving is there, was brilliant and at the same time of great depth and interest. . . . Coleridge's sentiments are formed on the Lutheran exposition of the Gospel scheme, which he considers to be derived from the exposition given by St. Paul and St. John, the two most gifted apostles. He conceives a genuine faith is the gradual substitution of Christ's reviving influence which causes the natural man to throw off as it were, by successive sloughs, the mortal vices. He conceives that an internal Church which 'cometh not by observation' is preparing in the minds of men; whilst an external Church must at the same time, by its salutary influence on the mind, keep up the internal action which would otherwise gradually wear out; that this was the scheme ordained from the beginning of our earth and the very object of its existence, at least after the fall; that the Jewish prophets looked forward to an eternal life by redemption, as the expressions of Ezekiel, for instance, 'that the wicked man turning away from his wickedness shall save his soul alive,'[6] have otherwise no meaning, because certainly physically incorrect; that evil is merely subjective, not objective; that it is falsehood, the devil, who is a liar from the beginning, wishing to reconcile the impossibilities of being at the same time a creature, and yet equal to the Creator. He finely illustrated the subjectiveness of evil producing objective good by supposing the parts of a machine in a manufactory to be animated, and anxious to tear and bruise each other, and the manufactured article, which, at last, however, arrives at perfection by this very means. This, it is true, leaves untouched the origin of evil, and perhaps favours too much the doctrine of necessity. [...]

January 29 [1829].−[...] In the evening with B. Montagu to Coleridge's. He had been seized with a fit of enthusiasm for Donne's poetry, which I think somewhat unaccountable. There was great strength, however, in some passages which he read. One stanza or rather division of his poem, on the 'Progress of the Soul,' struck me very much; it was, I think, the fourth, in which he addresses Destiny as the 'Knot of Causes.'[7] The rest of the poem seemed the effusion of a man very drunk or very mad.

Coleridge launched forth at some length upon Bacon's inductive method, at the request of Montagu. I think he clearly failed in his attempt to depreciate experiment. [...]

To use Coleridge's favourite simile, the human mind may be the kaleidoscope, but it is a dull instrument if there be no extrinsic object to work upon. He was happy in one image, not so much as an illustration, but as a pleasing touch of fancy. He said that Nature had for ages appeared to wish to communicate her stores of higher knowledge by the phenomenon of the compass, but that she was too distant from us, and we could only watch the trembling of her lips without catching the sound.

NOTES

[1] 26 February 1824; quoted in Una Taylor, *Guests and Memories. Annals of a Seaside Villa* (1924), 57.

[2] Lawrence Rogers, a police magistrate in London (p. 58).

[3] Merivale's son, later Under-Secretary for India.

4 Heraud printed two longer 'Monologues' (*Fraser's* XII (1835) 494-6; 619-29), more dictated essays than records of talk. An earlier memoir of Heraud's has this fragment (STC has been talking about the incompletion of 'Christabel'):

> A friend of ours, in company with another gentleman, paid a visit to Coleridge to get at the fact relative to this conclusion. 'By-the-bye,' answered Coleridge, 'that is a curious circumstance, — I'll tell you all about it, — ' and then digressed into some other topic, upon which he discoursed so fascinatingly that both himself and his questioners forgot the purport of their visit, and came away without the solution which they went to get. This is a type of Coleridge's conversation, and shews its singular power. ('Reminiscences of Coleridge [...]', *Fraser's* X (1834) 379-403, 393-4)

5 Cf. *TT*, I, 94-5. In a book effusively dedicated to STC's memory — in the 'Preface' to which he is described as 'the great religious philosopher, to whom the mind of our generation in England owes more than to any other man' — STC is recorded saying, 'in reference to those who almost deify her, *No! Nature is not God; she is only the devil in a straight waistcoat*' (Julius Charles Hare, *The Mission of the Comforter, with Notes* (2nd. [revised] edn.; Cambridge, 1850), xii-xiii, 410). And cf., too, the story told by Frederick Denison Maurice:

> [A] professor in conversation with Coleridge used the word Nature in a way which roused Coleridge to exclaim, 'Why do you say Nature, when you mean God?' On Dr. Buckland answering, 'I think it more reverent; but you think both words have the same meaning, do you not?' Coleridge indignantly rejoined: '*I* think God and Nature the same! I think Nature is the devil in a straitwaistcoat.' (Edward Strachey, 'Recollections of Frederick Denison Maurice', *Cornhill Magazine* NS II (1897) 536-47, 540-1)

6 Cf. Ezekiel 18.27.
7 Cf. Donne, 'Progress of the Soul', l.35 (which is indeed in the fourth stanza).

Encounters at Highgate, 1827-28

(i) HENRY NELSON COLERIDGE

From Specimens of the Table Talk, *I, 66-7n., recalling a day in June 1827.*

How well I remember this Midsummer-day! I shall never pass such another. The sun was setting behind Caen Wood, and the calm of the evening was so exceedingly deep that it arrested Mr. Coleridge's attention. We were alone together in Mr. Gillman's drawing-room, and Mr. C. left off talking, and fell into an almost trance-like state for ten minutes whilst contemplating the beautiful prospect before us. His eyes swam in tears, his head inclined a little forward, and there was a slight uplifting of the fingers, which seemed to tell me that he was in prayer. I was awe-striken, and remained absorbed in looking at the man, in forgetfulness of external nature, when he recovered himself, and after a word or two fell by some secret link of association upon Spenser's poetry.[1] Upon my telling him that I did not very well recollect the Prothalamion: 'Then I must read you a bit of it,' said he, and, fetching the book from the next room, he recited the whole of it in his finest and most musical manner. I particularly bear in mind the sensible diversity of tone and rhythm with which he gave: –

'Sweet Thames! run softly till I end my song,'

the concluding line of each of the ten strophes of the poem.

When I look upon the scanty memorial, which I have alone preserved of this afternoon's converse, I am tempted to burn these pages in despair. Mr. Coleridge talked a volume of criticism that day, which, printed verbatim as he spoke it, would have made the reputation of any other person but himself. He was, indeed, particularly brilliant and enchanting, and I left him at night so thoroughly *magnetized*, that I could not for two or three days afterwards reflect enough to put any thing on paper.

(ii) JOHN STERLING

From Julius Charles Hare's memoir, prefacing John Sterling, Essays and Tales *(2 vols.; 1848), I, xvi-xix; xxiv-xxvi. Sterling (1806-44), essayist and novelist, was at Trinity under Hare, a keen Coleridgean, who probably introduced the young man to Coleridge in late 1827.[2] Sterling soon became a follower.[3] Hare thought Sterling's notes of the master's talk 'the only record I have seen, which enables one at all to apprehend how his wonderful combination of philosophical and poetical powers manifested themselves in his discourse' (pp.xv-xvi).*

Mr. Coleridge happened to lay his hand upon a little old engraving of Luther with four German verses above it. He said, 'How much better this is than many of the butcher-like portraits of Luther, which we commonly see! He is of all men the one whom I especially love and admire.' Pointing to the first words of the German verses, he explained them, *Luther, the dear hero.* 'It is singular, (he said,) how all men have agreed in assigning to Luther the *heroic* character; and indeed it is certainly most just. Luther, however wrong in some of his opinions, was always right in design and spirit. In translating his ideas into conceptions, he always understood something higher and more universal than he had the means of expressing. He did not bestow too much attention on one part of man's nature to the exclusion of the others;

but gave its due place to each, — the intellectual, the practical, and so forth. He is great, even where he is wrong, — even in the sacramental controversy, the most unhappy in which he engaged; for his idea of Christ's body becoming infinite by its union with the godhead is entirely wrong.' Some one mentioned Calvin. He said 'Calvin was undoubtedly a man of talent; I have a great respect for him; he had a very logical intellect; but he wanted Luther's powers.'

He then began to speak of landscape-gardening, in consequence of some remark about the beautiful view behind the house in which he resides. 'We have gone too far in destroying the old style of gardens and parks. There was a great deal of comfort in the thick hedges, which always gave you a sheltered walk during winter. There is certainly a propriety in the gradual passing away of the works of man in the neighbourhood of a home. The great thing is to discover whether the scenery is such that the country seems to belong to man, or man to the country. Now among the lakes of Westmoreland man evidently belongs to the country: the very cottages seem merely to rise out of, and to be growths of, the rock. But the case is different in a country where everything speaks of man, houses, corn-fields, cattle. There your improvements ought to be in conformity with the character of the place. Man is so in love with intelligence, that where he is not intelligent enough to discover it, he will impress it. Some of the finest views about here (Highgate) are only to be seen from among the most wretched habitations. Luther said truly: *How different is a rich country from a happy country!* A rich country is always an unhappy, miserable, degraded country.'

He then went into a long exposition of the evils of commerce and manufactures; the argument of which, I think, is to be found in one of the Lay Sermons.[4] In the course of it he took occasion to say that the Legislature is defective. 'I don't mean anything about the nonsense of universal suffrage; but the land-proprietors have too great a proportion of power. Land is something fixed and tangible: if one man have more of it, another must have less. But this other kind of wealth, which is founded in the National Debt and so forth, — one man's having a million of it does not prevent another man's getting two millions of it; nay, it rather makes it more probable that he will do so. Thirty or forty years ago, it would have been a disgrace to a merchant to be seen on the Stock

Exchange. Now it is thought nothing of. There are only two remedies for the evil of our excessive increasing population. We have not virtue enough for the one, which is a plan of general and continued emigrations, in which the people would be perpetually going forth, headed by the priest and the noble. In every parish a certain portion of every family ought to live under the knowledge that at a certain age they were to emigrate. The other remedy is a perfectly free trade in corn; but this would only do for a time. More rich men are springing up in the country than the country can support: the Regent's Park is covered as it were with an enchanted city.

The division of labour has proceeded so far even in literature, that people do not think for themselves; their review thinks for them.' [...]

Mr. Coleridge is not tall, and rather stout: his features, though not regular, are by no means disagreeable; the hair quite grey; the eye and forehead very fine. His appearance is rather old-fashioned; and he looks as if he belonged not so much to this, or to any age, as to history. His manner and address struck me as being rather formally courteous. He always speaks in the tone and in the gesture of common conversation, and laughs a good deal, but gently. His emphasis, though not declamatory, is placed with remarkable propriety. He speaks perhaps rather slowly, but never stops, and seldom even hesitates. There is the stongest appearance of conviction, without any violence in his manner. His language is sometimes harsh, sometimes careless, often quaint, almost always, I think, drawn from the fresh delicious fountains of our elder eloquence. I have no doubt that the diction of much that I have reported is different from Coleridge's, and always of course vastly inferior. I have treasured up as many of his phrases as I could; they will easily be recognised. On one occasion he quoted a line of his own poetry, saying, 'If I may quote a verse of mine written when I was a very young man.' It was something to this effect: 'They kill too slow for men to call it murder.'[5] He happened to mention several books in the course of his remarks; and he always seemed inclined to mention them goodnaturedly.

I was in his company about three hours; and of that time he spoke during two and three quarters. It would have been delightful to listen as attentively, and certainly easy for him to speak just as well for the next forty-eight hours. [...] It is painful to observe in Coleridge, that, with all the kindness and glorious far-seeing intelligence of his eye, there is a glare in it, a light half unearthly, half morbid. It is the glittering eye of the *Ancient Mariner*. His cheek too shows a flush of over-excitement, the red of a storm-cloud at sunset. When he dies, another, and one of the greatest of their race, will rejoin the few Immortals, the ill understood and ill requited, who have walked this earth.

(iii) JOHN DUKE COLERIDGE

From E.H. Coleridge, Life and Correspondence of John Duke Coleridge[,] Lord Chief Justice of England *(2 vols.; 1904), II, 378-80 (first published in* 'Reminiscences by the Lord Chief Justice', Illustrated London News *103/2829 (8 July 1893).) John Duke Coleridge (1820-94) was the son of John Taylor Coleridge (for whom, see above).*

Two years (I think 1827 and 1828) my father, then a young barrister, was obliged by professional business to stay near London during the Long Vacation, and we occupied two houses in Hampstead—Netley Cottage one year and Bellevue the other—both, I think, still standing and both within a walk of the Grove at Highgate. My father went constantly, when he could find time, to see and hear his uncle, and on three occasions he took me with him, warning me to be on my best behaviour, for that his uncle was a great man; that he believed very few boys so young as I was ever went to see him; and that probably I should not understand all he said, but I must listen and be very quiet.

It is sixty-five or sixty-six years ago, but the scene is before me as clearly as if it had been yesterday—the scene, nothing more; for though he was (I believe always) most kind and gentle to children, and patted me on the head and kissed me (an honour which, as I have hated snuff all my life, I fear I did not properly appreciate), the discourse on each occasion was far out of my ken (probably at any time of my life, most certainly at that time), and I cannot recall a word nor even the subject of it.

Carlyle has given, in the too famous passage in his *Life of Stirling* [sic], a not inaccurate account of the Prophet and his audience as I remember them. He has not, I think, done justice—probably he did not feel the extraordinary melody of Coleridge's voice nor the gentle suasion of his manner—things which a child could feel and did feel. Nor, as I remember, does he describe adequately the suppressed murmurs of admiration when

Coleridge paused, as he sometimes did at the end of one paragraph (so to call it) before he set out upon another, 'That last was very fine.' 'He is beyond himself to-day.' This sort of thing I distinctly recollect, and the puzzle it was to me what it was all about.

I sat on a wooden stool near him, and on two occasions I seem to remember that the window was wide open, and the shutters half closed to keep out the sunlight. But I do not assert this positively, for it is quite possible that the window looked due north, and had no shutters.

Twice or three times I remember his dining with my father at a party necessarily small, for we lived at that time in Torrington Square. I was, of course, much too young to 'dine downstairs'; but I have the same recollection of his kindness and gentleness and of the sweetness of his voice during a few minutes I was in his presence while the guests were assembling before dinner. One piece of his conversation, at one of these dinners, I have heard so often repeated that I sometimes half persuade myself that I heard it, though I am bound to say that is impossible: 'Southey,' said Coleridge, 'is a curious person. He came to me to inform me that he had determined to write a History of Brazil. "Well, Southey," said I, "and what sort of a history do you intend to write? Do you mean to write of man as man, after the manner of Herodotus; or of political man, according to the fashion of Thucydides; or of technic man, as Polybius did?" And what do you think was his answer? He said: "Coleridge, I am going to write a History of Brazil."'[6]

(iv) HENRY CRABB ROBINSON
From Crabb Robinson, Diary, *II, 394.*

June 18th. [1828]—An interesting day. Breakfasted with Aders. Wordsworth and Coleridge were there. Alfred Becher also. Wordsworth was chiefly busied about making arrangements for his journey into Holland. Coleridge was, as usual, very eloquent in his dreamy monologues, but he spoke intelligibly enough on some interesting subjects. It seems that he has of late been little acquainted with Irving. He says that he silenced Irving by showing how completely he had mistaken the sense of the Revelation and Prophecies, and then Irving kept away for more than a year. Coleridge says, 'I consider Irving as a man of great power, and I have an affection for him. He is an excellent man, but his brain has been turned by the shoutings of the mob. I think him mad, literally mad.' He expressed strong indignation at Irving's intolerance. <He also expressed himself strongly about [Southey]. He said: 'He suffers himself to be flattered into servility by that one-testicled fellow Peel. He writes most servilely though very honestly.' I confounded their names together. 'Pray do not make such a blunder again. I should have no objection to your doing it with him.' (Pointing to Wordsworth.)>[7]

NOTES

[1] Spenser is the first item discussed in the table talk recorded for 24 June 1827.

[2] Carlyle (*Life*, 81) says that they met in late 1828; Anne Kimball Tuell (*John Sterling: A Representative Victorian* (NY, 1941), 240), says August 1827.

[3] They spread the word: see, e.g., *The Life and Correspondence of Arthur Penhryn Stanley*, ed. Rowland E. Prothero and G.G. Bradley (2 vols.; 1893), I, 106-14.

[4] Cf. *LS*, 169-70; 202-5, *etc.*.

[5] Cf. 'Religious Musings', ll.289 (*CPW*, I, 120).

[6] A story also told by Alexander Dyce: *Reminiscences*, ed. Schrader, 178.

[7] Words in angle-brackets from *On Books and Their Writers*, ed. Morley, I, 359-60.

The Continental Tour, 1828

(i) THOMAS COLLEY GRATTAN

From Thomas Colley Grattan, Beaten Paths; and Those who Trod Them *(2 vols.; 1862), II, 110-13; 113-14; 114-17; 118; 120-1; 121-2; 129-37. Grattan (1792-1864) encountered Wordsworth, his daughter Dora, and Coleridge, on their tour, passing through Brussels, on 25 June 1828, and joined them.*

There were several gentlemen of the party. Coleridge talked much and indiscriminately with those next him or about him. He did not appear to talk for effect, but purely for talking's sake. He seemed to breathe in words. Wordsworth was at times fluent but always commonplace; full of remark but not of observation. He spoke of scenery as far as its aspect was concerned; but he did not enter into its associations with moral beauty. He certainly did not talk well. But in fact he had no encouragement. He had few listeners; and what seemed rather repulsive in him was perhaps chiefly from its grating contrast to the wonderful attraction of Coleridge. His was a mild enthusiastic flow of language; a broad, deep stream, carrying gently along all that it met with on its course, not a whirlpool that drags into its vortex, and engulfs what it seizes on. Almost everything he talked about became the subject of a lecture of great eloquence and precision. For instance his remarks on grammar and its philosophy. His illustrations from chemistry and colours came here into play quite naturally, and led him on, but by no means abruptly into a complete, and it must be added a rather complex, essay on the nature of colour, prismatic effects and the theory of light. He was no doubt familiarly acquainted with Goethe's doctrine or theory of colours, and probably with an Italian translation of Aristotle's treatise, which neither I nor any of his listeners had more than passingly heard of. For in alluding to Newton's theory, which Goethe had written in refutation of, (comparing light to a closed fan, saying that a mixture of all colours made white, etc.) he called it 'an incubus on natural philosophy;' and he branched off from his main subject, to trace the analogy between natural grammar and colour, the whole of which he made very interesting if not very lucid, and as to its originality I am not competent to judge. It was difficult to believe that all this was uttered extempore, or indeed without much elaborate arrangement. The thoughts and words appeared stereotyped; and in the fanciful system, as in all his discourse, there was a strong flavour of Kantean transcendentalism and mysticism.

But on all the various topics touched on by Coleridge he said something to be remembered. A true Boswell would have found ample matter for record. I recollect a few of his remarks. He said of Rubens's picture of The Boar Hunt, in the Prince of Orange's collection, 'It is a perfect dithyrambic – every piece of it forms a separate epithet of beauty.'

'I like an occasional desert view in travelling,' said he; 'such scenes are the *punctuations* of a tour.'

Talking of the German language, on which subject he was quite at home, he bore testimony to its copiousness and power, by remarking that 'in reading the German translation of the Georgics if he did not pronounce the words he could believe that he was reading the original.' Of Schiller he said that 'he had reached the acme of his genius in the "Wallenstein." His previous works were too wild, his latter too formal. He was a man of deep feeling for moral beauty, and should have written half-a-dozen grand historical plays.' He observed that Frederick Schlegel,[1] (whom by the way he pronounced to be a consummate coxcomb) had told him that his translation of 'Wallenstein' was better than the original. 'If so,' said Coleridge, 'it is because I struck out a word from almost every line. Wherever I could retrench a syllable I did so, and I cleared away the greatest possible quantity of stuffing.' [...]

In almost everything that fell from Coleridge that evening there was a dash of deep philosophy — even in the outpourings of his egotism — touches not to be given without the whole of what they illustrated. In a word, the impression made on me by his voluptuous and indolent strain of talk, flowing in a quiet tone of cadenced eloquence, was that he was by far the most pleasing talker, but by no means the most powerful, I had ever heard. He led you on beside him by the persuasive elegance of diction, but never drove you forward by the impetuous energy of argument. 'He had,' as Bishop Burnet said of William Penn, 'a tedious, luscious way that was not apt to overcome a man's reason though it might tire his patience.' But Coleridge's talk was not absolutely tiresome, only somewhat drowsy. I thought it would be pleasant to fall asleep to the gushing melody of his discourse, which was rich in information and suavity of thought. But there was something too dreamy, too vapoury to rouse one to the close examination of what he said. Logic there no doubt was, but it was enveloped in clouds. You were therefore delighted to take everything for granted, for everything seemed to convince — because it took a shape and colour so seductive. [...]

At both Waterloo and Quatrebras, while Wordsworth keenly inspected the field of battle, insatiably curious after tombstones, and spots where officers had fallen (the Duke of Brunswick, Picton, Ponsonby, etc.), Coleridge spoke to me of the total deficiency of memorable places to excite any interest in him unless they possessed some *natural* beauty. He called this a defect. I thought it was, and a strange one in such a man, as associations of moral interest seem so fruitfully to spring in a poetic mind on the sites of memorable deeds. Coleridge took evident delight in rural scenes. He was in ecstasies at a group of haymakers in a field as we passed. He said the little girls standing with their rakes, the handles resting on the ground, 'looked like little saints.' Half-a-dozen dust-covered children going by the roadside, with a garland of roses raised above their heads, threw him into raptures. He murmured that 'it was a perfect vision.' It would be easy for a critic or a satirist to ridicule all this, to call it 'twaddle,' or by some such dishonouring epithet. Every little incident of the kind, or even glimpses of commonplace scenery, produced the same sort of effect. But there was no affectation nor *cockneyism* in it. It was evidently prompted by a deep sympathy with nature. It flowed quite naturally—and very pleasingly subsided.

At Namur we walked out by the light of a splendid full moon. We poked our way through the narrow streets to the bridge of the Sambre, then to that of the Meuse; Wordsworth, who took charge of his daughter, pioneering us along, bustling through, asking the way from every one we met; while Coleridge walked after leaning on my arm, and in a total abstraction of thought and feeling, indifferent as to whether we went right or left, but finding somewhat to admire in every glance of moonshine or effect of shade, and a rich fund to draw from in his own mind. He talked away on many subjects; and at last, the broad river, the lofty ridges of hills, and masses of wood, burst suddenly on us in the full light, as we emerged from a gloomy passage that opened on the quay.

Coleridge advanced towards the river, with quiet expressions of enjoyment at the beauty around him. Wordsworth stepped quickly on, and said aloud, yet more to himself than to us—

'Ay, there it is—there's the bridge! Let's see how many arches there are—one, two, three,' and so on, till he counted them all, with the accuracy and hardness of a stone-cutter.

The shadow of the bridge falling on the water gave to every open arch its clear reflection in the stream, which made each of course perfectly round, looking like a row of so many huge, limpid moons, or, as I happened to observe, in allusion to their vapoury appearance, 'so many ghosts of moons.' This hit Coleridge's fancy.

Very good!' said he, moving forward, [']that's a good observation—that's poetry. Let me see, let me see?'

He then paused till I rejoined him, when he took me by the arm, and in his low recitative way he rehearsed two or three times, and finally recited, some lines which he said I had recalled to his mind, and which formed part of something never published. He repeated the lines at my request, and as well as I could catch the broken sentences I wrote them down immediately afterwards with my pencil as follows,

> —— and oft I saw him stray,
> The bells of fox-glove on his hand—and ever

And anon he to his ear would hold a blade
Of that stiff grass that 'mid the heath-flower grows,
Which made a subtle kind of melody,
Most like the apparition of a breeze,
Singing with its thin voice in shadowy worlds. [...]

It was during this walk that he strongly urged me to study German, of which I had only the slightest smattering. He told me he had compiled a grammar, never published, containing, he said, in ten pages, all that was of the least use to a learner of intelligence. This led to his favourite topic, grammar. Every conversation on that subject was a general treatise on its philosophy, its construction, and its value. [...]

The next morning saw us up very early. The carriage was ready by seven o'clock, when we sat down to breakfast, Coleridge (as usual at that meal, or with his evening tea while travelling) despatching three eggs to his share, dressed according to his own recipe — two minutes in boiling water, then taken out and put into a hot napkin for two minutes more, then returned to the water, but not to *boil* again, for another minute — and then to be eaten. I unfortunately cannot state whether Coleridge was a big or a little-endian; but it was no small amusement to see the importance he attached to this arrangement of cookery, by which, as he maintained, the egg acquired an entirely superior flavour, the white part being done more thoroughly — and I forget exactly what advantage accruing to the yelk [*sic*]. [...]

Coleridge leant on my arm as we walked; and some observations of mine relative to the geology of the neighbourhood, called forth a long discourse on 'the great philosophical work' in which he said he had been twenty years engaged, and which he was then concluding and about to publish in conjunction with Mr. Greene [*sic*], the lecturer on natural philosophy. He talked of Nature and God, which he said 'so far from being the same were direct contrasts;' and of Religion, of which he said many things; among the rest that 'revealed religion was a pleonasm — there could be none other.' [...]

The point of most interest, in as far as he was personally concerned, which I touched on with Coleridge, was that of opium-eating. I, along with almost every one who had heard anything of him, had set him down as a regular glutton in that respect. I talked to him of his indulgence in this enjoyment as a matter of course.

On this he displayed infinitely more vivacity and energy than I had yet thought him suspectible of. He quite took the thing to heart. And, with an earnest anxiety to be rightly understood, and an evident hope that I would in some measure forward his views to that effect, he laboured to assure me that the most false notions existed on the subject. He admitted that he had at times taken opium, as the only means of relieving dreadful visitations of nightmare, which had frequently so afflicted him as to make him leap from his bed in agonies of undefinable terror. He might have quoted Milton (leaving out one word) —

> — 'Sleep hath forsook and given me o'er
> To (death's) benumbing opium as my only cure.'[2]

In speaking thus he seemed suddenly to recollect, and then recited, some lines which he said were never published, powerfully expressive of his sufferings, more so than his 'Pains of Sleep.' He shuddered and panted as he repeated them in a deep murmur, and gave me a vivid notion of the horrors to which he must have been habituated. But he solemnly protested against ever having taken opium in anything like excess, or for the purpose of mere excitement.

'It would have been a deep and wanton crime in me,' said he, raising his hands and eyes towards heaven, by no means a common movement with him, for he used but little gesticulation even when speaking with strong emphasis.

He spoke with absolute abhorrence of the 'Confessions of an English Opium-eater,' called it 'a wicked book, a monstrous exaggeration,' and dwelt with great reprobation on the author for 'laying open his nakedness to the world.' He considered him to have behaved grossly in bringing him (Coleridge) into the book, as an authority for the excesses he avowed;[3] and declared that 'when he suspected Mr. de Quincy [sic] of taking opium, he had on several occasions spent hours in endeavouring to dissuade him from it, and that gentleman invariably assured him in the most solemn manner that he did not take it at all, while by his after confessions it appeared that he was drinking laudanum as other men drink wine.'

I think it was on the day previous to this conversation, as we were driving along, that Coleridge was holding forth, in his oracular but not dogmatical tone and style on the decay of literature and the degradation of taste. It must be remarked that he avowedly never read any of the light literature of the day, being wholly engaged for years previously on his 'great work.' He however heard the names of successful novels and popular authors, and confounded them altogether in his brain, which was certainly no respecter of persons. He had heard of *me* as one of the herd, what he no doubt considered the 'small deer' of literature; but of what I had written he had not the slightest notion. As he was talking away, a quarter to us and three parts to himself, both Wordsworth and I caught the words, 'Yes, this may be truly called the penultimate stage of English literature—there may be one station lower. We have Waverley novels and their school, Highway and Byway tales and their imitators.—We have'—but a coarse laugh of full two-horse power bursting from Wordsworth, and an irresistible faint echo from me (while our charming female fellow-traveller blushed deeply) put a stop to his remarks.[4] I turned off the interruption much to his satisfaction by joining in his strictures, and leaning on the arm of his criticism, as it were, to crush with weightier pressure the victims of whom I myself made one. Wordsworth was highly amused.

In the evening, as we walked about the court-yard of the Hôtel de Flandre at Namur, Coleridge took me by the arm and said, 'I'll tell you a story.' He then proceeded.

'When my "Lyrical Ballads" first came out it was anonymously, and they made a good deal of noise. A few days after they were published I dined at Mrs. Barbauld's and sat beside Pinkerton the geographer.[5] We talked a good deal together, and I found him very amusing and full of general information. When we retired to the drawing-room he led me to a recess, having taken up a copy of the "Lyrical Ballads" which lay on the table.

"Pray, Sir," said he, "have you read this thing?"

"I have looked into it."

"Do you know the author?" asked he.

"Do *you* know the author?" echoed I, resolved not to be caught.

"No," said Pinkerton, "but I never read such utter trash as his book, particularly an extravagant farrago of absurdity called 'The Ancient Mariner.' Don't you think it insufferable?"

Coleridge: Intolerable!

Pinkerton: Detestable!

Coleridge: Abominable!

Pinkerton: Odious!

Coleridge: Loathsome!

Pinkerton: Sir, you delight me. It is really delightful to meet a man of sound taste in these days of our declining literature. If I have a passion on earth, it is an abhorrence of these "Lyrical Ballads," of which every one is talking, but most especially of this wretched "Ancient Mariner."

Coleridge: Hush, not a word more! Here comes our hostess. I know she is acquainted with the author, and she might be hurt.

Pinkerton (pulling Coleridge by the button, taking a huge pinch of snuff, and speaking in a whisper): I'll tell you what, Sir, we mustn't let this matter drop. Let's fix a day for dining together at the Turk's Head. We'll have a private room, a beef steak, a bottle of old port, pens, ink, and a quire of foolscap. We'll lay our heads together and review this *thing* – and if we don't give it such a slashing, such a tearing, such a –

"If we don't!" said Coleridge.

"Is it a bargain?"

"Most certainly!"

"Done!"

"Done!"[']

While Coleridge thus told his story, dramatizing it, it may be said, and with great humour and *gusto*, I was more amused than with the anecdote itself, by the anticipation of the pleasure I should have, by quoting for him the case in point, which had happened to myself this morning. But he disappointed me, by putting his hand on my shoulder, and saying in the kindest tone of frank good-nature, 'So you see, my dear Mr. Grattan, that I have been myself served as I, with less reason than Pinkerton, have served you. Wordsworth has told me of my misconduct. I have never read your works that I spoke so lightly of; but I shall make it a point of conscience to read every one of your tales, and I am sure the task will turn out a sincere pleasure.'

I passed the subject over by asking him how Pinkerton looked when they next met.

'I never saw him afterwards,' said he. 'He no doubt thought that I should hate him for the unintended affront – but that was because he was a Scotchman. But I have no dread of your hating *me.*'

'Why not?' asked I.

'Because you are an Irishman.'

This compliment to my country came out so graciously that I took it personally. But the only subjects seriously national on which we touched were the question of Catholic Emancipation and *Potatoes*.

Of the first he spoke, for the purpose of convincing me that he was not intolerantly opposed to the measure. But his reasoning on it was extremely confused. In his discourse there was a jumble of religion, politics, and metaphysics which I had not time to sift. He did not grapple with the subject, or take it by any strong or any weak point. I found it difficult to follow him, which is now happily of no consequence, even had the issue of the great question depended on his opinion one way or the other.[6]

Relative to potatoes, Coleridge told me the following anecdote, which I hope has not since then slipped into print.

A Lincolnshire lady of his acquaintance, wishing to secure for her only son (a boy-baronet) a most correct pronunciation, engaged a first-rate London governess at a high salary, to prepare him for his male teachers when a little more advanced. One day at dinner the child asked for a potato, with very distinct emphasis on each syllable.

'That's not it, my dear,' said the governess, 'try again.'

'Give me, please, a po-ta-to.'

'Once more, my dear, that's not right.'

'Indeed it is, though,' said the boy blubbering, 'I spelled it for Mamma to-day in a book—p, o, *po;* – t, a, *ta;* – pota;—t, o, *to;* – potato.'

'My dear, as far as the letters go you are right, but in the pronunciation you are wrong. You should say *petato, pe* – the lips compressed as I do mine—*pe!* There is no *po*, my dear, in the English language but *pochay!*'

'I make you a present of that,' said Coleridge, 'and it is not only original but true.'[7]

(ii) JULIAN CHARLES YOUNG

From Julian Charles Young, A Memoir of Charles Mayne Young, Tragedian [...] (1871; 2nd. edn.; 2 vols.; 1871), I, 116-18; 121-2; 122; 122-3. J.C. Young's Life of his father (1777-1856) incorporated pages (including the following) from his own journal. He met Coleridge's party at Godesberg, on the Rhine, in July.

I had scarcely entered the room, and was trying to improve a bad sketch I had made the day before when an old gentleman entered, with a large quarto volume beneath his arm, whom I at once concluded to be one of the anonymous gentry about whose personality there had been so much mystery. As he entered, I rose and bowed. Whether he was conscious of my well-intentioned civility I cannot say, but at all events he did not return my salutation. He appeared pre-occupied with his own cogitations. I began to conjecture what manner of man he was. His general appearance would have led me to suppose him a dissenting minister. His hair was long, white, and neglected; his complexion was florid, his features were square, his eyes watery and hazy, his brow broad and massive, his build uncouth, his deportment grave and abstracted. He wore a white starchless neckcloth tied in a limp bow, and was dressed in a shabby suit of dusky black. His breeches were unbuttoned at the knee, his sturdy limbs were encased in stockings of lavender-coloured worsted, his feet were thrust into well-worn slippers, much trodden down at heel. In this ungainly attire he paced up and down, and down and up, and round and round a saloon sixty feet square, with head bent forward, and shoulders stooping, absently musing, and muttering to himself, and occasionally clutching to his side his ponderous tome, as if he feared it might be taken from him. I confess my young spirit chafed under the wearing quarter-deck monotony of his promenade, and, stung by the cool manner in which he ignored my presence, I was about to leave him in undisputed possession of the field, when I was diverted from my purpose by the entrance of another gentleman, whose kindly smile, and courteous recognition of my bow, encouraged me to keep my ground, and promised me some compensation for the slight put upon me by his precursor. He was dressed in a brown-holland blouse; he held in his left hand an alpenstock (on the top of which he had placed the broad-brimmed 'wide-awake' he had just taken off), and in his right a spring of apple-blossom overgrown with lichen. His cheeks were glowing with the effects of recent exercise. So noiseless had been his entry, that the peripatetic philosopher, whose back was turned to him at first, was unaware of his presence. But no sooner did he discover it than he shuffled up to him, grasped him by both hands, and backed him bodily into a neighbouring arm-chair. Having secured him safely there, he 'made assurance doubly sure,' by hanging over him, so as to bar his escape, while he delivered his testimony on the fallacy of certain of Bishop Berkeley's propositions, in detecting which, he said, he had opened up a rich vein of original reflection. Not content with cursory criticism, he plunged profoundly into a metaphysical lecture, which, but for the opportune intrusion of our fair hostess and her young lady friend, might have lasted until dinner time. It was then, for the first time, I learned who the party consisted of; and I was introduced to Samuel Taylor Coleridge, William Wordsworth, and his daughter Dora.

The reported presence of two such men as Coleridge and Wordsworth soon attracted to Mrs. Aders's house all the illuminati of Bonn—Niebuhr, Becker, Augustus Schlegel,[8] and many others. It is matter of lamentation to me, now, to think that I have not preserved any traces of the conversations at which I was privileged to be present. But, alas! my ignorance of German, and my inaptitude for metaphysics, debarred me from much information that, but for those accidents, I might have obtained. I recall nothing but a few fragmentary remarks, which, for a wonder, I *could* understand. Schlegel was the only one of those I have named who spoke English, so that his were the only remarks I recollect, and they hardly worth [sic] repetition. I fancy I see him now, twitching his brown scratch wig, and twisting a lock of artificial hair into a curl, and going to the glass to see how it became him. He talked admirably, yet not pleasingly, for whatever the topic, and by whomever started, he soon contrived to make himself the central object of interest. The perfect self-satisfaction with which he told of his involuntary successes with the fair sex, was both amusing and pitiable. He said that when he lived with Madame de Staël at Copet, he supplied her with all the philosophical materials for her *L'Allemagne*. Coleridge told him that there never had been such a translation of any work in any language as his of Shakspeare. Schlegel returned the compliment, scratched *his* back in turn, and declared that Coleridge's translation of Schiller's *Wallenstein* was unrivalled for its fidelity to its original and the beauty of its diction. Both of them praised Cary's *Dante* highly. Schlegel praised Scott's poetry. Coleridge decried it, stating that no poet ever lived, of equal eminence, whose writings furnished so few quotable passages. Schlegel then praised Byron. Coleridge immediately tried to depreciate him. 'Ah,' said he, 'Byron is a meteor "which will but blaze and rove and die:"[9] Wordsworth, there' (pointing to him) 'is a "star luminous and fixed". During the first *furore* of

Byron's reputation, the sale of his works was unparalleled, while that of Wordsworth's was insignificant, and now each succeeding year, in proportion as the circulation of Byron's works has fallen off, the issue of Wordsworth's poems has steadily increased.'

I observed that, as a rule, Wordsworth allowed Coleridge to have all the talk to himself; but once or twice Coleridge would succeed in entangling Wordsworth in a discussion on some abstract metaphysical question: when I would sit by, reverently attending, and trying hard to look intelligent, though I did not feel so; for at such times a leaden stupor weighed down my faculties. I seemed as if I had been transported by two malignant genii into an atmosphere too rarefied for me to live in. I was soaring, as it were, against my will, 'twixt heaven and the lower parts of the earth. Sometimes I was in pure æther — much oftener *in the clouds*. When, however, these potent spirits descended to a lower level, and deigned to treat of history or politics, theology or belles lettres, I breathed again; and, imbibing fresh ideas from them, felt invigorated.

I must say I never saw any manifestation of small jealousy between Coleridge and Wordsworth; which, considering the vanity possessed by each, I thought uncommonly to the credit of both. I am sure they entertained a thorough respect for each other's intellectual endowments. [...]

The melody of Coleridge's voice had led me, as in the case of Scott, to credit him with the possession of the very soul of song; and yet, either from defective ear or from the intractability of his vocal organs, his pronunciation of any language but his own was barbarous; and his inability to follow the simplest melody quite ludicrous. The German tongue he knew *au fond*. He had learned it grammatically, critically, and scientifically at Göttingen: yet so unintelligible was he when he tried to speak it, that I heard Schlegel say to him one evening, 'Mein leiber Herr, would you speak English? I understand it; but your German I cannot follow.' Whether he had ever been before enlightened on his malpronunciation of German, I know not; but he was quite conscious that his pronunciation of French was execrable, for I heard him avow as much. He was a man of violent prejudices, and had conceived an insuperable aversion for the *grande nation*, of which he was not slow to boast. 'I hate,' he would say, 'the hollowness of French principles: I hate the republicanism of French politics: I hate the hostility of the French people to revealed religion: I hate the artificiality of French cooking: I hate the acidity of French wines: I hate the flimsiness of the French language: — my very organs of speech are so anti-Gallican that they refuse to pronounce intelligibly their insipid tongue.' [...]

I have heard Coleridge say, more than once, that no mind was thoroughly well organized that was deficient in the sense of humour: yet I hardly ever saw any great exhibition of it in himself. The only instance I can recall, in which he said anything calculated to elicit a smile, during the two or three weeks I was with him, was when he, Wordsworth, and I, were floating down the Rhine together in a boat we had hired conjointly. The day was remarkably sultry; we had all three taken a considerable walk before our dinner; and what with fatigue, heat, and the exhaustion consequent on garrulity, Coleridge complained grievously of thirst. When he heard there was no house near at hand, and saw a leathern flask slung over my shoulder, he asked me what it contained. On my telling him that it was Hock Heimer, he shook his head, and swore he would as soon take vinegar. After a while, however, finding his thirst increasing, he exclaimed, 'I find I must conquer my dislike — eat humble pie, and beg for a draught.' He had no sooner rinsed his mouth with the obnoxious fluid, than he spat it out, and vented his disgust in the following impromptu: —

> 'In Spain, that land of monks and apes,
> The thing called wine doth come from *grapes:*
> But, on the noble river Rhine,
> The thing called *gripes* doth come from wine.' [...]

After the trio had left Godesberg, and were returning homewards viâ Amsterdam and Rotterdam, they paid a visit to Haarlem. Mrs. Aders received a letter from Coleridge, dated from that place, in which he told her that they had not arrived many minutes at their hotel before one of the principal waiters of the establishment entered the room, and asked if they would like to accompany a few other persons in the house to hear the celebrated organ played, as a party was then in the act of forming for that object.

'Oh,' said Wordsworth, 'we meant to hear the organ! but why, Coleridge, should we go with strangers?' 'I beg your pardon,' interrupted the waiter, who understood and spoke English well, 'but it is not every one who is willing to pay twelve guilders (1*l*.); and as the organist will never play privately for less, it is customary for persons to go in parties, and share the expense between them.' 'Ah, then I think I will not go: I am tired,' said Wordsworth. 'Then you and I will go together, Dora,' answered Coleridge. Off they went, arm-in-arm, leaving Wordsworth behind them, reclining on a couch. They had not been long in the Church of St. Bavon, listening to the different stops which the organist was trying to display to the greatest advantage—the solo stop, the bell stop, the trumpet stop, the vox humana stop—before Coleridge was made sensible of the unwelcome intrusion of a strong current of air throughout the building. He turned his head to see the cause; and, to his amusement, descried his gentle friend, noiselessly closing the door, and furtively making his way behind one of the pillars, from whence he could hear without being seen, and thus escape payment. Before the organist had concluded his labours, Wordsworth had quietly withdrawn. On the return of his friend and his daughter, he asked them how they had enjoyed their visit to St. Bavon, but said nothing of his own!

NOTES

1 Friedrich von Schlegel (1772-1829), writer and critic. Grattan may be confusing him with his brother August Wilhelm (see below).

2 Milton, 'Samson Agonistes', ll.630-1.

3 '[O]ne celebrated man of the present day, who, if all be true which is reported of him, has greatly exceeded me in quantity': *Confessions of an English Opium-Eater* (1822), 4n..

4 Grattan was author of *High-ways and By-ways; or, Tales of the Roadside* (1823).

5 John Pinkerton (1758-1826), antiquarian, author of *Modern Geography* (1802).

6 STC opposed the Catholic emancipation legislation that was passed in 1829.

7 Southey also liked the joke ('Literally true': 3 December 1807; *Selections from the Letters*, II, 32). Lengthy consultation with colleagues has failed to discover exactly why it is funny. The butt is presumably the governess's false refinement: she refuses to utter the uncouth monosyllable 'po' (meaning 'chamber-pot') where it should (innocently) appear, but pronounces it freely in 'pochay', where (perhaps) it should not. *OED* has 'po' as 'chamber-pot' later in the century, but that is not decisive. 'Pochay' is an anglicised form of 'post-chaise' (perhaps a little *déclassé*?); alternatively, it might be a mispronunciation of 'poché' (presumably, an affected way of saying 'poached').

8 Barthold Georg Niebuhr (1776-1831) and Wilhelm Adolf Becker (1796-1846), classical historians; August Wilhelm von Schlegel (1767-1845), brother of Friedrich, critic and translator (and an influence on STC).

9 Cf. Matthew Prior, 'An English Ballad, On the Taking of Namur', l.132.

Late Sightings

(i) CHARLES AND MARY COWDEN CLARKE
From Clarke, Recollections of Writers, *63-4. Memories from 1830.*

In the same diary above alluded to there is another entry, under the date Friday, 5th March:—'Spent a wonderful hour in the company of the poet Coleridge.' It arose from a gentleman—a Mr. Edmund Reade, whose acquaintance we had made, and who begged we would take a message from him to Coleridge concerning a poem lately written by Mr. Reade, entitled 'Cain,'—asking us to undertake this commission for him, as he had some hesitation in presenting himself to the author of 'The Wanderings of Cain.' More than glad were we of this occasion for a visit to Highgate, where at Mr. Gilman's [sic] house we found Coleridge, bland, amiable, affably inclined to renew the intercourse of some years previous on the cliff at Ramsgate. As he came into the room, large-presenced, ample-countenanced, grand-fore-headed, he seemed to the younger visitor a living and moving impersonation of some antique godlike being shedding a light around him of poetic effulgence and omnipercipience. He bent kindly eyes upon her, when she was introduced to him as Vincent Novello's eldest daughter and the wife of her introducer, and spoke a few words of courteous welcome: then, the musician's name catching his ear and engaging his attention, he immediately launched forth into a noble eulogy of music, speaking of his special admiration for Beethoven as the most poetical of all musical composers; and from that, went on into a superb dissertation upon an idea he had conceived that the Creation of the Universe must have been achieved during a grand prevailing harmony of spheral music. His elevated tone, as he rolled forth his gorgeous sentences, his lofty look, his sustained flow of language, his sublime utterance, gave the effect of some magnificent organ-peal to our entranced ears. It was only when he came to a pause in his subject—or rather, to the close of what he had to say upon it—that he reverted to ordinary matters, learned the motive of our visit and the message with which we were charged, and answered some inquiries about his health by the pertinent bit already quoted in these Recollections respecting his immunity from headache.

(ii) ANNE CHALMERS

From Letters and Journals of Anne Chalmers, *edited by her daughter (1922),*
120-1. Thomas Chalmers (1780-1847), Professor of Theology at Edinburgh, and
his daughter Anne, met Coleridge on 31 May 1830.[1] *Anne's journal entry rec-*
ords her impression. According to later 'Autobiographical Notes', 'The effect of
his monologue was on me like that of listening to entrancing music. I burst into
tears when it stopped and we found ourselves suddenly in the open air' (p. 177).

We staid half an hour with Coleridge, and I can give no idea of the
beauty and sublimity of his conversation. It resembles the
loveliness of a song. He began by telling of his health, and of a fit
of insensibility in which he had lain thirty–five minutes, three
weeks before. Just as he came to consciousness, and before he had
opened his eyes, having heard the voice of his physician, he
uttered a sentence, which I regret that I do not remember exactly,
but it was about the fugacious nature of consciousness and the
extraordinary nature of man. His nephew was quite amused to
find the ruling passion strong in death, when he heard him utter a
piece of metaphysics. From this he went to a discussion on the soul
and the body, and brought in an ingenious little interlude about a
bit of wire. I did not understand him always, but I admired him
throughout. Then he inquired for Mr. Irving, and upon this subject
he was sublime.[2] He regretted that such a man as Irving should
throw himself away upon abstruse speculations while thousands
were hungering—were perishing for the common bread of life
(Matt. xi.28). This book on the human nature of Christ was minute
to absurdity;[3] one would imagine the pickling and preserving was
to follow, it was so like a cookery book. The Holy Spirit was the
only respectable personage of the three. Then he told us of his own
idea of the Book of Revelation, and that he had gone over the first
eight chapters of it with Mr. Irving, and explained every word and
every symbol; that he asked him if he was satisfied, and that Irving
said the idea was so new to him that he felt stunned by it; that he
had not seen Mr. Irving for a year and three months, but heard in
the meantime that he was launching out into all sorts of vagaries.
Talking of the Revelations, he had some fine climaxes. He said
Jesus did not come now as before, meek and gentle, healing the
sick and feeding the hungry and dispensing blessings around, but
He came on a white horse, and who were His attendants? Famine,
war, and pestilence. But I can give no idea of his voice or
eloquence. There was a lady in the room who seemed to admire

him as much as we, and who wisely did not talk to us, but left us at liberty to listen to him. I said to her that I wished he would be induced to publish his scheme of the Revelations, and she replied that they all wished it. The contrast between Coleridge and Bennet[4] is amusing from its absurdity. They are both engrossers, but the conversation of the one contains nothing; that of the other is replete with mind and eloquence. I have heard people say that it showed a disagreeable admiration of himself, Coleridge's flow of talk; but I should think that person very conceited who, after having been admitted to an interview with him, should feel inclined to talk rather than listen. For my own part, I could have listened much longer.

(iii) JOHN McVICKAR

From William A. McVickar, The Life of the Reverend John McVickar (NY, 1872), 131-2. McVickar, a professor at Columbia, visited in the summer of 1830.

His appearance is of a man over sixty, of powerful make, large head, massive features, and large and expressive eyes, though rather dreamy. There was no company, but his married daughter, Mrs. C——, one of the prettiest and most learned women in England. His conversation is that of a lofty religious enthusiast, but full of deep and original thought, with a flow and power of expression I have never heard equaled. His topics were varied, but with a continued tendency to the deep and personal truths of Christianity. [...]

In the course of the evening the Rev. E. Irving, who was one of our small circle, drew from his pocket a letter, and prefacing it by a call on Mr. Coleridge, to counsel him in his spiritual doubts, as 'being the man,' said he, 'from whom I have gained more wisdom than from all other men living,' proceeded to read a communication just received from the celebrated Thomas Erskine, of Edinburgh, containing the particulars of the first wonderful effusion of tongues, as it was termed, in the family of the Campbells, near Greenock.[5] The anxious inquiry of Mr. Irving was, 'How is this to be regarded?' Mr. Coleridge, to whom it probably was not new, being thus addressed as an oracle, answered with corresponding solemnity and certainty, without the ambiguity complained of in oracular responses of old, 'Sir, I make no question but that it is the work of the Holy Spirit, and a foretaste of that spiritual power which is to be poured forth on the reviving Church of Scotland.' Though evidently in a circle who eagerly hailed the decision, I felt myself obliged to speak, and press upon him its want of accord with the Scriptural account of the gift of tongues, and its unworthiness not alone of the wisdom of God but of the reason of man. To my protestation he listened respectfully, though evidently unwillingly, and immediately replied, 'Was not the case the same in the Apostles' days? Is not St. Paul's argument in the fourteenth chapter of First Corinthians founded upon the supposition that the saints often spoke in tongues which no man understood?' Pressed again by its incongruity with Scripture facts, more especially with the record of the first day of Pentecost, he finally cut short the argument with denying the genuineness of the chapter that contained it, and concluded with reiterating his first assertion. Such is Mr. Coleridge, and such are some of his wild opinions. But with all his errors he both was and is a wonderful man. 'Sir,' said Edward Irving to me after this interview, 'his words sink into my mind like seeds into the ground; they grow up afterwards, I know not how, and bear fruit.'

(iv) JOHN FRERE

From E.M. Green, 'A Talk with Coleridge, Cornhill Magazine *NS 42 (1917) 402-10, 402-3; 405-6; 407; 408-9. Frere was a student at Trinity, Cambridge, and a member of the 'Apostles', who were much influenced by Coleridge.*[6]

C. Is there anything stirring now in the world of letters, anything in the shape of poetry lately produced, for I see nothing of the sort, nor even a Review that is not a year old?
F. No, Sir, at least I have heard no talk of any such thing; these continual burnings occupy all men's thoughts and conversation.[7]
C. And what remedies are proposed? They talk I suppose of retrenchments, but what good can retrenchment do? Alas! revolutionary times are times of general demoralisation; what great men do they ever produce? What was produced by the late Revolutionary Spirit in France? There must be something uppermost to be sure in such disturbances; some military superiority, but what great—I mean truly great—man was produced?

In England the same spirit was curbed in and worsted by the moral sense, afterwards there followed times of repose, and the Muses began to show themselves. But now what is going forward? The depravity of the spirit of the times is marked by the absence of poetry. For it is a great mistake to suppose that thought is not necessary for poetry; true, at the time of composition there is that starlight, a dim and holy twilight; but is not light necessary before?

Poetry is the highest effort of the mind; all the powers are in a state of equilibrium and equally energetic, the knowledge of individual existence is forgotten, the man is out of himself and exists in all things, his eye is in *a* fine &c.[.][8]

There is no one perhaps who composes with more facility than your Uncle;[9] but does it cost him nothing before? It is the result of long thought; and poetry as I have before observed must be the result of thought, and the want of thought in what is now called poetry is a bad sign of the times. [...]

F. You have not read much of Keats, Sir, I think.

C. No, I have not. I have seen two Sonnets which I think showed marks of a great genius had he lived. I have also read a poem with a classical name — I forget what. Poor Keats, I saw him once. Mr. Green, whom you have heard me mention, and I were walking out in these parts, and we were overtaken by a young man of a very striking countenance whom Mr. Green recognised and shook hands with, mentioning my name; I wish Mr. Green had introduced me, for I did not know who it was. He passed on, but in a few moments sprung back and said, 'Mr. Coleridge, allow me the honour of shaking your hand.'

I was struck by the energy of his manner, and gave him my hand.

He passed on and we stood still looking after him, when Mr Green said,

'Do you know who that is? That is Keats, the poet.'

'Heavens!' said I, 'when I shook him by the hand there was death!' This was about two years before he died.[10]

F. But what was it?

C. I cannot describe it. There was a heat and a dampness in the hand. To say that his death was caused by the Review is absurd, but at the same time it is impossible adequately to conceive the effect which it must have had on his mind.[11]

It is very well for those who have a place in the world and are independent to talk of these things, they can bear such a blow, so can those who have a strong religious principle; but all men are not born Philosophers, and all men have not those advantages of birth and education.

Poor Keats had not, and it is impossible I say to conceive the effect which such a Review must have had upon him, knowing as he did that he had his way to make in the world by his own exertions, and conscious of the genius within him.

Have you seen, Mr F., anything of Lord Byron's poetry?

F. Nothing, Sir, but the translation of 'Faust'. [...]

Had you ever any thought of translating the 'Faust'?[12]

C. Yes, Sir, I had, but I was prevented by the consideration that though there are some exquisite passages, the opening chorus, the chapel and the prison scenes for instance, to say nothing of the Brocken scene where he has shown peculiar strength in keeping clear of Shakspear, he has not taken that wonderful admixture of Witch Fate and Fairy but has kept to the real original witch, and this suits his purpose much better. [...] There are other parts too which I could not have translated without entering my protest against them in a manner which would hardly have been fair upon the author, for those things are understood in Germany in a spirit very different from what they would infuse here in England. To give you an example, the scene where Mephistopheles [sic] is introduced as coming before the Almighty and talking with Him would never be borne in English and this whole scene is founded on a mistranslation of a passage in Scripture, the opening of Job.[13] [...]

It is evident that there is no suggestion, no evil in the officer at all — indeed the belief in Angels and that sort of poultry is nowhere countenanced in the Old Testament and in the New, nowhere else.

F. Indeed, Sir, I think I know a very strong passage.

C. Well, what is it?

F. Our Saviour tells his disciples when alone with them and apart that a certain kind of Devils goeth not out but by prayer and fasting.[14]

C. Well, and what has that to do with Angels?

F. I beg your pardon, Sir. I thought you included devils in your feathered fowl.

C. There is nothing I say in the New Testament to countenance the belief in Angels. For what are the three first Gospels? Every one must see that they are mere plain narratives, not of things as they are but of things as they appeared to the ignorant disciples — but when we come to John, Mr. F., there we find the difference.[15] He told things as they were, and therefore you must not believe everything that you read implicitly; and with respect to Devils entering into a man, why it is quite absurd. What do we mean when we say a thing is in another? Why 'in' is merely a relative term. [The argument, though I was compelled to assent to it, I am sorry to say was far above my comprehension, and therefore I could not catch it, still less bag it and carry it away, — however it proved that there could be no Devils and still less could there be Devils in a man.] Spirit therefore was not more in a man that it was out of him, the mistake arising from a misconception of the word *in.* As for all notions of men with wings, of course they are absurd in the extreme.

I return however to 'Faust.'

F. Did you ever see Shelley's translation of the Chorus in 'Faust' you were just mentioning?[16]

C. I have, and admire it very much. Shelley was a man of great power as a poet, and could he only have had some notion of order, could you only have given him some plane whereon to stand, and look down upon his own mind, he would have succeeded. There are flashes of the true spirit to be met with in his works. Poor Shelley, it is a pity I often think that I never met with him. I could have done him good. He went to Keswick on purpose to see me and unfortunately fell in with Southey instead. There could have been nothing so unfortunate. Southey had no understanding for a toleration of such principles as Shelley's.

I should have laughed at his Atheism. I could have sympathised with him and shown him that I did so, and he would have felt that I did so. I could have shown him that I had once been in the same state myself, and I could have guided him through it. I have often bitterly regretted in my heart of hearts that I did never meet with Shelley.

F. It is time to be gone now I fear, Mr. Coleridge, and when I come up again I hope you will allow me to bring a volume of Keats with me.

C. I shall be most happy to see you for any night you like to come, and any day before 12 o'clock. Thursday nights are over now, but any night whether Thursday or not I shall be most happy to see you.

F. I must not allow you to come out into the passage, Sir. Good night.

(v) WILLIAM C. HETHERINGTON

From 'Coleridge and his Followers'; in Lectures Delivered Before the Young Man's Christian Association [...] , in Exeter Hall, from November 1852, to February 1853 *(1853) 405-48, 415-17. Hetherington, minister of Free St. Paul's, Edinburgh, is respectful but sceptical of Coleridge's theology, criticising the 'excess of* subjectivity *in his system' (p. 432). They met once.*

Never shall we forget that interview. It was in the year 1831, that, having received an introduction from a mutual friend in London, we made our way to Highgate, and were admitted into the hospitable mansion of Mr. Gillman. There we were received by Mrs. Gillman herself, the poet's 'most kind hostess,' who stated that Mr. Coleridge was suffering under extreme weakness and pain, but would very soon be ready to receive us. She went out for an instant, then quickly returning, began in a soft, low, apologetic, half-pleading, half-persuading tone, to mention, 'that the state of Mr Coleridge's health was such as to render it extremely injurious for him to give way to that excitement in the flow of conversation so natural to him, which a very few minutes' converse with a congenial mind could not fail to produce; that she was convinced she needed but to hint the propriety of abstaining from the discussion of any exciting topics, and of not prolonging the interview to any length likely to be hurtful, for that, of course, no friends of Coleridge could wish to obtain gratification to themselves at the expense of injury to him;' then smiling, and requesting forgiveness, she retired. While we were admiring and mentally applauding her gentle prudence and her tender care, a door from another apartment slowly opened, and leaning on a smooth-worn staff, with short, feeble, and shuffling step, approached the poet and sage himself. A sickening pang of mingled surprise and sorrow shot through our heart to behold, in such a condition, the beloved and venerated man. The expression of his countenance was that of pain, subdued by resignation and sublimed by serious thoughtfulness. Still the poetic light was alive within the dreamy depths of his large grey eyes; and his broad, high, and compact forehead seemed still a fitting home for genius of the loftiest order. He spoke, and the tones of his voice were kindly but plaintive, as he apologised for his tardy approach, in consequence of his many and heavy infirmities. In a few seconds, resting himself in an easy chair which we had placed for him, he assumed a more cheerful tone and manner, and began conversing on a number of topics chiefly connected with Scotland and its literary men, displaying a very minute and accurate acquaintance with all of any celebrity. From that the transition was easy to the Rev. Edward Irving, on whom he passed a glowing eulogium, deploring at the same time his wayward will, and, consequently, wayward fate. The stream flowed on and began to widen. The interpretation of prophecy was the next topic on which he touched, making it evident that he had studied the subject with considerable attention. The multiform mellifluous monologue was now commenced. His eye began to kindle and dilate; the expression of pain and languor forsook his countenance; his forehead brightened and beamed, and even seemed to expand with the power of the mental workings within; his fine silvery locks waved more freely and gracefully, as if with young life, around his temples; and his voice poured out a strange rich, mellow, rhythmical, yet somewhat monotonous music, peculiarly suited to his ever-varying yet continuous flow of transcendent eloquence. It was with not less than mental agony that we perceived the forbidden limits to be well-nigh overpassed. We rose—hesitated—blushed—expressed our deep regret that we must most reluctantly tear ourselves away. He looked for a moment confused, surprised, half-disappointed, then smiling affectionately held forth his hand, saying, 'I understand your motive, and I appreciate it. I thank you; I have as yet sustained no injury—again, I thank you warmly; all my young friends are not so considerate. Farewell!—in the full meaning of that most emphatic word, fare well!' and we departed, feeling amply rewarded for our self-denial by his warm grasp and his full-hearted farewell.

(vi) EMMA WILLARD

From Emma Willard, Journal and Letters, from France and Great-Britain *(1833), 311-312. Willard (1787-1870), pedagogue and pioneer in women's education, met Coleridge in 1831, while on a European tour.*

This morning Mrs. B——, an interesting and fashionable American lady, resident in London, with whom I had dined the day before; took me to Hempstead [*sic*] to see Mr. Coleridge. He was boarding in a family with whom he had made his abode for a considerable time. Here we found a parlor looking into a garden, from the first floor. Mr. Coleridge, we were told, was ill. His pension I knew had been withdrawn, since the change in the ministry, and we supposed it probable that he might be out of spirits.[17] Mrs. B——, in sending our names to the poet, said that I was an American lady, and an admirer of his works.

After a little time he appeared. He has all the poet in his large dark eye, and intellectual face; and his manners seemed to me, such as suited his portly and dignified person. I was told that if he became fairly engaged in conversation, he would need but little response. He found in me a delighted auditor, and he was on subjects that interested him. The other ladies, (Mrs. B—— being an acquaintance of his hostess,) left us,—returned—and left us again, before the conversation was over. Yet, though I was delighted at the time, I cannot now recall many of his expressions, or even his ideas. Who that should hear twenty pages of Coleridge's metaphysics, could tell afterwards what it was; and yet who, but would feel that it was passing strange, and very grand. You look intensely for his ideas, as you look through the dark rolling cloud for the outline of the distant mountain. Sometimes you think you have caught it, but then comes another cloud,—and the view was too evanescent to admit of your making a sketch. Yet the clouds themselves are beautiful, and while they make the object behind it [sic] indistinct, they increase its apparent grandeur.

The subject of his conversation was nature, intellectual and material—the animals and vegetables—the heavens, and man with his noble faculties, looking with faith to his God and Redeemer,— and last of all—the angelic figure that took the loveliest light of the picture, was Heaven's best gift—beautiful, refined, intellectual, woman. How divinely good, ought we to become, to deserve all that the poets say of us!

(vii) HENRY NELSON COLERIDGE

From Specimens of the Table Talk, *I, 233-34n.. H.N. Coleridge describes his uncle at an exhibition at the British Gallery in Pall Mall, 24 July 1831.*

Mr. Coleridge was in high spirits, and seemed to kindle in his mind at the contemplation of the splendid pictures before him. He did not examine them all by the catalogue, but anchored himself before some three or four great works, telling me that he saw the rest of the Gallery *potentially*. I can yet distinctly recall him, half leaning on his old simple stick, and his hat off in one hand, whilst with the fingers of the other he went on, as was his constant wont, figuring in the air a kind of commentary of small diagrams, wherewith, as he fancied, he could translate to the eye those relations of form and space which his words might fail to convey with clearness to the ear. His admiration for Rubens, showed itself in a sort of joy and brotherly fondness; he looked as if he would shake hands with his pictures. What the company, which by degrees formed itself round this silver-haired, bright-eyed, music-breathing, old man, took him for, I cannot guess; there was probably not one there who knew him to be that Ancient Mariner, who held people with his glittering eye, and constrained them, like three years' children, to hear his tale. In the midst of his speech, he turned to the right hand, where stood a very lovely young woman, whose attention he had involuntarily arrested; – to her, without apparently any consciousness of her being a stranger to him, he addressed many remarks, although I must acknowledge they were couched in a somewhat softer tone, as if he were soliciting her sympathy. He was, verily, a gentle-hearted man at all times; but I never was in company with him in my life, when the entry of a woman, it mattered not who, did not provoke a dim gush of emotion, which passed like an infant's breath over the mirror of his intellect.

(viii) DAVID SCOTT

From William B. Scott, Memoir of David Scott, RSA, *58; 204-5. The painter and illustrator Scott (1806-49) approached Coleridge in the winter of 1831, to ask if he knew of a likely publisher for Scott's illustrations to 'The Ancient Mariner'; Coleridge's reply was forlorn (CL, VI, 875; 1057). (An edition finally appeared in 1837.) Scott subsequently visited; this is from his diary for 1832.*

He is a little clerical-looking man, but common in appearance, rather poor indeed, and without mark in the figure and face, except that he has most uncommonly snowy hair; it is perfectly white and long, but does not wave, which prevents its having much effect. His look is not especially poetic. The moment he is seated, as has been said, he begins to talk, and on it goes, flowing and full, almost without even what might be called paragraphic division, and leaving colloquy out of the question entirely. He talked of the effect Italy had upon himself, and wandered on about the Italian painters and poets. I mentioned my drawings from the Ancient Mariner, and he expressed his very favourable opinion of them.[18] I recollect upon calling, Mrs. Gillman requested me not to sit above half an hour, for Mr. Coleridge was unable to stand fatigue, and was apt, forgetting time, to talk too long. 'The old man eloquent' received me very kindly. His eye shone in tears as he spoke. He shook me kindly by the hand at parting, and hoped, if he lived, to see me again.

William Scott records more of the conversation:

The opinion of these designs [...] was, as far as we can recollect, to the following effect: – Dividing poetry as Descriptive, or dealing with outward nature, and Imaginative, or dealing with the forms of things in the mind, he thought that the first of these classes was to be illustrated directly by the painter, and that the one and the other should be coincident in their impressions. But in the latter class – that of the purely Imaginative – illustration by the painter was infinitely more difficult – that exact circumstantial illustration of such works was none at all, and that the only way in which the artist could work with them was by an adequate expression of the same imaginative sentiment, different in form or mode, according to the differing nature of his art. This, perhaps, is the true theory of the matter. The designs in question he thought a successful example in point.

(ix) SAMUEL CARTER HALL

From Hall, A Book of Memories, *43. The reference to 'thirty years' is obviously vague, but perhaps enough to date the encounter somewhen in the 1830s.*

I can recall many evening rambles with him over the high lands that look down on London; but the memory I cherish most is linked with a crowded street, where the clumsy and the coarse jostled the old man eloquent, as if he had been earthy, of the earth. It was in the Strand: he pointed out to me the window of a room in the office of the *Morning Post* where he had consumed much midnight oil; and then for half an hour he talked of the sorrowful joy he had often felt when, leaving the office as day was dawning, he heard the song of a caged lark that sung his orisons from the lattice of an artisan who was rising to begin his labour as the poet was pacing homewards to rest after his work all night. Thirty years had passed, but that unforgotten melody – that dear bird's song – gave him then as much true pleasure as when, to his wearied head and heart, it was the matin hymn of nature.

I remember once meeting him in Paternoster Row; he was inquiring his way to Bread Street, Cheapside, and, of course, I endeavoured to explain to him that if he walked on for about two hundred yards, and took the fourth turning to the right, it would be the street he wanted. I noted his expression, so vague and unenlightened, that I could not help expressing my surprise as I looked earnestly at his forehead, and saw the organ of 'locality' unusually prominent above the eyebrows. He took my meaning, laughed, and said, 'I see what you are looking at: why, at school my head was beaten into a mass of bumps, because I could not point out Paris in a map of France.' It has been said that Spurzheim pronounced him to be a mathematician, and affirmed that he could not be a poet. Such an opinion the great phrenologist could not have expressed, for undoubtedly he had a large organ of ideality, although at first it was not perceptible, in consequence of the great breadth and height of his profound forehead.

(x) HENRY BLAKE McLELLAN

From Henry Blake McLellan, Journal of a Residence in Scotland and Tour through England, France, Germany, Switzerland, and Italy *(Boston, 1834), 230-2. The young American McLellan (1810-33) visited Coleridge in 1832.*

Saturday, April 27th. Walked to Highgate to call on Mr. Coleridge. I was ushered into the parlor while the girl carried up my letter to his room. She presently returned and observed that her master was very poorly, but would be happy to see me, if I would walk up to his room, which I gladly did. He is short in stature and appeared to be careless in his dress. I was impressed with the strength of his expression, his venerable locks of white, and his trembling frame. He remarked that he had for some time past suffered much bodily anguish. For many months (thirteen) seventeen hours each day had he walked up and down his chamber. I inquired whether his mental powers were affected by such intense suffering; 'Not at all,' said he, 'my body and head appear to hold no connexion; the pain of my body, blessed be God, never reaches my mind.' [19] After some further conversation and some inquiries respecting Dr. Chalmers, he remarked, 'The Doctor must have suffered exceedingly at the strange conduct of our once dear brother laborer in Christ, Rev. Mr. Irving. Never can I describe how much it has wrung my bosom. I had watched with astonishment and admiration the wonderful and rapid developement of his powers. Never was such unexampled advance in intellect as between his first and second volume of sermons. The first full of Gallicisms and Scoticisms, and all other cisms. The second discovering all the elegance and power of the best writers of the Elizabethan age. And then so sudden a fall, when his mighty energies made him so terrible to sinners.' Of the mind of the celebrated Puffendorf[20] [*sic*] he said, 'his mind is like some mighty volcano, red with flame, and dark with tossing clouds of smoke through which the lightnings play and glare most awfully.' Speaking of the state of the different classes of England, he remarked, 'we are in a dreadful state; care like a foul hag sits on us all; one class presses with iron foot upon the wounded heads beneath, and all struggle for a worthless supremacy, and all to rise to it move shackled by their expenses; happy, happy are you to hold your birth-right in a country where things are different; you, at least at present, are in a transition state; God grant it may ever be so! Sir, things have come to a dreadful pass with us, we need most deeply a reform, but I fear not the horrid reform which we shall have; things must alter, the upper classes of England have made the lower persons, *things*;[21] the people in breaking from this unnatural state will break from duties also.'

(xi) HARRIET MARTINEAU

From Harriet Martineau's Autobiography *(1877; 2nd edn.; 3 vols.; 1877), I, 397–8. Martineau (1802–76) wrote on an immense range of subjects, including religion, economics, and mesmerism. She was not impressed by Coleridge.*

If Coleridge should be remembered, it will be as a warning, — as much in his philosophical as his moral character. — Such is my view of him now. Twenty years ago I regarded him as poet, — in his 'Friend' as much as his verse. He was, to be sure, a most remarkable-looking personage, as he entered the room, and slowly approached and greeted me. He looked very old, with his rounded shoulders and drooping head, and excessively thin limbs. His eyes were as wonderful as they were ever represented to be; — light grey, extremely prominent, and actually glittering: an appearance I am told common among opium eaters. His onset amused me not a little. He told me that he (the last person whom I should have suspected) read my tales as they came out on the first of the month; and, after paying some compliments, he avowed that there were points on which we differed: (I was full of wonder that there were any on which we agreed:) 'for instance,' said he, 'you appear to consider that society is an aggregation of individuals!' I replied that I certainly did: whereupon he went off on one of the several metaphysical interpretations which may be put upon the many-sided fact of an organised human society, subject to natural laws in virtue of its aggregate character and organisation together. After a long flight in survey of society from his own balloon in his own current, he came down again to some considerations of individuals, and at length to some special biographical topics, ending with criticisms on old biographers, whose venerable works he brought down from the shelf. No one else spoke, of course, except when I once or twice put a question; and when his monologue came to what seemed a natural stop, I rose to go. I am glad to have seen his weird face, and heard his dreamy voice; and my notion of possession, prophecy, — of involuntary speech from involuntary brain action, has been clearer since.

(xii) THOMAS MOORE
From Memoirs, *VI, 331; VII, 7-8 — entries for 4 August and 9 November 1833.*

[T]old of Coleridge riding about in a strange shabby dress, with I forget whom, at Keswick, and on some company approaching them, Coleridge offered to fall behind and pass for his companion's servant. 'No,' said the other, 'I am proud of you as a friend; but, I must say, I should be ashamed of you as a servant.'

[...]

Was too far from Coleridge, during dinner, to hear more than the continuous drawl of his preachment; moved up to him, however, when the ladies had retired. His subjects chiefly Irving and religion; is employed himself, it seems, in writing on Daniel and the Revelations, and his notions on the subject, as far as they were at all intelligible, appeared to be a strange mixture of rationalism and mysticism. Thus, with the rationalists, he pronounced the gift of tongues to have been nothing more than scholarship or a knowledge of different languages; said that this was the opinion of Erasmus, as may be deduced from his referring to Plato's Timæus on the subject. (Must see to this.) Gave an account of his efforts to bring Irving to some sort of rationality on these subjects, to 'steady him,' as he expressed it; but his efforts all unsuccessful, and, after many conversations between them, Irving confessed that the only effect of all that Coleridge had said was 'to *stun*' him, — an effect I can well conceive, from my own short experiment of the operation.

Repeated two or three short pieces of poetry he had written lately, one an epitaph on himself; all very striking, and in the same mystical religious style as his conversation. A large addition to the party in the evening, and music. Duets by Mrs. Macleod and her sister, which brought back sadly to my memory an evening of the same kind, in this same room, with poor Sir Walter Scott, before he went abroad for his health. One of the duets, in which the voices rose alternately above each other, Coleridge said reminded him of *arabesques*. With my singing he seemed really much pleased, and spoke eloquently of the perfect union (as he was pleased to say) of poetry and music which it exhibited: 'The music, like the honey-suckle round the stem, twining round the meaning, and at last over-topping it.' This 'over-topping the meaning' not a little applicable to his own style of eloquence.

(xiii) SIR WILLIAM ROWAN HAMILTON

From Robert Perceval Graves, Life of Sir William Rowan Hamilton [...] *(Dublin; 3 vols.; 1882-1889), I, 557; 601-2; II, 623. Hamilton (1805-65), prodigious mathematican and physicist, met Coleridge in the early 1830s. The passages are from letters: the first (28 May 1832) to Aubrey de Vere; the second (15 August 1832) to Lady Campbell; the last (2 September 1848) to J.W. Barlow.*

You are quite right in thinking that I was completely satisfied with Coleridge. It is true that in your own words, which I remember to have heard Francis Edgeworth also use, Coleridge is rather to be considered as a Faculty than as a Mind; and I did so consider him. I seemed rather to listen to an Oracular voice, to be circumfused in a Divine ὀμφή, than, as I did in the presence of Wordsworth, to hold commune with an exalted man. Yet had I human feelings too, and yearnings of deep affection, as I sat in the sick chamber and by the bed of the old and lonely Bard, the philosopher of whom the age was not worthy, the 'hooded eagle flagging wearily' through darkness and despair, the perishing outward man whose inward man was renewed day by day, and who, while feeding upon heavenly manna, could count in his indulgent love the visits of me among his 'consolations.' [...]

As to Coleridge and his obscurity in conversation, I assure you that whenever I thought him obscure I laid all the blame on myself. One day in particular he seemed so, when besides his being on the highest subjects which men can approach, I had tired myself before by walking out from London. Even then I did not behave like a puppy of a classical Archdeacon (don't tell this to the man's acquaintance), who, I hear, visited Coleridge; but piquing himself on the clearness of his ideas, and finding them grow somewhat confused, abruptly ran away. [...]

You may have heard that nobody ever talked with Coleridge; for the full and rapid torrent of his own eloquence of discourse soon absorbed all minor rivulets, such as other men could supply. However, I must acknowledge that he took very graciously, and in good part, any few words I ventured to throw in; and allowed them to influence, and in some degree to guide his own great, and sweet, and wondrous stream of speech. Presuming that he had forgotten those former visits of mine, which, however, he afterwards assured me that he had not done, I said to Coleridge, on being placed beside him by Dr. Thirlwall, at Cambridge,[22] that I had read most of his published works: but, by way of being very honest, I added, But, sir, I am not sure that I understand them all. 'The question is, sir,' said he, 'whether I understand them all myself.'

(xiv) SARA (FRICKER) COLERIDGE

From Minnow Among Tritons, *165. In a letter to Poole (16 August 1832), Sara describes the christening of Edith, daughter of the younger Sara.*

[W]hat will perhaps greatly surprize you as it did all his friends, the grandfather came from Highgate to be present, and to pass the rest of the day here! [...] His power of continuous talking seems unabated, for he talked incessantly for full 5 hours to the great entertainment of Mrs May and a few other friends who were present, and did not leave us till 10, when he was accompanied home by the Revd James Gillman, (son of his friends,) who performed the ceremony, and when Henry called to see him yesterday he appeared no worse for the exertion he had made.

Coleridge talked a good deal of you, as he always does when he speaks of [his] early days; he told me to let him know when I obtained any news from you.

(xv) RALPH WALDO EMERSON

From Ralph Waldo Emerson, English Traits *(1856; Riverside Edition, 1883), 13-16; 17. Emerson (1803-82), essayist, poet, philosopher, and former Unitarian, toured Britain in 1833, including a visit to Highgate.[23]*

It was near noon. Mr. Coleridge sent a verbal message that he was in bed, but if I would call after one o'clock he would see me. I returned at one, and he appeared, a short, thick old man, with bright blue eyes and fine clear complexion, leaning on his cane. He took snuff freely, which presently soiled his cravat and neat black suit. He asked whether I knew Allston, and spoke warmly of his merits and doings when he knew him in Rome; what a master of the Titianesque he was, &c. &c.[.] He spoke of Dr. Channing.[24] It was an unspeakable misfortune that he should have turned out a Unitarian after all. On this, he burst into a declamation on the folly and ignorance of Unitarianism, — its high unreasonableness; and taking up Bishop Waterland's book, which lay on the table, he read with vehemence two or three pages written by himself in the fly-leaves, — passages, too, which, I believe, are printed in the 'Aids to Reflection.'[25] When he stopped to take breath, I interposed that 'whilst I highly valued all his explanations, I was bound to tell him that I was born and bred a Unitarian.' 'Yes,' he said, 'I supposed so;' and continued as before. It was a wonder that after so many ages of unquestioning acquiescence in the doctrine of St. Paul, — the doctrine of the Trinity, which was also according to Philo Judæus the doctrine of the Jews before Christ, — this handful of Priestleians should take on themselves to deny it, &c., &c.[.] He was very sorry that Dr. Channing, a man to whom he looked up, — no, to say that he looked *up* to him would be to speak falsely, but a man whom he looked *at* with so much interest, — should embrace such views. When he saw Dr. Channing he had hinted to him that he was afraid he loved Christianity for what was lovely and excellent, — he loved the good in it, and not the true; — 'And I tell you, sir, that I have known ten persons who loved the good, for one person who loved the true; but it is a far greater virtue to love the true for itself alone, than to love the good for itself alone.' He (Coleridge) knew all about Unitarianism perfectly well, because he had once been a Unitarian and knew what quackery it was. He had been called 'the rising star of Unitarianism.' He went on defining, or rather refining: 'The Trinitarian doctrine was realism; the idea of God was not essential, but super-essential;' talked of *trinism* and *tetrakism* and much more, of which I only caught this, 'that the will was that by which a person is a person; because, if one should push me in the street, and so I should force the man next me into the kennel, I should at once exclaim, I did not do it, sir, meaning it was not my will.' And this also, that 'if you insist on your faith here in England, and I on mine, mine would be the hotter side of the fagot.'

I took advantage of a pause to say that he had many readers of all religious opinions in America, and I proceeded to inquire if the 'extract' from the Independent's pamphlet, in the third volume of the Friend, were a veritable quotation.[26] He replied that it was really taken from a pamphlet in his possession entitled, 'A Protest of one of the Independents,' or something to that effect. I told him how excellent I thought it and how much I wished to see the entire work. 'Yes,' he said, 'the man was a chaos of truths, but lacked the knowledge that God was a God of order. Yet the passage would no doubt strike you more in the quotation than in the original, for I have filtered it.'

When I rose to go, he said, 'I do not know whether you care about poetry, but I will repeat some verses I lately made on my baptismal anniversary,' and he recited with strong emphasis, standing, ten or twelve lines beginning, —

'Born unto God in Christ – '[27] [...]

I was in his company for about an hour, but find it impossible to recall the largest part of his discourse, which was often like so many printed paragraphs in his book, — perhaps the same, — so readily did he fall into certain commonplaces. As I might have foreseen, the visit was rather a spectacle than a conversation, of no use beyond the satisfaction of my curiosity. He was old and preoccupied, and could not bend to a new companion and think with him.

(xvi) MARY STUART

From Letters from the Lake Poets [...] to Daniel Stuart, Editor of The *Morning Post* and The *Courier*, 1800-1838 *(1889), 322-5. Mary Stuart, daughter of Daniel, Coleridge's old editor, recalls their last meeting, in 1834.*

It was a lovely afternoon in early summer when my dear father took me for a ride up to Highgate to pay what proved our last visit to Coleridge. We chatted pleasantly on the way till we drew up and dismounted under the large trees of The Grove, at Mr Gillman's gate, and were shown into his dining-room, whose shade and coolness were most refreshing after our dusty ride. My father sent up his card, and we waited some quarter of an hour, when the door opened, and the old poet (old! he was but sixty-two!) appeared, clad in black, leaning on his staff; much bent, his hair snow white, his face pale; but his eyes, those wondrous eyes! large, lustrous, beaming with intelligence and kindness. The first greetings over, we sat down, and my father and he were soon deep in politics. Disestablishment was their subject, against which Coleridge vehemently argued, citing widely from the Old Testament, and-mixing up the names of leading statesmen with those of Isaiah and the other prophets, especially Ezekiel, in what was to me a most bewildering maze. I may here mention that Ezekiel seemed his especial favourite. The first time I dined in company at my father's table, I sat between Coleridge and Mr. Hill[28] (known as 'Little

Tommy Hill') of the Adelphi, and Ezekiel then formed the theme of Coleridge's eloquence. I well remember his citing the chapter of the Dead Bones, and his sepulchral voice as he asked, 'Can these bones live?'[29] Then his observation that nothing in the range of human thought was more sublime than Ezekiel's reply, 'Lord! Thou knowest!' in deepest humility, not presuming to doubt the omnipotence of the Most High. But to return to Highgate. Profound as were his arguments, yet the tone, the earnestness, above all the constantly appealing expression of that inspired countenance, fascinated me, and I followed the thread of his discourse delighted, trusting to chance for what I might retain. My father was equally animated, and the conversation lasted upwards of an hour. When we rose to depart, Coleridge took us into the drawing-room to show us a portrait which had lately been taken of himself. He was much dissatisfied with it, and appealed to my father and me that it had not taken his *expression*. But what portrait ever did? He showed us several others, and we stood criticizing, — rather to my amusement, being then but in my teens! But his vanity, if such it might be called, had in it such a mixture of benevolence and fun, that one seemed to love him the better for it. At last we went back through the dining-room into Mr. Gillman's hall, where he took an affectionate leave of me, and stood talking to my father while I mounted my horse. I think the two old friends of nearly forty years' standing had each a feeling that it might be a last adieu. So loth did they seem to part, Coleridge coming out of the door and shaking hands with my father repeatedly. There he stood while my father mounted! We took our last look, exchanged the last farewell, and rode off. My father was very silent all the way back, while *my* young brain was busy arranging into order the conversation I had listened to, and which I noted down immediately on my return home.

(xvii) VISCOUNT ADARE

From Graves, Life of Sir William Rowan Hamilton, *II, 94–5 – from a letter of 30 June 1834. Edwin Richard Windham Wyndham Quin, later Earl of Dunraven (1812–71), was a student of Hamilton's, who sent him to see Coleridge.*

Up I went, feeling a mixture of pleasure and awe, and was shown into a small room, half full of books in great confusion, and in one corner was a small bed, looking more like a couch, upon which lay certainly the most remarkable looking man I ever saw; he quite surpassed my expectations; he was pale and worn when I first entered, but very soon the colour came into his cheeks and his eye brightened, and such an eye as it is! such animation, and acuteness! so piercing! He began by asking how you were, and telling me how ill he had been for three months, but he is now getting a little better; he said he was sure it would give you pleasure to know (as far as I could understand) that religion had alleviated very much his hours of pain, and given him fortitude and resignation. He then talked about the Church, but really I found it so difficult to follow him that I cannot recollect what he said, but even less can I remember what I should say were the subjects of conversation: this I think arises from a great want of method; but I say this, feeling I do him injustice: still it strikes me he rambled on; but I remarked how, when once or twice he was interrupted by people coming into the room and speaking to them, he resumed at the very word he left off at—he said he was sure you would feel very sorry at the line of conduct Thirlwall had pursued about some petition about the Dissenters,[30] and how it had pained him. Now and then he said something very droll, which made us laugh; and he conversed with so much vigour and animation, though he had difficulty in *speaking* at all. I ventured, when a pause came, to put in a word. This happened twice: the second time I asked him when we might hope for another work from him. He said he had one very nearly ready, and it would have been out, were it not for his illness. He gave me the plan of the book, but really he got so deep, using words in a sense not familiar to me, that I could not follow him, and I gazed on his eloquent and venerable countenance, as he went on describing the results of his thoughts. All I can tell you is, that his book is on *logic* of some particular kind, and is a sort of introduction to his great work, as he calls the one which Aubrey says exists only in his brain. He gave me a sketch of this also, very brief: the title I thought beautiful, and would have given anything to have written it down for you: indeed, much as I enjoyed the visit, I wished you could have been in my place, for I know you would have enjoyed it so exceedingly, and could have recollected all. He also spoke beautifully about Kant, who, as well as Bacon, was, he says, as Aristotelian; but I was unable to comprehend his explanation of the sense in which he said their methods were similar. He says he will get some one to look out for that work of Kant's for you, which he says is very valuable, and he told me how little Kant is known or read in proportion to what he ought to be. I

was with him more than half an hour—nearer an hour, I believe—
and could willingly, as you may suppose, have staid all day; but I,
with some resolution at last, got up and said something about
fearing I had interrupted him. [...] His head is finer than I had
expected, and his eye different. I supposed it black and rather soft,
instead of being grey and penetrating. He laughed a good deal
when he alluded to some comparison, I believe he said in the
Friend, about little toads, and the Emancipation Bill, and the Reform Bill[.][31]

(xviii) SARA COLERIDGE

From CL, VI, 991-2 — from a letter (5 August 1834) from Sara to Hartley.
Coleridge died on 25 July.

On the evening of the 19th he appeared very ill & on Sunday the
20th of July came a note—which I opened—Henry being at
Church. We sent to him there & he went to Highgate immediately.
My dear father had often seemed near death before so that it was
not impossible that he might rally. Still from the tone of the note I
mourned him as one about to be taken from us. Henry returned in
a few hours. My father since he felt his end approaching had expressed a desire that he might be as little disturbed as possible. He
took leave of Mrs Gillman & did not wish even to see his beloved
friend Mr Green. The agitation of nerves at the sight of those dear
to him disturbed his meditations on his Redeemer to whose bosom
he was hastening & he then said that he wished to evince in the
manner of his death the depth & sincerity of his faith in Christ.
Henry, however, was resolved to enter his room & see him for the
last time. He was just able to send his blessing to my mother & me,
though he articulated with difficulty & speaking seemed to increase his pain. Henry kissed him & withdrew—never to see him
living again. He continued to suffer much pain in the chest or
bowels & had an impression that there was water in the chest. Mr
Green brought a physician who examined him with a stethoscope
& thought there was not much water. Henry continued to visit the
Grove but made no attempt to see my father again, & we all agreed
that it would be useless for my mother & myself to go to Highgate
or for Derwent or you to come up. [...] My father had a most faithful & affectionate Nurse in Harriet, an old servant of the G's, & a
few hours before his death he raised himself a little in bed & wrote
six or seven lines recommending *her* for a legacy.[32] [...] On Thursday Henry brought word that by injections of laudanum the medi-

cal attendants had succeeded in easing my father's sufferings. This was a great relief indeed to our minds. He was able to swallow very little—but had taken some arrow-root & brandy & a dose of Laudanum. He had told Harriet that he had no feelings of dissolution upon him & feared his end would be long & painful. Thank God this was not so. On Wednesday—no Tuesday he saw Mrs Gillman for the last time & took leave of James Gillman. James then saw him raise his head in the air—looking upwards as in prayer—he then fell asleep —from sleep into a state of coma, Torpor, as I understood it, and ceased to breathe at half past six in the morning of Friday. Mr Green was with him that night till he died. In the middle of the day on Thursday he had repeated to Mr Green his formula of the Trinity. His utterance was difficult—but his mind in perfect vigour & clearness—he remarked that his intellect was quite unclouded & he said 'I could even be witty'.

NOTES

1 The account in *Memoirs of the Life and Writings of Thomas Chalmers*, ed. William Hanna (4 vols.; Edinburgh, 1849-52), III, 261-2, adds little of substance.

2 Irving had worked with Chalmers in Glasgow before coming to London.

3 Irving was author of *The Orthodox and Catholic Doctrine of Our Lord's Human Nature* (1830). He also wrote about Revelation, in *The Last Days* (1828).

4 George Bennet, a verbose man who had circumnavigated the world.

5 An outbreak of speaking in tongues in Scotland attracted great curiosity. See John Beer, 'Transatlantic and Scottish Connections: Uncollected Records'; in Richard Gravil and Molly Lefebure (eds.), *The Coleridge Connection: Essays for Thomas McFarland* (Basingstoke, 1990) 308-43, 327-8.

6 Arthur Hallam (1811-33), also an Apostle, included a portrait of STC in his 'Timbuctoo': 'a face, whose every line / Wore the pale cast of Thought; a good, old man, / Most eloquent, who spake of things divine. / Around him youths were gathered, who did scan / His countenance, so grand and mild; and drank / The sweet, sad tones of Wisdom' (*Poems* (1830), 74). See John Beer, 'Tennyson, Coleridge and the Cambridge Apostles'; in Philip Collins (ed.), *Tennyson: Seven Essays* (Basingstoke, 1992), 1-35.

7 Autumn 1830 saw an outbreak of rick-burning, part of the Reform crisis.

8 *A Midsummer Night's Dream*, V.i, l.12.

9 Presumably, John Hookham Frere (1769-1846), translator and poet.

10 Cf. *TT*, I, 325, where Keats is described as a 'loose, not well dressed youth'. Keats met STC in 1819 (see above) and died in 1821. STC said the same ('Alas! there is death in that hand!') about his young disciple Steinmetz (*CL*, VI, 920).

11 A brutal review in the *Quarterly* had finished Keats off (or so said Shelley in the preface to *Adonais* (1821)).

12 STC had proposed a translation of *Faust* to Murray in 1814 (*CL*, III, 521-2).

[13] Cf. Crabb Robinson, *On Books and their Writers*, ed. Morley, I, 107.

[14] Cf. Matthew 17.18-21.

[15] Cf. STC in 1831: 'He told the young enthusiast for German philosophy that he had thrown all such speculation overboard, and found perfect satisfaction for every inquiry in the first chapter of the Gospel of St. John' (Anna M. Stoddart, *John Stuart Blackie. A Biography* (2nd. edn.; 2 vols.; Edinburgh, 1895), I, 129).

[16] Shelley translated two scenes, published in *Posthumous Works* (1824). Byron reported Shelley saying that 'the translator of "Wallenstein" was the only person living who could venture to attempt it;—that he had written to Coleridge, but in vain. For a man to translate it, he must think as *he* does' (*Medwin's Conversations of Lord Byron [...]*, ed. Ernest J. Lovell (Princeton, NJ, 1966), 261).

[17] STC had been awarded an annual grant by the Royal Society of Literature in 1824. It was discontinued under William IV, with some public noise, including pieces in *The Times* (see *CL*, V, 343; VI, 854-7).

[18] That was kind: elsewhere, STC said Scott had blundered badly in representing the Mariner as an old man at the time of his voyage (*TT*, I, 273-4).

[19] Cf. 'Poor man, he has been for two months past under the influence of cholera and other extra disorders, by which he seems sadly enfeebled and even crippled. One heard from him, however, things which could have come from no one else; not such continuous and unintermitted eloquence as I have sometimes heard from him, but the "flash and outbreak of a fiery mind" from time to time' (*Correspondence of Henry Taylor*, ed. Edward Dowden (1888), 39-40).

[20] Samuel von Pufendorf (1632-94), political and legal philosopher.

[21] For the ethical distinction between persons and things, see *F*, I, 189-90.

[22] Connop Thirlwall (1797-1875), later Bishop of St. David's. STC attended the 1833 meeting of the British Association in Cambridge: see Robert Aris Wilmott's anonymous *Conversations at Cambridge* (1836), 1-6 (*TT*, II, 449-68).

[23] 'Almost nobody in Highgate knew his name. I asked several persons in vain; at last a porter wished to know if I meant an elderly gentleman with white hair? Yes, the same. "Why, he lives with Mr. Gillman." Ah yes, that is he' (*Journals of Ralph Waldo Emerson 1820-1872*, ed. Edward Waldo Emerson and Waldo Emerson Forbes (10 vols.; 1910-14), III, 174).

[24] William Ellery Channing (1780-1842), Unitarian and Wordsworthian. He met STC in 1823: see *Memoir of William Ellery Channing* (1851), 205-6.

[25] Presumably the long note in *AR*, 312-15, which draws on Waterland.

[26] *F*, I, 411-14; cf. *CM*, IV, 675-6. Passages from William Sedgwick's *Justice upon the Armie Remonstrance* (1648) appear in *The Friend*, altered a good deal.

[27] A version of 'My Baptismal Birthday' (*CPW*, I, 490-1).

[28] Thomas Hill, Hook's butt (see above), whose chambers were in the Adelphi.

[29] Ezekiel 37.3.

[30] Thirlwall's *Letter on the Admission of Dissenters* (1834) argued in favour.

[31] Surinam toads appear in *The Friend* (*F*, II, 212).

[32] *CL*, VI, 990.

Index